Boutwell

Boutwell

RADICAL REPUBLICAN
AND CHAMPION OF
DEMOCRACY

JEFFREY BOUTWELL

W. W. NORTON & COMPANY
Independent Publishers Since 1923

For information about permission to reproduce selections from this book, write to Permissions,
W. W. Norton & Company, Inc., 500 Fifth Avenue, New York, NY 10110

For information about special discounts for bulk purchases, please contact W. W. Norton Special Sales
at specialsales@wwnorton.com or 800-233-4830

Manufacturing by Sheridan Chelsea
Book design by Chris Welch
Production manager: Julia Druskin

ISBN 978-1-324-07426-7

W. W. Norton & Company, Inc., 500 Fifth Avenue, New York, NY 10110
www.wwnorton.com

W. W. Norton & Company Ltd., 15 Carlisle Street, London W1D 3BS

1 2 3 4 5 6 7 8 9 0

Mickey, Gene, and Kit Rachlis,
For your love of the written word

Buthaina Shukri,
For your love

Contents

Author's Note

In the 1820s, my great-great-grandfather, Rodney Cleaves Boutwell, was a teenager growing up on his family's farm in southern New Hampshire. Thirty miles farther south across the Massachusetts border, his cousin, George Sewall Boutwell, was also a farm boy. Though the two men lived only miles apart for many decades, they likely never met. Rodney would have known about George, though, who in 1851 became the youngest-ever governor of Massachusetts and then a key figure in American politics during the Civil War, the Reconstruction era, and later the Spanish-American War.

I also grew up in Massachusetts but knew little about George Boutwell until I was well into my forties. My family never mentioned that we had an illustrious relative, and George was very much absent from books on American history. When I did come across his memoirs later in life, the two-volume *Reminiscences of Sixty Years in Public Affairs*, I found the writing often ponderous and George uncharitably critical of many of his contemporaries. The photograph of George I saw most often depicted a seemingly stuffy and self-satisfied civil servant.

Then, in the 1990s, my young family and I lived for a few years in George's hometown of Groton, Massachusetts, just a few hundred yards from the Governor Boutwell house that still stands on Main Street and is home to the Groton Historical Society. I learned a bit more about George in those four years, in part by serving as a board member of the Groton Public Library, which George had helped establish in 1854.

But, it was only in 2010, while reading Nicholas Lemann's *Redemption: The Last Battle of the Civil War*, that I began to truly appreciate George Boutwell's political significance and courage. I was deeply moved by Lemann's account of Boutwell's US Senate investigation of white supremacist violence against Black Americans during the 1875 political elections in Mississippi. Public support for Reconstruction was coming to an end, yet George Boutwell traveled to Jackson and Aberdeen, Mississippi, to document the organized campaign of intimidation and violence carried out by white Democrats to "redeem" their state. The painful testimony from victims of that violence that was collected by his Senate committee kindled my own memory as a teenager of the brutal killings in 1964 of civil rights workers James Chaney, Andrew Goodman, and Michael Schwerner in Philadelphia, Mississippi, the same area where George had traveled some ninety years before.

Prompted by Lemann's book, I began to read up on George. Newly published histories of the birth of the Republican Party, Abraham Lincoln and the Emancipation Proclamation, the impeachment of Andrew Johnson, and the presidency of Ulysses Grant have frequently cited Boutwell as an important if underappreciated figure during the Civil War and the Reconstruction era. When I learned that, at age eighty, he was called on to lead the opposition to America's annexation of the Philippines being orchestrated by William McKinley and Teddy Roosevelt, I knew there was a good deal more to George's story. This book is the result.

Boutwell

Introduction

George Boutwell looked up as his aide handed him a note on White House stationery. Unfolding it, he saw the signature of Orville Babcock, private secretary to Ulysses S. Grant. "The President desires me to say that he will visit the Capitol today at twelve o'clock and will be pleased to have you call here and ride up with him in his carriage."[1]

As treasury secretary overseeing a mammoth government department, Boutwell had spent the morning checking the government's gold and bond sales and reviewing any pending congressional legislation that might affect the nation's economy. Suddenly, the remainder of Boutwell's day would be anything but routine. The note he had just received would set in motion events that would shape America down to the present day.[2]

IT WAS THURSDAY, March 23, 1871. Boutwell left his office and made the few minutes' walk to the White House. He and the president conferred briefly before climbing into the presidential carriage for the ride up Pennsylvania Avenue. During the twenty-minute drive to Capitol Hill, Boutwell implored Grant to stand firm against his critics. Congress was considering a bill to strengthen federal enforcement in the South of civil rights protections for America's Black citizens, some four million of whom had been enslaved just a few years previously. The Reconstruction program seeking to reshape southern society to provide equality of opportunity for Blacks as well as whites was in trouble. Two weeks earlier, white vigilantes had killed more than thirty Black men and women following a courtroom brawl in Meridian, Mississippi. In South Carolina, racial violence perpetrated by the Ku Klux Klan and other white supremacist groups was so widespread that the state governor was pleading for assistance from the US Army.

It was six years since the end of the Civil War. A growing number of Americans were tiring of federal intervention in the South to protect the gains of the Fourteenth and Fifteenth Amendments that guaranteed voting and political rights to many of the country's Black citizens. "Reconstruction fatigue" was spreading, even in Grant and Boutwell's Republican Party, leading to calls that the South should be left to tend to its own affairs. As the president told Boutwell on the way to the Capitol, "the public mind is already disturbed by the charge that I am exercising despotic powers in the South." Ulysses Grant was having the same doubts that, a century later, would beset Dwight D. Eisenhower and John F. Kennedy as they decided whether to employ federal marshals to enforce school integration in Little Rock, Arkansas, in 1957 and Oxford, Mississippi, in 1962.[3]

Once they reached the Capitol, Grant and Boutwell conferred with Attorney General Amos Akerman and other cabinet members as well as with Massachusetts congressman Benjamin Butler, author of the original KKK bill. They all joined Boutwell in urging the president to stay the course. After an hour-long discussion, the president sat down and composed his message, "without pause or correction," calling upon Congress to enact legislation that "shall effectually secure life, liberty and property, and the enforcement of law, in *all* parts of the United States."[4]

Congress acted swiftly on Grant's request, and less than a month later the president returned to Capitol Hill to sign the Ku Klux Klan Act. Known formally as the Third Enforcement Act, the law gave the federal government additional measures with which to combat the widespread violence and voter intimidation being inflicted on Blacks and their white Republican supporters by the KKK and other white vigilante groups in the South. Ulysses Grant was given the authority to suspend the writ of habeas corpus and deploy US troops in those situations where local authorities in the South were unable, or unwilling, to deal with the violence. The law also made it illegal to use "force, intimidation, or threat" to prevent government officials, such as members of Congress, federal judges, and federal marshals, from performing the duties of their office.[5]

In the short term, the KKK Act and resulting federal prosecutions helped disband and disperse the Klan and other white supremacist groups throughout the South. President Grant had to invoke martial law only once, in nine South Carolina counties in 1871, but it proved effective in reducing the violence.[6]

Quite soon, though, "Reconstruction fatigue" returned. The country became preoccupied with the economic recession that followed the "Panic of 1873." Three years later, when it was time to celebrate the nation's one hundredth birthday, Americans wanted to look to the future, not revisit the Civil War in defense of Black civil rights. Following that year's presidential election, Rutherford B. Hayes took office on the tacit understanding that he would reduce federal interference and let the South take care of its own affairs. By 1883, a Supreme Court that was increasingly hostile to Reconstruction declared that the KKK Act applied only to state actions, not those of individuals, thus gutting the law of much of its power. Through the end of the 1800s and into the twentieth century, the legalization of "Jim Crow" in the South and rigid racial discrimination in the rest of the country destroyed the Reconstruction goal of an equitable multiracial society.[7]

THE AMERICA WE KNOW TODAY was shaped by the decisions and political battles fought at the end of the Civil War and during its tumultuous aftermath, the Reconstruction era. This period is now called the "Second Founding" by many historians and legal scholars, given that the original protections found in the US Constitution for personal liberty and equal rights were expanded to cover a much broader array of American citizens. No longer were the ideals of the Declaration of Independence—life, liberty, and the pursuit of happiness— confined to white males with property. As Lincoln had proclaimed at Gettysburg, America would have "a new birth of freedom."

This "new birth" began with the abolition of chattel slavery by the Thirteenth Amendment in 1865. Then, the Fourteenth Amendment in 1868 made citizens of the four million newly freed Black Americans who were previously enslaved by the authority of the Constitution. This amendment also extended "equal protection" and "due process" of the laws to all American citizens, now defined as anyone born in America or properly naturalized. In 1870, the Fifteenth Amendment sought, with some flaws, to extend the right to vote to all (male) citizens of whatever race or color, with the aim of strengthening America as a representative democracy.[8]

As much as any public figure during this seminal period in American history, George Boutwell fought to redeem the promise of America as an equitable, multiracial society. In 1860, he helped write the Republican Party's national platform and nominate Abraham Lincoln for president, events that foreordained an agonizing civil war. As an increasingly important leader of the Radical wing of his party, he identified slavery as the cause of that war and its abolition as the only policy that could reconstruct the Union as a true representative democracy. Sixteen years later, in 1876, he stood on the floor of the US Senate, warning that white supremacist violence in Mississippi was destroying the civil rights protections for America's Black citizens, and thus weakening the rights of all Americans, over which the Civil War had been fought.[9]

During the years in between, Boutwell worked closely with Abraham Lincoln and Ulysses S. Grant to abolish slavery and accord citizenship rights to Black Americans while helping to write and enact, as a member of Congress, the Fourteenth and Fifteenth Amendments to the Constitution. When Andrew Johnson threatened these rights by seeking to unilaterally restore white control in the South, Boutwell helped initiate and then lead the impeachment proceedings against the president, which failed by only one vote in May 1868. Thirty years later, in a remarkable third act to his career, he again fought for the ideals of American citizenship and representative democracy in opposing the annexationist policies of William McKinley and Theodore Roosevelt following the Spanish-American War.

Born to a farming family outside of Boston, Massachusetts, and with only a "common school" education, George Boutwell is the most consequential public figure Americans have never heard of. Little known is that Boutwell was a trusted advisor to Abraham Lincoln during the darkest days of the Civil War, helping to prepare the country for the Emancipation Proclamation of January 1, 1863. Or that George Boutwell and Ulysses Grant developed a strong friendship as they sought to protect the equal rights gains of Reconstruction, such that, in 1885, Boutwell was one of six civilian pallbearers during the Grant funeral procession that was witnessed by more than a million and a half people in New York City. Then, in 1898, still trim and fit at the age of eighty, Boutwell became president of the Anti-Imperialist League, the country's first mass antiwar movement protesting America's subjugation and proposed annexation of the Philippine Islands. With prominent figures such as Mark Twain, Andrew Carnegie, Booker T. Washington, Jane Addams, and William James, Boutwell was still leading that campaign when he died of pneumonia at the age of eighty-seven at his home in Groton, Massachusetts, in 1905.

All of which invites the question: If George Boutwell was so consequential, why is he so little known? In 1989 he was the subject of a modest though well-researched biography published by his hometown historical society, but it is only recently that Boutwell has emerged from the shadows as historians have begun to illuminate the central role he played in American politics.[10]

For most of the twentieth century, Boutwell was either ignored or dismissed. In the 1930s, for example, one of the deans of American history, Allan Nevins, wrote that George Boutwell "was as thin, acrid, and rustling as a dead elm leaf," whose "intellectual poverty" contrasted sharply with the acumen of his betters from Boston society. Another eminent historian, Samuel Eliot Morison, belittled Boutwell for meddling with the governance of Harvard College while serving as governor of Massachusetts. When Boutwell was mentioned at all, it was usually as "a nondescript public functionary of limited imagination" or "a narrow-minded, intense partisan always on the make."[11]

Why, then, has Boutwell been hiding in plain sight for so long? First is his persona. Growing up on a Massachusetts farm, Boutwell absorbed the values of hard work, perseverance, attention to detail, and civility. But he also was pure Yankee: reserved, correct in his relations with others, at times morally smug. While politically ambitious, he preferred working behind the scenes; thus the description of him as "a nondescript public functionary." Passionate about the causes he believed in, he was easily labeled "an intense partisan," even a fanatic, by opponents. Though at times a gifted writer and speaker, Boutwell often droned on far too long, trying the patience of listener and reader alike. One colleague described him as "a steady wind blowing aft." Too often he was curtly dismissive in assessing the talents of others, coming across as "honest and sincere . . . but too much of a scold."[12]

In public life, George Boutwell was not an attention seeker. Compared to many of his Republican colleagues in Congress—Charles Sumner, Thaddeus Stevens, Roscoe Conkling, and Benjamin Butler—Boutwell did not seek the limelight. He was not an elegant orator like Sumner, a political firebrand like Stevens, or a wily political machine boss like Conkling or Butler. Rather, he was respected by his colleagues as an effective legislator, adept at conciliating opposing viewpoints, and a superb administrator, mastering the complexities of economic policy and international law. Even Allan Nevins grudgingly admired Boutwell's political skills, writing that "nobody knew better how to run with the hare and hunt with the hounds."[13]

With his working-class background, Boutwell was often scorned by the Harvard-educated, Boston intellectual elite. Henry Adams, descendant of two presidents and member of a still powerful Massachusetts political family, described Boutwell as "a somewhat lugubrious joke." To critics such as editors Horace Greeley of the *New York Tribune* and E. L. Godkin of *The Nation* magazine, Boutwell was a rabid partisan seeking to expand the power of the national government in the service of the Radical Republican goals of reshaping southern society and protecting Black rights. As the country moved on from the Civil War, Boutwell was seen as out of step with the business of America getting on with its business.[14]

AS FOR AMERICAN HISTORIANS for most of the past 150 years, they have viewed George Boutwell as being on the "wrong" side of history in four major episodes of American life.

First was his role in the impeachment of Andrew Johnson, which for decades was portrayed as an extralegal attempt by fanatical Radical Republicans to remove a sitting president merely because they didn't like his policies. Only recently have scholars been giving more credit to the arguments of Boutwell and others that, as impeachment is more a political process than a legal one, it is justifiable to judge a president on gross malfeasance in office, even if such conduct doesn't rise to the level of criminally indictable offenses.[15]

Second, Boutwell's role as treasury secretary for Ulysses Grant from 1869 to 1873 meant that he suffered from the anti-Grant sentiments that long characterized American historical writing. Henry Adams was responsible for much of this bias, writing in his widely acclaimed and influential autobiography, *The Education of Henry Adams*, that Grant was "pre-intellectual, archaic, and would have seemed so even to the cave-dwellers." Even into the 1990s, professional historians ranked Ulysses Grant as one of our country's worst presidents, keeping company with James Buchanan and Warren G. Harding. It is only in recent decades that the Grant presidency and Boutwell's role in it have received a far more positive assessment.[16]

Third, there is George Boutwell's leadership of the Anti-Imperialist League protesting America's military occupation of the Philippines following the Spanish-American War. This first mass antiwar movement in the country's history was seen at the time, and for many years after, as a quixotic quest led by elder statesmen woefully out of touch with the dynamism of an imperial America, personified by Teddy Roosevelt, at the dawn of the twentieth century. Today, in the wake of our country's tragic interventions in Vietnam, Iraq, and Afghanistan, Boutwell's warnings about the folly of nation-building through military occupation appear positively prescient.[17]

Fourth, and most important, was Boutwell's leadership of congressional Reconstruction policies in the 1860s and 1870s that sought to extend political and civil equality to the nation's four million Black citizens, the great majority only recently freed from slavery. For the next one hundred years, the triumph of the myth of the southern "Lost Cause" meant that Reconstruction was seen by most Americans as a travesty imposed by rapacious northern carpetbaggers and their southern Black allies, orchestrated by fanatical Radical Republican politicians such as George Boutwell. Indeed, less than a year after Lee's surrender to Grant at Appomattox, the Virginia writer Edward Alfred Pollard had coined the phrase, writing that white supremacy was not a "Lost Cause" at all but would soon be "redeemed" throughout the South. Evoking John Milton's *Paradise Lost* for his white audience, Pollard argued that, because the "permanent inferiority of the Negro" is a biological given, all attempts by Radical Republicans to legislate and promote Negro equality were doomed to failure as "experiments against nature."[18]

In the decades that followed, Pollard's theme was spread by historians such as William Archibald Dunning of Columbia University and in popular culture through magazines, advertisements, and movies such as the wildly successful and patently racist *Birth of a Nation,* given a White House showing by President Woodrow Wilson in 1915. All advanced the argument that Reconstruction had been a "dark, unpleasant interlude of failure." Even in the 1950s, popular books such as John F. Kennedy's *Profiles in Courage* were describing the Reconstruction period, with unintended irony, as "a black nightmare the South could never forget."[19]

ONE PROMINENT "LOST CAUSE" historian who denigrated George Boutwell was Benjamin B. Kendrick, a Dunning disciple at Columbia University. In 1913 Kendrick wrote his PhD thesis on what many regard as the most important congressional committee ever created, the Joint Committee on Reconstruction (1865–1868), which battled President Andrew Johnson for control over the future of America's race relations. George Boutwell was one of the most important members of that committee, thus one of Kendrick's favorite targets, described as "perhaps the coldest, most calculating and yet unreasonable fanatic" of all the Radical Republicans, the one who advocated "the most extreme measures in dealing with the South." In the years that followed, Kendrick and other purveyors of the "Lost Cause" myth, criticized by famed American writer Ambrose Bierce as "literary bearers of false witness in the aftertime," would help propel the Democratic Party back into power in national politics.[20]

Contemporaneous with Kendrick, there was a young African American historian, Benjamin Arthur Quarles, a graduate student at the University of Wisconsin, who would help set in motion a new interpretation of Reconstruction politics. The son of a railway porter from Boston, Quarles wrote his master's thesis, "George Sewall Boutwell: A Radical with Reasons," in 1933. In the decades ahead, Quarles became one of the most prominent historians of the Black experience in America, writing the first modern biography of Frederick Douglass and publishing numerous studies highlighting the roles played by Black Americans during the Revolutionary War, the Civil War, and the growth of modern America.[21]

In writing about George Boutwell, Quarles selected the (white) person he thought was the strongest supporter of Black civil rights during the Reconstruction period. As a proponent of "Black agency," the concept that Blacks themselves had much to do with advancing American democracy, Quarles praised George Boutwell's "indefatigable" support for the twin pillars of Black self-reliance: the right to vote and universal public education. As Quarles wrote, "few Congressmen in the [1860s] had a greater interest in the welfare of the Negro than Boutwell . . . long before Radicalism had solidified into a coherent formula, Boutwell had shown a high degree of courage by voicing his views on the Negro." Quarles recognized that Boutwell's support for Black suffrage and education combined the practical advantage of winning their votes for the Republican Party with the moral imperative of demanding equal rights for all American citizens.[22]

In 1935, two years after Quarles wrote his thesis, W. E. B. Du Bois published his pathbreaking *Black Reconstruction in America*, emphasizing the theme of Black agency to which Quarles would devote his life. This was followed in 1961 when the African American historian John Hope Franklin published his seminal *Reconstruction: After the Civil War*. It would take many more decades, however, for American historians, white and Black, to dismantle the narrative of southern white redemption of the Dunning School and publish far more balanced accounts of Reconstruction, both its successes and failures. This in turn has led to a far greater appreciation of Boutwell's role in promoting Reconstruction, now viewed as the well-meaning if lost opportunity for America to advance the goals of a more equitable, multiracial society.[23]

DURING HIS SEVEN DECADES of public service, from the presidency of Martin van Buren in the 1830s to that of Theodore Roosevelt in the early 1900s, George Boutwell sought to redeem the American promise of equality of opportunity and equal protection of the laws for every citizen. His story, one of successes, setbacks, and constant striving during some of the most turbulent times in American history, remains both relevant and inspiring today. So much so that, in 2021, George Boutwell made a cameo appearance in the Pulitzer Prize–winning novel *The Netanyahus*, by Joshua Cohen, as the greatly admired subject of a fictional biography by the novel's main character, Ruben Blum, an economic historian who rightly saw in George Boutwell a kindred soul and a champion of democracy.[24]

PART ONE

FROM MASSACHUSETTS
TO WASHINGTON, DC,
1818–1860

1

Young Mr. Boutwell

In August 1817, several months before George Boutwell was born on a farm in the village of Brookline in eastern Massachusetts, there died in neighboring Boston a man who helped light the spark of America's industrial economy. Francis Cabot Lowell, member of a Boston blue-blood family, had returned home in 1812 after two years abroad in England, where he meticulously studied the great textile mills of Manchester. In an audacious feat of technology transfer (or theft, if you will), Lowell used his prodigious memory to evade British laws in bringing the designs and specifications of the power loom home to Massachusetts.

In what we now call reverse engineering, Lowell pioneered construction of the first vertically integrated woolen and cotton mills in America, including what would become, after his death, the namesake city of Lowell, northwest of Boston. By the 1820s, when these and similar mills in New England and the American North were linked by canals, the telegraph, and the railroad, the industrial potential of the young American republic began to take off.[1]

This was the America that shaped George Boutwell's formative years. The rapid advances in manufacturing, transportation, and communication were greatly altering home life and working conditions, giving rise to religious and temperance movements and increased demands for women's rights. The telegraph and ever-increasing numbers of newspapers spread information to all corners of the country, helping solidify a sense of national identity. Book publishing and the popularity of public lectures and organized adult education, known as the lyceum movement, helped disseminate knowledge and ideas to a far greater number of Americans.

The composition of American society itself was changing with rapid increases in immigration. By the 1840s, annual Irish and German immigration had increased from the tens to the hundreds of thousands, injecting nativist prejudice into American society and politics. The Irish tended to settle in the cities of the Northeast, the Germans in the Midwest. Contributing valuable labor to eastern factories and midwestern farms and small businesses, the two immigrant communities helped fuel America's expanding economy, albeit one that was leading to greater and greater wealth disparities.

The one constant during this period was the country's sectional divide over slavery. Protected by the US Constitution, slavery entrenched itself in the American South as the invention of the cotton gin and other mechanical aids fueled the growth of the cotton industry. The number of enslaved Blacks tripled from 700,000 in 1790 to over two million by 1830. Their labor made possible a 400 percent increase in the production of cotton, which made fortunes not only for southern plantation owners but for northern textile manufacturers such as the family of Francis Cabot Lowell and the New England traders who shipped the cotton to England.

Seeking to counter the political clout of the southern Slave Power was an increasingly vocal and activist abolitionist movement throughout the North. Inspired by tales of enslaved Blacks escaping via the Underground Railroad, and knitted together by newspapers and the lyceum movement, abolitionism led by whites and free Blacks became a major political force across America's political landscape. By the 1850s, when the storm clouds of conflict were gathering, the hypocrisy of a nation founded on individual liberty that treated an enslaved people as second-class human beings would become the defining issue of George Boutwell's life.[2]

HIS ROOTS WERE modest. Born on January 28, 1818, to a Massachusetts farm family, George was the second of that name to be born to Sewell and Rebecca Boutwell; his mother was five months pregnant with him when the first-born George died of cholera at the age of twenty months. A little over two weeks after George's birth, Frederick Douglass would be born into slavery on the eastern shore of Maryland.[3]

Sewell Boutwell managed a farm for a prominent Boston physician, Dr. John Phillips Spooner. George remembers his father as "a practical man and a gentleman by nature. With him civility was innate. He was a close observer and something of a philosopher . . . of even temper and of an imperturbable spirit." George Boutwell would come to embody these traits himself.[4]

Boutwell's mother, Rebecca Marshall, came from a prominent farming family in southern New Hampshire. Described as having "unusual intellectual endowment, and of great rigidity of opinion," Rebecca encouraged her son's reading and book learning. As was usual at the time, George attended the local district school both winter and summer until he was ten, after which he devoted summers to working on the farm.

George had two younger brothers (Jacob and Micah) and two younger sisters (Abby and Olive). All of them were born after the family moved in 1820 to Lunenburg, forty-five miles west of Boston, where his father had purchased a 113-acre farm with commanding views of nearby Mount Wachusett.

Sewell Boutwell's farm produced nearly all the family needed: meat, milk, butter, cheese, grain, fruit, and vegetables. In those days, wood and timber were abundant and money was scarce. George remembered vividly how the debt on the family home weighed heavily on his father; the son would carry this Yankee disdain of indebtedness with him when he became secretary of the treasury, charged with paying down the country's monumental Civil War debt.

Thrift and hard work were staples of growing up on a New England farm. With money little in use, and few goods to buy, Boutwell remembers that borrowing and lending with one's neighbors "extended to nearly every moveable thing that anyone possessed." Friction matches had not yet been invented, so he was often sent "on a flying visit to a neighbor's house" to borrow fire for the hearth. Even shoes were a luxury; after tending the oxen barefoot on frosty mornings in the early autumn, George would look for a stone warmed by the sun to stand on.

In helping his father tend the farm, Boutwell learned a variety of skills, including, by the age of ten, the grafting and budding of apple, cherry, and peach trees. When time allowed, there was hunting and fishing. George recalled vividly how he and his father would catch pigeons in nets that were baited with grain soaked in aniseed oil and how, for a ten-year-old boy, "wringing their necks [was] a brutal business."

Even into his eighties, Boutwell never stopped being a farmer. He came to own six hundred acres surrounding his future home in Groton, Massachusetts, raising cattle and growing fruits and vegetables. In 1860 on the eve of the Civil War, Boutwell was president of the Middlesex (County) Agricultural Society when he chaired a meeting featuring the historic talk by Henry David

Thoreau that drew on principles of the recently published *On the Origin of Species* by Charles Darwin. In 1897, when he was almost eighty years old, a Boston newspaper reported that "Ex-Governor George Boutwell will send to market this fall 2,000 baskets of peaches grown on his farm."[5]

THE BOUTWELL FAMILY was not especially religious, though his mother was a devout Bible reader. Rebecca would read passages every day with her son standing in front of her; George thus learned the art of reading print upside down, a useful talent for a budding lawyer and politician. His father Sewell openly disparaged the concepts of hell and eternal damnation and believed that the Bible was mostly valuable as "a record of events, and the expression of human thought and feeling, rather than as a message of Divine will." The family did attend church on a regular basis, but more out of form than conviction.

All around them, however, religious fervor—known as the Second Great Awakening—was brewing. Boutwell's memoirs recount the squabbles and controversies between Methodists, Universalists, agnostics, and others. He was coming of age at a time when, as described by historian Jill Lepore, a religious revival was recasting "America from the secular nation at its founding to a Christian nation." Between 1775 and 1845, the number of preachers and ministers in America swelled from 1,800 to 40,000, confirming the prediction of James Madison that the Constitution's prohibition of an established state religion would allow a diverse religious expression to thrive. The result in the opening decades of the 1800s was that "Americans founded new sects, from Shakers to Mormons, and rival Protestant denominations sprang up in town after town." All this would inform George Boutwell's fundamental belief in the freedom of Americans to worship as they wished, grounded in the separation of church and state. He would act on those beliefs in the 1880s when he represented the Church of Jesus Christ of Latter-day Saints, despite his disagreement with Mormon customs such as polygamy.[6]

IN 1830 AT THE AGE of twelve, Boutwell moved out of the family house to begin an apprenticeship with the Lunenburg postmaster, Simon Heywood. In return for his room and board and the chance to continue his schooling during the winter months, Boutwell kept the accounts in the post office while helping Heywood manufacture small hats made of palm leaf. The hat-making process was intricate as well as dangerous as it involved stripping the palm leaves by hand and then bleaching them with sulfur in large boxes.

Three years into his apprenticeship, the teenager witnessed what's rightly been called one of the "astronomical wonders of the modern era." Rising as usual at 2 a.m. on a cold November morning to receive the mail from a passing stagecoach, Boutwell looked up to the heavens to see the "Great Meteor Storm of 1833," the famous Leonid meteor shower that generated tens of thousands of meteors per hour, all visible throughout the country east of the Rocky Mountains. Running through the town to tell his neighbors of the celestial display, Boutwell would remember how the local butcher, Abijah Whitney, "came out to commence preparations for his morning rounds, but conceiving that the day of judgment had come, he returned into the house and gave up business for the day."[7]

Abijah Whitney was in good company. Near Independence, Missouri, the Mormon leader Joseph Smith "beheld the stars fall from heaven like a shower of hail stones," believing it a literal fulfillment that the coming of Christ was close at hand. Native American nations including the Cheyenne and Lakota would in future hold ceremonies and reset their calendars in honor of the event. Abraham Lincoln, Harriet Tubman, and Frederick Douglass all remember witnessing the spectacle from their homes in Illinois and Maryland, with the young Douglass being "awe-struck" at the "bright, descending messengers from the sky."[8]

Boutwell finished his Lunenburg apprenticeship in December 1834. He then signed on as a teacher at the one-room schoolhouse in Shirley, Massachusetts, where, at sixteen, he was younger than some of his students. When the high cost of firewood forced the school to close, Boutwell made one of the most momentous decisions of his life: he moved to the neighboring town of Groton, Massachusetts.[9]

In February 1835, Boutwell answered an ad in the *Lowell Journal* and took a job with Benjamin Dix in Groton, about ten miles east of Lunenburg and well situated on the travel routes coming out from Boston and Cambridge toward Worcester and southern New Hampshire. As he signed on for a clerkship of three years in the shoe and leather store, the move at first seemed disastrous: Dix went bankrupt, and within six months George was unemployed.

But good fortune intervened when Boutwell was able to sign on with another Groton trader, Henry Woods, who in just two years thought well enough of George's skills and work ethic to make him a partner in the business, with 25 percent of the net profits. In addition to farm tools, clothing, and hardware, Boutwell (a lifelong teetotaler) and Woods did a thriving business in the cultivation and sale of hops, a major staple in central Massachusetts.[10]

His work with Henry Woods had the added benefit of introducing George to his future wife, Sarah Adelia Thayer (Henry's sister-in-law), who came from a prominent family in nearby Hollis, New Hampshire. Their marriage in 1841 might not have been consummated had Boutwell followed through with an earlier decision to leave Groton and study law at what is today Phillips Academy in Exeter, New Hampshire. In 1837, he had all but secured a place at the Academy when Henry Woods convinced the teenager to stay in Groton, offering him the partnership. George worked long hours, learning the ropes of the business while building a nest egg and using his spare time to read the law with the help of several prominent Groton lawyers. While doing so, he was exposed to the literary community of Groton, including Margaret Fuller and her family, as well as to the wider intellectual world of Ralph Waldo Emerson and the Transcendentalists.

BY THE LATE 1830S, Groton was a growing community of two thousand residents, home to several prominent Massachusetts families and a network of well-connected lawyers, and second only to nearby Concord in political importance west of Boston. It also boasted a vibrant intellectual community based on the local Lyceum, part of the circuit of public education and entertainment locales from Massachusetts to Illinois given prominence by Ralph Waldo Emerson and the Transcendentalist movement.

Emerson is now considered the country's "first modern public intellectual," and his writings and lectures impacted American culture across such diverse areas as literature, religion, philosophy, race relations, and concepts of American identity. From Concord, midway between Groton and Boston, Emerson developed his credo of individual self-sufficiency combined with the German Romantics' love of nature and a Unitarian theology of a direct, personal relationship with God; all designed to help individuals transcend the daily cares and machinations of life. In 1836, these became the intellectual foundation of the Transcendentalist Club, which, although its life span was short, would greatly influence American philosophy and literature. Emerson soon published two of his most famous works, *Nature* (1836) and *The American Scholar* (1837), the latter considered by Oliver Wendell Holmes Sr. as America's "intellectual Declaration of Independence." Through the Lyceum network, supplemented by the profusion of newspapers, pamphlets, and books available at the time, Emerson was able to reach tens of thousands of Americans. Consisting of a core group that included Henry David Thoreau, Bronson Alcott (father of

Louisa May), Nathaniel Hawthorne, and Margaret Fuller, the Transcendentalists were the social disrupters of their time, riling religious conventions and
needling the conscience of the Protestant establishment.[11]

Prominent among these was Fuller, soon to become one of the leading literary intellectuals of nineteenth-century America and only twenty-three when
she moved to Groton in 1833. Her father, Timothy, had been a member of Congress who suddenly abandoned politics and his law practice to take up farming. He failed to prosper and died of cholera two years later, just as George was
arriving in town, leaving Margaret and the family in difficult straits.

Boutwell remembers the Fullers "for their odd manners and style of dress,"
not surprising as the family had reluctantly followed Timothy in leaving behind
the intellectual environment of Cambridge and Harvard College. Margaret
didn't take kindly to her new country home at first, but soon found herself
drawn to the beauty of the rolling countryside. As for the Groton townsfolk,
she came to admit that "the people here are much more agreeable than in most
country towns; there is no vulgarity of manners . . . and I hear no gossip."[12]

In short order, Margaret made the acquaintance of Waldo Emerson (as he
preferred to be called) from nearby Concord. Through Emerson she befriended
Thoreau, the Alcotts, and especially Nathaniel Hawthorne. Until her untimely
death in 1850 in a shipwreck off Long Island while returning from Europe,
Fuller would help spread the concepts of individual self-reliance and devotion
to nature that the Transcendentalists infused into American society prior to
the Civil War.

In Groton, Margaret taught Sunday school at the First Parish Church,
which George attended; the two would often meet at Sunday evening teachers'
meetings. Admiring her lively intellect, George recalled how Margaret would
"set forth her opinions with great frankness, and in a style which assumed they
were not open to debate." George also worked with one of Margaret's younger
brothers, Eugene, in the law office of Groton attorney George F. Farley.

Boutwell was twenty-one and Margaret Fuller was just turning thirty when
she, her mother, and siblings left Groton in April 1839 and moved to Jamaica
Plain near Boston. She soon became editor of the Transcendentalist journal,
The Dial, while George became a newly elected member of the Massachusetts legislature. With a shared commitment to progressive causes that were
assuming increased importance at the time, such as improving the conditions
of prisons, mental hospitals, and women's educational facilities, Margaret
would go on to become a widely read columnist for Horace Greeley's *New*

York Tribune, while George would lead legislative fact-finding investigations into conditions at Massachusetts's schools and hospitals. In Boutwell's home library at the time of his death in 1905 was a complete collection of Margaret Fuller's works, one of them inscribed to George by another of Margaret's younger brothers, William.[13]

DURING HIS SIX YEARS working with Henry Woods, Boutwell would manage the store each day until 10 p.m., then read and write until well past midnight. If he started falling asleep, he would splash his face with cold water. He devoured the classics of philosophy and literature: Plutarch, Adam Smith, Shakespeare, and John Locke. He took a special interest in constitutional law, reading the *Federalist Papers* of Hamilton and Madison and the French theorist Jean Louis De Lolme on the English Constitution. With this grounding in law, finance, and politics, he began writing articles for publications such as the Bay State *Democrat*. As for languages, George taught himself the Hebrew alphabet while also reading Virgil, Cicero, and Caesar in Latin with a local physician, Dr. Amos Bancroft. He later learned French with a tutor during his first years in the Massachusetts legislature.[14]

In addition to being a voracious reader, Boutwell developed relationships in his teens and early twenties with lawyers in Groton who helped expand his horizons. Principal among these was Judge Samuel Dana, lawyer and member of Congress during the War of 1812, and patriarch of the extended Dana family that included Richard Henry Dana Jr. (author of *Two Years Before the Mast*), who himself would play an important role in Boutwell's career.

Of the Groton lawyers he came to know, Bradford Russell was the one most responsible for Boutwell's education in the law. With an office a few doors away on Main Street, and a small library above, Russell hired George for five dollars a day to help with debtors' cases when Insolvency Court was in session. A good lawyer but poor business manager, Russell relied on the young Boutwell's mastery of detail to keep track of the cases that came in from throughout Middlesex County and to report on their adjudication in court. It was a practical apprenticeship in the law that far surpassed what he could have learned at any academy. By the age of twenty, then, Boutwell was already co-owner of a dry goods business, learning the law, and coming to know Groton's most prominent citizens.[15]

In town, the Groton Lyceum was an especially important part of Boutwell's education and his contacts with the wider world. His daughter Georgianna later described how her father, even at age eighteen, began writing a paper each year for the Lyceum. Soon, these articles began appearing in national publications such as *Hunt's Merchants Magazine*, the leading business and commercial journal of its time.[16]

If you had seen George Boutwell on the streets of Groton at that time, walking from the dry goods store to a local lawyer's office and then home, you would have witnessed a young man of medium height, muscular but trim, with dark black hair. What especially stood out to contemporaries was that George, somewhat of a loner, "was serious, always attentive, ever observant." A visiting abolitionist from New York, having met Boutwell at antislavery meetings in town, was surprised when told that George was a store clerk, thinking that Boutwell's "studious face marked him as a member of one of the professions, and most likely that of the law."[17]

IN AUGUST 1841, Frederick Douglass first appeared in Groton, three years after having made his escape from slavery on the eastern shore of Maryland. The man who would become America's most visible and vocal opponent of slavery, Douglass was the same age as George Boutwell. Though they came from different worlds, each would play a major role in seeking the abolition of slavery and securing political and civil equality for Black Americans.[18]

In one sense, though, their worlds were not so different. The slavery in Maryland which shaped Frederick Douglass had deep roots as well in Massachusetts and throughout the North. Soon after the first enslaved people arrived in Boston in 1624, the Massachusetts Bay Colony led by a Puritan, John Winthrop, himself a slave owner, enacted the first law legalizing slavery in 1641. So began the infamous "triangle trade" that enriched many a New England family. Ships carrying rum and "African iron," small pieces of metal used as currency on the Gold Coast of Africa, would sail to what is modern-day Ghana and Guinea, where they picked up cargoes of enslaved Black Africans, pepper, and gold dust. From there they sailed to Barbados and the West Indies to exchange their human cargo for sugar and molasses that they would transport back to New England, on occasion bringing some enslaved Africans with them. Although Britain sought to monopolize this slave trade in the late 1600s and 1700s, Yankee ship captains easily evaded capture by using the small coastal harbors along the thousands of miles of New England shoreline.[19]

In the 1700s, there were an estimated 4,500 enslaved Blacks in

Massachusetts. Native Americans had also been enslaved by the colonists beginning in the 1630s. When taken captive during the Pequot War of 1636–1638 and then King Philip's War of 1675–1678, Native Americans were either kept locally or sold and shipped to the West Indies. The wealth generated by slave labor and the triangle trade would contribute to the building of some of Massachusetts's most famous landmarks, including Boston's Faneuil Hall, synonymous with the spirit of liberty and the Revolutionary War, as well as Harvard Law School and the House of the Seven Gables in Salem, immortalized by Nathaniel Hawthorne.

Beginning in the mid-1700s, some enslaved Blacks were able to sue successfully for their freedom. Groton at the time was still home to some dozen enslaved people, but also to numerous Black freedmen, one of whom, Barzillai Lew, was among three dozen free Blacks who fought with the colonial army against the British at the Battle of Bunker Hill in June 1775.

In 1780, when future president John Adams helped enact the Massachusetts Constitution, he made sure it enshrined the principle of "all men" having "certain natural, essential, and unalienable rights," which accelerated the process of enslaved people being able to win their freedom in the courts. Still, the practice died out slowly, with many enslaved people sold off or shipped to the Caribbean so their owners would not suffer financial loss.

Home to the Fuller, Dana, and other progressive families, Groton organized one of the first local chapters of the Massachusetts Anti-Slavery Society, founded in the 1830s by William Lloyd Garrison, editor of the abolitionist newspaper, *The Liberator*. At its peak, the Groton chapter had two hundred members, male and female, representing 10 percent of the population. Its local agent was Luther Boutelle, a minister of the Adventist Church and a distant relative of George's. Meetings were held in Groton's Liberty Hall, which George later bought with his good friend Daniel Needham as both an investment and a locale for antislavery meetings, such as the two-day session on August 31 and September 1, 1841, featuring Frederick Douglass.[20]

Douglass returned to Groton in March 1842, one of forty-two towns he visited during a two-month speaking tour in the Northeast, "often visiting two towns in a single day and lecturing twice in the same place in a single day." But it was his third visit in February 1844 that was especially memorable.[21]

At the time, the same passions that were fueling the religious revival of the 1830s and 1840s were stimulating the equally fervent temperance and abolitionist movements. Included in this mix was the appearance of Second

Adventism, a creed that espoused the second coming of Christ and the end of the world. Also known as "Millerism" for its chief apostle, William Miller, it predicted that Christ would appear for his thousand-year reign in the twelve months between March 21, 1843, and March 21, 1844.[22]

By early 1844, with that window closing, the local Millerite community in Groton was becoming ever more anxious as Frederick Douglass arrived in town to speak as part of the "Massachusetts Hundred Conventions" tour, a grueling four-month stint organized by Wendell Phillips and the American Anti-Slavery Society. Speaking on February 24, Douglass was disappointed by the empty seats in front of him. On March 6, he lamented to Garrison that "Groton abolitionism is not where it once was," adding that "Millerism in Groton" had "thrown itself across the path of anti-slavery" and deprived him of his audience. Douglass regretted having to report "a somewhat dark and despondent picture of the state of our cause in Groton."[23]

When Christ failed to appear as promised, the local Millerites lost members and then disbanded, selling their meeting hall in Groton to Boutwell and Needham, a Quaker abolitionist. Rechristened as Liberty Hall, the two men moved it to the center of town, using it as a Lyceum for antislavery and other lectures. Liberty Hall was also a business venture, housing shops on the first floor and the large meeting space on the second available for rent.[24]

Despite Douglass's "despondent picture," Groton in the 1840s became increasingly active as part of the Underground Railroad network, locally and with ties to Washington, DC. Groton resident William Chaplin, who moved to the District of Columbia in 1848 to take a leadership role in the national organization, would become famous for organizing a daring but unsuccessful escape of seventy-seven enslaved people down the Potomac River on the schooner *Pearl*. The incident provoked riots in Washington, led to the banning of the slave trade (but not slave ownership) in DC, and helped inspire Harriet Beecher Stowe's *Uncle Tom's Cabin*.[25]

IN 1839, GEORGE BOUTWELL had his first opportunity to enter the world of politics, and to experience firsthand the degradations of slavery. Thanks to an 1836 act of Congress that granted pensions to a certain class of Revolutionary War widows, and given that Groton and the surrounding towns had supplied many colonial Minutemen, Boutwell began canvassing for potential clients. Taking advantage of his legal training with Bradford Russell, he was able to secure more than fifty applicants. He sent their petitions to Washington, but the process was slow. As many a lawyer has lamented, Boutwell complained that his frustrated clients had become "anxious and their visits and importunities were annoying."

To speed up the process, Boutwell made his first trip to Washington, DC, in January 1839, traveling with local stagecoach owner Gen. Thomas Staples, as he later described:

"From Groton to Boston by stage, and from Boston to Stonington, Conn., by rail; from Stonington to New York by steamboat; from New York to Perth Amboy by steamboat; from Perth Amboy by rail, I think, but possibly by stage to a town on the Delaware River, Franklin perhaps. From that point to Philadelphia, by steamboat. Our journey from Philadelphia to Washington was by rail in part and in part by stage."[26]

In Washington, General Staples introduced Boutwell to their local congressman, Democrat William Parmenter, who in turn arranged a meeting with President Martin Van Buren. Parmenter also used his influence at the Pension Office so that the novice lawyer was able to clear up his docket of applications in a few weeks and satisfy his clients back home. It was a lesson in the benefits of political connections that Boutwell would take back with him to Groton.

Boutwell's Washington trip included visits to the Supreme Court and the US Senate, hearing speeches and arguments by Daniel Webster and Henry Clay on one side of the slavery question, and John C. Calhoun and Kentucky senator John J. Crittenden on the other. He also visited the House of Representatives and heard former president John Quincy Adams, now a Massachusetts congressman, denounce what Adams called the southern Slave Power.[27]

As memorable as any of his Washington experiences was a chance meeting with a Black woman, "fifty years or more of age, a slave." As a reader of the abolitionist newspaper *The Liberator*, Boutwell was familiar with the writings of William Lloyd Garrison, Wendell Phillips, and the British abolitionists William Wilberforce and Thomas Clarkson. He had not yet, however, personally experienced the inhumanity of slavery.

ONE SUNDAY MORNING, George Boutwell walked from his hotel to one of the city's major "slave pens"—jails for holding enslaved Blacks about to be sold—at Seventh Street and Independence Avenue, a building he described as "of brick, enclosed within a brick wall, and all of a dingy straw color." He met there an elderly Black woman, in tears, who said that her eighteen-year-old daughter had been taken from her, sold, and was being transported to Louisiana the next morning. When told that her master was "Mr. Blair, of the *Globe*," Boutwell would have known that the woman was referring to Francis Preston Blair Sr., editor-in-chief of the *Washington Globe* and patriarch of one of Washington's preeminent political families.

Boutwell would never forget the anguish of a mother having her daughter "sold down the river" to even harsher conditions in the Deep South. By the time he abandoned the proslavery Democrats in 1854 to help create the Republican Party, he would remember that, as a Democrat, "I never said anything in favor of the system of slavery." If he had ever been tempted to do so, "the interview with that old woman would have restrained me."[28]

Boutwell's chance meeting with the enslaved woman illustrated the deeply embedded nature of the institution of slavery in the nation's capital. The "dingy straw color" described by Boutwell is what gave the slave pen, owned by the notorious slave trader W. H. Williams, its other name—the "Yellow House." Located on the south side of what is now the National Mall, in 1841 the Williams slave pen was where Solomon Northrup, a free Black from New York, was imprisoned after being kidnapped and then sold into slavery, a tale he recounted in *Twelve Years a Slave.* Another slave pen nearby, Robey Tavern, was on land adjacent to today's L'Enfant Plaza Metro station. Both slave pens had unobstructed views of the US Capitol Building being renovated and enlarged on the hill above them.[29]

Several years after Boutwell's visit, in 1847, construction began on the original home of the Smithsonian Institution, made of beautiful Seneca red sandstone and located diagonally across the street from the "Yellow House." Known as "The Castle," it was designed by James Renwick Jr., also responsible for St. Patrick's Cathedral in New York City. It was completed in 1855 and thus, for several years prior to the start of the Civil War, the officials and scholars who worked in and visited the building would have walked by the Williams slave pen to get there.[30]

The building's iconic red sandstone came from the Seneca Mills quarry, twenty-three miles northwest of Washington along the Potomac River in Virginia. The quarry was owned by John Parke Custis Peter, great-grandson of George Washington's wife, Martha Custis. Historical records show that he owned twenty-three slaves at his mansion, called Montevideo, and it is probable that many of them were quarry workers. Enslaved Blacks were also likely involved in the construction of the Smithsonian as carpenters, masons, or laborers, akin to their "employment" for the White House, the US Capitol Building, and other government structures. As they were leased out by their masters at $1.25 a day, a nice profit was turned by those owning five or ten slaves.[31]

The domestic trade in enslaved Blacks was also crucial in sustaining the city's and the region's economy. From 1790 to 1860, more than 600,000 enslaved people were sold and relocated from the Upper South to the prime cotton-growing regions of Alabama, Mississippi, and Louisiana. Much of this trade was consummated in the nation's capital. With slaves commanding prices of around $500 to $2,000 each in 2020 dollars, the total trade in enslaved persons would amount to $300 million to $1.2 billion.[32]

A prominent and still existing example of slavery's economic importance is the house of Thomas Peter, father of the quarry-owning John Peter. Thomas was a wealthy merchant in the early 1800s who built one of the most magnificent mansions in America at the time, Tudor Place, in Washington's Georgetown district. Thomas owed much of his fortune to the selling of slaves belonging to his wife, Martha Parke Custis, who inherited them from her grandmother, Martha Custis Washington, wife of our first president.

Today, the Tudor Place Historic House and Garden is one of Washington's premier mansion museums, sitting on five acres at Q and Thirty-First Streets in Georgetown, just off Wisconsin Avenue. Its collection of 18,000 decorative objects documents six generations of the family of Mary Custis Washington and is the largest collection of Washingtonia apart from Mount Vernon. It is well worth visiting and is aptly described, perhaps with unintended irony given the importance of enslaved labor to white wealth-building, as "Tudor House: America's Story Lives Here."[33]

IN JANUARY 1839, Boutwell returned from his trip to Washington chastened by his introduction to the realities of slavery but excited about the political world he had seen. He had met his first president, Martin Van Buren; sixty-five years later, he and Theodore Roosevelt would meet in Boutwell's hometown of Groton. In the intervening decades, he would work closely with two of our greatest presidents, Abraham Lincoln and Ulysses S. Grant, while becoming an implacable foe of one of our worst, Andrew Johnson. First, though, Boutwell had a political apprenticeship to serve in Massachusetts politics.

2

Rising Star in
Massachusetts Politics

The city of Boston was draped in black on March 10, 1848. American flags were at half-mast and a steady rain muddied the streets. An artillery company on Boston Common began firing its cannons shortly after one o'clock. Bells tolled from the Park Street Church nearby. Six black horses pulling an empty caisson met the funeral train arriving from Washington that bore the body of John Quincy Adams. Several days of rain canceled the planned parade through Boston's streets, so the caisson proceeded directly to Faneuil Hall for a magnificent memorial service. Twenty-four members of Congress, each representing a different state of the Union, accompanied the casket from Washington and joined Massachusetts officials and Boston citizens in honoring the country's sixth president (1825–1829) and, remarkably at age eighty, a US congressman. Adams's body lay in state overnight in the historic hall that recalled the revolutionary days of his father and second president, John Adams. Taken by rail the next day to the family homestead in Quincy, south of Boston, John Quincy Adams received a final eulogy and was buried in the family tomb.[1]

George Boutwell met the funeral train from Washington as a member of the delegation responsible for hosting the visiting congressmen and overseeing the funeral arrangements. His guest and traveling companion for the ceremonies was Congressman John Wentworth of Illinois. As he sat with Wentworth at the banquet that night and on the rail trip to Quincy the following day, he thought back to his first visit to Washington, DC, in 1839. From the spectator gallery above the House floor, Boutwell had been transfixed by the parliamentary maneuvering of John Quincy Adams in foiling the attempts of southern

congressmen to deny him his constitutional right to offer petitions condemning slavery.[2]

Boutwell had marveled at the political theater unfolding before him,
with John Quincy Adams the leading man. On leaving the White House in
1829, Adams had made the remarkable decision to run for Congress, where
he served in the US House from 1831 until his death in 1848 (he suffered a
stroke on the floor of the House on February 22 and was moved to the Capitol rotunda, where he died the next day). As slavery became a contentious
issue in the 1830s, Adams took the lead in submitting petitions from northern
abolitionists seeking an end to slavery in the District of Columbia. Violent
arguments broke out in Congress as southern defenders of slavery sought to
rule these petitions out of order, even going so far as to institute what Adams
himself famously called the "gag rule" preventing open debate.[3]

In the debate in January 1839 that Boutwell likely witnessed, Adams presented two petitions that expressed his political and moral outrage over the
institution of slavery. The first recommended moving the nation's capital out
of the District of Columbia "to some point North, where the principles of the
Declaration of Independence are not treated as a mere rhetorical flourish."
The second proposed appointing a "committee on color" that would examine
the pedigrees of all the members of Congress. Should any member be found
to "have the least drop of colored blood in their veins, they shall be expelled
from office, and their places filled by persons of pure Anglo-Saxon blood."
Although the official record of that day's debate described Adams's petition as
"of a humorous character," Adams was in deadly earnest.[4]

Just shy of his twenty-first birthday, George Boutwell was witnessing one
of the great dramas in American political history: the ongoing struggle in the
halls of Congress between the Slave Power of the South and northern congressmen like Adams who continued to hammer home the inconsistencies of slavery
with the principles of the Declaration of Independence. In the 1830s, Adams
may have been fighting a lonely battle against slavery (his petition was voted
down 117 to 24), but the courage and passion displayed by the former president
would inspire the young Boutwell to think seriously of a career in politics.

ON HIS RETURN from Washington, Boutwell began his apprenticeship in
Massachusetts politics by running for local office. In the spring of 1839, he
won a seat on the Groton school committee, where he advocated a secular,

modernist approach to "common school" public education that he would later implement statewide in the 1850s as secretary of the Massachusetts Board of Education. Instead of having local ministers play a dominant role in setting educational norms and practices in Groton and other Massachusetts towns, Boutwell successfully initiated a campaign for the school committee to be composed of schoolteachers and other secular citizens.[5]

His political appetite whetted, Boutwell next set his sights on the Massachusetts House of Representatives. Coming from a family that abstained from alcohol, Boutwell joined the Temperance Party, a force that was significant in state politics but overshadowed by the dominant Whig and Democratic Parties. A central issue in the 1839 election was the recently enacted Massachusetts Fifteen Gallon Law, which prohibited the sale of alcohol in fewer than fifteen-gallon quantities. Given how blatantly the Whig-inspired law discriminated against working-class Democrats who couldn't afford to buy liquor in bulk, it was both unpopular and short-lived. Boutwell's opposition to the law, however, wasn't enough to win the election as a third-party candidate; he realized he would have to join one of the two main political parties—Whigs or Democrats—if he were to have any chance of future electoral success.

His farming background and "common school" education made him a natural for the Democratic Party, which supported him in the 1840 election on a platform of shortening the workday, reducing the poll tax, adopting a secret ballot voting system, abolishing imprisonment for debt, and extending voting hours to make it easier for laborers to vote. These were the issues Boutwell championed against the Whig opposition, dominated as it was by textile and business owners and Boston's old-money Brahmins. Despite the support of a major party, Boutwell lost that election as well, largely a victim of the Whig tide that swept William Henry Harrison into the White House over the incumbent president, Martin Van Buren.[6]

The disappointment of losing his first two elections was soon followed by far deeper troubles, starting with the death of his business partner and friend, Henry Woods, in January 1841. Woods, a Democrat, had been Groton's postmaster, with Boutwell enjoying the political and business benefits of helping to run the post office out of their store. With a new Whig administration in power in Washington, that would soon end. Given that George was also actively courting Henry's sister-in-law, Sarah, the personal loss was pronounced. Boutwell did serve as postmaster for a few months before the Whigs made a new appointment. But by April, not only had George Boutwell lost his good friend and business partner and the benefits of being postmaster; he had also taken on the guardianship of Henry Woods's two daughters and would soon have a wife.

A contemporary described Boutwell at the time as despondent, but George rebounded quickly, helping the Woods family by moving in with them. Then, on July 8, he married Sarah Adelia Thayer in a simple ceremony in town.[7]

Four years his senior, Sarah had attended the local private school, Groton Academy, later rechristened Lawrence Academy thanks to donations from the wealthy Lawrence family. Becoming a teacher who matched her husband's intellectual curiosity, she was plagued by ill health for much of her life. George and Sarah had two children, a daughter, Georgianna (1843), and a son, Francis (1847). Georgianna would stay single her entire life, joining her father for much of his time in Washington, DC, and becoming an important partner in his career. Francis worked variously in the woolen trade and the law before marrying late in life. Neither had any children, so this part of the Boutwell line ended when Georgianna died in 1933.

In November 1841, Boutwell ran a third time for the Massachusetts House and won. Political luck played a role, as the Whig Party had split badly following the death of President Harrison, after just thirty-one days in office, the previous April. Whigs in Massachusetts with their antislavery views were loath to support the new president, the former Democrat and Virginia slave owner John Tyler. With local Whigs fractured, Boutwell squeezed out a one-vote victory and was on his way to the Massachusetts legislature on Beacon Hill in Boston.

GEORGE BOUTWELL SERVED seven terms of one year each as a Democrat in the Massachusetts House, from 1841 to 1844 and 1846 through 1850. A detail-oriented legislator, Boutwell supported the ten-hour workday and other workers' rights issues advanced by the party's labor-oriented "Loco Foco" wing (the nickname comes from a type of match made famous when workers lit them after Tammany Hall bosses shut off the lights during a political meeting in New York City). But he also favored more conservative positions on the need for protective tariffs and a sound currency. Seen by colleagues as studious and reserved, Boutwell did have a wry sense of humor; one story he often told described a House session where a colleague's "opening sentence was: 'I rise, Mr. Speaker, and throw myself into the crackling embers of the debate.'" Boutwell concluded that, "in the judgment of the House, he never emerged."[8]

As a freshman legislator, Boutwell didn't hesitate to confront racial issues in general and the explosive issue of interracial marriage in particular. William Lloyd Garrison and his *The Liberator* newspaper had sought for years to repeal a 1705 Massachusetts statute forbidding mixed marriages. Opponents argued that legalizing interracial marriages was but one small step on the path to full civil equality for Blacks. By 1842, support for repeal was growing, with Boutwell leading such efforts along with legislative colleagues Henry Wilson and Charles Francis Adams. The following year, Boutwell was joined in the effort by his father, Sewell, newly elected to the House, representing Lunenburg in Worcester County. By then, prospects for repeal of the ban had improved, despite the opposition's mobilizing likely fictitious petitions from "colored women" who complained that repeal of the ban would lead to their husbands deserting them to marry white women.[9]

In March 1843, George and his father joined the majority in repealing the statute by a vote of 174 to 139. The opposition predicted a collapse of social morals and rampant miscegenation; in fact, the new law helped energize efforts to outlaw discrimination and segregation throughout the Commonwealth on railway and streetcars, in public schools, and in the militia.[10]

That same month, Boutwell took on another controversial issue when he introduced a bill to reduce the state poll tax, a fee charged to those registering to vote or at the polling stations themselves, from one dollar to fifty cents. First known as a "per capita" tax in colonial times that was imposed on all citizens and became part of the cry of "no taxation without representation" which ignited the American Revolution, by the 1840s it had become more of a general means of raising revenue than a mechanism for regulating voting. Nonetheless, it could still be used by the party in power to determine who could, and could not, vote.

This was what Boutwell argued before his colleagues in the House when he charged that such taxes were being applied indiscriminately by "irresponsible assessors" to keep laborers and the poor, i.e., Democrats, from voting. In heavily Whig Massachusetts, the Democrats relied for support on immigrant Irish Catholics, whose numbers were increasing with the immigration following the great potato famine in Ireland in the 1840s. Responding to derogatory comments about immigrants during debate in the House, Boutwell retorted, "who in this community [is] not descended from foreigners? If foreigners come here ignorant . . . let them not be treated like enemies. The sooner they [are] placed upon a footing to exercise the rights and duties of citizenship, the better it [will] be for the community."[11]

Following the Civil War, when poll taxes were used in the South to keep Blacks from voting, Boutwell would use similar arguments about the poll tax being nothing more than "a relic" that had no business "in the policy of free States."[12]

A third cause Boutwell championed, one he shared with Margaret Fuller and the abolitionists William Lloyd Garrison and Wendell Phillips, was abolishing capital punishment. In early 1843, he supported a bill that ultimately was voted down, but not before a mischievous colleague inserted a provision that, should capital punishment not be abolished, then that "portion of the clergy who are the most zealous advocates of judicial murder" should do the hanging themselves.[13]

Boutwell's initial stint in the Massachusetts legislature came to an end when he lost the 1844 election due, as he admitted, to "some political sins of my own." In truth, the "political sin" was an example of Boutwell doing the right thing but with adverse political consequences. The year before, he had introduced a bill requiring banks and corporations to reveal to local tax assessors the names of all stockholders residing in each city and town, along with the numbers and par values of their shares. Not surprisingly, these stockholders "who had theretofore escaped taxation were enraged." This included well-to-do Whigs in Groton who had previously supported him but now helped vote him out of office in the 1844 election.[14]

Boutwell finished his first three terms in the Massachusetts House with a growing reputation as a no-nonsense, detailed-oriented legislator who took his work seriously. With black, slick-backed hair and a sharp chin not yet graced with a beard, he could easily be mistaken for one of the many accountants scurrying among the banks and merchant houses of Boston. Legislative sessions in those days lasted three months, from January through March, giving Boutwell and his colleagues the rest of the year to make a living. Back in Groton, he built up his dry goods business while relishing the role of new father with namesake daughter Georgianna, born in May 1843. Most importantly for his future political prospects, he studiously cultivated the support of his fellow townsmen through his work on the school committee and other local activities.

AMERICA IN THE 1840S was feeling the tremors of the sectional split over slavery that had temporarily been quieted by the Compromise of 1820, which admitted Missouri as a slave state, Maine as a free state, and permitted slavery in the new Louisiana territories below the 36°30′ parallel (Missouri's southern border, extending westward toward the Pacific Ocean). In Massachusetts, antislavery societies and *The Liberator* newspaper sparked the flames of abolitionism. For his part, George Boutwell introduced a bill in 1843 in the Massachusetts legislature condemning the three-fifths provision of the US Constitution, the compromise engineered by the South in 1787 to increase its political power in Washington by having enslaved persons count as "three-fifths" of a person in order to increase the southern states' numbers in Congress and the Electoral College. Boutwell's admittedly symbolic measure did pass and was introduced in the US Congress by John Quincy Adams, but it died in committee.

Boutwell's "three-fifths" measure had been sparked by the furor in October 1842 over the arrest in Boston by federal authorities of a fugitive slave named George Latimer. Boston abolitionists led by Garrison and Phillips gathered more than 60,000 names on petitions denouncing the federal government's Fugitive Slave Act, which mandated the arrest and return of enslaved persons escaping from the South. Frederick Douglass applauded what he referred to as the "monster petition" that was delivered to the Massachusetts legislature, which itself passed a "personal liberty law" forbidding state authorities from participating in the arrest of fugitive slaves. Such opposition availed little, though, as the US Supreme Court had ruled in a case from Pennsylvania that federal authorities must comply with the law and were not to be interfered with by state or local officials. Powerless to prevent federal marshals and courts from sending Latimer back to his master in Virginia, Boutwell and his colleagues in the Massachusetts House could only register symbolic but ineffective protests in Washington, DC.[15]

Equally futile was Boutwell's opposition as a member of a House committee with Charles Francis Adams concerning the admission of Texas in 1845 as a slave state. Tensions with Mexico over the status of Texas and the delineation of its boundaries then sparked the US-Mexican War of 1846–1848. Many in the North rightfully saw the conflict as having been stoked by the Slave Power in the South seeking new territory for slavery. A devout believer in America's Manifest Destiny, President James K. Polk engineered an incident on the

Texas-Mexican border that all but ensured war. By February 1848, victory over Mexico led to the third largest acquisition of territory in American history, surpassed only by the 1803 Louisiana and 1867 Alaska Purchases, encompassing the present-day states of California, Nevada, Utah, and parts of Arizona, New Mexico, Colorado, and Wyoming.

War with Mexico put Boutwell in a tough position politically. Although opposed to slavery, he felt duty-bound as a Democrat to support the president's prosecution of the war. Accordingly, he cast a key vote in the Massachusetts House in 1847 approving a $20,000 appropriation for the raising of a state regiment to send to Mexico. Lloyd Garrison and *The Liberator* newspaper pounced, gleefully announcing that Boutwell had revealed the true nature of the Democrats as "a profligate pro-slavery party."[16]

Admittedly, Boutwell was seeking to have it both ways, being a loyal Democrat while expressing his antislavery views. He did so by echoing the party line that the Mexican war, with its potential for vast land acquisitions south to the Rio Grande and west to the Pacific Ocean, had little relevance for the expansion of slavery. He supported President Polk's rationalization that, as slave-based agriculture was ill suited to the arid deserts of the Southwest, the issue itself was an abstraction.[17]

At the time, there was a freshman congressman in Washington, DC, who felt very much the same: thirty-nine-year-old Abraham Lincoln, who was campaigning in Massachusetts within miles of Boutwell's home. Though a member of the more antislavery Whig Party, Lincoln "did not share the fears of abolitionists that the annexation of Texas would lead to the spread, and hence the perpetuation, of slavery." Abolitionists in Massachusetts and elsewhere were outraged by such views, fearing that extending slavery into the western territories would forever embed it in the fabric of the union. In Lincoln's case, as a newcomer in Washington, he gave priority to working with southern Whigs, not wanting "to stir up sectional animosities." While Lincoln did give a famous speech accusing Polk of "the sheerest deception" in provoking Mexico into war, the Illinois congressman joined Boutwell in repeating the fatuous contention that Polk wasn't seeking to extend slavery into America's Southwest (which the president most certainly was).[18]

As noted by the historian David Potter, Boutwell and Lincoln were subject to "the gravitational pull of party loyalties" in giving priority to the national aims of the Democratic and Whig parties, respectively, over regional concerns with slavery and abolitionism. While it was precisely this moderating function

of the parties at the national level that allowed the country to contain sectional divisions and forestall any serious debate over slavery from 1820 to 1850,
that consensus was nearing an end. Lincoln's refusal, and that of other prominent Whigs, to identify slavery as a cause of the Mexican War deepened a rift
in the party, leading many so-called "Conscience" Whigs to bolt and support
the creation of a new party, the Free Soil Party, to contest the 1848 election.
As for George Boutwell, his attempt to balance his antislavery conviction with
allegiance to a national Democratic Party that was controlled by the southern
Slave Power was becoming increasingly untenable in Massachusetts.[19]

In the short term, Lincoln and Boutwell tried to make the best of their
political quandaries. Lincoln, campaigning in Massachusetts for the Whig
presidential nominee, Gen. Zachary Taylor, insisted that the Whigs were the
true antislavery party. Such protestations did little, however, to stem the deepening divisions between southern "Cotton" Whigs and their northern mercantile allies and the "Conscience" antislavery Whigs, many of whom were
deserting to the Free Soil Party (so named because it opposed any extension
of slavery into the western territories). For his part, George Boutwell in 1849
would help craft a strong plank at the Massachusetts Democratic State Convention condemning slavery and its extension into the territories, but increasingly, he felt alienated in a party that at the national level became even more
strident in its defense of slavery. In just a few short years, both Boutwell and
Lincoln would be seeking new political homes.

BOUTWELL WON BACK his seat in the Massachusetts House in November
1846, having strategically enlarged his base of support in the community
by winning election as Groton town clerk the previous March. Methodical and focused, he was educating himself on those issues—transportation,
finance, and education—of greatest concern to his constituency. In 1845 he
was appointed by the governor to the Massachusetts Railroad Commission,
just as the extension of the Fitchburg Railroad to Groton and Concord, with a
station near Henry David Thoreau's cabin on Walden Pond, was transforming
life in these communities. In Thoreau's case, this was not progress—he hated
the railroad. But for George Boutwell, a trip from Groton to the State House in
Boston that had taken several hours each way in the early 1840s by stagecoach
now took only an hour by rail.

He also spent these years reading and writing extensively about labor
and economic issues. Believing that "labor was the only source of wealth,"

he favored measures to increase investment in domestic production, limit the public debt, and improve working conditions for common laborers. His articles in statewide and national publications on economic as well as foreign policy issues, such as the Oregon boundary dispute with England, spread his name beyond the borders of Massachusetts. Later in the decade, Boutwell became one of three bank commissioners, charged by the legislature with examining the Commonwealth's banking institutions and their charters, as well as investigating fraud.[20]

Boutwell also threw himself into progressive causes, such as examining the deplorable conditions at the state's one hospital for those deemed "insane," in Worcester. Similar to the investigative journalism that Margaret Fuller was doing for Horace Greeley's *New York Tribune* (she once spent a night at Sing Sing prison for background on a story), Boutwell visited hospitals in Rhode Island and New York. In none of these, Boutwell wrote, were patients ever "naked or confined in a cell." By contrast, he was "shocked" at the conditions at the state facility in Worcester, "by the sight of women . . . who had no bedding but straw . . . no clothing whatever . . . and their arms tied so as to limit the use of the hands." He and his colleagues advocated forcefully for more humane treatment, which was gradually adopted.[21]

Boutwell's main passion, though, was education. In 1847, he attracted the attention of colleagues when, as a member of the House Committee on Education, he convincingly dissected the deficiencies of a bill proposed by his own committee chair, John Lothrop Motley. A Harvard graduate, Motley was seeking to take funds promised to the primary and secondary common schools that Boutwell had attended and give them instead to state colleges.

Oliver Wendell Holmes Sr., the famed American writer, physician, and father of the Supreme Court justice of the same name, recounted what transpired in his memoir of Motley. Holmes wrote that Motley was convinced that he had presented a "most masterly report . . . elaborate. . . . unanswerable." There then rose to speak "a young man from some country town," who "demolished the report." Holmes wrote how Motley dejectedly described himself as being cast "on his own dunghill, ignominiously beaten." Motley would later write that he was greatly impressed with "the speech-making faculty of a Representative of a common school education." For his part, Boutwell would tell Holmes that Motley "espoused the weak side of the question and the unpopular one," adding a bit smugly, "failure was inevitable."[22]

Back home in Groton, Boutwell's support for public education was opposed by those who favored the town's private school, Lawrence Academy. Spearheading efforts in 1848 to establish a local public high school, Boutwell argued that it should not be subsumed under Lawrence Academy, and that "we need a [separate] High School which shall be as an Academy *for us all*." The effort took over a decade, but the Groton public high school opened its doors in 1860.[23]

IN THIS SECOND stint in the Massachusetts legislature, Boutwell plunged into two of the most incendiary issues having to do with slavery: the question of states seceding from the Union and the domestic slave trade (the import of slaves had been banned under the US Constitution since 1808). Both illustrated the controversial nature of slavery and its growing consequences for the nation. And for Boutwell, both revolved around what he considered one of the pillars of democracy and one championed by John Quincy Adams: the right of individual citizens to petition their government for redress of grievances.

With its origins in the Magna Carta signed in 1215, the right of petition has been refined through the centuries, giving first the English nobility, then Parliament, and finally individual citizens the right to demand of their government (or monarch) the lawful execution of its powers. As such it is one of the bedrocks of the First Amendment and American democracy. Little used in America until the 1830s, petitions to Congress "began flowing . . . in a constantly increasing stream" to abolish slavery in the District of Columbia. In the years following, abolitionists in Massachusetts adopted the same tactic, submitting petitions that would require the legislature "to devise measures for a peaceable secession of Massachusetts from the Union" if slavery was not abolished.[24]

This was provocative stuff indeed, given occasional threats from southern states to leave the Union over states' rights issues such as slavery and tariffs. In the Massachusetts House, legislators responded to one such petition by demanding that debate be shut off and the measure tabled, but Boutwell objected to the motion being denied a hearing. Invoking the rights of citizens to petition their government, even for unpopular causes, he asked that it be referred to the Judiciary Committee. Once in committee, however, Boutwell refused when asked to sponsor the measure himself, asserting his belief in the sanctity of the Union and the Constitution. Abolitionists including William Lloyd Garrison had a field day, criticizing Boutwell for seeking to have it both ways ("how disinterested the action, how exact the calculation!") in affirming the right of petition while standing for union over slavery. For

George Boutwell, that was exactly the point, to support both the right of petition and the sanctity of union.[25]

Few Americans today realize that such threats to dissolve the Union first
originated, not with South Carolina and the other southern states, but with
Yankee Federalists in New England in the early 1800s. At the time, northern commercial and political interests were becoming increasingly concerned
with the growing influence of southern Slave Power, represented for them by
the policies of the "Virginia dynasty" presidents—Thomas Jefferson, James
Madison, and James Monroe—who served continuously from 1801 to 1825.
When the War of 1812 with Britain led to financial hardship for Yankee shipping and other sectors of the economy, the New England states almost voted
for secession at the Hartford Convention of 1814, but retreated.[26]

There was a second, far more unusual case, where Boutwell defended the
right of petition. In February 1849, a farmer on Cape Cod caused an uproar in
the state legislature when he submitted a petition to allow him "to import one
or two slaves from the South" and hold "them in perpetual servitude" to help
him on his farm. Although slavery had never been formally outlawed in Massachusetts, the practice had all but died out prior to 1800; local abolitionists
were proud of the fact that the official state census for 1790 listed no enslaved
people. Over the years, civil courts had repeatedly awarded freedom to Blacks
brought into the state by their masters, and Massachusetts had become a hot-
bed of northern abolitionism. Accordingly, many House members deemed the
petition "an insult to the dignity of the House" and demanded that it be withdrawn. Yet for George Boutwell, the principle of the right of petition was again
at stake. Answering those colleagues who denounced the petitioner, Boutwell
emphasized the right of petition as "extended to every citizen of this Commonwealth" by both the Massachusetts Constitution of 1780 (Article 19) and
the US Constitution of 1787 (First Amendment). Even if he disagreed with its
intent, the petition nonetheless deserved to be referred to the Judiciary Committee, to be treated the same as the "petitions presented daily for the secession of Massachusetts from the Union."

William Lloyd Garrison and the abolitionist community again howled in
protest, accusing Boutwell of playing "the demagogue" and being "willfully
blind to all moral distinction." Nonetheless, he stood firm on the principle of
the right of petition; in the event, no slaves were ever imported to Cape Cod.[27]

This commitment to principle, even when it cost him politically, would be
a recurring feature of Boutwell's career. No matter how strongly he felt about

an issue, he always conceded the basic importance of conforming to constitutional norms as fundamental to the preservation of American liberties.

AS HE NEARED the end of his political apprenticeship in the Massachusetts House of Representatives, Boutwell was well positioned to seek higher office. Having recently turned thirty, he was a recognized leader of the Democratic Party and easily won the party's nomination for governor in 1849. At the Democratic convention held in Springfield in September, Boutwell engineered the passage of resolutions condemning slavery and its extension into the western territories. This made possible increased political cooperation with the state's new Free Soil Party, led by disaffected Whigs such as Charles Francis Adams who were strenuously antislavery. In the election that November, Boutwell lost badly to the Whig candidate, but the fact that the combined Democrat–Free Soil vote surpassed the Whig total provided tantalizing hints of what a future coalition might accomplish.

Personally, Boutwell had forged close political relationships with two fellow House members, Nathaniel Banks (future Speaker of the US House of Representatives and Civil War general) and Henry Wilson (future US senator and vice president to U. S. Grant in 1873), that would serve him well in Massachusetts politics and subsequently on the national scene. All three men were from modest origins, supported temperance and opposed slavery, and had strong connections with working-class voters. Of the three, Boutwell was considered the most astute politically, a "nimble-witted party manager" who was skilled at debate and a master of legislative detail. Even newspapers outside of New England were taking notice; the *New York Daily Herald* reported that "Mr. Boutwell . . . enjoys an enviable reputation . . . he is little more than thirty years old but has been a prominent public man here for the last eight years."[28]

AT MID-CENTURY, GEORGE BOUTWELL had seen the country grow from a fledgling republic of nine million people in 1818 to a continental nation of twenty-three million. There were now thirty-one states in the Union, spanning nearly three million square miles—the size of Australia. The American economy, largely stagnant between 1790 and 1820, had exploded by more than 50 percent between 1820 and 1850, and would continue at that rate in the decade ahead. The US railroad network was expanding at breakneck speed, while the telegraph and newspapers were bringing news almost instantaneously to all parts of the country.[29]

Far from dying a natural death, as some of the Founding Fathers might have hoped, slavery had entrenched itself even more firmly in the American economy. With southern cotton comprising 40 percent of all US exports and 80 percent of the global cotton trade, the number of enslaved Blacks needed to harvest what many called "white gold" now numbered three million.

But politically, the uneasy compromise over slavery was fraying badly. The Missouri Compromise of 1820 was three decades old and the Slave Power in the South was looking to expand into the newly won western territories. Northern acquiescence to slavery, whether based on racial prejudice or the wealth generated by cotton, was weakening due to the twin assaults of the abolition movement and the emergence of new political movements such as the Free Soil Party. Political realignments were in progress, and George Boutwell was about to take advantage of them.

3

Governor of Massachusetts

George Boutwell detested the month of March in Boston. Skies were uniformly gray, snow was turning to slush in the streets, and the trees in the Public Garden were weeks away from beginning to flower. Back home in Groton, the planting season wouldn't begin for another two months.

All this was forgotten on March 8, 1850, as Boutwell made his way down the wide granite steps of the State House with colleagues Henry Wilson and Nathaniel Banks to take a stroll around Boston Common. What they discussed that day would upend Massachusetts politics and launch the careers of all three men onto the national scene.

The day before in the nation's capital, Massachusetts senator Daniel Webster had thrown a hand grenade into the sectional politics of slavery. In his famous Seventh of March Speech, Webster spoke to a packed gallery in the US Senate, declaring his support for a grand compromise that sought to heal the deepening rift between North and South. Proclaiming to speak "not as a Massachusetts man, nor as a Northern man . . . but as an American," Webster urged the adoption of a package of measures put together by Senator Henry Clay of Kentucky that both men hoped would quiet the growing calls for secession in the South and the ever-strident voices of abolitionism in the North.[1]

Henry Clay, known as "The Great Compromiser" for his decades-long efforts to keep the Union from imploding over slavery, had worked with Senators Stephen Douglas of Illinois and John C. Calhoun of South Carolina on separate pieces of legislation that, when passed in September, would come to be known as the Compromise of 1850. These included: admitting California as a free state; using "popular sovereignty" referendums to determine whether slavery would be permitted in the New Mexico and Utah territories; banning the slave trade in the District of Columbia (administered by the federal government); and implementing a more stringent Fugitive Slave Act.

Webster was immediately criticized, especially in his home state of Massachusetts, for supporting a compromise that would permit slavery to expand far beyond the South. Abolitionists such as William Lloyd Garrison and Wendell Phillips, fearful that four new slave states might be created out of territory stretching from Texas to California, charged Webster with capitulating to the southern Slave Power. The long-revered Massachusetts senator, one of the great orators in American politics, had hoped he could "dispense the threatening storm" of sectional disunion. Instead, he was accused by some of "whoring after southern support" for his widely known presidential ambitions. His speech did little to placate the South whereas it further deepened the divide between his "Cotton" and "Conscience" Whig colleagues. With one speech, Webster had made far easier the prospect of a winning coalition between the Democratic and Free Soil Parties, which was precisely what Boutwell, Wilson, and Banks were discussing as they turned down Beacon Street and walked into Boston Common.[2]

Nathaniel Banks was a fellow Democrat and supporter of Boutwell's efforts in 1849 to strengthen the antislavery plank of the state Democratic Party. Henry Wilson was a former Whig who left the party in 1848 to help establish the Free Soil Party, a refuge for "Conscience" Whigs and antislavery Democrats. Wilson, still seething the day after Webster's speech, took the initiative in seeking to revive the idea of a Free Soil–Democratic coalition to contest Whig supremacy in Massachusetts. Banks, recalling that similar efforts in the previous year's election had come to nothing, was skeptical, asking Wilson "if he was fool enough" to cross Daniel Webster, still a formidable political power in the Bay State. Boutwell reportedly had little to say during the walk, but was clearly intrigued that such a coalition could improve his chances of becoming governor.[3]

Over the next several months, events conspired to strengthen the political feasibility of Democrats and Free Soilers coalescing to defeat the Whigs in the November election. In July, Whig President Zachary Taylor died and was replaced by a Compromise supporter, Millard Fillmore, further alienating "Conscience" Whigs. In Massachusetts, one of the rising stars of the antislavery movement, the brilliant Harvard-educated lawyer Charles Sumner, was gaining prominence within the Free Soil Party as a passionate abolitionist.

Sumner had recently gained national attention for representing a Black family, the Roberts, in the case of *Roberts v. City of Boston*, challenging the legality of the city's segregated schools. Sumner and the Roberts lost in court, but in 1855 the Massachusetts legislature would mandate racially integrated schools throughout the Commonwealth.[4]

As for the Democrats, George Boutwell began crafting legislative proposals with Free Soiler Henry Wilson on issues that would appeal to farmers and laborers in Massachusetts and strengthen coalition building in local communities across the Commonwealth. These included increased appropriations for common school education, limiting working hours, stricter regulation of corporations and railroads, introducing the secret ballot, poll tax reduction, and seeking greater public oversight of Harvard College.[5]

AS THE ELECTION CAMPAIGN got under way in the fall of 1850, divisions remained between conservative Democrats and the more liberal, antislavery Free Soilers. A bad pun making the rounds told of a Free Soil man, asked whether he supported the Democrat Boutwell for governor, responding with "no, our state government is a 'bout-well' enough as it is." Still, Henry Wilson made it known that the Free Soil leadership would support Boutwell for governor in return for sending a Free Soil man, most likely Charles Sumner, to promote the antislavery cause in the US Senate.[6]

The Whigs, meanwhile, howled with indignation at the prospect of losing the governorship, control of the state legislature, and the US Senate seat long held by Daniel Webster. Incredulous that working-class Democrats and abolitionist Free Soilers were putting an end to Whig dominance, textile magnate Abbott Lawrence exposed his Protestant nativist prejudice by slamming the Boston Irish for supporting Boutelle (*sic*) for governor. The Whigs were especially alarmed over the coalition's support for the Ten-Hour law (workers' hours at the time were unregulated), as well as the secret ballot, both of which Boutwell had supported in the legislature and both of which would weaken Whig control of factory workers.[7]

Come November, the coalition prevailed, winning a majority of seats in both the Massachusetts House and the Senate. The Whig candidate for governor did win a plurality of the vote in a three-person race (47 percent to Boutwell's 30 percent), but he failed to gain the 50 percent majority needed to win outright. Accordingly, the gubernatorial election would be decided in the Massachusetts legislature, where Boutwell's election was all but assured.

Joining Boutwell as governor would be Henry Wilson as the new president of
the Massachusetts Senate, and Nathaniel Banks as Speaker of the Massachusetts House. Rounding out the grand bargain, the Free Soil Party would send a
staunch antislavery senator, Charles Sumner, to Washington for the full term
of six years. If only things had gone that smoothly.

EVEN BEFORE THE November election, prominent members of both parties
were expressing doubts about their coalition partner. Free Soilers distrusted
Boutwell for what they saw as political opportunism in watering down con-
demnations of slavery by the Massachusetts legislature. Democratic Party
leaders such as Caleb Cushing feared that likely Senate candidate Charles
Sumner's strong abolitionist views would undermine the Compromise of 1850
and fracture the country.[8]

When the Massachusetts legislature convened in January 1851, it moved
quickly to elect Boutwell, not yet turned thirty-three, as the Commonwealth's
youngest-ever governor. But the grand bargain then fell apart. Henry Wilson
was furious as Cushing and other prominent Democrats, known as Hunkers
(the term comes from "hanker," as in "hankering" after political spoils), continued to oppose Sumner's election to the US Senate. The Free Soil poet and
editor John Greenleaf Whittier had warned of this just days after the November election, writing that "without some *positive* assurance [that Democrats
would support Sumner] . . . I for one wd never vote for Geo. S. Boutwell."[9]

As the newly installed governor, George Boutwell could have used his
influence to pressure his Democratic colleagues to elect Sumner, but he chose
not to, knowing he would need the help of Cushing and others to enact his
domestic legislative program for Massachusetts. Prominent antislavery activists were outraged; Samuel Gridley Howe, husband of Julia Ward Howe, disparaged Boutwell as "a timid, cunning, time-serving trimmer."[10]

Following a stalemate that lasted months, Henry Wilson ultimately engineered Sumner's election to the US Senate. Antislavery advocates such as William S. Robinson, editor of the *Lowell American*, were jubilant, asserting that
the "year of darkness and doubt cast . . . by the great treachery of the 7th of
March, 1850" was over. The author of that "treachery," Daniel Webster, died in
October 1852, his legacy in Massachusetts forever compromised.[11]

Sumner received the news of his election while dining with Free-Soil
colleague Charles Francis Adams at the Adams family mansion on Beacon Hill. Seated at the table that night was middle son Henry Adams,

twenty-one years old, who had enjoyed a front row seat to all the political horse-trading that he would later characterize as "jockeys selling a race . . . a flagrantly corrupt political bargain." Thus began Henry's lifelong disdain for political wheeling and dealing (more so when his side came up short) and for politicians such as George Boutwell, whom he loved to scorn.[12]

IN HIS FIRST ADDRESS as governor, George Boutwell denounced slavery while acknowledging that he was legally bound to uphold the laws of the land. This included the Fugitive Slave Act, no matter how repugnant he thought it. Foreshadowing the secession of South Carolina in 1860, he warned that, "If a state has a right to nullify, or a citizen to resist an act of Congress, our government ceases to be a government of laws." As with Abraham Lincoln, his reverence for the Constitution and for the sanctity of the Union was nothing less than a "civil religion."[13] In his inaugural address on January 16, the young governor declared that time was on the side of the abolitionists. He noted how, with California having joined the Union as a free state, "the entire coast of the Pacific is dedicated to freedom." He pointed out that "the commerce of the country is in the hands of the North" and that the economic advantages of a free-labor system would only grow over time compared to the slave-based agriculture of the South. Declaring that he regarded slavery as "a moral, political, social and industrial evil," he cautioned that "actual conflict" over slavery "would end in the destruction of the American Union."

Abolitionists thought Boutwell's remarks spineless and criticized them accordingly. *The Liberator* castigated Boutwell as "a precious specimen of Northern doughface-ism, political hypocrisy, and benevolent twaddle!" The poet Whittier, who had reluctantly worked for Boutwell's election, was equally furious: "I have read the message of Gov. B. It is, under the circumstances, insulting and monstrous. May God forgive us for permitting his election!"[14]

Boutwell's refusal to actively oppose the capture and return to slavery of fugitive Blacks also soured his relationship with his Free Soil coalition partners and the newly elected senator, Charles Sumner. Wanting the Free Soil Party to establish its own identity, Sumner warned his colleagues that Boutwell "is in our way." While respecting Boutwell's antislavery credentials, the new senator feared that the young governor's ultimate allegiance to a national Democratic party that was very much proslavery would taint the Free Soil Party among Massachusetts voters. Sumner's fears turned out to be well founded; the coalition never did coalesce effectively and would last only two more years. Not until Sumner and Boutwell joined forces to create the new Republican Party in the mid-1850s would they begin an effective political partnership seeking to abolish slavery.[15]

WITHIN A MONTH of becoming governor, Boutwell faced his first real test on the issue that was tearing the country apart. Boston had been in a state of turmoil for months, its citizens deeply divided over how far to oppose federal authorities in carrying out the Fugitive Slave Act. Hundreds of formerly enslaved Blacks were making their way through Boston en route to Canada, fleeing southern bounty hunters and federal marshals and heading north from Maryland, Pennsylvania, and New York. Local Black leaders urged Boston's Black community to arm themselves and to once again "make Massachusetts a battlefield in defense of liberty" by physically resisting enforcement of the hated law. Fights broke out in Faneuil Hall when pro-Unionist supporters of Daniel Webster tried to break up antislavery meetings.[16]

Then, on February 15, federal marshals arrested Shadrach Minkins, an escaped slave who'd been living in Boston for a year while working in a coffee-house near Boutwell's office in the State House. Minkins was arraigned before a US magistrate but managed to escape to Canada when Black supporters spirited him out of the courtroom to Montreal via the Underground Railroad.[17]

As Minkins was making his way to Montreal, another escaped slave, Thomas Sims, was hiding out on a sloop arriving in Boston from Savannah. Sims managed to evade authorities for his first two months in the city, but was arrested in April, held in chains, and brought before a federal commissioner. He was ordered to be sent back to Georgia where a whipping administered by his owner was well publicized in the North. Following the proceedings from the governor's office, Boutwell felt powerless to act when Magistrate Judge George Curtis returned Thomas Sims to bondage and physical torture.[18]

The Sims affair convulsed Boston. Local protests were organized by the Boston Vigilance Committee, founded a year earlier in Faneuil Hall, with speakers including Frederick Douglass urging resistance to the Fugitive Slave Act. Reports that armed abolitionists would seek to free Sims led authorities to seal off the US Court House with chains. Boutwell could see the thousands of antislavery protestors on Boston Common from his State House office, but he felt powerless to intervene. William Lloyd Garrison heaped scorn on the governor's inaction while Ralph Waldo Emerson noted in his journal that "we shall never feel well again until that detestable law is nullified in Massachusetts and until the Government is assured that once and for all it cannot and shall not be executed here."[19]

With the country preparing to celebrate the seventy-fifth anniversary of the Declaration of Independence, the fact that southern slave owners, with the blessing of the federal government, were sending armed agents into the North to forcibly retrieve their "property" made a mockery of the concept of "all men being equal." In Boston above all, the cradle of liberty, the sight of Thomas Sims being led in chains to be sent back to Georgia vividly portrayed the inhumanity of slavery even for those who had never been to the South. George Boutwell was constrained by the Constitution from intervening, and he was roundly criticized for his inaction. But the Sims affair left its mark, and soon he would more forcefully stand up to the southern Slave Power.

THE PUBLICATION OF *Uncle Tom's Cabin* by Harriet Beecher Stowe in 1851 helped fuel the North's growing revulsion against slavery. Frederick Douglass described the book's reception to that of lighting "a million campfires in front of the embattled hosts of slavery." Abraham Lincoln as president may or may not have later greeted Stowe by saying, "So you're the little woman who wrote the book that made this great war." More than anything, Stowe's portrayal of enslaved people as human beings, and of the inhumanity of the slave catchers, helped fan abolitionist flames among northern whites.

Questions of American identity and citizenship—of who counted as "American" and who did not—were becoming more and more pronounced in the 1850s. Of four million Blacks in the country, three and a half million of them—men, women, and children—were enslaved, representing 30 percent of the population of the South. Not one was considered "American," or even a person, being merely the property of their owner. The remaining 500,000 "free" Blacks, more than 50,000 of whom also lived in the South, had only limited legal rights and citizenship status. One of the most persuasive rallying cries of the abolitionists, especially through church networks, was the imperative of conferring dignity and personhood to Black "Americans."

Growing immigration from abroad added to the debates about identity and citizenship. The arrival of several hundred thousand Irish (fleeing the ravages of the 1840s potato famine) and German immigrants set off a nativist backlash among white Protestant Americans. On the west coast, the influx of mainly Chinese immigrants sparked similar animosities and the passage of state codes and laws restricting their rights. By 1860, America had four million immigrants out of a total population of thirty-one million people.

And before any of these, there were the original inhabitants of America, the Indigenous peoples who were constantly being uprooted and pushed west as the country fulfilled its Manifest Destiny of expanding to the Pacific Ocean. Their population in 1860 was 340,000, none of them considered either a citizen or "American."

So, fully one-third of the total US population of 31.5 million—Blacks, immigrants, and members of Indigenous tribes—was told they had little or no claim to being "American" or a citizen. But their numbers were growing, especially Blacks and immigrants, as was the social friction and outright conflict engendered by their presence. White plantation owners in the South were fearful of slave uprisings, anti-immigrant riots were occurring in major northern cities, and the Plains Indians were violently resisting the encroachment of white settlers seeking gold and farmland. More and more, the question of who qualified as "American," and with what benefits as a citizen, was coming to dominate the national discourse.

ONE OF THOSE pondering the question was Ralph Waldo Emerson. By the 1850s, the brief burst of Transcendentalist influence had begun to decline, but for Emerson, a new phase in his life was beginning, characterized by a much more activist, antislavery stance, fueled by his outrage over the Fugitive Slave Act. Emerson the philosopher of "self-reliance" was becoming Emerson the defender of the need for "a thoroughgoing democratic cultural pluralism." No longer just a philosopher, he began engaging far more actively in abolitionist and other political issues of the day, including supporting George Boutwell's candidacy for the US House of Representatives in the late 1850s.

As was true of many abolitionists, Emerson's antislavery stance was tainted by his belief in the racial and cultural superiority of the Anglo-Saxon race. Drawing his inspiration from the great German and English romantics and the Scottish philosopher Thomas Carlyle, Emerson believed that Anglo-Saxons were "the natural rulers of other races." In passionately supporting abolition in the 1850s, he did so as much from his belief that the institution of slavery was corrupting white, Anglo-Saxon ideals of freedom and liberty as from a concern for the welfare of several million enslaved Blacks.[20]

Over time, Emerson did reject the more extreme "scientific racism" theories of Swiss naturalist Louis Agassiz and others on the innate inferiority of

Blacks. While still believing in the cultural superiority of whites, Emerson wrote that "you cannot draw a line where a race begins or ends." For the "Sage of Concord," culture was the determinant of identity, not race. And as America became more culturally diverse in the 1850s, Emerson's "instinct was to embrace diversity rather than reject it."[21]

IN NOVEMBER 1852, Boutwell as governor spoke to these issues of American identity when he gave the dedication speech at a local monument commemorating the deaths of colonial settlers during King Philip's War in the late 1600s. On a snowy November morning in Sudbury, Massachusetts, Boutwell recalled how that conflict, between the English settlers of southern New England and the Wampanoag and other Indian tribes led by the chieftain Metacomet (commonly referred to by his anglicized name, King Philip), had been a defining experience in the evolution of an "American" identity. In a war that destroyed farmland, hunting grounds, and Native American encampments and settler villages, including Boutwell's hometown of Groton, thousands on both sides died from wounds, disease, and famine. As Boutwell noted, if the "[American] Revolution was a struggle for *freedom*; the contest with Philip was for *existence . . .* it was a war of extermination."[22]

In the late 1600s, the 40,000 to 60,000 colonial settlers living in New England had only just begun the process of becoming "American." No longer "English," they received no help from the mother country during the conflict and lived a frontier existence, where boundaries were constantly shifting between their world and that of their Wampanoag, Algonquin, and other Native American neighbors. In the decades following, the publication of hundreds of letters, diaries, and chronicles testified to the conflict's importance in shaping the colonists' sense of identity. The most famous of these was Mary Rowlandson's account of her three-month captivity by the Nipmuck tribe and her "redemption" after being ransomed for twenty pounds; her book was published in 1682 and became the first "best seller" in American history.[23]

Reminding his audience that "the Past is not dead. By a mysterious cord it is connected with the Present," Boutwell summarized the devastation that overtook both settler and Native American alike, including kidnappings of white settlers and the selling of Indian women and children into slavery. In dedicating a memorial to slain settlers, Boutwell surprisingly focused on the conflict's catastrophic consequences for Native Americans. He pointed out how the settlers themselves helped bring on the conflict by promoting trade in alcohol and weapons. He noted how relations between the two peoples were strained by the forcible acquisition of Indian lands by the colonists, even when legal, and by settler attempts to convert Indigenous peoples to Christianity, which produced "neither conviction of the head nor conversion of the heart." In closing, Boutwell emphasized the inevitability of conflict, given that "Philip . . . saw his people dispossessed of their hunting grounds, and an unknown religion zealously pressed upon them. To him there was in the present only humiliation and disgrace, in the future only ignominy and death."[24]

These were remarkable assessments coming from a thirty-four-year-old governor of the Commonwealth of Massachusetts, speaking to a white audience while dedicating a memorial to white settlers. Boutwell also criticized later colonial accounts of King Philip's War, which were based, he said, on "prejudiced sources" such as the contemporary perspectives of two New England icons, the rival ministers Samuel Hubbard and Increase Mather, that were "often strangely barbarous in spirit."[25]

For historian Jill Lepore, Boutwell's speech that day reflected white American attitudes that romanticized the Wampanoags of King Philip while being contemptuous of contemporary Native Americans, caricatured as either savages or innocents as they often were in popular literature and on the stage. In calling Philip's defeat "the first great step in the red man's solemn march to the grave," Boutwell predicted, paternalistically, that Philip's descendants would never again be "a proud and free race." Ravaged by European diseases and constantly pushed westward, the remaining several hundred thousand Native Americans were viewed by white Americans as either a romanticized memory or impediments to their own newly forming identity based on Manifest Destiny.[26]

REGARDING LOCAL POLITICS in Massachusetts, Boutwell promoted issues that he had emphasized in his 1851 inaugural address: strengthening of "common school" education across the Commonwealth, the condition of the public debt, a more equitable valuation of tariffs, reform of the statewide electoral system, and changes in the governance of Harvard College. He expressed satisfaction that Massachusetts, with a population now exceeding one million, was thriving commercially, its seaports connected by an ever-expanding system of railways to Canada and the Great Lakes. Good Unionist that he was, Boutwell took pride in the fact that no section of the country had benefited more than New England from the "existence, stability and general policy of the national government."[27]

Speaking to the interests of his farming and working-class supporters, he emphasized the duty of government "to secure to every man an equal opportunity to acquire property, and equal rights in the possession of property." To that end, Boutwell was committed to improving educational opportunities for all, having a more equitable system of elections and representation, and removing barriers to voting, such as the poll tax.

No two issues were more important to George Boutwell than education and the ballot. He fought for the viability of the state's common schools by proposing to fund them through the sale of public lands then jointly held by Massachusetts and Maine. To protect voting integrity, he urged adoption of the secret ballot so that Whig mill owners couldn't exercise undue influence over how their workers marked their ballots at the polls. Boutwell also championed electoral reform to reduce Whig dominance in "winner take all" cities like Boston, where a simple majority of the total vote could result in winning most or all of the contested seats.[28]

During his first term, Boutwell achieved modest legislative success, aided by Henry Wilson in the Senate and Nathaniel Banks in the House. Bills were passed calling for a convention to amend the Massachusetts Constitution, institute the secret ballot, and reform the issuing of bank charters, previously a Whig monopoly. By the autumn of 1851, though, tensions within the coalition were mounting. Conservative Democrats opposed Boutwell's antislavery stance, which annoyed the Free Soilers. But as the incumbent, Boutwell was able to secure the Democratic nomination; when the November election returned a comfortable Democrat–Free Soil majority, the new legislature in January duly reelected him.

Political missteps then began to plague him. The most serious concerned his veto of a law prohibiting the sale of alcoholic beverages which, as a temperance man, he was expected to sign. Boutwell supported the bill but insisted it be approved via secret ballot in a public referendum. As the bill specified open voting, he vetoed it. When the Senate overrode his veto and sent him a new bill with no referendum requirement at all, he signed it, he admitted, "as a point of expediency." His actions ended up pleasing no one.[29]

THE MOST POLITICALLY controversial issue of Boutwell's second term was the Harvard Reorganization Act, which had become law in May 1851 and now awaited implementation. While still a legislator, Boutwell had argued for greater government oversight of the college, citing Massachusetts charter law that Harvard was a public, not a private, institution (Harvard was founded in 1636 by the General Court of the Massachusetts Bay Colony). He produced detailed statistics showing that the Boston-based student body and high tuition resulted in Harvard no longer being a "college of the people and the state" but one that had been captured by the Whigs and the Boston mercantile and professional elite. Henry Wilson was less diplomatic, accusing the Whigs of desiring "to keep Harvard College from the influences of outside barbarians."[30]

As governor, Boutwell put his weight behind the Harvard Reorganization Act, which he hoped would "democratize" and "secularize" the institution through reform of the Board of Overseers. When it became law on May 22, 1851, it took away the power of electing the thirty regular members from the Board itself and gave it to the legislature, thus strengthening what Boutwell considered "public oversight." To reduce what the governor considered undue Unitarian and Congregational Church influence on the college, the act also eliminated any mandatory number of clerical members. As a Democratic governor whose electoral base consisted of mill workers and farmers from medium- and small-sized towns, Boutwell felt he had made good on his promise to improve public oversight of the state's premier educational institution.[31]

Though it aroused much passion at the time, the controversy soon faded, and the election of overseers was soon transferred to the Harvard alumni, where it resides today. In the 1930s, Boutwell's role in reorganizing the governance of Harvard was resurrected by famed American historian Samuel Eliot Morison, who accused Boutwell of being "hostile" to Harvard and of setting in motion forces that impinged on Harvard's academic freedom. In a lecture to the Massachusetts Historical Society that echoed long-standing Boston Brahmin prejudice, Morison erred in blaming Boutwell for the denial of tenure of a respected academic.[32]

BY THE SUMMER OF 1852, the Democrat–Free Soil coalition was fraying badly enough that Boutwell decided not to seek reelection; in November, the dominant Whig Party reclaimed the governorship. Having been in state government for nine of the eleven years since 1841, Boutwell planned to spend more time on his law practice and on a project of special importance, the upcoming Massachusetts Constitutional Convention, called for by an act he had championed as governor.

When it convened in the spring of 1853, the convention focused on amending those articles of the original Massachusetts Constitution (drafted by John

Adams and adopted in 1780) relating to legislative electoral districts and life-time tenure for judges. It would also consider an amendment abolishing poll taxes in line with Boutwell's conviction that "the right of voting is in the man himself," not for reasons of property or literacy.[33]

Most important, Boutwell wanted the convention to protect the sanctity of the secret ballot from legislative meddling. He detested open ballot voting, where preferences marked by voters could clearly be seen by election super-visors and others at the polling places. For years, the Whig Party had abused the system by having mill owners in cities like Lowell tell their employees that their jobs would be dependent on how they voted. When Boutwell as governor had enacted the secret ballot law, some Whigs howled in protest that requir-ing citizens to "vote with a sealed bag, or not at all, is an act of despotism."[34]

Boutwell knew that, now back in power, the Whigs would seek to abolish the secret ballot, both for future state elections and for the upcoming vote to select delegates to the convention. Using bare-knuckle tactics to ram a new law through the Massachusetts legislature, one Whig editor declared piously how only "those who are afraid or ashamed to have it known how they voted" would avail themselves of sealed ballots. The new law took effect just five days prior to voting for delegates to the convention and was roundly criti-cized by Democrat and Free Soil spokesmen as opening the door for reviving the "intimidation, coercion, or bribery" that had characterized previous Whig practices. In this case, though, the Whigs were bucking public opinion. On March 7, the third anniversary of Daniel Webster's fateful speech that tore the party apart, the Whigs won only 30 percent of the delegates, giving George Boutwell and his Democratic and Free Soil colleagues a decided majority at the convention that opened in May.[35]

BOUTWELL CONSIDERED HIS EFFORTS at the convention some of the most important of his life. Working closely with Henry Wilson and skilled lawyer Richard Henry Dana, Boutwell was reunited politically with his father, Sewell, who at age sixty-eight was elected as a convention delegate from Lunenburg. Among the delegates whom Boutwell described as "the ablest body of men that ever met in Massachusetts" were Charles Sumner, Ebenezer Rockwood Hoar (future US attorney general), Charles Francis Adams Jr., and Nathaniel Banks.[36]

Meeting during an unusually hot summer, convention delegates rep-resented the interests of Whig merchants and businessmen, Democratic and Free Soil artisans, farmers and laborers, and the recent influx of Irish immigrants to the Commonwealth. Historian Samuel Shapiro captured the anti-immigrant prejudices of the time in writing that "the arrival of the Irish, with their propensity for strong drink, their high rate of disease, pauperism, and prostitution, their alien religion and foreign priests, accentuated the social tensions attendant upon the industrial revolution in the state."[37]

George Boutwell and Richard Dana were the two primary drafters of the new Constitution, which Boutwell described as "the most exacting labor of my life." The two would work until midnight following each day's proceedings, not leaving "our little close bed-chambers" at Adams House, one of the finer hotels in Boston. Dana remembered how Boutwell's "self-possession, thorough knowledge of the subject, calmness and clearness of statement and explanation commanded the admiration of all."[38]

Despite months of effort, the draft Constitution was narrowly rejected by the voters of Massachusetts in a November referendum by 51 to 49 percent. Reasons for the defeat included the difficulty of voters having to decipher more than twenty changes to the Constitution among eight different propositions. Not only did the Whig establishment oppose changes that would decrease their overweighted representation in cities like Boston and Cambridge, but religion intruded as well. The Catholic bishop of Boston likely sealed the new Constitution's fate when he made known his opposition to an amendment that would bar public support for parochial schools.[39]

Yet Boutwell's efforts were not in vain. Just a few years later, Massachusetts voters approved a new Constitution that included many of the measures he deeply believed in, including establishing the secret ballot, abolishing the poll tax, and enacting a ban on using public funds for religious schools.

AT THE BEGINNING of 1854, Boutwell might have anticipated that the tempo of life would ease, allowing him to concentrate on his law practice, his dry goods business, and spending more time with his family in their new home. In 1851 at the start of his term as governor, he had built a handsome center-entrance, side-gabled italianate house on Main Street in Groton. Designed by a young Gridley James Fox Bryant, soon to become Boston's preeminent architect of the mid-nineteenth century, the house was well situated on Main Street at the head of Station Avenue, just a few hundred yards from Groton's train depot. Not only would Boutwell have an easy walk to catch the train to his law office in Boston, but his house would be the first thing that arriving passengers saw as they departed the station. Similarly, Boutwell could see them from his second-floor study, especially those coming to visit the ex-governor.[40]

Boutwell's daughter Georgianna was now ten and son Francis was six. Georgie remembers her father as an even-tempered man who prized civility above all: "[W]e were never ordered to do anything—we were asked in the same spirit that one would ask a friend." She fondly recalled family dinner conversations where "as we grew older we took part . . . on an equality as to our opinions." Book learning was always emphasized, with the admonition "never to take anyone's opinion but to find out for ourselves." As their relationship deepened, Georgianna remembers that "I always criticized or questioned his statements with the same freedom that I would one of my mates, and I think that instead of losing, I gained respect for him by his methods."[41]

Son Francis wasn't the student his sister was, but as a youngster, he helped out on the family farm that his father was expanding in the fields between the house and Martins Pond, raising livestock, harvesting vegetables, and cultivating fruit trees. He would soon begin the town's first milk delivery service.

As the Massachusetts winter enveloped Groton that January, George Boutwell's political future was uncertain. With seven years as a state legislator and two as governor, he had hit the ceiling of Massachusetts politics. There were seismic shifts occurring among the political parties, both in the Commonwealth and nationwide, that greatly complicated his options. Given his anti-slavery views, he could no longer stomach remaining in the Democratic Party. The Free Soil Party would have been his obvious home, but it was disintegrating with the rise of the anti-immigrant Know-Nothing Party, which swept the 1854 Massachusetts state elections. Soon enough, the incendiary politics of slavery would give birth to the Republican Party, with George Boutwell playing a pivotal role.

4

Birth of the Republican Party

I n the streets below George Boutwell's law office on State Street in Boston, hundreds of angry citizens were protesting the arrest of nineteen-year-old Anthony Burns, a fugitive slave from Stafford County, Virginia. A few days later, the crowd was even bigger at Boston's Court House when Burns appeared in chains before a federal commissioner, with lawyer Richard Henry Dana at his side.

Violence broke out when a group of armed abolitionists tried to break into the court house and free Burns, as had happened three years before with Shadrach Minkins. On this day, May 29, 1854, a deputy US marshal was fatally stabbed. President Franklin Pierce, a New Hampshire Democrat, thundered law and order pronouncements from Washington, DC, and sent US Marines into Boston. When a federal commissioner ordered Burns returned to slavery in Virginia, it took 1,500 soldiers to hold back the crowd of 50,000 people. Boutwell's friend and Groton native Amos Adams Lawrence expressed the outrage of many: "We went to bed one night old-fashioned, conservative, compromise Union Whigs & waked up stark mad Abolitionists."[1]

THE BURNS INCIDENT fueled antislavery anger already ignited by the Kansas-Nebraska Act of 1854, signed just a few days earlier. The brainchild of Illinois senator Stephen Douglas, the act repealed the Missouri Compromise of 1820 and opened the door for slavery in the western territories. Touting his concept of "popular sovereignty" as the essence of democracy, Douglas said that popular referenda, not Congress, should decide whether slavery should be permitted in Kansas and Nebraska. Almost immediately, Kansas became a battleground between abolitionist-led settlers and proslavery vigilantes from neighboring Missouri.

In response, prominent literary figures gave voice to the antislavery frenzy sweeping across the North. In his famous poem, "The Rendition," Whittier described the scene in Boston as "Liberty marched handcuffed down that sworded street." At a Fourth of July commemoration in Framingham, Massachusetts, William Lloyd Garrison sacrilegiously burned copies of the US Constitution. Henry David Thoreau published "Slavery in Massachusetts," bemoaning the loss of America's moral integrity. And Ralph Waldo Emerson pronounced the Fugitive Slave Law "a filthy enactment . . . I will not obey it, by God."[2]

With the politics of slavery again taking center stage in mid-1854, Boutwell knew he could no longer remain in the proslavery Democratic Party. He conferred with political colleagues Henry Wilson, Nathaniel Banks, and Richard Henry Dana on whether a new political party dedicated to opposing slavery might arise from the chaotic jumble of Whigs, Free Soilers, Know-Nothings, and even the Know-Somethings (an offshoot of the anti-immigrant Know-Nothings that was explicitly antislavery) that characterized state and national politics. In a few short months, the Republican Party would begin to emerge from the celestial dust of America's fractured politics, and George Boutwell would be "present at the creation."

FREE SOILERS, BARNBURNERS, Hunkers, and Loco Focos; "Cotton" and "Conscience" Whigs; Know-Nothings and Know-Somethings; Temperance Men and Rum Democrats. These were the factions whose colorful epithets described the patchwork quilt of American party politics in the 1850s. As such, they represented something entirely new in American society.

America in its early days had two main parties: the Federalists of Alexander Hamilton, who favored a strong central government and the growth of a national infrastructure and economy, and the Democratic-Republicans of Thomas Jefferson, agrarian champions of states' rights. By the 1820s, the Federalists had been transformed into the new business-oriented National Republican cum Whig Party of John Adams. The Democratic-Republicans became the populist, working man's Democratic Party of Andrew Jackson.

By the 1840s, the Democrats and Whigs were each divided into northern and southern factions, primarily over the issue of slavery but also due to disagreements about immigration and the need for national infrastructure

improvements. Due to party discipline, the Democrats were better able to survive these divisions than were the rank-and-file Whigs, whose primary loyalty
was to party leaders such as Henry Clay or Daniel Webster. The patronage
benefits of Democrat Franklin Pierce's victory in the 1852 presidential election
further solidified the party while the Whigs were fracturing into their "Conscience" and "Cotton" factions, with the latter increasingly allying themselves
with southern, proslavery Democrats.[3]

Fissures over slavery and immigration also led to the rise of splinter parties; the Free Soil Party led by disaffected "Conscience" Whigs had been crucial to George Boutwell's election as governor in 1851. The "Know-Nothing"
Party, originally a loose collection of secret societies in Massachusetts and
New York that were violently anti-Catholic (Know-Nothing members were
instructed to keep quiet about their activities, responding to any questions
with "I know nothing"), became the nativist American Party in 1855. Capitalizing on opposition to Irish immigration, the party appealed to rural
Protestants in the North who were both anti-immigrant and antislavery. At
the time, Abraham Lincoln highlighted this contradiction when he wrote to
law colleague Joshua Speed, "How can anyone who abhors the oppression of
negroes be in favor of degrading classes of white people? . . . As a nation, we
began by declaring that 'all men are created equal.' We now practically read
it 'all men are created equal, except negroes.' When the Know-Nothings get
control, it will read 'All men are created equal, except Negroes and foreigners
and Catholics.'"[4]

The Know-Nothings scored their biggest successes in 1854–1856, electing
governors and mayors in Pennsylvania, Maryland, Illinois, and especially Massachusetts, where they swept an astounding 397 out of 400 seats in the Massachusetts legislature. But their attempts to severely regulate alcohol, impose
Protestant standards on public schools, and impose strict residency requirements for officeholders soon produced a backlash, and few Know-Nothings
were reelected. Their influence would live on, however, as many of them took
their nativist views into the new Republican Party, helping to elect Lincoln
in 1860.[5]

The Free Soil Party was experiencing a similar rise and fall, unable to
broaden its support beyond its antislavery emphasis. In Massachusetts,
increased divisions between Free Soilers and Democrats had convinced Boutwell not to run for reelection in 1852. By 1854, those "Conscience" Whigs who
had jumped to the Free Soil Party were looking for a new home.

LATE SUMMER THUNDERSTORMS heralded the opening of the Republican state convention in Worcester on September 7, 1854. Declaring that he had "come from the tainted breath of Slavery [in Washington, DC] to breathe the pure air of Freedom here in Massachusetts," Charles Sumner warned that the southern Slave Power was not content to push slavery into the western territories; it was also casting covetous glances at Cuba and Haiti. What was needed, Sumner urged, was a new party that could challenge the supremacy of southern white Democrats in the nation's capital.[6]

At first, the Massachusetts Republican Party struggled to gain traction. Henry Wilson ran a distant fourth in the November election for governor, which was swept by the Know-Nothings. With the aim of reaching out to disaffected Free Soilers, Whigs, and Democrats, Boutwell and the Republicans by the summer of 1855 began building a solid political organization.

MEANWHILE, BOUTWELL WAS tending to business at home. Recovering from the labors of the constitutional convention and its referendum, he focused on his law practice, joining Boston patent lawyer Joel Giles. In Groton, he served as justice of the peace, helped create the town library, and chaired the Groton school committee, where he urged the initiation of teacher testing and the hiring of more female teachers.

Passionately devoted to public education, Boutwell promoted modern methods of teaching throughout the Commonwealth as a member of the State Board of Education, becoming its secretary in 1855. In doing so, he continued the progressive policies of his illustrious predecessor, Horace Mann, one of the leaders in shaping modern public education in America beginning in the 1830s. During Boutwell's five-year tenure, he organized twelve teachers' institutes a year, bringing in distinguished academics from Harvard to lecture on natural history and physical geography. Describing the state's educational bureaucracy as "little nurseries of selfishness and intrigue," Boutwell sought to break up the vested interests that thrived on nepotism in the selection of teachers, the repair of schoolhouses, and even the supply of firewood.[7]

Boutwell also championed female education, giving the dedication address in September 1854 at the Salem Normal School, a pathbreaking teachers' training institute in Salem, Massachusetts (modeled after the École normale supérieure of France), which he had helped create as governor. One of the school's most famous graduates, Charlotte Forten, later to become a prominent African American antislavery activist and a distinguished writer and poet, was living in Salem at the time with the family of Black abolitionist Charles Lenox Remond and would soon enter the Salem Normal School. Ten years later, when *The Atlantic Monthly* published, to wide acclaim, her account of teaching formerly enslaved Blacks on the Sea Islands off the coast of Georgia, Boutwell would cite Charlotte Forten as an example of the necessity of expanding public education opportunities for America's Blacks.[8]

Boutwell also supported penal reform. In August 1856, he presided at the opening of the country's first progressive female state reform school, the Lancaster Industrial School for Girls. Rather than incarcerate young female delinquents in jails as was the prior practice, the Lancaster school would house some forty young women between the ages of seven and sixteen, and their teachers, in three-story cottages with both dorm and individual bedrooms. Boutwell used his self-taught French to model the school on the Mettray youth facility in France, west of Paris, which opened in 1840.[9]

In 1858, Boutwell gave the fifteenth anniversary address at America's first female high school in Newburyport, north of Boston, in which he supported the "intellectual and moral training" of young women. But he also used the occasion to firmly oppose any notion of women's suffrage.

Why would Boutwell support women receiving all the benefits of a liberal education, yet not the vote? His attitude, common for the time, was that "the family, not the man or the woman, is the unit of the state" and "the ballot is the judgment of the family." As head of the family, the husband should exercise the vote. By the same logic regarding taxation, "if woman does not vote because she is woman, so . . . she is not subject to personal taxation."

Boutwell then asked himself the obvious next question, "Why, in the eye of the state, shall the man stand as the head of the family, rather than the woman?" His answer: "Because God has so ordained it." To his credit, Boutwell did pose the difficult question of why "the elective franchise is exercised by men *without* families and denied to those women who . . . *preside* in homes where the father's face is seen no more." His weak reply was that "the law universal can recognize only the general condition of things." One suspects that, with daughter Georgie on her way to becoming a vocal proponent of women's suffrage, there were contentious discussions around the dinner table.[10]

ON A WARM AUGUST EVENING in 1855, George Boutwell strode out of a Boston hotel believing that the future had brightened for a United States free of slavery. Boutwell was one of the principal organizers of a series of "Fusion for Freedom" meetings that brought together disaffected Whigs, Free Soilers, Democrats, and Know-Nothing Party members with the aim of supporting the nascent Republican Party in Massachusetts. Similar Fusion meetings were taking place across the North, led by prominent political figures such as Salmon Chase in Ohio and William Seward in New York. With the aim of first stopping the spread of slavery to the territories and then abolishing it entirely, the movement was spreading alarm among slaveholders: "[T]hese are signs of a . . . perilous future for the South," predicted *The Times-Picayune* in New Orleans.[11]

In Boston, Boutwell worked closely with Charles Francis Adams to craft an appeal to the people of Massachusetts declaring that "the time has fully come when a united and determined resistance must be made to the aggressions of the slave power, lest . . . the republic itself become a slave power in the family of nations." In meetings at the National Hotel, the press noted that Boutwell emerged as one of the most visible leaders of a party pledged to "restrain the alarming encroachments of slavery."[12]

The Fusion effort directly threatened both the Whig and the Democratic Parties in Massachusetts. The Whigs, already greatly weakened by the rise of the Know-Nothing movement, would cease to exist within a year. Symbolic of their demise was the death of the textile industrialist and Whig leader, Abbott Lawrence, in his Boston mansion on August 16 just as the Fusion meeting was taking place a few blocks away.[13]

As for the Democrats, party leaders were furious with Boutwell's participation in the Fusion meetings, claiming he had lied to them regarding his "party fidelity" and that he was "deceiving the friends who have been true to him." What these Democrats could not or would not stomach was that George Boutwell could no longer support a party which, at the national level, defended slavery.[14]

That year, the Republican candidate for governor finished a respectable second, increasing his vote sixfold from six thousand the year before. Throughout the North, the Republican Party was emerging as a credible force, opening the way for George Boutwell to begin his ascent to the national political stage.[15]

STEP ONE OF THAT ascent occurred early in 1856 when Boutwell's friend and colleague Nathaniel P. Banks won the longest-ever contest for Speaker of the US House of Representatives, defeating the proslavery candidate, William

Aiken of South Carolina, on the 133rd ballot. Then, in June, Boutwell was chosen as a delegate to the first national Republican Party convention, in Philadelphia, which would select the party's presidential candidate for the 1856
election. Surprising many of his colleagues, he reluctantly declined the offer,
believing it a conflict of interest with his nonpartisan position as secretary of
the Massachusetts Board of Education. When accepting the Education post
a year earlier, Boutwell had written to Richard Henry Dana that, although
he would "refrain from any active part in politics," he remained committed
to assisting the creation of an antislavery party to combat "the selfish, controlling policy of the slaveholders in the government of the country." Boutwell
recommended and hoped that Ralph Waldo Emerson would take his place, but
Emerson was unable to attend.[16]

Meeting in Philadelphia, the Republican convention nominated western
explorer John C. Frémont as its presidential candidate. With the party struggling to meld together antislavery and anti-immigrant views, Frémont ended
up losing badly in the November election to Democrat James Buchanan of
Pennsylvania, who promised to vigorously enforce the Fugitive Slave Act and
to promote slavery in the territories.

It was in those western territories that escalating conflict helped propel
the Republican Party forward. The Kansas-Nebraska Act had ignited guerrilla
fighting between pro- and antislavery forces in the Kansas territory. With Senator Douglas promoting the concept of "popular sovereignty"—let the local
population decide—a Kansas already rife with land speculation and political
rivalries became a battleground between proslavery vigilantes from neighboring Missouri and armed abolitionists from New England.

On May 21, violence burst into the national consciousness with the "Sack
of Lawrence" by proslavery forces and the revenge murder of five proslavery
men by John Brown's family a few days later in Pottawatomie. Throughout the
North, moderate Democrats and others who had hoped for a peaceful resolution over issues of extending slavery were outraged and began defecting to the
Republican Party.[17]

For George Boutwell, news of the attack on Lawrence hit hard. The town
was founded in 1854 by New England abolitionists seeking to keep Kansas a
free state and was named for Amos A. Lawrence, born in Groton, nephew
of Abbott, and a lifelong friend of Boutwell's. With money from his family's
textile fortune, Lawrence bankrolled the New England Emigrant Aid Society, which sent settlers, supplies, and weapons to the Kansas territory. For his

part, Boutwell lent his prestige as an ex-governor by endorsing a Kansas land agency selling property lots to antislavery men in and around Lawrence.[18]

The fighting in "Bleeding Kansas" soon provoked violence back in Washington. On May 22, Charles Sumner was viciously attacked on the floor of the US Senate by a South Carolina congressman. Sumner almost died after being clubbed on the head with a gold metal–topped cane by Representative Preston Brooks while other southerners in the Senate chamber cheered. Brooks claimed he was defending his region's honor after Sumner, notorious for his impassioned speeches, mocked the South for having "a mistress ... who ... though polluted in the sight of the world, is chaste in his sight—I mean the harlot, Slavery."[19]

Severely injured and with lasting head trauma, Charles Sumner was unable to resume his duties for several years. Throughout the North, he became a martyr to the cause of abolitionism who helped raise the visibility of the Republican Party. Massachusetts voters and the legislature reelected him and kept his Senate seat vacant as a potent symbol against slavery. Sumner returned to the Senate in 1859 as George Boutwell and other party leaders prepared for the 1860 Republican national convention that would ultimately result in the election of Abraham Lincoln as president.

WITH THE REPUBLICAN PARTY gaining prominence at the national level, Boutwell was helping to shape its fortunes in Massachusetts. In 1858, he sought the party's nomination for Congress, but lost narrowly by 66–63 to Charles R. Train at the party convention. What transpired afterward made for an amusing story involving electoral fraud and Ralph Waldo Emerson.[20]

Boutwell supporters alleged that eleven extra votes had mysteriously made their way into the final tally. The matter was forgotten until 1860 when Boutwell sought the nomination again. At a caucus held in Concord, Waldo Emerson collared a local Republican heavyweight, declaring that "Mr. Boutwell was cheated out of his nomination two years ago." When it came time to vote, party officials found "the transcendentalists [out] in force, surrounded by a deep fringe of farmers from all parts of the town." Emerson spoke: "The first four names on that paper are for Mr. Train. The second four names are for Mr. Boutwell. We are for Mr. Boutwell, and our friends will be careful not to vote for the first four names, but to vote for the second four names." As Boutwell would remember, "Mr. Emerson's policy prevailed, and as far as I knew, this was his only appearance in Concord politics."[21]

Despite winning the nomination, Boutwell decided not to run for Congress that year—for reasons that remain unclear—and he released his delegates to Charles Train at the state convention. When Boutwell did run for Congress in 1862, he noted with satisfaction how "Mr. Emerson gave me his support and during my term I received many letters from him in approval of my course [especially regarding the abolition of slavery], which to many others seemed extreme and unwise."[22]

THE REPUBLICAN PARTY came of age in the midterm elections of 1858. The collapse of the nativist American Party and the fracturing of the Democrats over the issues of slavery and violence in Kansas gave the Republicans a 113–83 edge in the House of Representatives. One issue hobbling the national Democrats was the Lecompton Constitution, a measure to protect slavery in Kansas which was so rigged that even Senator Stephen Douglas opposed it. Boutwell had written to Ohio governor Salmon Chase urging a boycott of the referendum by Kansas antislavery forces; the measure was ultimately defeated, clearing the way for Kansas to enter the Union as a free state in January 1861.[23]

The Republicans also reaped the benefits of widespread revulsion in the North over the *Dred Scott* decision of the US Supreme Court in March 1857. Scott had been living with his Missouri slave owner in the 1830s in Illinois, a free state. In 1846, he sued for his freedom on the grounds that Illinois did not recognize the property rights of slaveholders. By the time his case reached the Supreme Court, attracting national attention along the way, newly inaugurated President James Buchanan was hoping that a decision against Scott could settle the issue of slavery once and for all. Having seen his two predecessors in the White House politically wounded, Millard Fillmore by the 1850 Fugitive Slave Act and Franklin Pierce by the 1854 Kansas-Nebraska Act, Buchanan was hoping to avoid a similar fate, going so far as to lobby some of the justices for a favorable verdict.[24]

Favorable, of course, meant denying Dred Scott his freedom, even though a lower court had ruled in Scott's favor. Chief Justice Roger B. Taney, however, was determined to go much further. In a decision uniformly criticized to this day, Taney ruled that all African Americans, whether enslaved or free, had no claim on US citizenship and no right to sue in federal court. In writing the majority opinion, Taney described Blacks "as beings of an inferior order," having "no rights which the white man was bound to respect."

Not content to stop there, Taney challenged the authority of Congress by saying it had no right to outlaw slavery in any territories the country might acquire. The Missouri Compromise that had banned slavery from the northern territories for decades was thus ruled unconstitutional. Taney's decision allowing slave owners to take their "property" into states that had banned slavery also seemed to imply a "nationalization" of its legality in both North and South.

A firestorm of protest swept over the Mason-Dixon line. The South triumphantly declared slavery "the supreme law of the land," while northern newspapers like Horace Greeley's *New York Tribune* cited the decision's "detestable hypocrisy." Northern pastors and ministers warned their parishioners that "they disobey God" in accepting Taney's ruling. In the end, President James Buchanan got more than he bargained for in scheming for a favorable opinion from the Supreme Court as northern Democrats had difficulty defending the decision and suffered accordingly in the 1858 midterm elections.[25]

Even before the *Dred Scott* decision had become public, George Boutwell was warning friends that the issue of slavery might well destroy the Union. Anticipating the start of the Civil War by three years, he wrote to abolitionist Amos Lawrence in February 1858 that the Slave Power of the South "will always and necessarily be aggressive and offensive," and "in self-defense people will make war on it."[26]

Despite losing the Republican nomination for Congress in 1858, Boutwell was now a recognized party leader in Massachusetts. He used his status as an ex-governor to good advantage in networking with friends and colleagues, especially in April 1859 at a remarkable dinner in Boston.

THE PARKER HOUSE is one of Boston's grand, old hotels. Like the Fifth Avenue Hotel in New York, Willard's Hotel in Washington, DC, and the Palmer House in Chicago, it reigned supreme in the 1800s as a political watering hole. Still standing at a far corner of Boston Common, it's but a short stroll to the gold-domed Massachusetts State House on Beacon Hill.

In the early afternoon of April 13, Boutwell made his way along the city streets from his office to the Parker House, where he would preside over one of the most significant political meetings of his life. Early spring weather had come to Boston. Crocuses were pushing up in Boston's famed Public Gardens,

and a mild breeze was caressing the leaves on the majestic elm and linden
trees surrounding the green expanse of the Common. Today was the 116th
anniversary of Thomas Jefferson's birth, and Boutwell had the honor of presiding over the Republican Party's Jefferson Birthday dinner.

A who's who of the city's political and business elite sat down for a midday
dinner at 3 p.m., and shortly after 5 p.m., "the intellectual entertainment was
opened by Mr. Boutwell." By this time the crowd in the Parker House ball-
room had swelled to several hundred. The guests of honor sitting on either
side of Boutwell included US Senator Henry Wilson and John Andrew, soon to
become Massachusetts governor. A special guest who spent fifty hours traveling by train to join them was Carl Schurz of Wisconsin, future Civil War
general and later senator from Missouri.[27]

Anticipation was already building toward the 1860 presidential election.
With the Democratic Party splitting along sectional lines over the issue of
extending slavery to the territories, the newly formed Republican Party had a
very real chance of capturing the presidency.

As master of ceremonies, Boutwell directed that messages of regret at not
being able to attend be read from a quartet of the most prominent Republican politicians in the land: Senator William Seward of New York, Governor
Salmon Chase of Ohio, Representative Francis (Frank) Blair Jr. of Missouri,
and Abraham Lincoln of Illinois.[28]

Of the four, Seward and Chase were the best-known and were already
jockeying for the party's presidential nomination for 1860. The powerful Blair
family was supporting a third potential Republican nominee, Judge Edward
Bates of Missouri. As for Abe Lincoln, he had been a one-term congressman in
the 1840s and now was practicing law in Springfield, Illinois. Six months earlier, though, he had made a name for himself in the Lincoln-Douglas debates
during his losing campaign for Douglas's US Senate seat from Illinois. The
eloquence with which Lincoln staked out positions on slavery and the sanctity
of the Union had brought him tremendous national attention.[29]

In his keynote speech, Boutwell pronounced that "the great issue of slavery
is upon us. We cannot escape it." Paying tribute to Thomas Jefferson's belief
that the rights of man were superior to those of states, and that justice was the
foundation of the Union, he warned that "slavery is the enemy of justice; and
therefore, it is the enemy of Union." Contrasting the free labor society of the
North with the servitude of southern plantation agriculture, he called for the

necessary extinction of "an institution dangerous to the welfare of the people and hostile to the perpetuity of the Union."[30]

Speeches then followed from Wilson, Andrew, and Carl Schurz, the guest of honor, who had been invited to shore up the party's support from German Americans. Next was the reading of the letters from Seward, Chase, Blair, and Lincoln, each containing words of welcome to those assembled and effusive praise of Jefferson who, in Seward's words, they were honoring for promoting "the rights of human nature."[31]

The irony of Republicans in Massachusetts, political heirs to John Adams and the Federalists, paying homage to Jefferson, the exemplar of states' rights and Adams's arch nemesis, was not lost on anyone. Lincoln wrote that it was "curious and interesting" that Republicans, descended "from the party opposed to Jefferson, should now be celebrating his birthday in their own original seat of empire [Boston]." He compared the situation to that of two drunks (Republicans and Democrats) getting into a fight and going at it so helter-skelter that each "fought himself out of his own coat and *into* that of the other." Lincoln's point was that Jefferson's original "devotion to the *personal* rights of man, holding the rights of *property* to be secondary only," was now the credo of the Republican Party, not the Democrats. The latter, he charged, now "hold the *liberty* of one man to be absolutely nothing, when in conflict with another man's right of *property*." It is the Republicans who "are for both the *man* and the *dollar*, but in cases of conflict, the man *before* the dollar." Lincoln also used his letter to emphasize the centrality of the Declaration of Independence and its "abstract truth [of equality], applicable to all men and all times," a proposition he said that Democrats now labeled "self-evident lies" that are only applicable to "superior races."

In his brief letter, Lincoln set down the principles that helped shape his candidacy for the Republican presidential nomination a year later. And for any who doubted that he believed, fervently and providentially, in the ultimate extinction of slavery, Lincoln wrote one of his most memorable phrases: "[H]e who would be no slave, must consent to have no slave. Those who deny freedom to others, deserve it not for themselves; and under a just God, cannot long retain it."[32]

A FEW MONTHS LATER, Lincoln gave a speech at the Wisconsin Agricultural Fair that helped clarify the principles of the Republican Party for the

American electorate. Lincoln chose as his theme a proslavery speech given in 1858 by South Carolina senator James Henry Hammond that disparaged the working class, both white and Black, as the "mudsill" of society. To Hammond, such laborers were but the lowly foundation used by white planters and other capitalists to build and control the country's politics and economy.

Lincoln focused his remarks on individuals having "natural rights" to be rewarded with the fruits of their labor. Rather than a "mudsill," "free labor" was the bedrock of a free society. Articulating the Republican Party position that wealth is created by farmers and laborers, Lincoln stressed that upward mobility is *the* unique feature of American society, with public education and government initiatives promoting a level economic playing field so that all are given the opportunity to advance.[33]

The moral and economic arguments articulated by Boutwell and Lincoln, of slavery being the enemy of justice and the southern plantation economy being inimical to the country's economic potential and the rights of the individual American worker, were coalescing in the Republican Party as the 1860 national elections approached. Soon, George Boutwell would give expression to them when he helped draft the party platform at the national convention in Chicago.[34]

TWO WEEKS AFTER Lincoln spoke in Milwaukee, the abolitionist John Brown seized the US government arsenal at Harper's Ferry, Virginia, with a band of twenty-one armed men. Hoping to spark a slave revolt throughout the South, Brown's plan to distribute weapons to enslaved Blacks flocking to join him failed miserably. Less than thirty-six hours after it began on a Sunday night in October, the raid was over, Brown's men having been surrounded by local militia. US Marines commanded by Col. Robert E. Lee then stormed the arsenal warehouse early Tuesday morning, killing ten and arresting Brown and six others, all of whom would be executed for treason; the others escaped.[35]

Brown's raid and subsequent trial, where he received the martyrdom he welcomed, electrified the country. Americans were able to follow news of the event on a daily basis via telegraph dispatches from reporters who arrived by train in Harper's Ferry almost as quickly as the US Marines from their barracks in Washington, DC. Northern public opinion began to swing behind the Republican Party's opposition to slavery, while southerners exulted that Brown had torn away the fiction of gradual emancipation and revealed the North's true motives: the total abolition of slavery and destruction of the planter class.[36]

Suddenly, southern talk of secession, until then largely rhetorical, took on a deadly seriousness. Threats from the South to leave the Union helped consolidate the Republican Party in the North, but produced a final fracture between the northern and southern wings of the Democratic Party. The following April, the Democrats deadlocked at their presidential nominating convention in Charleston; two months later in Baltimore, Stephen Douglas became their official presidential candidate while a breakaway southern faction nominated John Breckinridge of Kentucky. A fourth party, the Constitutional Unionists, nominated John Bell of Tennessee. The Republican Party was the clear winner as this sectional discord among Democrats played itself out; whoever the Republicans nominated at its convention in April 1860 would likely be the next president.[37]

FOR SHEER PANDEMONIUM, few events in American political history can surpass the 1860 Republican Party convention in Chicago. Meeting in a grand, hastily constructed hall known as the Wigwam, more than ten thousand convention delegates, attendees, and spectators partied and horse-traded and gossiped and schemed to the point of exhaustion. Boutwell arrived by train on May 14 with members of the Massachusetts delegation; two days later, the Wigwam was filled to bursting, with many of the delegates and spectators having to bring their own chairs.[38]

Boutwell had pledged his support for favorite son candidate Nathaniel Banks, but he knew full well that the race would be between Seward and Lincoln. When Seward's lead of seventy-one delegates collapsed to just three on the second ballot, delegates from Ohio and then Massachusetts swung to Lincoln. Victory was assured for the candidate known as "the splitter of rails and the mauler of Democrats."[39]

Earlier, as one of thirty-seven members of the all-important Resolutions Committee, Boutwell had been chosen by his peers to be on the seven-member subcommittee that wrote the party platform. Others included Horace Greeley (from New York but representing Oregon as a proxy), Carl Schurz (Wisconsin), and Gustave Koerner, Lincoln's man from Illinois. When finished, according to historian James McPherson, the Republican platform was one of the most effective documents of its kind in American history.[40]

As adopted, the platform balanced a nod to state sovereignty with criticism of the Buchanan administration for "subserviency [sic] to the exactions of a sectional interest" that defended the Slave Power's assertion of "an unqualified property in persons." It castigated the "dangerous political heresy" of Chief Justice Taney's dogma that would carry slavery into all existing and future American territories. Attempts to reopen "the African slave trade, under cover of our national flag, aided by perversions of judicial power" were branded "a crime against humanity and a burning shame to our country and age." Finally, in declaring that "no persons should be deprived of life, liberty, or property without due process of law," the platform anticipated the adoption in 1868 of the Fourteenth Amendment, which Boutwell, then in Congress, would also help draft.[41]

Seeking to broaden the party's appeal beyond the slavery issue, the platform promised protective tariffs to advance "the industrial interests of the whole country," a national plan for river and harbor improvements, a railroad to the Pacific Ocean, and the Homestead Act to provide free land for those willing to settle the western territories. In an appeal to immigrants, the party opposed any change in the country's naturalization laws, declaring itself "in favor of giving a full and efficient protection to the rights of all classes of citizens."[42]

This last issue provided one of the convention's more humorous moments. Boutwell was sitting next to soon-to-be Massachusetts governor John Andrew when the naturalization plank, containing criticism of the Bay State's limits on immigrant voting rights, was read aloud. As related by Gustave Koerner, who was sitting directly behind Boutwell and Andrew, the latter shouted, "That will never do! This is aimed at our State." Andrew jumped up, demanding to be recognized by the chair, but "Boutwell at once laid hands on Andrew's shoulders and sought to push him down, while I . . . took hold of his coat tails and held him down." Boutwell and Koerner restrained the astonished Andrew long enough for the immigration plank to be approved by a voice vote and the next one introduced, thus saving the German American vote for the party.[43]

As news of Lincoln's nomination spread to an astonished America, Chicago streets were filled with celebration. "Bonfires glared red upon the heavens . . . and rockets clove through the air like fiery telegrams to the stars." Receiving the news of his defeat at home in Auburn, New York, William Seward was devastated, turning "pale as ashes."[44]

THE DAY AFTER the convention, Boutwell traveled downstate to Springfield with Republican Party leaders, to congratulate Lincoln and officially confer the nomination. It was Boutwell's first meeting with the future president.[45]

Upon arriving at the Springfield train station, the delegation of party notables was swept along by a jubilant crowd to the Illinois State House where, as recounted by Lincoln secretary John Hay, "the genial Gov. Boutwell of Massachusetts" gave one of several "brief and effective speeches." Hay knew Boutwell from two years earlier, when Boutwell had given a commencement speech—one that emphasized "the equality of rights guaranteed by our political institutions"—to Hay's graduating class at Brown University in Providence, Rhode Island. Following the State House celebration, Boutwell and his colleagues, who included Francis P. Blair Sr. and his two sons, Frank and Montgomery (the latter had represented Dred Scott before the Supreme Court and would serve as postmaster general in Lincoln's cabinet), walked to the two-story Lincoln home at Eighth and Jackson Streets where they were playfully received by Lincoln's sons, Tad and Willie.[46]

Once they were inside the house, the atmosphere in the front parlor turned a bit tense when Lincoln said he would need time to study the particulars of the party platform before he could officially accept the nomination. Sensing discomfort among his guests, Lincoln employed his usual humor to lighten the atmosphere. Going up to a lanky Pennsylvania delegate, William D. Kelley, Lincoln asked how tall he was. "Six feet three," Kelley replied, to which Lincoln chuckled and said, "I beat you. I am six feet four without my high-heeled boots." Kelley responded graciously, "Pennsylvania bows to Illinois. For years my heart has been aching for a President that I could *look up to*, and I've found him at last in the land where we thought there were none but *little* giants" (the common nickname for Lincoln's nemesis Stephen Douglas).[47]

Assuring his guests that "the Platform will be found satisfactory, and the nomination accepted," Lincoln shook hands and chatted a bit with each of the delegation members. Boutwell turned to a colleague and remarked, "they told me he was a rough diamond—nothing could have been in better taste than that speech." Lincoln was a good half foot taller than Boutwell, but when the two shook hands, they likely recognized in each other the modest farming and self-educated backgrounds that had shaped their characters.[48]

GEORGE BOUTWELL RETURNED to Chicago for the long train ride back to Groton. Soon after, he was asked to serve as president of the Massachusetts state Republican convention that would convene in Worcester in August. At that meeting, and in remarks aimed at a wider audience, Boutwell emphasized that those who thought the newly created party would be short-lived would be "doomed to disappointment." Criticizing Lincoln's likely opponents for the presidency as seeking "the triumph of slavery," Boutwell campaigned for Lincoln across Massachusetts that summer and fall, warning that "war was impending."[49]

During those anxious months, with the South threatening secession if Lincoln was elected, Boutwell took time to preside over what would become a landmark event in the annals of American environmental and literary history. On September 20, as president of the Middlesex (County) Agricultural Society, he introduced Henry David Thoreau as the featured speaker at that year's autumn farm and cattle show. Torrential rain and a bout of cattle disease limited the show's outdoor activities, but Thoreau more than made up for it by giving a talk in the town hall of his native Concord, Massachusetts, that he would later revise into one of his most famous and widely read essays.

Thoreau's address that afternoon, "The Succession of Forest Trees," was by turns prosaic, tinged with his well-known deadpan humor, and revelatory. He welcomed his audience by announcing that "every man is entitled to come to a Cattle-show, even a transcendentalist." He then explained the benefits to farmers of adhering to nature's practice of regular crop rotation. Through years of observation, Thoreau had deduced that pine forests, when cut down, are replaced—not by new pines—but by oaks, maples, and other hardwoods whose seeds are spread by wind, water, and animals. This was nature's way of ensuring soil fertility through the rotating of different types of flora; unless, of course, man got in the way and planted new stands of pine. As one of the first Americans to have read and been captivated by *On the Origin of Species*, available only months before in America, Thoreau was enlarging upon the concept of natural selection being advanced by Charles Darwin.[50]

Thoreau's talk was music to Boutwell's ears. Taught by his father to graft fruit trees at the age of ten and now the owner of a thriving cattle, vegetable, and fruit farm in Groton, Boutwell had always taken time, even while busy with his dry goods business and political career, to keep up with modern agricultural methods. When Thoreau had finished, Boutwell praised the talk for its "careful study of natural phenomena" and urged his fellow husbandmen to "exhibit a little of the spirit shown by Mr. Thoreau in his experiments and researches" in order to propagate modern methods of agriculture. Thoreau's talk was published a few weeks later by Horace Greeley in the *New York Weekly Tribune* and would become the most widely reprinted of the philosopher naturalist's essays. With its warnings about humans as agents of environmental change, even if unintended, Thoreau's essay became a totem of the environmental movement a century later in the 1960s.[51]

Just as relevant, Darwin's theories of evolutionary development became additional ammunition for northern antislavery spokesmen. For Thoreau and fellow abolitionists, the possibility "that all humans were biologically related [monogenesis] . . . seemed to refute once and for all the idea that African American slaves were a separate, inferior species." Such ideas were critical at a time when apologists for the Slave Power sought to justify the brutal institution by invoking the work of Louis Agassiz and other natural scientists who were promoting the theory of polygenesis, claiming that different peoples had naturally occurring differences in physical and mental faculties that allowed for the subjugation of one group by another.[52]

This was the backdrop as the country headed into the November election hopelessly fractured over slavery. Stephen Douglas was the Democratic nominee while John Breckinridge represented the party's dissident southern faction and John Bell was the candidate of the newly formed Constitutional Union Party, made up of disaffected Whigs and Know-Nothings.

As election day neared, South Carolina threatened to secede should Lincoln become president. When Lincoln was elected on November 6 with 40 percent of the popular vote and 180 out of 303 electoral votes, the die was cast.

PART TWO

ABRAHAM LINCOLN AND THE CIVIL WAR, 1860–1865

5

Organizing for War

Groton was blanketed by an early snow as Christmas approached. Wreaths and red ribbon sashes adorned the doorways on Main Street, candles lighted the windows of the First Parish Church in the center of town, and the townsfolk were doing their best to ignore the dire warnings of secession coming from the South.

In the Boutwell home, George was writing to Lincoln, assuring the president-elect of "my confidence that you are destined to restore peace to the country and redeem the American people from the suspicion that they are incapable of self-government." He was also preparing a major speech that he would give after the holidays in Charlestown, adjacent to Boston and the site of the Battle of Bunker Hill in June 1775. He was certain war was coming. What most troubled him was the prospect of Southern secessionists seeking to block Lincoln's inauguration on March 4 in Washington, or worse, assassination.[1]

The day after the November 6 election, crowds in Charleston, South Carolina, had surged through the streets carrying torches, hanging Lincoln in effigy with a placard mockingly anointing him "First President of the Northern Confederacy." Newspapers and politicians throughout the Deep South outdid each other in their outrage over what a Lincoln presidency would mean, not just for slavery in the territories, but for its very survival at home. Even Northern papers like the *New York Times* carried blatantly false reports that quoted Lincoln as saying he was in favor of both abolishing slavery in the South and promoting full social equality between Blacks and whites.[2]

In the nation's capital, there were constant rumors of conspiracy and possible attempts to overthrow the government by kidnapping President Buchanan. At the time, there were only several hundred Marines stationed in what is now the Navy Yard in southeast Washington, and their allegiance was uncertain. Representative Henry Dawes of Massachusetts heard of Southern plots to "seize the Capitol and the Treasury . . . and prevent the counting of the electoral vote" in Congress that would certify Lincoln's election.[3]

On December 20, South Carolina had taken the first step in splitting the Union by declaring that increased Northern hostility to slavery left it no other choice but to issue an ordinance of secession, which was formally adopted on Christmas eve. In the weeks following, the Palmetto state was joined by Mississippi, Florida, Alabama, Georgia, Louisiana, and Texas. On February 4, delegates from the seven states met in Montgomery, Alabama, to create the Confederate States of America. Jefferson Davis became the Confederacy's first president, with Alexander Stephens of Georgia as vice president. Lincoln's inauguration was still a month away.

As the secession dominos were falling, Boutwell's Charlestown speech delivered a stinging rebuke of slavery in the shadow of the Bunker Hill monument, where men from Groton had died fighting the British in 1775. He spoke of the mounting danger to the nation's capital, surrounded as it was by the slave states of Virginia and Maryland. As a precaution, he called for "the free States . . . with official declarations that no offensive movement will be undertaken," to pledge the mustering of a hundred thousand soldiers, ready to be sent to Washington at the first sign of danger. Newspapers criticized the speech as unnecessarily alarmist.[4]

Boutwell made clear that "the institution of African slavery" as embedded in the Constitution was the cause "of our public and national troubles." He brushed aside those who said that states' rights and sectional honor were paramount, declaring that "these could never have disturbed the harmony of our national relations" if not for the scourge of slavery.

To southerners invoking a constitutional right to secession, Boutwell replied that, if such a right existed, then "a mere majority of the citizens of the smallest State in the Union (could) decide whether the Union shall [no] longer exist." If secession was illegal, it followed that those taking up arms against the national government "are rebels and traitors."

Boutwell returned home to Groton where his wife and children asked anxiously if the country was headed to war. Daughter Georgianna, now seventeen, and son Francis, thirteen, were old enough to understand the severity of the situation. States including Georgia had already begun confiscating federal property, including customs houses and a US Treasury revenue ship-cutter. Boutwell was confident that the Bay State's recently inaugurated governor, John Andrew, would stand behind the national government, but he wasn't so sure about other political leaders in the North. As for whom Lincoln would pick for his administration, Boutwell was sending out feelers signaling his availability.[5]

BY EARLY FEBRUARY, no other slave states had seceded, yet. Of these, Virginia was by far the most important; its political heritage, location, and resources would be critical to the viability of a breakaway Southern confederacy. Thus, when former president and Virginia native John Tyler proposed a convention in Washington of slave and free states to discuss ways of preserving the Union, there was some room for hope, even though a steady stream of pro-secessionist congressmen, including Mississippi senator Jefferson Davis, had already left the capital and were heading south, "some with swagger, some with sadness."[6]

The Virginia Peace Convention that convened on February 4 at Willard's Hotel in Washington had little prospect of success. The seven secessionist states refused to attend and were meeting that very day in Montgomery, Alabama, to put together a Confederate government. In Virginia, a referendum was being held to authorize the holding of a secession convention. Georgia's senator, Robert Toombs, voiced the existential fear of the slaveowners: "we must expand or perish."[7]

A few days earlier from his Senate desk, Charles Sumner had written to Boutwell, soon to depart from Groton as one of seven members of the Massachusetts delegation to the convention. Sumner was blunt: "I see the future clearly, Va. [Virginia] will secede, and will carry with her the rest" (meaning North Carolina, Tennessee, and Arkansas). Writing to Boutwell that "I shall always value any suggestions from you," Sumner opposed any talk of compromise. The Massachusetts senator knew he had no cause to worry about Boutwell. Likewise, Governor John Andrew had selected Boutwell precisely for his uncompromising views, even if that meant that "New England must stand *alone*."[8]

As the delegates arrived at Willard's Hotel, many in their sixties and seventies, skeptics were already deriding the gathering as "The Old Gentleman's Convention." Having celebrated his forty-third birthday just weeks before, Boutwell was one of the youngest. Chairing the meeting was the

seventy-year-old Tyler, a member of one of Virginia's oldest slaveholding families, assisted by the equally arch-secessionist James Seddon, soon to become
the Confederacy's secretary of war. Their hope was to induce Northern concessions or, failing that, to at least discourage the Union from contemplating
military action. When he first arrived, Boutwell made it a priority to meet with
Seddon to better learn his views. The Virginian insisted that allowing slavery
into the territories was a matter of life and death for the South: "You have one
form of civilization, and we have another . . . but our culture is exhausting,
and we must have new lands." Boutwell could see that Seddon feared Northern military intervention above all and was anxiously seeking assurances that
"in no event should there be war."[9]

A few days into the convention, Boutwell and the other delegates went to
Capitol Hill to see whether Lincoln's election would be certified by Congress.
The mood in Washington was tense: the electoral votes had not yet been
officially counted, seven Southern states had already seceded, and rumors
abounded of plots to assassinate the president-elect and blow up public buildings. For the first time in American history, the peaceful transfer of power
from one president to the next was anything but certain. Inside the House
chamber, the boxes containing the ballots were in the custody of Vice President John Breckinridge of Kentucky, one of the three defeated presidential
candidates in the recent election, who some thought might betray his trust.
Outside the Capitol, General of the Army Winfield Scott deployed two bat-
teries of cannon on First Street, promising to "manure the hills of Arlington"
by firing body parts across the Potomac River of anyone who attempted to
obstruct the vote. Scott took the threat of violence so seriously that he infiltrated several hundred armed plainclothes police into the crowds surrounding
the Capitol. At the end of the day, Breckinridge performed his constitutional
duty, reading the tally and making Lincoln's election official.[10]

Back at Willard's Hotel, debate resumed on numerous resolutions that
might forestall the looming conflict. Having been chosen as their spokesman
by the Massachusetts and New York delegations, Boutwell rose on February
18, the very day that Jefferson Davis was inaugurated as president of the Confederacy in Alabama, and gave the most significant speech at the convention.
As reported in newspapers across the country, Boutwell "declared against all
compromise or concessions" by listing three conditions that everyone knew
the South could never accept: abandoning the doctrine of secession, accepting

the legality of Mr. Lincoln's election, and recognizing the legitimacy of the national government.[11]

Driving his point home, Boutwell demanded to know exactly what the North had done to justify secession. Advancing "slowly up the aisle until I could look into the faces of the Virginia delegation," Boutwell put the issue starkly: "[T]he North will never consent to the separation of the States. If the South persists on the course on which she has entered, we shall march our armies to the Gulf of Mexico, or you will march yours to the Great Lakes. There can be no peaceful separation."[12]

The final days of the convention were little more than debate and posturing as delegates sought to prevent the breakup of the Union. The best they could do was to repackage the components of the decidedly pro-Southern Crittenden Compromise of the previous December. Authored by Kentucky senator John J. Crittenden, that deal had promised an end to Southern threats of secession in return for permanently embedding slavery in the Constitution, strengthening the capture of fugitive slaves, reinstating the now nullified Missouri Compromise of 1820, and even giving the South a veto over the acquisition of any foreign territory (for example, Cuba) unless slavery was permitted there. Crittenden's deal had already been rejected by Republicans and President-elect Lincoln. In its new form, it was equally unpalatable to Boutwell and many Northern delegates.[13]

The Virginia Peace Convention disbanded as secession rhetoric grew more incendiary. Hotel keepers J. C. and H. A. Willard, forgoing any rent, hoped in vain that the use of their facilities might "be sanctified by restoring peace to the Union."[14]

ABRAHAM LINCOLN HAD arrived in Washington at 6 a.m. on February 23, wearing a disguise due to the fear of assassination. His chief of security, famed detective Allan Pinkerton, traveled with Lincoln in a special rail car from Philadelphia, passing through secessionist-leaning Baltimore in the middle of the night. The president-elect was met at the B&O station on New Jersey Avenue by his close friend and Illinois colleague, Congressman Elihu Washburne, who escorted him to Willard's Hotel. Acknowledging that he was "now public property," Lincoln refused to stay in a private residence where security would be easier to provide, preferring "a public inn . . . where people can have access to me." For the next week Lincoln was "overwhelmed with callers." His secretary, John Hay, was amazed that his boss wasn't "torn to pieces" by the crush of visitors, even as Lincoln was putting the finishing touches on his inaugural address and making final decisions on his cabinet.[15]

At the end of that long first day in Washington, having earlier called on President Buchanan at the White House, Lincoln met at the hotel with members of the Peace Convention. Knowing that many of the Southern delegates were looking forward to the reception, where they could "nourish their contempt for the 'rail-splitter,'" Vermont delegate and convention rapporteur Lucius Chittenden marveled at how Lincoln's "wonderful vivacity surprised every spectator." More than a few of the Southern delegates, meeting Lincoln for the first time, came away impressed. William Rives of Virginia felt that Lincoln "has been both misjudged and misunderstood by the Southern people. They have looked upon him as an ignorant, self-willed man, incapable of independent judgment, full of prejudices, willing to be used as a tool by more able men. This is all wrong. He will be the head of his administration, and he will do his own thinking."[16]

George Boutwell met with Lincoln upstairs in Parlor Six, the second-floor corner suite overlooking Pennsylvania Avenue, where the president-elect had been joined by his wife Mary and their sons, Robert Todd, Willie, and Tad. Among many topics, they discussed the nomination of Salmon Chase to be secretary of the treasury. Having worked with Chase as a fellow delegate at the peace convention, Boutwell supported the choice and was delighted when Chase was appointed, writing to the Ohioan of his "sincere personal gratification" at hearing the news. There were reports that perhaps Boutwell might join Chase at Treasury, but he quashed any such rumors. He was anxious to return to Massachusetts and did so without staying for Lincoln's inauguration on March 4. Little did Boutwell know he would soon return to the nation's capital, entrusted with a crucial mission.[17]

SIX WEEKS LATER, on April 13, Maj. Robert Anderson ordered his men to lower the American flag flying over Fort Sumter in Charleston harbor. Under fire for thirty-four straight hours by Confederate cannon, Anderson made the painful decision to surrender the fort to Gen. P. G. T. Beauregard in what was the opening salvo of the Civil War.

With war declared, Washington, DC, found itself surrounded by Virginia to the south and pro-secessionist Maryland to the north, with precious few troops to defend it. President Lincoln made an emergency appeal to the Northern states for 75,000 troops, and Massachusetts was the first to respond. Aided by a group of wealthy Boston businessmen who helped provide funds for militia training and to support families of men going off to war, the vigor of the effort surprised the abolitionist Wendell Phillips, who admitted he had been mistaken in thinking that the Boston business elite put profits above patriotism, that it was not "wholly choked with cotton and cankered with gold."[18]

A few days later, George Boutwell was walking through a produce market hall in Boston, talking with the men of Company B of the Sixth Massachusetts Regiment as they waited for their orders to proceed to Washington. Boutwell recognized many friends and neighbors among this group, who were dubbed the Groton Artillery. Mustered the same day that Fort Sumter fell, they would soon be on their way to the capital as the advance guard of tens of thousands of soldiers from all over the North. As one of the men said to Boutwell, "many of us will never see Massachusetts again."[19]

Boutwell spoke with his Groton neighbor, Dr. Norman Smith, surgeon for the Sixth Regiment, whose great-grandfather, Lt. Abraham Stickney Jr., had marched to Concord with the Minutemen on April 19, 1775. Departing by train the next day, the Sixth Regiment arrived in secessionist Baltimore on the morning of April 19 and was attacked by rock-throwing Confederate sympathizers. Five soldiers were killed (one was in civilian clothing), becoming the first fatalities of the war. On the same day in 1775, Middlesex County men had been the first to die at Concord and Lexington.

When the regiment reached Washington, the exhausted soldiers, with more than forty injured, slept on the floor of the Senate chambers in the Capitol Building. Norman Smith sawed off the leg of Lt. Moses Herrick under the dome of the Capitol Rotunda, the first of tens of thousands of amputations performed during the war. President Lincoln, who was anxiously waiting for troops promised by New York and Pennsylvania, visited the men of the Massachusetts Sixth at the Capitol. He told them simply, "*You* are the only Northern realities."[20]

On hearing the news of the Baltimore violence, Governor Andrew turned to Boutwell "as the man for this crisis," knowing of Boutwell's "influence, acquaintance with the Cabinet, [and] knowledge of Eastern public sentiment." Andrew instructed Boutwell to leave immediately for Washington to coordinate an additional supply of troops and military supplies to defend the capital.[21]

Boutwell traveled first to New York, equipped with "a hundred dollars in gold, an improvised cipher-code for telegrams, and a small revolver loaded," where he consulted with a Union general, John E. Wool. Lincoln's safety in Washington was thought so precarious that the two agreed to summon Vice President Hannibal Hamlin immediately from Maine, to take charge in the event "of the death or capture of Mr. Lincoln, of [whose safety] we then knew nothing." Writing to his wife Sarah from New York's Astor Hotel, Boutwell admitted that "there is great reason to fear for Washington, and the position of the Massachusetts troops is perilous." Trying to maintain an optimistic air, Boutwell was concerned; "this week is full of danger . . . the present may be disastrous."[22]

Boutwell continued his journey, having to detour around dangerous Baltimore by sailing down the Chesapeake Bay from Havre de Grace to Annapolis, where Massachusetts militia troops were being ably organized by Gen. Benjamin Butler. Not knowing of Boutwell's detour, and hearing nothing but "blank silence" from the nation's capital, Governor Andrew sent another emissary from Boston with offers of additional troops. While waiting for a troop train at Annapolis Junction, Boutwell slept on the floor of a small house with his briefcase as a pillow. He then traveled with soldiers of the Twelfth New York Regiment, witnessing burned bridges and railroad track torn up by Confederate sympathizers. Fearing sabotage on the tracks ahead, the train moved slowly at night, no further than the length illuminated by its headlight so men out in front could inspect the track. Boutwell arrived in Washington on April 27 to find District residents in a panic over whether more troops were on the way. When additional militias from Massachusetts and other Northern states began arriving in the next few days, he was able to notify Governor Andrew that "the President and the Cabinet are gaining confidence."[23]

IN WASHINGTON, BOUTWELL met with Lincoln and Gen. Winfield Scott, the seventy-three-year-old commander of the Union army and hero of the Mexican-American War. Boutwell found the infirm Scott splayed on a chaise longue and thought him "in no condition to organize or lead armies." Briefing members of Lincoln's cabinet, Boutwell emphasized the need for protecting the rail lines running north and proposed an immediate blockade of Southern ports to help choke off the rebellion. When he left on May 1 to return to Boston, he had the permission he wanted to raise two additional and sorely needed Massachusetts regiments.[24]

The next several months were anxious ones for the Union. The Confederacy was mobilizing an army of up to 100,000 men that threatened to overwhelm poorly defended Washington. In early June, Union and Confederate forces fought their first armed skirmish of the war near Philippi, Virginia (now West Virginia). A month later, two inexperienced armies of more than twenty thousand men each were approaching each other near the railhead at Manassas Junction in northern Virginia, less than thirty miles from Washington.

In Boston, George Boutwell was urging Governor Andrew and those organizing the Commonwealth's militias to speed up the delivery of men and supplies to Washington. He was particularly concerned about Confederate raids on Union shipping. Just days after Fort Sumter, Confederate president Jefferson Davis had authorized the outfitting of private vessels operating out of North and South Carolina to prey upon Union cargo ships. Calling the threat one of "utmost importance," Boutwell repeatedly emphasized the need to "purchase at least three steamers and equip them for coastal defense" and to deploy them in the waters off Wilmington and Charleston in the Carolinas.[25]

Boutwell returned to Washington in May and then again at the end of July, arriving in the capital just days after the calamitous Union defeat at the Battle of Bull Run at Manassas. In between those two visits to Washington, he gave yet another significant speech, denouncing slavery for being the cause of the conflict, in one of America's most venerated lecture venues.

THE PHI BETA KAPPA oration at Harvard College was first given in 1788 by future president John Quincy Adams. In 1837, the lecture was delivered by Ralph Waldo Emerson and later published as one of his most famous works, *The American Scholar*. The lecture series continues to this day.

On July 18, a crowd filled the pews of the First Congregational Church just off Harvard Square in Cambridge. Although the lectures are most often literary or scientific in nature, the *Boston Evening Transcript* noted how, for this occasion, three months after Fort Sumter, George Boutwell had requested to be allowed to speak on "the present rebellion." The title for his talk was plain enough: "The Conspiracy: Its Purposes and Its Power." Among the students attending Harvard College at the time was Robert Todd Lincoln, the president's eldest son, who may well have been sitting in the audience.[26]

As he had in his Charlestown speech the previous January, Boutwell blamed slavery for the Southern "conspiracy" that was seeking to destroy the Union. Although secessionist sentiment might have different shadings in Virginia as compared to the border states or the Deep South, he said it was slavery that sought to destroy "the integrity of our territory" and the sanctity of the

American Constitution. He quoted the Irish political philosopher Edmund Burke, who described slave owners as having "a haughtiness of domination" that translates into believing that "liberty is a privilege, not a right." For Boutwell, this flatly contradicted the "theory of our government, that liberty is a right, and not a privilege."

Looking ahead to the war's end, Boutwell warned that anything less than "the extinction of slavery" would only lead to renewed conflict in the future. This was "a war for national existence."[27]

AT THE TIME, few northerners felt that the nation's existence was at stake. Most believed that the war would be a short one, and that a mere demonstration of the Union's superior economic and industrial strength would cow the South into submission. But then came the Battle of Bull Run.

Boutwell arrived back in Washington on July 23, two days after Gen. Stonewall Jackson and the Confederates had routed the Union troops, sending them—and the civilians with their picnic baskets who had come to watch them—fleeing back to Washington. President Lincoln was informed by telegram: "[T]he day is lost. Save Washington and the remnants of the Army." In the days that followed, Boutwell gathered as much information as he could amid the chaos. At Charles Sumner's house, he met Gen. Joseph Hooker, newly arrived from the west, who was vainly boasting that, if only given command, he "would take Richmond." Hooker was only one of many Union generals early in the war who would be tried and found wanting. Charged by Governor Andrew with providing a realistic appraisal of the situation, Boutwell wrote that the "rebels are weaving a network around Washington . . . and its surrender is not improbable." He pleaded with Andrew to institute a draft of ten thousand or twenty thousand men, believing that "other states will follow." Returning to Boston, Boutwell urged even more haste in overcoming the obstacles that were preventing the deployment of Union troops in the field.[28]

For the remainder of 1861, Boutwell continued to help coordinate the Massachusetts military contribution as the Union and Confederacy focused on equipping and training their troops. He was tireless in promoting the message that only the destruction of slavery and full emancipation for enslaved Blacks would destroy the rebellion. In December, he helped organize the inaugural meeting in Boston of the Emancipation League, which Frederick Douglass welcomed for emphasizing emancipation as both a moral imperative and a military necessity. Seeking to win over conservative Northern businessmen,

Boutwell emphasized that cotton production for their mills would be far more productive with a free-labor system. *The Liberator* newspaper, so disdainful of Boutwell as governor a decade before, reprinted his speech in full, noting that the standing-room audience listened with "profound attention, broken, however, by frequent applause."[29]

In the spring of 1862, Union setbacks in the Peninsula campaign against Richmond, and in Virginia's Shenandoah Valley, again made Washington vulnerable to Confederate attack. Out west, the Union had its one good piece of news when newly promoted Ulysses S. Grant defeated Confederate forces at Forts Henry and Donelson. Grant had been given command by Gen. John C. Frémont, the famed explorer of California and Republican Party candidate for president in 1856 who had taken command of the Department of the West in July 1861.[30]

AT HOME IN GROTON in June 1862, Boutwell left his house early one morning to catch the train into Boston to continue his work on the war effort. It was a day that would change his life. Daughter Georgie remembers being surprised at seeing her father walk through the front door just hours later at noon, explaining that he had received a telegram from Edwin Stanton, the new secretary of war, ordering him to report immediately to Washington. The next morning, he took the first train south. Neither he nor his family knew that, for the next three decades, Boutwell would spend a substantial part of each year in Washington; as Georgie wrote, "thirty-four years of life changed in a single moment upon receipt of a telegram."[31]

On arriving in Washington two days later, Boutwell took a hackney cab to the War Department, where Stanton ordered him to Cairo, Illinois, to investigate festering problems in the Western War Department that were undermining the Union war effort. Frémont, an unpopular commander, had been relieved of duty by Lincoln the previous October due to Frémont's highly controversial decision to unilaterally abolish slavery in his area (which risked driving Kentucky into the Confederacy). There were also ongoing accusations of fraud and graft in the tendering of army contracts that were weakening morale.[32]

After meeting Stanton, Boutwell was summoned to the Executive Mansion, where an even bigger surprise awaited. The president told Boutwell that, if Congress passed legislation authorizing new taxes to help pay for the Union war effort, Lincoln would ask him to become the country's first revenue commissioner. Strongly recommended by Secretary Chase for his "highest obtainable ability and integrity," Boutwell would get the job even though Lincoln had initially favored another candidate.[33]

ARRIVING IN CAIRO, Boutwell joined fellow commission members Charles A. Dana (former editor of the *New York Tribune* and cousin of Richard Henry Dana) and Stephen Logan (Abraham Lincoln's ex–law partner) to evaluate claims of fraud against the Western War Department. In letters home, he described the hot and humid conditions in the town, at the junction of the Mississippi and Ohio Rivers where the borders of Illinois, Missouri, and Kentucky meet. Almost every evening, he wrote, there would be a "collision of thunder showers, one coming down the Mississippi, and the other down the Ohio." Although extensively protected by levees, Cairo was often flooded. Sickness and disease were rampant among both the troops and civilians, George wrote, with army refuse and dead animals covering the ground. He sought to reassure Sarah and the children that, by drinking only "tea and water from Iowa ice . . . I preserved my health."[34]

When completed, the commissioners' report was highly critical of Frémont's command. In fairness to Frémont, he had taken charge in 1861 in a Missouri rife with Confederate guerrillas and sympathizers, and with inadequate military resources. Nonetheless, the imperious and ostentatious Frémont engaged in highly questionable favoritism in the letting out of military contracts. Surrounding himself with a personal guard in lavish uniforms, Frémont managed to alienate both his own soldiers and local citizens.[35]

On July 8, Boutwell celebrated his twenty-first wedding anniversary, sharing it not with his wife but with the ever-present mosquitos that smothered the low-lying river town. Writing to Sarah, he regretted not being home with her, Georgie, and Frank, though he did want to tell her about "one of the best jokes of the times [that] has just transpired."

At that time, enslaved Blacks who escaped into the Union camp were given jobs and discarded "secesh" (Confederate) uniforms to wear, as many of them wore rags "hardly enough to cover their nakedness." The local mayor, a Confederate sympathizer, was helping Missouri slave owners recapture some of their "property." Learning of this, the Union commander, Gen. William K. Strong, intervened immediately and ordered that all forcibly taken ex-slaves be released immediately. When the mayor protested, General Strong declared them free on the technicality that they were wearing Confederate uniforms and thus were the army's responsibility. He then put the mayor in the guardhouse, where he remained for several days. Boutwell noted how, upon being released, the mayor "has had nothing more to do with negro catching . . . and the negro catchers have made tracks for Missouri. Love to all, George."[36]

Humor aside, Boutwell picked up valuable intelligence while in Cairo about the Confederate use of enslaved Black labor. On a journey down the Mississippi River, he saw the Confederate earthworks around Columbus, Kentucky, a strategic "key to the valley of the Mississippi," which had been built by hundreds of Black laborers. Boutwell realized that similar use of enslaved Blacks at "Memphis, Vicksburg, Corinth, Manassas, and Richmond" was freeing up thousands of white southerners to fight on the front lines. He was convinced that depriving the Confederacy of this military asset must be a major Union war aim. It soon would be when, a few months later, President Lincoln declared his intention to issue the Emancipation Proclamation.[37]

As he celebrated a humid and lonely Fourth of July, Boutwell assumed he would be in Cairo through the end of the month. In less than two weeks, however, with Lincoln having signed the Revenue Act of 1862 on July 1, Boutwell was headed back to Washington, where he would have the opportunity to press his views on the military advantages and moral necessity of emancipation to the president himself.

ARRIVING IN THE CAPITAL on July 16, Boutwell was sworn in as revenue commissioner the next day by Supreme Court Justice James Moore Wayne. A Georgian and former congressman, Justice Wayne had supported Roger Taney's *Dred Scott* decision. Though Boutwell likely bristled at having to take the oath of office from Wayne, Lincoln's new revenue commissioner would soon be able to let the entire country know precisely where he stood on the issue of emancipation.

6

Financing the War

Despair permeated the city; the war was going badly. In the revolving door of Union army commanders, Gen. George B. McClellan was the latest to disappoint Lincoln, having been stymied in the Virginia Peninsula campaign after failing to take the Confederate capital at Richmond. In the western theater, Union forces captured Nashville, New Orleans, and Memphis, seizing control of much of the Mississippi River, but still faced the daunting task of subduing Vicksburg.

Politically, there was growing dissatisfaction with Lincoln's leadership and fears among Republicans that they might lose badly in the 1862 midterm elections. Residents in the capital were demoralized by the constant sight of sick and wounded soldiers and by the scarcity of goods and rising wartime inflation. Thousands of fugitives from slavery were in the city, needing to be housed and fed. The president and his cabinet also had to deal with the sky-rocketing cost of the war and how to pay for it, which was why George Boutwell had been summoned to Washington.

In 1861, Congress had gone into emergency session to seek ways of financing the Union war effort. Seeking to spread the burden evenly between rich and poor, and eastern merchant and western farmer, legislation was proposed that would increase tariffs on sugar, tea, coffee, and alcohol (affecting the less well-off); impose a direct tax on the states totaling $20 million (greatly affecting farmers); and implement a flat income tax of 3 percent on incomes over $800 (primarily affecting the more well-off). President Lincoln signed the bill on August 5, 1861, triggering a run on gold as depositors sought to redeem paper currency issued by state banks that was falling in value. To stabilize the situation, Congress in February 1862 authorized issuing a total of $300 million in "greenbacks" (so-called for the green ink used in printing them) to help the government pay for war supplies and replace the confusing array of currency notes printed by state banks.[1]

By early 1862, war costs had escalated to $2 million a day and more money was needed. Lincoln was complaining that Treasury Secretary "Chase has no money, and he tells me he can raise no more. The bottom is out of the tub." Prior to becoming revenue commissioner, Boutwell had said $150 million a year would be needed, and that nothing was more important than solidifying the government's financial stability: "[D]efeats in the field we may recover from more easily than discredit on the exchange." To address the shortfall, the proposed Revenue Act of 1862 would levy a new tax on manufactured goods (primarily affecting the poor) while introducing a new graduated income tax that would tax middle-class Americans in addition to the wealthy. In spreading the tax burden, Lincoln and Chase hoped that northerners would be more emotionally invested in the Union war effort.[2]

Signed by President Lincoln on July 1, the Revenue Act of 1862 was an extraordinary measure for desperate times. Previously in American history, government revenues had consisted of tariffs on imported goods, excise taxes on domestically manufactured goods and raw materials, and the sale of public lands. Although the idea of a tax on wages, property, and investments had been raised earlier to help pay the country's debt from the War of 1812, it was only with the dire situation facing the Union in the early days of the Civil War that the concept was revived. Even then it was controversial, with many in Congress complaining that "an army of officials" would be needed to collect a broad array of taxes in a highly intrusive operation disrupting the private lives of ordinary Americans. As congressional leader Thaddeus Stevens remarked, the Union faced a choice "between these disagreeable" taxes or the "annihilation of this government."[3]

In addition to Congress's deciding whether personal taxes should focus on incomes or on property and rents (which would hit farmers especially hard), there was the question of whether the federal government could even collect such taxes. Knowing that hundreds if not thousands of tax assessors and collectors would have to be hired, Treasury Secretary Chase doubted whether the money collected would even offset the cost of collecting it. Yet with the war need so great, the Revenue Act was passed, creating the office of commissioner of internal revenue within the Treasury Department.[4]

BEING CHOSEN TO OVERSEE this monumental effort at a critical time in American history was a signal event in George Boutwell's life. When he arrived in Washington, he hadn't even read the Revenue Act, which, "at twenty thousand words," he described as "the longest and most detailed statute the country had ever seen."[5]

Having spent most of that first night reading the new law, Boutwell arrived at the Treasury Building on July 17 and was given a small office on the ground floor. He immersed himself in the details of the tax code, which he deemed "sensible and wise but incompletely and imperfectly thought out." Assisted by three clerks assigned to him from other divisions of the department, he began hiring additional staff. One was Marshall Conant, a former school principal from Massachusetts who had the responsibility of handling millions of dollars in tax revenues in the coming months, at a salary of $1,200 a year.[6]

Next, Boutwell began the daunting task of working with Treasury Secretary Chase to appoint more than three thousand tax assessors and collectors to be deployed throughout the twenty Union and four border states. Inundated with candidate recommendations from members of Congress and party bosses such as Thurlow Weed of New York, Boutwell was given some latitude by Secretary Chase in filling the positions, though not to the extent, as he claimed in his memoir, that "Mr. Chase took no part in the appointment of collectors and assessors." Both Chase and President Lincoln took a decidedly hands-on role, given the need to satisfy different factions of the Republican Party and monitor the sensitive process of tax collection in the border states of Maryland, Delaware, Kentucky, and Missouri. As Lincoln reportedly said about any issue that might drive the slaveholding border states into the arms of the Confederacy: "I would hope to have God on my side, but I must have Kentucky." Even in the loyal states, the administration of the new tax law would be "both delicate and arduous," as Americans would be sensitive to this new army of revenue officials probing their financial affairs.[7]

And what an army it was. By early 1863, the Internal Revenue workforce was an astounding 3,882 persons, most of them tax assessors and collectors in the field. On the second floor of the immense Treasury Building, which was still only half completed, Boutwell's clerks sat at single desks, giving "the appearance of a day school for boys . . . the only sound being the smooth scratch of the goose quill . . . gliding over multitudinous sheets of paper." By war's end, the Revenue Bureau dwarfed even its parent Treasury Department in terms of employees.[8]

As commissioner, Boutwell had to both oversee this hiring effort and interpret the Internal Revenue Act and its application across a wide range of products, licenses, and income tax questions and disputes. The incoming inquiries and questions were voluminous, given the public's confusion over the variety of taxes. Boutwell established a rigorous daily system for dealing with them. First, the hundreds of inquiries flowing into the office would be dealt with each evening by the heads of divisions. When solutions and answers were agreed on, outgoing letters were dictated the next morning by Boutwell with the aid of "two short-hand writers." He would then read over the finished letters in the afternoon before signing them, while making sure copies were given to heads of "the respective divisions for future guidance." By October, he estimated that as many as eight hundred letters a day were being sent out from the Bureau.[9]

Very quickly, the name of George Boutwell was as well known to the business community and the general public as that of any other government figure in America, save the president. Newspapers across the country would feature Boutwell's tax decisions on their front page, all to help educate the public. From small-town papers like the *Daily Whig* in Bangor, Maine, to the big-city *Free Press* in Detroit, Michigan, readers learned of the latest tax decisions on everything from the difference between billiard tables in private homes and those in public pool halls (Boutwell loved billiards) to the manufacture of everything from horseshoes to wine, all signed with Boutwell's name.[10]

The complexity of the issues facing businesses and tradesmen was illustrated by one such item in the *Chicago Daily Tribune*. An association of Chicago manufacturers wrote to Boutwell urgently seeking answers to two questions: (1) the difference in tax rates for products made directly from raw materials as opposed to previously manufactured components, and (2) whether the tax on gross sales would be adjusted if component parts of those products had previously been taxed. In their letter, the businessmen pleaded that "some rule of interpreting the law be early adopted . . . and made public."[11]

Boutwell's effort in organizing the Internal Revenue office was herculean; the work was continuous, seven days a week, generally into the evenings. His colleague Hugh McCulloch, who became comptroller of the currency in February 1863, marveled that "there was really more hard and difficult work done in a single year in a single bureau—the Bureau of Internal Revenue (for the admirable organization of which the country is indebted to George S. Boutwell)— than was done in the whole [Treasury] Department from the establishment of the Government up to 1861." (In 1972, the newly renovated auditorium on the top floor of IRS headquarters in Washington, DC, was named the Boutwell Auditorium in George's honor.)[12]

BOUTWELL DESCRIBED HIS workdays as going "to the office before breakfast, then during the day, and then again in the evening. My only exercise was a ride on horseback after hours and before dinner," often with Lincoln secretary John Hay. Boutwell lived alone for the first several months—his family would join him in December 1862—in the Foggy Bottom neighborhood about eight blocks west of the Treasury Building, where he maintained and paid for the servants. One, an elderly cook named Monaky, had worked for and become greatly attached to Senator Daniel Webster and his family. Boutwell recalled Monaky's distress when she learned that Webster's son, Fletcher, a colonel in the Twelfth Massachusetts Volunteer Infantry, had been killed at the Second Battle of Bull Run, just six weeks after arriving in Washington with his regiment.[13]

The Treasury Building that Boutwell walked to each day was both a construction site and an armed fortress. Even in wartime, work continued on the building's new western facade facing the White House (known then as the Executive Mansion or the President's House). The east and south wings had been completed by 1860, and the north wing on Pennsylvania Avenue would be constructed from 1867 to 1869. In addition to hundreds of construction workers, there were military units camped all around the building, including the Fifth Massachusetts Regiment. Treasury staff were organized into a self-defense militia, the Treasury Guard, which drilled each day in the inner courtyard. In the event of a Confederate attack that breached the outer ring of forts surrounding Washington, the Treasury Building and Executive Mansion complex would become one of three key defensive positions in the city, along with the Capitol Building and City Hall (today's Judiciary Square). Should the rebels overwhelm the city, the Treasury Building would be the final citadel.[14]

When his family came to join him in December, they found a life totally alien from the one they had left in New England. Poor sanitation and widespread disease plagued the city's seventy thousand inhabitants, symbolized by the Washington Canal that bypassed the White House as it ran from the Potomac River to the Anacostia, full of "rats, mildew and foul smells." Boutwell sketched a city "filled with troops, the hospitals, churches and other buildings were crowded with the wounded; the streets were stuffed with ambulances, baggage wagons, artillery, and the material of war. The hills were dotted with tents, and the officers and men were discontented and almost in a state of mutiny." Daughter Georgianna, only nineteen, described how "crossing the street meant to hopelessly traverse an acre or more of mud in a vain attempt to find the . . . avenue you had just left." Cows and pigs pastured on the public squares. Visiting her father at the Treasury Building, Georgie watched construction crews building a bridge from the new west wing to the east corner of the White House "over which messages were sent to the President."[15]

Despite the hardships and the war, Washington continued to maintain its social scene. With her father working late at the Treasury almost every evening, Georgie recalled how she and her mother would arrive at the building after dark and walk past armed guards through long, underground tunnels to his office to fetch him. Her mother Sarah was often ill with respiratory ailments because of the unsanitary conditions, so Georgie found herself more and more being her father's sole "companion" at dinners and receptions. Often, the other guests would mistake her for George's wife. Writing of one party hosted by Secretary of State William Seward, Georgie noted with resignation, "father introduced me as his daughter, but it did no good" as the other guests kept referring to her as Mrs. Boutwell. Having inherited her father's wry sense of humor, however, she turned it to her advantage. Writing to her Aunt Abby back in Groton in a Jane Austen tone, she said that yes, guests coming to their house "persist in calling me Mrs. Boutwell. [But] it is almost as good as having a husband, and I have no doubt that he [my imaginary husband] is quite equal to any I should be likely to obtain." Letters home were also filled with social gossip, including less than flattering descriptions of the famous people they were meeting, including William Seward ("an ordinary man . . . not good looking"), Salmon Chase ("rather flashy and well proportioned"), and Mary Todd Lincoln ("short, rather stout").[16]

During the day, as was common for women during the war, Georgie and her mother volunteered at the civilian and army hospitals in the city, including Campbell General Hospital, which had nine hundred beds. Supplies at the hospitals were always running low, so Sarah would write home, asking her sister-in-law to send items like gum tea and sugar that the wounded men find "very beneficial after amputation."[17]

THE MOST NOVEL ASPECT of the 1862 Revenue Act was the introduction of a graduated personal income tax for the first time in American history. A progressive tax, it was zero percent on the first $600 of income (considered the poverty line); 3 percent on incomes between $600 and $10,000; and 5 percent on incomes greater than $10,000. In 2023 dollars, the amounts would be equivalent to no tax on the first $18,000; 3 percent up to $300,000; and 5 percent over $300,000.

The tax was to be levied on both workers and investors; on "any kind of property, rents, interest, dividends, salaries, or from any profession, trade, employment, or vocation whatever." As noted by Sidney Ratner in his 1942 classic, *American Taxation*, the Revenue Act adopted "the seemingly radical principle of progressive taxation . . . even if in a very moderate manner."[18]

Given his working-class roots, George Boutwell personally favored a higher tax rate on wealthy Americans, such as a middle tier of 4 percent on incomes between $5,000 and $10,000. Surprisingly, Boutwell's Radical Republican colleague, Thaddeus Stevens, thought progressive taxes "unjustly discriminatory," while the successful banker Augustus Frank endorsed rates as high as 10 percent on the wealthiest Americans. In the end, the debate was a bit academic, as only 10–15 percent of all Union households, those with incomes over $600 annually, were ever subject to any income tax at all. What Boutwell considered most important was that Americans were complying with their tax payments, whether on income or on goods and services.[19]

Boutwell's belief in the necessity of citizens meeting their tax obligations was illustrated by one case involving Gen. Winfield Scott and Frederick Douglass. Scott, the hero of the Mexican War, presidential candidate in 1852, and commanding general of the US Army, had retired at full pay in November 1861. In March 1863 he wrote to Boutwell, asking that he be exempt from paying the 3 percent income tax. The general pointed out that, by presidential fiat, his salary could never be reduced. Reporting on this story in his newspaper, *Douglass' Monthly*, Frederick Douglass noted with satisfaction that "Commissioner Boutwell" said no, the income tax was not a reduction in salary, it was a tax. Douglass editorialized that Scott's request was "very small business" for a former commanding general and agreed with Boutwell that exempting Scott would set a poor example for other US military officers.[20]

During his tenure from July 1862 to March 1863, Boutwell oversaw a tax collection effort that was crucially important for the Union army, bringing in $37 million the first year and $109 million for fiscal year 1863 (in 2023 dollars, an increase from $1 billion to over $3 billion). By 1864, the tax collection process Boutwell had put in place was, for the first time in the country's history, raising more revenue in domestic taxes than in import duties and tariffs. Later, as a member of Congress, his appeal for an additional income tax tier was vindicated when the Revenue Act of 1864 set rates of 5 percent over $600,

7.5 percent over $5,000, and 10 percent over $10,000. By war's end, Union victory was made possible in part by the tax collection operation that Boutwell and Chase implemented with their army of Revenue agents. More than 20 percent of all federal expenditures during the war, military and civilian, were covered by income and other taxes. The Confederacy, by contrast, had difficulty collecting even the miniscule taxes that it levied on real estate and other personal property, which covered only 5 percent of its expenses.[21]

Assessing his eight months' tenure as revenue commissioner, Boutwell wrote that there were no hints of scandal in the vast patronage machine that was put at his disposal, nor were many of the Bureau's tax decisions ever overturned by the courts. Among all his rulings, he was most proud of the one that declared that, if slaves were "liberated by the last will and testament of their masters, they were not to be treated as personal property and were not subject to the tax," whatever existing state law might say. Even this early in his Washington career, Boutwell was proclaiming that enslaved persons were human beings, not property, while also asserting the primacy of federal law over states' rights.[22]

GEORGE BOUTWELL RESIGNED his position on March 4, 1863, when he was sworn in as a new member of Congress, despite Chase asking him to stay on as commissioner until Congress officially convened in August. Boutwell could have done so legally, but refused, concerned about the appearance of a conflict of interest. More than that, Boutwell offered to compile a tax manual "without compensation," bringing together the 1862 Revenue Act, his decisions as commissioner, information on the assessment and collection of taxes, and various forms and regulations, to help guide the future work of the Bureau. An impressive achievement, *The Manual of the Direct and Excise Tax Systems of the United States*, at more than three hundred pages, is still available today. Boutwell did have the good sense to ask Chase for the copyright, a wise move given that the tax manual underwent multiple printings.[23] Many years later, in his law office in Boston, Boutwell would open a copy of the manual given him by a junior colleague, one noted for his sense of humor, and read the inscription, "DEDICATION: To the Memory of Caesar Augustus in whose reign there went forth the decree that all the world should be taxed."[24]

Prone to be overly judgmental of his colleagues, Boutwell would write of Salmon Chase that "Mr. Chase's mental processes were slow, but time being given, he had the capacity to form sound opinions." Working closely together,

Boutwell fully appreciated that Chase was tasked with creating an entirely new financial system for the US government, in time of war, that included establishing a national banking system, issuing legal tender notes (greenbacks) as the country's first paper currency, and raising $500 million through war bonds.[25]

It was no secret at the time that Chase still harbored designs on the presidency; he had sought the Republican Party nomination in 1856 and 1860 and might do so again in 1864. Unfortunately for Chase, his constant political maneuvering caught up with him in the spring of 1864. He had tendered his resignation to Lincoln one too many times in an attempt to upstage the president. This time it was accepted, damaging Chase's political credibility. Following the November election, Lincoln nominated Chase to be chief justice of the Supreme Court, replacing Roger Taney, who had died in October.[26]

Putting Chase on the Supreme Court was a great example of Abraham Lincoln's political skills in maneuvering between the Radical and conservative wings of the Republican Party. Despite his 1864 reelection, the president needed the support of conservative Republican leaders such as Francis P. Blair Sr., who wanted the Supreme Court vacancy for his son, Postmaster Montgomery Blair. Apprehensive over how the younger Blair might rule on the constitutionality of the Emancipation Proclamation, Lincoln connived the elder Blair into believing that opposition from his cabinet officers gave him no choice: "If the strongest horse in the team *would* go ahead, he *cannot*, if all *the rest hold back*." By nominating Chase, Lincoln also gained credit with the Radical Republicans for nominating a man who had been one of the country's strongest antislavery advocates.[27]

Lincoln's choice of Chase was significant given that the court might soon be ruling on both the constitutionality of the Emancipation Proclamation and the legality of greenbacks, two issues of great importance to George Boutwell. Talking with Boutwell, by then in Congress, Lincoln said that while he certainly hoped that Chase would provide a crucial fifth majority vote on such issues, the president would never ask Chase to commit himself beforehand. In a famous quote that is now referred to almost every time a president is considering a new Supreme Court nominee, Lincoln told Boutwell: "[W]e cannot ask a man [how he might vote] . . . if we should, and he should answer us, we should despise him for it. Therefore, we must take a man whose opinions are known." Lincoln was assuming that Chase, as a longtime Radical Republican, would rule favorably on emancipation, and, as the treasury secretary who had introduced greenbacks, would do likewise on the legal tender issue. The president would be only half-right.[28]

Shortly after becoming chief justice, Salmon Chase had the privilege of performing a signal act on behalf of his country. On February 1, 1865, with Senator Charles Sumner standing nearby, Chase admitted attorney John S. Rock of Massachusetts to the bar of the Supreme Court. Having officially credentialed the first Black attorney to practice before the court, Roger Taney's successor as chief justice had set a bold new precedent in America's race relations.[29]

REGARDING THE ISSUE of greenbacks, Salmon Chase as treasury secretary had been as responsible as anyone for giving the Union army the resources it needed to win the war. Despite some reservations on its legality, Chase had supported the Legal Tender Act and the printing of greenbacks. By 1870, though, Chase had changed his mind, thinking that not only did the war not give the government such authority, but that doing so represented an impairment to the enforcement of contracts. In *Hepburn v. Griswold* (1870), Chase spoke for the 5–3 majority in ruling that greenbacks did not have to be accepted for the payment of contracts agreed to prior to the passage of the law on February 25, 1862, thus sowing confusion in the American economy until his colleagues on the court overruled him a year later.[30]

The person having to deal with the consequences of Chase's change of mind was none other than George Boutwell, appointed secretary of the treasury by President Ulysses Grant in 1869. In an unusual move that would be highly controversial today, Chase gave Boutwell a heads-up about the impending decision, fearing chaos on America's gold exchanges.[31] As for the income tax that Boutwell helped introduce, it survived the war by only a few years. Congress first reduced the tax in 1867 (Boutwell by then was a congressman from Massachusetts) and then repealed it altogether in 1872. It was revived in 1894 but then ruled unconstitutional by the US Supreme Court in 1895. It was only when President William Howard Taft proposed a constitutional amendment in 1909 that would allow Congress to tax incomes directly, and the Sixteenth Amendment became law in 1913, that the national income tax was reinstated.

Prior to the income tax being reinstated, taxes on alcohol and tobacco had been two of the main sources of federal government revenue. By the early 1900s, however, the temperance movement in America was again on the march. Given the declining sales of liquor, the federal government needed a new revenue stream, thus bolstering the political argument for an income tax.

By the time it was fully introduced in 1916, Congress found it much easier to enact a total ban on alcohol. Prohibition began when the Eighteenth Amendment became law in 1919.

Boutwell, of course, had begun his political career in Groton in 1839 by joining the Temperance Party. Then, in the 1860s, he was revenue commissioner. When Congress passed the Volstead Act in 1919 to implement the Eighteenth Amendment, it gave the commissioner of the newly formed Internal Revenue Service, Boutwell's old job, the primary responsibility for enforcing Prohibition. Agents of the bureau, appropriately known as "Revenuers," roamed the land arresting bootleggers and destroying illegal stills. In an ironic twist that Boutwell would have enjoyed, mobsters such as Al Capone were ultimately sent to jail, not for illegal bootlegging but for evasion of income taxes, the very instrument that the abstinent Boutwell had helped bring into being in 1862 as head of the Revenue Bureau.

EVEN AS HE was working day and night in the Treasury Building in the autumn of 1862, Boutwell was keeping an eye on his congressional district back in Massachusetts. His first love in politics was the give-and-take of crafting legislation and representing his constituents. When he was offered the nomination for a House seat in the Seventh Congressional District, he jumped at it. Despite being absent from his district for many months, and despite some opposition to his strident calls for Black emancipation, Boutwell won the election in November with 55 percent of the vote. He would be joining the new Congress in March 1863 with an opportunity to make history.

7

The Promise of Emancipation

I t was but a short walk to the Executive Mansion from Boutwell's office in the Treasury Building at the corner of Fifteenth Street and Pennsylvania Avenue. Mornings, afternoons, or evenings, he and the president could be conferring on a moment's notice to review the appointment of tax collectors and assessors and how well these officials were doing in keeping the national government afloat. But the two men would also meet frequently when each stopped by the War Department, just beyond the White House at Pennsylvania and Seventeenth Street, to check on the latest news of the military campaigns being waged in Virginia, Tennessee, and Mississippi. The president was a constant presence in the War Department's telegraph office, hoping that the most recently appointed Union military commander was at last taking the initiative against the Confederates. George Boutwell was a frequent visitor as well, wanting to catch up on the latest news from the front.[1]

As the two men came to know each other better, the president would seek Boutwell's views and the two would talk at length about the conduct of the war. Long before the president's death in April 1865, George Boutwell had become, in the words of Lincoln scholar Allen C. Guelzo, "a devoted friend to Abraham Lincoln." Oddly enough, that friendship deepened in the same month that Boutwell directly challenged the president, in front of a crowd of ten thousand people, to move more quickly on emancipation. The occasion was one of the most important speeches Boutwell ever gave, in early August 1862, on the grounds of the US Capitol.[2]

BOUTWELL HAD BEEN IN Washington but three weeks when he was invited to be one of the main speakers at a massive public rally being held on August 6 to boost badly sagging morale in Washington. The war, now more than a year old, was not going well. The Army of the Potomac was once again retreating from a failed campaign in Virginia, sick and wounded troops were bivouacked all over the city, wartime expenses were escalating, and friction was rife between Secretary of War Stanton and Gen. George McClellan, commander of the Army of the Potomac.[3]

Washington was suffering its usual summer heat and humidity on that Wednesday as bells throughout the city began to peal at 4 p.m., calling citizens of the District to attend the Great War Meeting on Capitol Hill. The Stars and Stripes adorned public buildings and private residences alike, and the Marine Band was playing before a crowd of ten thousand people as the proceedings began. As advertised, President Lincoln and some of his cabinet—Secretary of the Treasury Salmon Chase and Attorney General Edward Bates—were sitting on the platform, though they were not scheduled to speak. George Boutwell was on the speaker's list, slated to appear second.

As the initial speaker turned to take his seat, the crowd began chanting for Lincoln. "The call for the President was irresistible," the next day's paper noted, and "after a brief consultation with Secretary Chase and Attorney General Bates, he good naturedly came forward."[4]

In this, his first major public appearance since giving his inaugural address the year before, the president's impromptu remarks were pure Lincoln: short, humorous, and self-effacing. Seeking to put the crowd at ease, Lincoln made light of the quarrels being reported between McClellan and Stanton, observing that "Gen. McClellan is not to blame for sometimes asking for what he wanted and needed, and the Secretary of War is not to blame for not giving when he had none to give." As commander-in-chief as well as president, Lincoln remarked that he alone bore ultimate responsibility. Moving to his seat, Lincoln told the crowd, "I have talked longer than I expected. I avail myself of my privilege of saying no more."[5]

George Boutwell then rose to take the podium, telling the audience that "I am a stranger to you, and I do not know any good reason why your committee should have undertaken to introduce an acquaintance between us."[6]

Lincoln was taking his seat as Boutwell began his address, provocatively entitled, "Treason the Fruit of Slavery." The president heard his revenue commissioner say, "Speaking for the first time in the free, open air in the city of Washington, if it had not been for slavery, there would have been no treason; and when slavery should cease to exist, there will be no traitors. That is the beginning and the end of this war, slavery in the beginning, freedom in the end." Boutwell next told the crowd spread out below him that the president and his cabinet would receive "the reward and gratitude of their countrymen . . . the faster he and they march on towards the conclusion when slavery shall have ceased to exist."[7]

In this, the first great public rally of the war, Boutwell was the only speaker of more than a dozen who directly addressed slavery as a cause of the war and emancipation as a solution. Here was the newly appointed internal revenue commissioner, unknown to all but a few, declaring support for emancipation policies that the president himself was not yet able to voice publicly. It was only two weeks before, on July 22, that Lincoln had even raised such issues with his full cabinet, showing them a draft of his proposed, and very limited, emancipation proclamation. Although the military necessity for freeing the slaves in Confederate territory had been occupying Lincoln's thoughts for months, he was reluctant to move forward for fear of alienating Northern public opinion and possibly losing the allegiance of the slaveholding border states of Missouri, Kentucky, Delaware, and Maryland.

As Lincoln had explained in that July 22 cabinet meeting, his Emancipation Proclamation would only apply to enslaved Blacks in states and territory still under Confederate control. Nonetheless, the president's proposal came as a shock to his cabinet members. Public opinion was not yet ready for measures that even hinted at Black civil or social equality. Even though personally committed to emancipation, Lincoln had to publicly frame the war effort as one whose only object was to preserve the Union. As he famously declared one month later in an open letter to Horace Greeley on August 22, "my paramount object in this struggle is to save the Union and is not to either save or to destroy slavery. If I could save the Union without freeing any slave, I would do it."[8]

Thus, for George Boutwell on August 6 to publicly declare that "we shall never crush the rebellion until we crush slavery" was bound to generate controversy. The conservative *New York Herald* noted how the speeches that day, with only one exception, "reflected the policy of the administration, to prosecute the war for the Union, to crush out the rebellion first, and attend to other matters [i.e., slavery] afterwards. This exception [was] the speech of Governor Boutwell." The paper noted how the president himself avoided any reference to the "negro question."[9]

Was it just a coincidence that Boutwell was not only invited to speak but prominently placed second, so that newspaper reports of the meeting would carry his remarks at the top of their stories? Did the president know and welcome what Boutwell was going to say? Lincoln was certainly familiar with Boutwell's views, as voiced at the Virginia Peace Convention and in his Phi Beta Kappa lecture. Did Lincoln welcome Boutwell being one of the speakers, knowing that his revenue commissioner would speak of the military necessity of eradicating slavery, a policy that the president could not yet voice? With his presence on the stage, was the president tacitly endorsing Boutwell's call for the Union to "take slavery by the throat and destroy it"?[10]

For his part, Boutwell was surprised to have been invited at all. As he wrote to Charles Sumner a few days after the rally, he fully expected to be disinvited, having accepted the invitation but telling the organizing committee that he would "speak my own sentiments" on the need for complete abolition and on slavery being the cause of the war. He told Sumner that the committee "faltered one day" before agreeing to have him speak; perhaps its members needed a day to clear the invitation with the president?[11]

Boutwell's speech may well have been a testing of the waters for public acceptance of emancipation as necessary for winning the war. As a member of Lincoln's government but not having the visibility of a cabinet member, Boutwell was well-placed to say what others couldn't. And he said it, plainly: "I say, my friends, that this doctrine of emancipation in the eleven seceded States— immediate, unconditional, universal—is the solution of the difficulty of the war, and consequently the conclusion of peace."[12]

Interestingly, a similar scenario had played out eight months earlier in Boston when Governor John Andrew, knowing that he could not yet publicly support emancipation, had asked Boutwell to replace him as a speaker at the inaugural meeting of the Emancipation League before a packed audience in Tremont Temple in December 1861. As Andrew explained to the meeting organizers, "[ex-]Governor Boutwell can say and do usefully what I could not, without injury to our own cause." Andrew knew that Boutwell's speech to the League that night would emphasize the military necessity of emancipation, "for the salvation of the government."[13]

IF BOUTWELL'S SPEECH was intended to provoke a positive response, it succeeded; his remarks were met with cheers and cries of support from the crowd. Pro-administration newspapers such as the *National Republican* noted how

Boutwell "did not hesitate to say that it is slavery" that was the cause of the rebellion. The *New York Times* and *New York Tribune* reported that Boutwell was interrupted often by "applause, cries of 'Good, good,' and cheering." In Boston, the *Evening Transcript* was laudatory: "Gov. Boutwell's strong emancipation speech . . . is much talked of. It was a stirring and able off-hand effort, and was very well received," although "his sentiments, thus openly and sharply defined . . . *surprised some of his hearers* [emphasis added]."[14]

The response from the free Black community was equally enthusiastic. In Elisha Weaver's *The Christian Recorder*, the country's leading African American newspaper, Minister Henry McNeal Turner of the African Methodist Episcopal Church wrote that all "the speakers were generally very eloquent, but the Hon. G. S. Boutwell was the only one out of all, who dared to take a bold stand in favor of the colored man." Frederick Douglass praised Boutwell for proclaiming that abolishing slavery was, as Douglass put it, "the only wise solution of our present national troubles." In his report on the Great War Meeting, Douglass once again criticized Lincoln for avoiding the emancipation issue altogether, describing the president's remarks as "full of repetitions and remarkably careless."[15]

Boutwell's speech was similarly well-received overseas, especially in Britain. Newspapers from London to Leeds to Liverpool applauded Boutwell's call that "slavery has ceased" should be the Union "war cry." Such sentiments played well with the antislavery British public, as was likely the intention, given the necessity of preventing the United Kingdom from recognizing the Confederacy. In the trying days of summer 1862, it helped greatly to have British public opinion offsetting the pro-Confederate tendencies of English woolen manufacturers and the landed gentry, who tended to identify culturally and economically with Southern plantation owners.[16]

Throughout his political career, Abraham Lincoln believed that "public sentiment is everything. With public sentiment, nothing can fail; without it, nothing can succeed." In its way, Boutwell's speech was an example of the president's conviction that "he who moulds public sentiment, goes deeper than he who enacts statutes or pronounces decisions." The response to Boutwell's speech demonstrated that Northern public opinion was moving, albeit slowly, toward recognizing slavery as the crux of the conflict. As Lincoln would shortly write to Horace Greeley, the president might even think of freeing *"all* the slaves" if he thought that would save the Union.[17]

Lincoln biographer Michael Burlingame has written that the president "was hardly a reluctant emancipator." In 1861 and 1862, Lincoln was juggling the realities of a divided Republican Party, Northern white racism, calls from the Black community and white abolitionists for faster progress, and constitutional constraints, all while managing a war effort led by a succession of cautious and incompetent generals. Boutwell himself, as Burlingame notes, believed that Lincoln only *"appeared* to follow rather than to lead the Republican Party" and that the president, Boutwell believed, "waited patiently and confidently for the healthy movements of public sentiment which he well knew were in the right direction." The Great War Meeting and Boutwell's speech on August 6 may well have been an important part of that process.[18]

IN DENOUNCING SLAVERY to the crowd that day, however, Boutwell did not shy away from confronting the Achilles' heel of Northern support for the Union war effort: the prejudice of working-class whites against Blacks in general and Black laborers in particular. In raising the issue, he reminded the crowd of how, just two days earlier in Brooklyn, "there was a riot between the free white laborers and the colored men." He mentioned similar "conflicts in Cincinnati and elsewhere throughout the North."[19]

Boutwell asked rhetorically, "what is the solution of this difficulty between the white and the colored races of the North?" He answered simply, "freedom to the Blacks." He then sketched a scenario in which, if the seceded South was brought back into the Union with slavery intact, Northern whites would continue to face competition for jobs from large numbers of Blacks escaping to the North. Far preferable was "to give them a home on territory which they and you have fought for, in the coast region of the South."

Boutwell was clearly appealing to racial prejudices to convince undecided whites that emancipation was in their interest. "You . . . have to take the choice," he said. "[A]bolish slavery in these seceded States, give the negroes a home there, and carry them out of the North by the mild power of persuasion, or else allow the North to be overrun by escaped fugitives from the South." He then played the race card even more overtly in predicting that newly freed Blacks would naturally gravitate to the "cotton fields and the rice-plantations of the South" and the territory and climate they preferred, "leaving to the white people of the North entire freedom from competition in labor." He was painting far too rosy a picture of emancipation, but one that prompted loud applause and cheers from the crowd.[20]

Allen Guelzo has written that Boutwell was advocating the equivalent of modern "Bantustans (the supposedly independent black states created by the South African apartheid regime)" through the "forced removal of the white population of South Carolina and Florida, and turning these states over to the freed slaves." Yet Turner in *The Christian Recorder* applauded Boutwell's proposal that "the states of South Carolina, Georgia, and Florida should be dedicated to the black race . . . and the mild power of persuasion . . . used to get the intelligent [Black] people from the north to emigrate there and establish a nationality [what Boutwell would call a majority]." As Boutwell would argue elsewhere, what he was promoting was the transfer of confiscated Confederate property to Blacks in South Carolina, Georgia, and Florida to which they would move voluntarily in order to establish viable farms and livelihoods in areas where they were a majority and not subject to white economic control. This indeed is what became the policy of the Freedmen's Bureau in a few years, to set aside confiscated and abandoned lands so that formerly enslaved Blacks could begin to build wealth as landowners. Not only this, Boutwell would make the more sophisticated argument later, one that has relevance for our own times, that it made most sense to establish majority Black electoral districts in various parts of the South so that Black freedmen, when suffrage came, could concentrate their political power and not have it diluted across a South still dominated by whites.[21]

Nonetheless, in making these arguments, Boutwell was clearly playing on the racial anxieties of Northern whites who opposed emancipation. He also supported the president's declared policy of providing compensation to slave owners in the border states who voluntarily emancipated their slaves, but, he added, never "shall the treasury of this country be opened to compensate rebels for the loss of their slaves." Concluding his remarks, he declared that "either slavery must die, or the government is at an end."[22]

Boutwell left the podium as subsequent speakers exhorted the crowd to give "three cheers for the Union." The Marine Band played "Yankee Doodle" and fireworks lit up the sky as the festivities came to a close at 11 p.m. Many in the crowd had been on their feet for more than six hours. Boutwell made his way back to his quarters on Twenty-First Street, ready to resume the pressing business of organizing the Internal Revenue office the next morning. He did so with a much higher political profile than when he had come into town from Cairo, Illinois.

A FEW WEEKS LATER, Boutwell was at the White House with Lincoln to review the hiring of tax assessors and collectors. Union forces under Gen. John Pope had just been decisively defeated at the Second Battle of Bull Run in Manassas, the battle in which Daniel Webster's son, Fletcher, died. Boutwell remembers being with Lincoln on "the darkest day of the sad years of the war . . . our losses of men had been enormous, but most serious of all was the loss of confidence in commanders."[23]

When the two men had finished reviewing their tax business, the president asked Boutwell for his opinion as to army commanders. After replying that he favored restoring McClellan to command, Boutwell voiced his opinion that "emancipation seemed the only way out of our troubles." Lincoln replied, "must we not wait for something that looks like a victory? Would not a proclamation now appear as *brutum fulmen* [harmless thunderbolt, empty threat]?" Boutwell remembered it as "the only Latin I ever heard from the President." What Lincoln did next convinced Boutwell that the president was indeed committed to emancipation, and sooner rather than later. Reading aloud two letters from supporters who opposed any type of emancipation, Lincoln said simply, "they cannot expect me to give up this Government without playing my last card." As Boutwell knew, emancipation was the president's last card in letting the South know that the Union would be fighting for total victory and that Lincoln was waiting for good news on the war front to issue his proclamation. That same night Boutwell wrote to Charles Sumner, voicing the premonition that "I have special reasons for thinking that a victory by our troops would bring a policy that we desire."[24]

TWO WEEKS LATER, on September 17, Lincoln got the victory he was seeking, but at a horrific cost. Outnumbering Robert E. Lee's 38,000 Confederate troops at Antietam in Maryland with a Union force of 80,000, McClellan was only able to blunt the Confederate advance and drive them back across the Potomac River into Virginia. More than 22,000 soldiers—Union and Confederate—were killed, wounded, or missing in what remains the bloodiest day in American military history.

Prior to the battle, Boutwell shared the public's anxiety that Lee's army, which had crossed into Maryland on September 3, was hoping to rouse pro-Southern sentiment in Maryland and perhaps even encircle the capital. Voicing the fears felt in Washington, Boutwell wrote to Sarah that perhaps "direct communication with the North will be cut off. If this happens you and Georgie and Frank must be of good cheer, for though no one can foretell what will happen, it is not wise to despair or to fear calamities that may never happen."[25]

Anxiousness turned to relief when McClellan fought Lee to a draw at Antietam, but this quickly turned to frustration when McClellan missed a golden opportunity, with Lee's fatigued soldiers having to cross a Potomac River swollen by heavy rains, to decimate the Confederates. Boutwell was especially disappointed given his recommendation to the president just weeks before about restoring McClellan to command.[26]

Antietam did give the president the opportunity he wanted to issue his Emancipation Proclamation on September 22, to take effect on the first of January 1863. Coming just prior to the congressional midterm elections on November 4, the Union "victory" at Antietam and the issuing of the Emancipation Proclamation provided Lincoln and the Republican Party with a much-needed morale boost. Writing to his wife, Boutwell was ecstatic: "[A]t the moment I write this you cannot have heard of the President's Proclamation of Emancipation . . . there ought to be great rejoicing throughout the North; it is the most important American event of history."[27]

For a brief period, the president's spirits improved. At the end of October 1862, Boutwell was about to leave Washington to help with the Republican canvass for the all-important 1862 midterm elections when he again saw the president. Lincoln was in a playful mood, recounting for Boutwell his strategy for issuing the Emancipation Proclamation: "[W]hen Lee came over the river [to Maryland], I made a resolution that if McClellan drove him back I would send the proclamation after him [Lee]." On confirming that Lee had indeed retreated into Virginia, Lincoln told Boutwell that he polished the Emancipation Proclamation on Sunday and then on Monday, "I let them [Lee and the Confederacy] have it." As for George McClellan, he was sacked by the president the day after the midterm elections.[28]

The Union's fortunes soon deteriorated again when the Army of the Potomac, now commanded by Gen. Ambrose Burnside, suffered a bloody defeat in December at Fredericksburg, Virginia, with waves of US soldiers cut down by Confederates firing from behind the stone wall along the Sunken Road at the base of Marye's Heights. Once more, there were miles of Union troops retreating toward Washington from central Virginia, with Lincoln commenting, "If there is a worse place than hell, I am in it." Shortly after the defeat, Boutwell had dinner in Washington with a family friend from Groton, Dr. Peter Pineo, a surgeon with the Union army. Dismayed that Union forces were unable to take Richmond, Boutwell and Pineo lamented that "the General for the occasion [must be] found."[29]

Following months of winter stalemate between the Union and Confederate armies, Boutwell and Lincoln met one evening in the spring of 1863 on the steps of the Executive Mansion, Boutwell asking, "Mr. President, have you any news?" Lincoln replied, "Come in and I will tell you!"

Lincoln became animated as he recounted how General Grant's forces had crossed the Big Black River in Mississippi and were now in the rear of Vicksburg. Boutwell remembered that "it was evident that his faith in our ultimate success had been changed into absolute confidence." For several frustrating months, Grant and Adm. David Porter had been unsuccessful in drawing the noose around Vicksburg, which would ensure the city's capitulation and the opening of the entire Mississippi River to Union forces. When Vicksburg finally surrendered to Grant on July 4, just a day after Union forces under Gen. George Meade had defeated Lee at Gettysburg, ultimate Union victory was but a matter of time.[30]

IN MARCH 1864, George Boutwell would meet the hero of Vicksburg for the first time when Ulysses Grant came to Washington to receive his promotion to lieutenant general and commander-in-chief of all the Union armies. The evening reception at the White House on March 8 is a famous affair, as it was also Grant's first meeting with Lincoln. Having arrived that afternoon at Willard's Hotel, his clothes still dusty from travel, Grant strode up Pennsylvania Avenue to pay his respects to the president.[31]

Hundreds of Washington notables attended that evening's reception. The welcome was so boisterous that, after being introduced to the president and Mrs. Lincoln, Grant was led by Secretary of State William Seward out of the Blue Room into the much larger East Room where he pulled Grant up onto a sofa so the general could be better seen.

Georgianna Boutwell's recollection of the evening begins at this point, having arrived a bit late with her father for the festivities: "I heard cheers . . . something unusual was happening." When she and George entered the Blue Room, "No one [was] there but the President and Mrs. Lincoln, and the master of ceremonies [Secretary of War Edwin Stanton]." Georgie remembers how "Mr. Lincoln was in the best of spirits and at once remarked, 'The "Lion" is in the other room. You must go into the East Room to see Gen. Grant.'" Admonished a second time by the president, Georgianna and her father went into the East Room, where "Gen. Grant was standing on a sofa . . . Secretary Seward was presenting the company to him. The General was brown from exposure and

wore a uniform which had evidently seen hard service, with two stars only."
Grant would receive his commission as lieutenant general, and its additional
star, the next day at the White House, becoming only the second full lieutenant
general in US history up to that time, George Washington being the first.

The historic nature of the occasion, when Union victory seemed certain but
there was much hard fighting and death still to come—the terrible Battles of
the Wilderness and Spotsylvania Court House in central Virginia were only
two months away—is captured in Georgie's refreshingly naïve perspective:

"It was an unusual gathering of prominent men, even for Washington,"
she wrote; they all "anxiously scanned the face of the new leader, to see what
promise it gave of succeeding in the great plan assigned to him." She writes of
"Lincoln the Emancipator, Stanton the great War Secretary, Chase the financier of the war period, Sumner the fearless advocate of freedom, and Elihu
Washburne, life-long friend of Gen. Grant. They were all there to do honor to
our new hero."[32]

For George and Georgianna Boutwell, it was the beginning of a two-decade
relationship with Ulysses Grant and his family that deepened into friendship
well before Grant's death in 1885.

IN 1863, BOUTWELL had joined the Thirty-Eighth Congress as a committed
Radical Republican, supporting Thaddeus Stevens and others in calling for
the destruction of slavery and extending political equality to the formerly
enslaved. He also advocated the raising of Black troops as soon as possible. In
a speech in June to the National Union League Association, he proclaimed,
"They are Americans by birth. They have a future on this continent. They are
men." He called for Black officers to lead them, one of the few in Congress to
do so. During debate on a conscription bill in February, Boutwell objected to
provisions for Black regiments being "commanded by white officers." In urging that Black soldiers be allowed to show what they could do "with honor to
themselves and advantage to the country," Boutwell was an early advocate of
the famed, all-Black, Fifty-Fourth Massachusetts Infantry Regiment.[33]

Once Massachusetts governor John Andrew and Secretary Stanton gave
the go-ahead to begin recruiting for the Fifty-Fourth, Boutwell enlisted the
support of his Seventh Congressional District in Massachusetts, while Frederick Douglass and other Black abolitionists began traveling throughout the
North to sign up recruits. Douglass believed that once the Black man had "an
eagle on his button, and a musket on his shoulder, and bullets in his pocket,

there is no power on earth . . . which can deny that he has earned the right of citizenship." He helped recruit more than a hundred of the Union army's first black soldiers, including two of his sons, twenty-two-year-old Lewis and eighteen-year-old Charles.[34]

Based at Camp Meigs in Readville, to the west of Boston and just south of Boutwell's district, the Fifty-Fourth Regiment reached its full complement of 1,007 soldiers in May, with recruits coming from as far away as Canada and the West Indies. At least thirty of them were former slaves. Once the Fifty-Fourth had sailed from Boston to deploy in South Carolina, surplus recruits were organized into its sister regiment, the Fifty-Fifth. In Washington, Boutwell continued to object to the whites-only regulation for officers, writing to Governor Andrew on June 10 that "If these four million black people enter into this contest and make sacrifices . . . they have a right to share in the benefits . . . public service by men capable of performing it is the right of the people, black and white."[35]

On July 18, just weeks after the Union victories at Gettysburg and Vicksburg, the Fifty-Fourth took part in the bloody assault on Fort Wagner outside of Charleston. Leading his men over the parapets, the white commander Col. Robert Gould Shaw was killed and his Black adjutant, Sgt. William Carney, was wounded. Carney would be decorated with the Medal of Honor for his heroism in returning the regimental flag to Union lines. Some 280 Union troops were killed, and Lewis Douglass was among the more than 800 wounded. Also wounded that day was a neighbor of Boutwell's from Groton. Adrastus Hazzard was a free Black farmer, eighteen years old, when he enlisted in the Fifty-Fourth Massachusetts Regiment in April 1863. He would succumb to his wounds in a military hospital in Beaufort, South Carolina, in April 1865.[36]

The fame earned by the Black soldiers at Fort Wagner and throughout the war validated Boutwell's belief that, in seeking the extinction of the institution of slavery, "who more than the slave should share in the dispensation of a divine justice due to the master as the oppressor of the black man?"[37]

Following the battle, Colonel Shaw earned unintended honors when the Confederates refused to return his body, thinking they were disrespecting the white officer by burying him in a mass grave with his fallen Black troops. In response, Shaw's father, Francis—a committed abolitionist and friend of Margaret Fuller and other Transcendentalists—declared that "we can imagine no holier place than that in which he lies, among his brave and devoted followers, nor wish him better company."[38]

AT THE END OF 1863, in his annual message to Congress, Abraham Lincoln issued his Proclamation of Amnesty and Reconstruction. The document pleased Radical Republicans by declaring that the South must accept emancipation as a condition for rejoining the Union and that those enslaved people freed by the Emancipation Proclamation would never be reenslaved. As John Hay noted in his diary, Boutwell "was looking over [the president's message] quietly & saying, It is a very able and shrewd paper. It has great points of popularity; & it is right."[39]

But Boutwell and his Radical Republican colleagues soon began criticizing the president for seeking to entice Confederate states back into the Union with the promise of pardons and the restoration of property, excepting slaves. Known as the "Ten Percent Plan," Lincoln's offer required that 10 percent of a rebel state's voters from the 1860 election list approve a state constitution declaring loyalty to the Union. Boutwell thought the plan far too lenient and in February 1864 supported the Wade-Davis Bill that would require approval from 50 percent of the state's white male residents who had taken a loyalty oath, and the promise of Black suffrage. Opposed to allowing those southerners who had actively rebelled to keep their land, Boutwell wanted to use it to establish Black farms and homesteads. Like other Radical Republicans, he also advocated a greater role for Congress in setting the terms of postwar reconstruction. He was especially adamant about instituting Black suffrage and was disappointed when Lincoln killed the Wade-Davis Bill with a pocket veto in July 1864.[40]

Boutwell was also seeking ways to extend freedom to those enslaved Blacks in the border states who were not covered by the Emancipation Proclamation. By combining emancipation with military enlistment, he and Thaddeus Stevens hoped an amendment to the 1863 Enrollment Act would ease the recruitment of Black soldiers once their freedom had been "purchased" from owners who had been loyal to the Union. The proposal was a novel twist on Lincoln's various plans for compensating slave owners in Kentucky, Missouri, Maryland, and Delaware. Although disagreements over how much to offer in compensated emancipation were finally settled at $100 per enslaved person, the plan was of little interest to border state enslavers.[41]

During these debates, Boutwell went well beyond his colleagues in proposing a series of declaratory resolutions regarding postwar Union reconstruction that would affirm the requirement of "freedom to the black man" on a par with whites. Accused by critics of offering "humbug propositions," Boutwell's motions went nowhere. In May 1864, his House colleagues sought to silence him when Boutwell proposed suffrage for newly freed Blacks to aid in the reconstruction of the Southern states. Saying that Blacks should be given "local political power" with which to "defend themselves" in South Carolina, Georgia, and Florida, the House Speaker's "hammer fell" and cut him off as the congressman from Massachusetts demanded justice so that Blacks could "enjoy the fruits of their labor and their capacity."[42]

LIKE MANY OF his Republican colleagues, Boutwell was uneasy with the president's lukewarm support for Black equality and his conciliatory attitudes toward reconstructing a Confederacy that was on the verge of defeat. During congressional debates in early 1864 over the proposed Thirteenth Amendment abolishing slavery, for example, Lincoln adopted a hands-off attitude. The president also seemed to favor restoring Southern lands to Confederates who took a loyalty oath, which Boutwell and others feared would greatly reduce the amount of land available for redistribution to the formerly enslaved. The one thing Lincoln and his critics did agree on was final repeal of the hated Fugitive Slave Act, previously rendered moot in the Confederacy by the Emancipation Proclamation and then finally abolished in the border states in June 1864.[43]

Despite his differences with the president, Boutwell appreciated the political realities confronting Lincoln in advance of the presidential election in November. Disaffected Republicans called for abandoning Lincoln; many met with pro-Union Democrats in Cleveland to nominate a third party candidate, Lincoln bugbear Gen. John C. Frémont, whose candidacy went nowhere. Boutwell remained loyal to Lincoln and attended the Republican Party convention in Baltimore, where he denounced the Democratic Party for its "moral and political treason" in calling for a negotiated peace with the Confederacy and for nominating as its candidate another Lincoln nemesis, Gen. George B. McClellan. In the fall campaign, Boutwell stumped vigorously for himself and the president, with both he and Lincoln winning almost 70 percent of the vote in Boutwell's Massachusetts district. Rescued politically by General Sherman's capture of Atlanta in September, the president easily won reelection, defeating McClellan, whose longtime political aspirations burst on the national scene but were seen no more. The Democrats, deeply divided between pro-Unionists and the Copperheads, who favored peace with the South at any price, won only three states to Lincoln's twenty-two, and lost the popular vote by 55 to 45 percent.[44]

With the North inching closer to final military victory in late 1864, the president and Republican congressional leaders debated how to readmit the defeated Confederate states into the Union and "reconstruct" the country. Boutwell believed that, when the war ended, it would be up to the national government, and primarily Congress, to govern the Southern states "as seemed expedient and readmit them into the Union at such times and upon such terms as the Government should dictate." He thought it important, not only to extend full civil and political equality for the four million formerly enslaved Blacks, but to ensure their proper representation in Congress. In a speech to the Emancipation League in Boston in early 1865, he repeated what he had previously proposed in the House, that Congress reorganize South Carolina, Georgia, and Florida as territories following the war, "and the colored people [be] invited to settle there—not in any way compelled to do so— and build up States of their own, from which they might in a few years send black representatives to Congress."[45]

Even before the war had ended, George Boutwell was anticipating the difficulties that Blacks would have in executing their franchise in the South once they obtained it. Fearing that the Southern white plantation elite might find ways of retaining political control, Boutwell was advocating a type of "packed gerrymandering" where Blacks could concentrate themselves to increase their political power rather than have it diluted across the entire South. In our own time, there have been similar proposals for a "reverse migration" of Blacks from the north to select areas of the south where their voting power could be magnified.[46]

Boutwell was also among those pushing to create a Freedmen's Bureau to help provide jobs, housing, and education to the four million newly freed Blacks once the war ended. Working with Charles Sumner, Boutwell sought to counter the arguments of those in Congress who, despite their support for emancipation and Black citizenship, opposed what they deemed a federal "system of guardianship and pupilage and overseership." Boutwell had criticized the initial legislation for its paternalistic treatment of newly freed Blacks that proposed a contract system of labor that would greatly limit their freedom of movement and options in finding work. As one of six members of the House-Senate conference committee charged with revising the bill, Boutwell helped write language that "envisioned the freedmen as independent farmers" having the option of ultimately owning the forty acres of land that might be allotted to them from the confiscated and abandoned estates of former Confederates.

As enacted, the bill creating the Bureau of Refugees, Freedmen, and Abandoned Lands was "to continue during the war of the Rebellion and for one year thereafter." President Lincoln signed the bill on March 3, 1865, one of his last official acts as president.[47]

MUCH HAS BEEN WRITTEN about Abraham Lincoln's second inauguration, both for the spirituality of his inaugural address that insisted on "malice toward none, and charity for all," and for the inebriated, incoherent condition of his vice president-elect, Andrew Johnson, whose address preceded Lincoln's. With her father below her on the Senate floor, Georgianna watched from the upstairs gallery as Andrew Johnson rose to speak. From a revealing essay written in 1895, Georgianna remembers:

"It was not easy to see what was taking place there, but I had the advantage of facing all the audience. Soon I heard what seemed to be the speech of a drunken man and asked a lady in front of me, 'who was speaking?' Her reply that it was 'the Vice President' was appalling. I can see the scene now. The intense excitement, the fear that the ceremonies should not proceed; the relief which we were beginning to feel when everything had gone well thus far, and then the shock when we realized that we had made as successor to Abraham Lincoln, a man who could not control himself on even such a day and such an occasion. There was a look of consternation upon all faces; two especially. Utter disgust on the face of Mr. Sumner and the sadness and helplessness on the face of Mr. Lincoln."

When Johnson had mercifully finished, the notables inside the Senate chamber proceeded outside to hear Lincoln's inaugural address while Georgie remained inside, staring out through a window. The rain that had been falling all morning ceased, with the sun breaking through the clouds in what to many seemed an auspicious omen for a nation soon to emerge from a terrible civil war. Georgie was only able to hear some of Lincoln's inaugural address, interrupted as it was by a crowd estimated at up to 50,000 people. What she most remembered, admittedly with the clarity of hindsight, was not Lincoln's hopeful poetry, but her own "fears for the future . . . and the tragic extent of the difficulties" that lay ahead with Andrew Johnson as president.[48]

A little over a month later, on a Saturday morning, Abraham Lincoln succumbed to the gunshot wound he suffered the evening before at Ford's Theater. Andrew Johnson was sworn in as the country's seventeenth president. Entrusted with the fearsome task of reuniting a war-torn country, Johnson was given the oath of office by Chief Justice Salmon Chase at Kirkwood House, a five-story hotel midway between the White House and the Capitol.

Newspaper reports described Andrew Johnson that day as "dignified, composed, and sober." The new president promised continuity and reassured the public that he would keep most of Lincoln's cabinet members, including Edwin Stanton, whose friends urged him to delay retirement, pleading that "the country cannot spare you . . . stand your ground . . . there is work for you yet to do."[49]

Within weeks, though, Andrew Johnson's presidency spiraled out of control as he sought to sideline Congress and implement his "presidential" version of reconstruction to bring the defeated Confederacy back into the Union. Johnson felt it was imperative to reunite the country as quickly as possible, based on the "restoration" of white state governments so long as they "pledged" loyalty to the Union. This put him at odds with the Republican majority in Congress, and with figures like Stanton, who emphasized the protection of Black rights in the South under the guidance of "Congressional Reconstruction." As the drama unfolded, the secretary of war would find himself in the president's crosshairs, with George Boutwell playing a pivotal role in the struggle.[50]

JUST DAYS BEFORE Lincoln's assassination at the hands of John Wilkes Booth, George Boutwell had traveled home to Groton to see his family before returning to Washington for the important work that lay ahead. He was absent when the city went into shock at the news of the president's death and the attempted murder by Booth's co-conspirators of Secretary of State William Seward. As he made plans to return to Washington, Boutwell was asked to deliver a eulogy for the slain president in the nearby city of Lowell, the birthplace of America's textile industry and itself symbolic of the wealth the country had derived from cotton and the slave economy of the South.

On Wednesday morning, April 19, four days after Lincoln's death, George Boutwell took the thirty-minute train ride from Groton to Lowell, arriving at the Merrimack Street Depot. It was four years to the day that soldiers from the Sixth Massachusetts Regiment had died in Baltimore, becoming the first fatalities of the Civil War. Two of them were Lowell natives, Luther Ladd and Addison Whitney, and their bodies were buried in Monument Square near where Boutwell alighted from the train. As he walked with the mayor of Lowell to Huntington Hall to give his speech, Boutwell thought of the slain president that he had come to know well and whose company he cherished. He may also have thought of the farmers from surrounding Middlesex County who died on that date ninety years before at Concord and Lexington, fighting to establish "government of the people, by the people, and for the people."

Boutwell voiced the grief of millions of his fellow citizens that day, extolling Lincoln's virtues and calling for justice, not vengeance, in seeking those responsible for "this unparalleled crime." Declaring that "he who destroyed slavery was himself by slavery destroyed," Boutwell called upon the nation "to purify itself from this foulest of sins." With Lincoln no longer there to help guide the country, America had to begin the process of redeeming itself from the sin of slavery.[51]

PART THREE

ANDREW JOHNSON AND RECONSTRUCTION, 1865–1868

8

Reconstruction and the Fourteenth Amendment

T he war was over and the Union victorious, thanks in large part to the modern production methods established in Lowell, Massachusetts, decades earlier, which had transformed the North into an industrial powerhouse. When combined with advances in steam technology, the telegraph, and the railroad, the industrial output of the states above the Mason-Dixon Line dwarfed that of the South. The North produced vastly more in everything from pig iron to textiles to firearms, churning out 3,200 rifles and pistols to every 100 produced in the southern states. Immigrants from overseas settled mainly in the North, giving it a total population advantage of 23 million to 9 million in the South, 4 million of whom were enslaved Blacks. The South did have wealth, but it was tied up in cotton and was dependent on slave labor. Whether in banking and finance or education and the development of technology, the South simply lacked the North's capability to wage modern war.

By early 1865, it was only a matter of time before the South capitulated. Union armies led by Ulysses S. Grant in Virginia, William Tecumseh Sherman in Georgia and the Carolinas, and George H. Thomas in Tennessee were devastating the Confederacy's dwindling resources in manpower, agriculture, and industrial production. Atlanta and Savannah had fallen in September and December 1864, Charleston surrendered in February 1865, and Grant was tightening the noose around Richmond in March. Following the surrender of the Confederate capital on April 3, Robert E. Lee and the Army of Northern Virginia had no choice but to capitulate to Ulysses Grant at Appomattox Court House on April 9. The final battle of the war took place in mid-May near Brownsville, Texas, the only state in the Confederacy where slavery remained legal. On June 19 the last vestige of slavery was outlawed by order of the local Union commander, and one hundred fifty-six years later, Juneteenth was proclaimed a federal holiday.[1]

Total war dead from the conflict surpassed 700,000, more than all the Americans who had died or would die in past and future conflicts. The South lost 20 percent of its adult (white) male working population, with 300,000 dying from wounds, disease, or malnutrition. A greater number of Union soldiers, white and Black, died in the conflict, but they represented 8 percent of working-age males.

Waged mainly on southern territory, the effects of the war were especially devastating for the states of the Confederacy. As early as 1862 in areas under Union control, such as New Orleans and the coastal islands off South Carolina, white plantation culture was upended while economic devastation was impoverishing both white and Black alike. As Union armies moved through Mississippi, Virginia, and Georgia, crop fields were ruined or left untended, while rail lines and factories were torn up and destroyed.

By 1865, the acute labor shortage caused by white southerners having gone off to war was magnified by hundreds of thousands of newly free Blacks who were leaving the plantations to seek long-separated family members or a better future. Similar numbers of whites, primarily small farmers and residents of devastated cities and towns, were also displaced and on the move. The effects of declining crop prices, a northern blockade that crippled trade with Europe, and the physical destruction of agriculture and industry combined to reduce the Confederacy to a barter economy. And the social revolution ignited by Abraham Lincoln's Emancipation Proclamation had only just begun.[2]

AT WAR'S END, a close friend of the Boutwell family witnessed these conditions while serving with Union forces on Hilton Head Island near Savannah, Georgia. Dr. Peter Pineo was a lieutenant colonel in the army medical corps stationed on the island, which had been in Union control since 1861 and used as a base for blockading the ports of Charleston and Savannah. He, his wife, and young daughter were neighbors of the Boutwells in Groton in the 1850s and would remain friends for decades after.

On April 14, Good Friday, Pineo took part in the Union victory celebration at Fort Sumter, witnessing Maj. Gen. Robert Anderson raise the same Stars and Stripes that he had lowered four years earlier when surrendering the fort. Unbeknownst to the hundreds of whites and Blacks who had ferried out to

Sumter for the celebration, Abraham Lincoln was shot that evening at Ford's Theater, dying the next morning.

Two days later, on Easter Sunday, Pineo attended a packed church service in Charleston to hear the Reverend Henry Ward Beecher, one of the invited guests for the Fort Sumter ceremony. That night, in a letter to Abby Boutwell, George's sister back in Groton, Pineo described his feelings toward the newly freed Blacks he had encountered in the city. He wrote of how Beecher preached to "an immense congregation of white & black people of every variety of shade, and very promiscuously placed and seated." Pushing his way toward the pulpit, Pineo spoke of his "proximity to the contraband [Blacks], of extensive odor."[3]

Pineo's letter reveals much about northern attitudes that would undermine Black political and civil equality in the years to come. "Directly before me, and within the rails of the sanctum, [were] two colored brethren . . . one of them [wearing] *Major's straps!* Now, my friend, I am a pretty good Abolitionist, but if that negro had worn the insignia of higher rank than myself, I should have felt impelled to at once resign my commission, for the idea of being liable to receive commands, and being obliged to obey the order of a negro, black as *Erebus*, is too much for my Abolition Stomach."

Peter Pineo was an educated white professional whose grandfather had served on the staff of Gen. George Washington during the Revolutionary War. If white northerners such as he refused to countenance equitable promotion for Blacks in the military, much less any semblance of social equality, then the road to racial redemption for America would be long indeed. This degree of white northern prejudice, combined with overt southern racism and resistance, would ultimately prove fatal to the goal of reconstructing the country on the principles of political and civil equality for all.

ABRAHAM LINCOLN'S DEATH on April 15 was the first severe setback suffered by Reconstruction and its goal of Black equality. Not that Lincoln himself could have ensured the success of reconstructing the Union on the foundation of racial equality, but the loss of his stewardship meant that the country would be in the hands of the fundamentally racist Jacksonian Democrat from Tennessee, Andrew Johnson.

In the aftermath of war, a grieving country faced the daunting prospect of reuniting a nation consisting of an economically prostrated and white supremacist South and a North that itself was deeply ambivalent over the goal of racial equality for free and formerly enslaved Blacks. Thaddeus Stevens summarized the feelings of George Boutwell and the Radical Republicans in saying: "We . . . are about to turn loose, four million slaves, without a hut to shelter them or a cent in their pockets. The diabolical laws of slavery have prevented them from obtaining an education, understanding the commonest laws of contract, or of managing the ordinary business of life. The Congress is bound to look after them until they can take care of themselves."[4]

Congress had taken this first step when it created the Freedmen's Bureau in March. Located in the War Department, the Bureau had the immense task of assisting newly freed slaves with food, housing, medical care, education, and family reunification. Led by Gen. Oliver Otis Howard, a Medal of Honor recipient known as the "Christian General" for his religious piety, the Bureau's efforts were supplemented by hundreds of northern doctors, missionaries, and teachers, many of them women, who spread throughout the South. Although most of these northerners were well-meaning, there were some—corrupt Bureau agents and "carpetbagger" businessmen—looking to profit from the South's misfortune. More important in reducing the Bureau's effectiveness was active opposition by local whites to any effort that might improve the lot of the formerly enslaved.[5]

AT THE TIME of his death, some Radical Republicans believed that Lincoln had been too moderate in his plans for Reconstruction, as evidenced by the Ten Percent Plan, and hoped that Andrew Johnson would take a harder line in bringing the rebellious states back into the Union. Andy Johnson had, after all, been a staunch Unionist in Confederate Tennessee and had demanded the death penalty for Jefferson Davis and other such traitors. A vocal opponent of slavery during the war, Johnson as a middle-class white had long bitterly resented the southern plantation elite. In the first few weeks after Lincoln's death, the new president met with the acknowledged leader of the Radical Republicans, Charles Sumner, who found Johnson "firm and determined" on the issue of Black suffrage.[6]

George Boutwell was more cautious. True, Boutwell wholeheartedly agreed with Johnson on the treasonous behavior of the Confederate leaders, even initially supporting the death penalty for Jefferson Davis and Robert E. Lee. Less than a week after the assassination, Boutwell was writing to his colleague Benjamin Butler that, should evidence be found linking Davis and others "with the plot to assassinate the President, [then] indictments should be found that we may follow them to other countries" (some Confederate officials were fleeing to Canada). In Congress, Boutwell would zealously investigate links between the Confederate leadership and the Booth conspirators. But, as a former Democrat who knew the party's ideology all too well, Boutwell distrusted Johnson's commitment to Black equality and considered wishful thinking the president's belief that the southern states led by white Democrats would voluntarily grant Black suffrage.[7]

Thus, Boutwell was not surprised when it took only a few weeks for Andrew Johnson to show his true colors by advocating a restoration of the southern states to their previous place in the Union without any substantial social reconstruction of their societies. On May 9 the president issued an executive order recognizing Virginia as a "loyal" state and followed that on May 29 with a Presidential Amnesty Proclamation offering pardons to most of those who had rebelled against the Union. That was the same day that Boutwell was in Boston, presenting his vision of Reconstruction that would maximize the effectiveness of the Black vote in the South.[8]

In the nation's capital, the president was announcing plans for reorganizing the state government of North Carolina with its antebellum white power structure intact. On returning to Washington, Boutwell demanded to see Johnson, objecting that voluntary promises by North Carolina to institute Black suffrage were not sufficient. Told by the president that "the step was experimental" and "that no other State would be reorganized until the experiment in North Carolina had been tested," Boutwell later admitted that he made the mistake of taking the president at his word. He would soon realize that Johnson had no intention of having North Carolina be a test case and that his own acquiescence to the president's policy had emboldened Johnson "to pursue the policy against which I was protesting."[9]

The only conditions specified by Johnson for allowing southern states to rejoin the Union consisted of ratifying the Thirteenth Amendment abolishing slavery, agreeing not to ask the national government to pay Confederate debts incurred during the war, and expressing "regret" over having seceded. As Congress would not reconvene until December, the president knew he would have a free hand for months to pursue his policy of southern "restoration." In short order, he unilaterally established provisional state governments in Mississippi, Georgia, Texas, Alabama, South Carolina, and Florida. White southerners soon realized that Johnson was allowing them to re-create their state governments with little regard for empowering their former slaves or worrying about congressional interference. Florida governor William Marvin summed it up nicely: Blacks should not think "that emancipation implied civil equality or the vote," and he advised the "freedmen to return to the plantations, labor diligently, and call your old Master—'Master.'"

Formerly enslaved Blacks might be "free," but they now had little in the way of homes, jobs, and the means to sustain themselves. In Mississippi it was estimated that 400,000 Blacks roamed the countryside, lacking food and work. The *Jackson Daily News* declared, "we must keep the ex-slave in a position of inferiority. We must pass such laws as make him feel his inferiority." These were the "Black Codes" that, across the South, would strictly regulate whether and how Blacks could own property, seek jobs, serve on juries, and conduct their daily lives.[10]

Helping to enforce the Black Codes were white state militias and roving bands of vigilantes, self-appointed "regulators" seeking to resurrect white supremacist dominance. In some ways, formerly enslaved Blacks were worse off than before. As "property," they at least could count on their owners' economic self-interest to keep them fed, housed, and healthy enough to work. Now, Blacks were subject to the laws and norms of white society. In a tragic irony, where non-slave-owning whites would never have touched a plantation owner's property, now they were free to do so, and did. Gen. George A. Custer described in Texas what was happening across the South; Blacks were being killed on the streets for refusing to step aside for a white man, or for no reason at all. In 1865 alone, an estimated 5,000 Black men, women, and children were murdered, while hundreds of Black churches, businesses, and schools were burned. Despite this paroxysm of racial violence, Andrew Johnson insisted that the US Army be withdrawn from the South.[11]

Boutwell and the Radical Republicans criticized the president's planned withdrawal of troops and were equally outraged by Johnson's policy of decriminalizing former Confederates and restoring their property. In the summer of 1865, this consisted of some 850,000 acres of land controlled by the Freedmen's Bureau. Initial plans had been to grant the freedmen forty-acre plots; the phrase "forty acres and a mule" likely originated with Gen. William Tecumseh Sherman's plan in early 1865 to set aside land in coastal South Carolina for the exclusive settlement of Blacks. But by September, Johnson had issued an executive order restoring confiscated lands to their pardoned former owners and suspending scheduled land sales in Virginia and South Carolina.[12]

FOR THOSE SURPRISED by Andrew Johnson's retreat from protecting Black rights in the South, they only had to remember his words from the previous May: "there is no such thing as reconstruction." The president believed merely in *restoring* the southern states to their proper place in the Union, with renewed representation in Congress, "provided always they [now] elect loyal men," meaning white men. It would be up to the newly constituted white state governments to provide for "voluntary Black suffrage" as they saw fit, without interference from the national government.[13]

During the summer of 1865, as America celebrated its first peacetime Fourth of July holiday in five years, there were some who still believed that the president might be, as he had famously called himself in a Nashville speech in 1864, a "Moses" leading the Blacks from bondage to freedom. Boutwell's friend and Massachusetts colleague, Senator Henry Wilson, as strong a supporter of Black rights as any, told a holiday gathering near the White House that the president would "complete the great work of emancipation and enfranchisement" that Lincoln had begun.[14]

Back home in Massachusetts, George Boutwell felt differently. In a remarkably prescient speech given on Independence Day in the town of Weymouth, south of Boston, Boutwell spelled out what should be required of the rebellious states to rejoin the Union and the dire consequences of the South's regaining control of the national government should Andrew Johnson's "restoration" plan be implemented.

Entitled "Reconstruction: Its True Basis," Boutwell criticized Johnson's policy of leaving it up to southern white governments to voluntarily grant suffrage to Blacks. It was illusory, he said, to think of giving such power to "the men who have been in arms against the republic . . . and contaminated by . . . the crime of slavery. Full negro suffrage is essential to the security of the Union, as well as to the protection of the negroes themselves." He dismissed literacy tests and other restraints on voting, saying that Black voting power was now as important as his "bayonet was essential to us during the war."

Boutwell then addressed the political calculus of the Black vote, pointing out that denying the vote to Blacks in the South would increase the political power of white southerners, diluting that of the North. If southern states were allowed to count Blacks as full citizens (no longer three-fifths of a person) but deny them the vote, they would gain an additional thirty seats in the House of Representatives and thirty extra votes in the Electoral College. This would make a mockery of the "one man, one vote" principle as "two voters in the South will have equal power in the government of the country with three voters in the North." Absent the Black vote, the Democratic Party would be able to control the South and would need to win only one northern state, New York, to win a majority in the Electoral College and capture the presidency.

Boutwell was pushing an admittedly partisan argument. He was blunt about the Republican Party losing its majority in Congress if southern white Democrats were allowed to deny Black suffrage. In closing, he promoted a Reconstruction policy that he thought equitable. In exchange for allowing Black male suffrage, the government would restore full civil and political rights to southern whites, even those who had been in rebellion against the Union.

Evoking the ideals of Lincoln's Gettysburg Address, Boutwell called for renewed efforts to redeem America's promise through a "new birth of freedom." Because the protection of slavery in the US Constitution was responsible for contributing to "the woes through which we have passed," he told his audience, it was now clear that "justice, justice, is the only . . . security for national life."[15]

To further help the country solve "the great social problems of the day," Boutwell was also involved that summer in creating the American Association for the Promotion of Social Science. Meeting in Boston in October, Association members set a lofty goal of using the latest research and quantitative data to examine issues in law, education, criminal justice, public health, and poverty that could assist a country recovering from civil war.[16]

WITH CONGRESS IN RECESS until December, ex-Confederates knew they had carte blanche from Andrew Johnson to fashion state governments to their liking. Boutwell and fellow Radical Republicans Charles Sumner and Thaddeus Stevens asserted that "the executive was approaching usurpation," as Stevens put it, of legislative authority. They pointed to Johnson's policy of granting pardons to high-ranking Confederate political and military officials, and landowners (mainly plantation owners) with assets of more than $20,000, if these individuals appealed directly to him. It became common knowledge that the White House was full of "ex-Confederate soldiers, con men, and conspirators, all seeking a presidential dispensation." Walt Whitman reported seeing southern women supplicating on behalf of husbands, sons, and brothers. With Congress sidelined, Johnson by the end of summer had dispensed more than 2,500 pardons.[17]

Boutwell was convinced that Johnson was revealing his innate bias as a white Tennessee Democrat. Johnson freely admitted as much to intimates, proclaiming that only the Democratic Party could ensure a successful "white" Reconstruction of the South. Still, some Republican moderates felt that Boutwell and other Radical Republicans were overreacting. James A. Garfield, Ohio congressman and future president, spoke for many when he complained that "Sumner and Boutwell . . . and some foolish men among us are . . . bustling up for a fight and seem to be anxious to make a rupture with Johnson."[18]

Undeterred, Boutwell escalated his attacks on the president. In December, at a meeting of the National Equal Suffrage Association, Boutwell reminded his listeners that the nation had "accepted the blood of these [Black soldiers] . . . their bones bleach[ing] upon the plains of the South." In return, he demanded, "they have earned in the noblest manner, and with the largest sacrifices, the right to call this their country."[19]

WHEN CONGRESS RECONVENED that month, Thaddeus Stevens and Edward McPherson, clerk of the House of Representatives, took the bold step of refusing to seat dozens of newly elected southern representatives, including from Johnson's home state of Tennessee, which outraged the president. Many of these were ex-Confederate military and political figures, most of them elected under rules set by the white state governments "restored" by the president. After the Senate followed suit, Stevens called for the creation of a Joint Committee on Reconstruction to report on conditions in the former Confederate states and that would give primacy to Congress, not the president, in deciding when and how southern states would be readmitted to the Union. A Democratic newspaper bemoaned that Stevens and the Radical Republicans had "strangled the infant 'Restoration.'" After eight months of having a free hand, Andrew Johnson had been momentarily checked by the Republican Congress, setting the stage for a two-and-a-half-year battle of wills over how to reintegrate the South, and four million newly freed Blacks, into the Union.[20]

Boutwell was chosen as one of nine House members of the joint committee, along with six senators, and he quickly emerged as one of its leaders, perhaps second only to Stevens. Boutwell was also a member of the House Judiciary Committee, and in that role he rose on December 13 to make the very first motion for what would ultimately become the Fifteenth Amendment to the Constitution, giving Black men the right to vote.[21]

When the Joint Committee on Reconstruction (JCR) met several weeks later in January, its members began what many historians believe is the most significant body of work ever undertaken by Congress, resulting in, among other achievements, the Civil Rights Act of 1866, originally introduced by Senator Lyman Trumbull, chair of the Judiciary Committee, and the Fourteenth Amendment to the Constitution.[22]

To evaluate conditions in the South, the JCR split into subcommittees, with Boutwell chairing the one responsible for Georgia, Alabama, Mississippi, and Arkansas. Over the next three months, Boutwell interviewed thirty-nine of the subcommittee's forty-four witnesses, primarily US Army officers, Freedmen's Bureau agents, and southern Unionists, but also former Confederates, including CSA vice president Alexander H. Stephens. African American historian Benjamin Quarles has written that Boutwell "was never absent from committee meetings and he was not averse to playing the role of inquisitor," especially in probing the attitudes of whites toward formerly enslaved Blacks in the war-torn South. When the JCR couldn't decide on the conditions for readmitting Tennessee, a particularly sensitive issue because it was the president's home state, Boutwell was asked to chair that committee as well, with Roscoe Conkling of New York and George Williams of Oregon.[23]

On the all-important Fourteenth Amendment, the crown jewel of the JCR's efforts, Boutwell took a leading role in drafting section two, defining the nature and rights of American citizenship, including the right to vote. As he had in December, he proposed language that "no State shall make any distinction in the exercise of the elective franchise on account of race or color." That same day, January 12, John Bingham of Ohio, the primary drafter of section one, submitted the language that all citizens should have "equal protection in their rights of life, liberty, and property." Much work remained to finalize the amendment, but when completed in June, the constitutional precepts of "due process," "equal protection of the laws," and "the privileges and immunities of citizens of the United States" were ready to be incorporated into the fabric of American life.[24]

Black Americans were finally on the verge of becoming full citizens, given that the amendment defined citizenship as applying to those "born or naturalized in the United States." As citizens, they would be counted among a state's total population to determine representation. But, as Boutwell was warning, southern states could reap a bonanza of at least thirty extra House members and presidential electors if they denied Blacks the vote.

To prevent this, Boutwell and his colleagues debated the relative merits of "positive" versus "negative" guarantees of Black suffrage. "Positive" guarantees were straightforward: Black males must have the same voting rights as white men. "Negative" guarantees were those that imposed a penalty for preventing Blacks from voting, such as reducing a state's number of House seats by its proportion of Black citizens if that state were found to have "denied or abridged" the right to vote "on account of race or color." Admittedly less forceful, "negative" guarantees were favored by those committee members who were wary of Congress intruding on the rights of individual states to set voting requirements. Initially, this wasn't enough for Boutwell, who argued that only "positive guarantees" would prevent states from controlling suffrage based on race or color if they instituted measures like literacy tests and poll taxes that could be applied to all voters but that would fall disproportionately on Blacks.[25]

THE THIRTEENTH AMENDMENT "banning slavery and involuntary servitude," one of Andrew Johnson's minimal conditions for allowing southern states back into the Union, had become law in December 1865 when the president pressured the "restored" white governments of Georgia, South Carolina, Alabama, and North Carolina to ratify it. First proposed in December 1863 and passed by Congress in January 1865, the amendment had been signed by Abraham Lincoln as a nod to history, even though presidential certification was not required.[26]

With slavery abolished, the crux of the debate between presidential "restoration" and congressional "reconstruction" became one of who should determine how much "equality" to grant the newly freed slaves: the states or the national government. Symbolic of the debate were the conflicting views of Missouri senator John B. Henderson ("we give them no rights except his freedom and leave the rest to the states") and Indiana representative William Holman ("the mere exemption from servitude is a miserable idea of freedom").[27]

Southern white governments, aided and abetted by the president, took Henderson's pronouncement to heart, and began implementing "a miserable idea of freedom." One way they did so was by exploiting an exemption contained in the Thirteenth Amendment, whereby "involuntary servitude" was allowed "as a punishment for crime whereof the party shall have been duly convicted." This was already happening with the "Black Codes" that limited Black labor rights, freedom of movement, and firearms ownership. Even minor violations of these and other restrictions allowed local and state authorities to arrest and

convict Blacks for petty "crimes" that would strip them of their rights. Southern vagrancy laws were particularly pernicious; at a time when Blacks were on
the move throughout the South, looking for work and searching for family, it
became easy to arrest and jail them for vagrancy and then either put them on
work gangs or lease them out to white farmers and other employers. Despite
the landmark nature of the Thirteenth Amendment in abolishing chattel slavery, Boutwell and the Radical Republicans knew that additional federal protections would be needed for Blacks to achieve true equality.[28]

BY EARLY 1866, even moderate Republicans in Congress were coming to
share Boutwell's growing pessimism with the president's "restoration" policies. Andrew Johnson continued to appoint former Confederates to positions
in state governments, which in turn continued to enact Black Codes. White
supremacist vigilantes across the South were killing and maiming hundreds if
not thousands of Blacks in the spring and summer of 1866: the two most notorious massacres occurred in Memphis in April and New Orleans in July, with
more than forty Blacks killed and hundreds wounded in each.

The New Orleans massacre, which took place on July 30, was an especially
significant turning point in the rupture between Andrew Johnson and congressional Republicans. Local Republicans, white and Black, were gathering
for a political rally that the Democratic mayor considered illegal and had
promised to prevent. Without provocation, an armed mob of whites, led by
the city sheriff, shot down and butchered unarmed and wounded men in and
around their meeting site at the Mechanics Institute. Gen. Philip Sheridan
reported to Grant that what occurred was "no riot" but "an absolute massacre
by the police, which was not excelled in murderous cruelty [even] by that of
Fort Pillow" (the infamous slaughter by Confederate troops in 1864 of more
than a hundred mostly Black Union soldiers trying to surrender). What distinguished the New Orleans massacre politically was that Andrew Johnson not
only expressed no remorse whatsoever for the victims, but blamed Thaddeus
Stevens, George Boutwell, and other Radical Republicans for the "blood that
was shed . . . they are responsible for it." From then on, there was no doubt that
the president had become, in the words of historian Fawn Brodie, "the partisan champion of the white South."[29]

Yet public revulsion in the North over the New Orleans massacre soon
faded, replaced by the contentious issue of whether to expand Black suffrage
in the North itself. Attempts to extend the Black vote beyond the five New

England states where it existed (which did not include Connecticut) were successful in only two of thirteen states, Iowa and Minnesota. In New York, Pennsylvania, and Illinois, sizable numbers of Black voters continued to be largely disenfranchised.[30]

As for northern textile manufacturers and bankers, they were eager to get back to business as usual and urged a speedy resumption of southern cotton production. Until "white gold" again flowed north, southerners would not be able to "repay their prewar debts, New England textile factories would have to close," and the national government would lack the increase in exports needed to pay down its Civil War debt. Despite representing a district with major textile interests, Boutwell refused to give priority to "white gold" over his support for Black suffrage and political rights.[31]

The one place where Black voting rights came into immediate play was the federal District of Columbia, subject to control by Congress. Though members found it more expedient to accept Black suffrage in the nation's capital than in their home states, many still insisted on requirements for voting such as military service, property ownership, and/or literacy tests.

George Boutwell strongly disagreed. In an eloquent speech on the House floor on January 18, he pointed out the hypocrisy of those seeking to neuter Black voting rights. First, since Blacks were prohibited from becoming soldiers until late in the war, "it is with ill grace that we decline to allow the vote of any man because he has not performed that service." Second, property qualifications were outdated and an affront to democracy, "remnants of a time when the landed aristocracy dominated politics." Most outrageous of all were literacy tests: how could members of Congress "justify refusing suffrage to men who have been denied the privilege of an education, and whom it has been a crime to teach."[32]

Boutwell's final warning to his colleagues has echoed down through the years: "[I]f you leave these four million people to the care and custody of the men who have inaugurated and carried on this rebellion, then you treasure up, for untold years, the elements of social and civil war, which must not only desolate and paralyze the South, but shake this government to its very foundations."[33]

Energized by Boutwell's speech, the House rejected all but a few minor voting qualifications and passed the bill by a two-to-one margin, generating "loud demonstrations of applause" from the Black spectators in the gallery. It was finally approved by the Senate many months later after the Republicans increased their House and Senate majorities in the midterm elections. As threatened, President Johnson vetoed the bill, but Congress overrode the veto, and the bill became law on January 8, 1867.[34]

A FEW WEEKS AFTER Boutwell's January 1866 speech, Andrew Johnson suffered a public relations disaster while meeting with Frederick Douglass and a delegation of Black civic and religious leaders at the White House. The president was hoping to generate favorable press coverage by hosting the group, but things went badly from the start. The president began with a rambling monologue, filled with condescending remarks about his own experience as a slave owner, boasting that he had never sold an enslaved person nor broken up a family. He then warned the Douglass group that promoting Black civil rights could so anger whites that it might ignite a race war, resulting "in the certain extermination of the negro population." Perhaps, the president said, it would be best for Blacks to emigrate out of the South. Johnson then indulged in the bizarre speculation that giving Blacks the vote would somehow lead to an alliance between "the colored man and his master," with the two groups conspiring to keep poor whites "in slavery," denying them a portion "of the rich land of the country." As Douglass and his colleagues took their leave of the president, they had no illusions on where Johnson stood. Once the group was out of earshot, the president exploded (as quoted at the time): "Those d——d sons of b——s thought they had me in a trap! I know that d——d Douglass; he's just like any nigger, & he would sooner cut a white man's throat than not."[35]

MEANWHILE, ON CAPITOL HILL, the status of Tennessee and its readmission to the Union was the major issue being considered by Boutwell and his colleagues on the Joint Committee. Johnson, having lived in the Volunteer State since his teens and served as its military governor during the war, was certain that he best understood its people, white and Black.

In advance of other southern states, Tennessee had adopted a state constitution in February 1865 that rejected secession and abolished slavery, thus fulfilling Lincoln's Ten Percent Plan for rejoining the Union. A year later, the Joint Committee was about to approve Tennessee's readmission to the Union when George Boutwell objected, insisting that Blacks in the state should also be given the right to vote. His motion was defeated by one vote in the JCR, opposed by members such as Roscoe Conkling of New York, fearful of upsetting white voters back home.[36]

Boutwell was particularly disappointed that his longtime friend and colleague, Henry Wilson in the Senate, went along with the majority in favoring the immediate accession of Tennessee. In July, Boutwell again offered an amendment to the bill requiring Tennessee to establish "an equal and just system of suffrage for all male citizens . . . not less than twenty-one years of age." Boutwell asked his colleagues: If Congress won't use its power to demand that Tennessee extend the vote to its Black citizens, what will happen when the other southern states seek readmission? His plea fell on deaf ears; Tennessee was readmitted to the Union by a House vote of 125 to 12.[37]

As friction mounted with the president that spring and summer, Boutwell expressed dismay regarding Johnson's mental state, writing to his wife that "the city is full of rumors as to Johnson's condition and conduct. If half is true of what is said, never was there so unfit a man for the office." Boutwell had heard rumors of how Johnson lived in fear of assassination and even had a personal taster to make sure his food wasn't being poisoned. His conviction was growing that it would soon be time to move against the president.[38]

IN APRIL, CONGRESS PASSED the Civil Rights Act of 1866, legalizing the concept of "birth citizenship," which would soon become enshrined in the Fourteenth Amendment. At a stroke, Congress invalidated the 1857 *Dred Scott* decision and moved to protect those "civil" rights that Blacks were being denied by local and state authorities: the right to travel and seek work, sign contracts, own property, and sit on juries and give testimony against whites. The Act did not cover political rights such as voting and the holding of public office, as these were considered the responsibility of individual states, nor did it outlaw racial discrimination by individuals or companies in providing goods or services. Once more, Andrew Johnson vetoed the bill, but Congress quickly overrode the veto.

While the civil rights legislation was easier to enact than a constitutional amendment, which would require two-thirds votes in the House and Senate and ratification by three-quarters of the states, the Act could of course be undone by a future Congress. Accordingly, work continued on the Fourteenth Amendment as the ultimate guarantor of Black civil and political rights.[39]

THE FOURTEENTH AMENDMENT begins with the concept of birthright citizenship, whereby *"All persons born or naturalized in the United States and subject to the jurisdiction thereof, are citizens of the United States and of the State wherein they reside."* As one legal scholar has written, "These twenty-eight words reversed the twenty thousand words of Chief Justice Taney's *Dred Scott* opinion" in giving former slaves and free Blacks "legal rights equal to those of whites." Section 1 of the amendment also prohibited the individual states from denying those rights (also known as "privileges or immunities") without "due process of law" and "equal protection of the laws" being accorded to all American citizens. Quite simply, Section 1 revolutionized American constitutionalism by giving the national government the power to protect the rights of individuals from abuse by local and state authorities. Based on his conviction that Americans were citizens of the country first and only then residents of the individual states, and having been part of the three-member subcommittee that wrote the amendment, Boutwell could convincingly say that "these words were chosen with care." Otherwise, he believed, the country would have to accept "the fact that there are States in this Union whose citizens cannot be protected by the power of the United States."[40]

In our own time, the Fourteenth Amendment's "due process" and "equal protection" provisions have become central to a wide range of issues in American life, including abortion, affirmative action, and same-sex marriage, with much controversy over whether these rights fall within the jurisdiction of the national or the state governments.[41]

Sections 2 and 3 of the amendment went beyond the Civil Rights Act in addressing the issues of voting and political representation. Section 4 addressed the issue of the national government's debt arising from the war, and section 5 gave Congress the "power to enforce, by appropriate legislation, the provisions" of the amendment.

Mindful of the sensitivity of states' rights issues in both South and North, committee members knew they would have to set clear limitations on the provisions of the Fourteenth Amendment in order to gain passage in Congress and ratification by the states. Once again, debate focused on the more forceful *positive power* of the federal government—"Congress shall have the power to make all laws"—and wording that implied a less intrusive *negative power*, whereby "no state shall make or enforce any law." To come up with acceptable language, members turned to a subcommittee consisting of Boutwell, John Bingham, and Democrat Andrew Rogers of New Jersey.

Section 2, on seeking to protect the voting rights of newly created Black citizens, illustrated the difficulty. Given his firm commitment to Black voting rights, Boutwell proposed decidedly positive language: "Congress shall have the power to abolish any distinction in the exercise of the elective franchise in any State." This was rejected by the committee as being too intrusive on the ability of states to decide the conditions for voting and elections. So, the final wording of Section 2 called for a negative penalty of reducing a state's representation in Congress if such voting rights were "in any way abridged."

Boutwell realized that this negative penalty was the most that was achievable at the time, but Charles Sumner thought otherwise; the Massachusetts senator almost torpedoed the Fourteenth Amendment over the weak language in Section 2. Meeting with Sumner, Boutwell had to convince his colleague that "the country—the loyal states—were not then ready" to "extend the franchise to the blacks," which was true. Boutwell emphasized that the important issue was protecting the Black vote in the South, where the federal government at least had the power to institute "negative" prohibitions against state governments for restricting Black suffrage. Sumner peppered Boutwell with seventeen drafts of his proposal, "not one of which," Boutwell knew, "would have been accepted by Congress or the country." After a marathon session, Boutwell finally persuaded Sumner to support the amendment.[42]

REGARDING SECTION 4 of the amendment, it might seem odd to include a provision confirming the validity of the nation's war debt, but there were good reasons for doing so. Knowing how strongly many in the North felt about not repudiating the "sacred" Civil War debt that had helped win the war, Boutwell and his colleagues felt that this provision would help offset any qualms about extending civil equality to formerly enslaved Blacks. By making the debt a point of national honor, the Republicans could build support for the amendment. The same was true in declaring Confederate debt illegal, given public anxiety over the scenario of a future coalition of southern and northern Democrats forcing the national government to assume a Confederate States of America debt of $1.4 billion.[43]

The Republican political calculations were good ones given that Andrew Johnson was showing his Democratic colors during the 1866 midterm election campaign by calling on individual states to reject ratification of the Fourteenth Amendment, which only alienated moderate and conservative Republicans. Come November, Republicans routed the Democrats, winning two-thirds, veto-proof majorities in the House and Senate. Emboldened by the results, Boutwell and the Radical Republicans looked forward to continuing the battle with Andrew Johnson over Black civil rights.

It is true that, when passed by Congress in June 1866, the Fourteenth Amendment did not contain what Boutwell most desired: ironclad guarantees of Black suffrage. He admitted that "it was impossible to do more" given that white northerners were not yet ready for Black civil or political equality, many out of a fear that this would lead to social equality. His disappointment was shared by Frederick Douglass, who publicly opposed the amendment on the grounds that "equal" citizenship without the positive right to vote was "but an empty name." Strong federal protection of the Black vote would have to wait for the Fifteenth Amendment in 1869, when Boutwell again would play a central role. In the interim, the country would experience the first impeachment of a US president in American history.[44]

9

Impeaching the President

Apolitical cartoon from 1868 portrays President Andrew Johnson as Caesar in Shakespearean garb (see illustration in insert). The seven House impeachment managers are the conspirators, seeking Caesar's downfall. The malevolent looking, hunch-backed Thaddeus Stevens conjures Richard III. Benjamin Butler is a bombastic Falstaff. And George Boutwell is there also, a perfect Cassius with, as Shakespeare famously wrote, his "lean and hungry look, He thinks too much; such men are dangerous."[1]

THROUGHOUT THE SPRING of 1866, Boutwell and his colleagues on the Joint Committee on Reconstruction took testimony from more than one hundred witnesses regarding conditions in the South. Union officers and officials of the Freedmen's Bureau, former slaves and plantation officers, Confederate officers—even Robert E. Lee—appeared before them. They continued to draft the Civil Rights Act of 1866 and the Fourteenth Amendment, finishing their work in June.[2]

The report they issued was blunt about the need to *reconstruct* southern society as a multiracial democracy prior to the former Confederate states rejoining the Union. It flatly contradicted Andrew Johnson's contention that "once a state, always a state," and that *restoration* could occur merely by renouncing secession and accepting the Thirteenth Amendment. Describing how "the people of these States . . . rose in insurrection against the United States," the report said it was a "mockery" to think that such states could "resume at their own will and pleasure, all their privileges within the Union."[3]

That same month, the Fourteenth Amendment was approved by Congress and sent to the states for ratification. Andrew Johnson urged the southern states to reject it.

The president soon raised the stakes in his battle with the Republican Congress by announcing the formation of a new party to contest the 1866 midterm elections. In August, the National Union Convention met in Philadelphia, attended by Democrats, former Confederates, and some disaffected Republicans looking to rally behind Johnson. The gathering came to be known as the "Arm-in-Arm Convention" when two men from Massachusetts and South Carolina linked arms and strode to the podium as a symbol of national reconciliation and support for Johnson's pro-southern policies. A newspaper editor back in the Bay State asked sarcastically if the two gentlemen were handcuffed to one another, adding that perhaps the convention delegates were singing "Sumner to hell . . . and Stevens and Boutwell and Greeley as well. Rebels, good cheer, office is near!"[4]

President Johnson was also cleaning house back in Washington, dismissing several Republican cabinet members and filling several thousand patronage jobs with Democrats. The president actively supported congressional candidates who opposed ratifying the Fourteenth Amendment. In September he embarked on his famous "Swing Around the Circle" speaking tour through the mid-Atlantic and Midwest, hoping to whip up public support in advance of the midterm elections.

Johnson's erratic and belligerent behavior during that tour stoked fears of public violence if not civil war. Rumors spread that the president was asking his attorney general about the legality of establishing an alternative Congress comprised of northern Democrats and southern representatives. Ulysses Grant warned Philip Sheridan, army commander in the South, that Johnson might be preparing to "declare [Congress] itself illegal, unconstitutional, and revolutionary."[5]

George Boutwell was also worried, voicing his fears at a Republican caucus that the president might be conspiring to turn the government "over to the Southern rebels." In October, Boutwell took those fears public, publishing an article entitled "The Usurpation" in *The Atlantic Monthly*. Using language he knew would enrage the president, Boutwell accused Johnson of being a "slave" to the passions of fear, hatred, and ambition, with little hope of ever freeing "himself from their malign influence." Alleging that Johnson was using "the immense patronage of the government . . . for the restoration of the Rebel States to authority," Boutwell accused the president of seeking to illegally admit southern representatives to the House and Senate so he could "usurp" the powers and privileges of Congress.[6]

Boutwell's article perhaps gave Johnson more credit for duplicity than the president deserved. Speculating that Johnson would first "restore" white southerners to Congress to block any possibility of impeachment, Boutwell wrote that Johnson would seek to win the presidency in 1868 with the electoral votes of southern states and New York, aided by his Secretary of State William Seward, still an ally.

If this was Johnson's plan, the president was his own worst enemy in seeking to implement it. The "Swing Around the Circle" tour was a disaster as the president alienated voters with ranting speeches that many speculated were fueled by alcohol. Shortly after Boutwell's *Atlantic Monthly* article appeared, the autumn midterm elections rewarded the Republicans with veto-proof majorities as Congress prepared to reconvene in December.

True to character, Johnson became yet more intractable and imperious. His annual statement to Congress in December brooked no compromise. He again called for the immediate seating of southern representatives and made no mention of the Fourteenth Amendment, whose ratification had temporarily stalled with approval from only six states.[7]

NOT BACKING DOWN, George Boutwell pushed ahead on two fronts: promoting the ratification of the Fourteenth Amendment and calling for the impeachment of a president for the first time in US history. Fearful that Johnson would withdraw US troops from the South so that ex-Confederates could more easily organize state governments, Boutwell conferred with Thaddeus Stevens and Secretary of War Edwin Stanton. A top priority was insulating General of the Army Ulysses Grant from the president's attempt to circumvent the congressional policy of maintaining military protection for Blacks in the South.[8]

Boutwell spent Thanksgiving with his family in Groton, then headed back to Washington, stopping first in Philadelphia. He had been invited by well-known Black abolitionist William Still to give the first in a series of lectures in National Hall; Frederick Douglass would present the second about a month later. On Friday evening, November 30, Boutwell spoke to an enthusiastic audience of several hundred prominent Black Philadelphians. His call for unconditional suffrage for Black men in the South generated sustained applause, as did his warnings about universal amnesty being granted to former Confederates and his insistence that President Johnson be impeached and removed from office. A constitution and a government founded on slavery, he declared, "has ceased to exist. It can never be restored." Boutwell was sharpening his argument that the president was seeking nothing less than the restoration of the Slave Power in controlling the national government.[9]

Arriving in Washington the next day to attend a caucus of fifty congressional Republicans, Boutwell proposed that a committee be formed to investigate the president's conduct, including Johnson's possible involvement in the Lincoln assassination conspiracy. Writing to his wife Sarah that the effort was "well received," Boutwell joined Stevens, Charles Sumner, and Representative James M. Ashley of Ohio to request House Judiciary Committee hearings on proposed articles of impeachment.[10]

During the caucus Boutwell received a message that Edwin Stanton wanted to see him "at the earliest moment possible." The next morning at the War Department, Stanton told Boutwell that his *Atlantic Monthly* article on "usurpation" "[has] affected Johnson more than anything that has [been] written." Stanton added that he had recently learned that the president wanted to manufacture an excuse to send General Grant to Mexico to get him out of Washington, the better to bypass Grant when issuing orders to military commanders in the South. Stanton said he shared Boutwell's fears that Johnson might seek to take control of the government by assembling a rogue Congress made up of "members from the seceding States and Democratic members from the North." Stanton then asked Boutwell to take down language that could be inserted into the upcoming Army Appropriation bill, making it a "a crime for the president to issue military orders that did not go through the General of the Army." Working with Thaddeus Stevens, Boutwell would later include language stipulating that "the General of the Army shall not be removed, suspended, or relieved of command, or assigned to duty elsewhere than at said headquarters, except at his own request, without the previous approval of the Senate."[11]

These were bold steps indeed, representing what many believe was an unconstitutional power grab seeking to limit Johnson's powers as commander-in-chief. As written, the law would make it a misdemeanor for the president to issue orders to any military officer except through the general of the army, or for any officer to obey such an order. Johnson may have been guilty of bypassing Grant in the chain of command, but as commander-in-chief he had that authority. Amazingly, Stanton's language survived. The president, not wanting to veto a military funding bill, signed it on March 2. For the moment, Johnson had been checked by Congress on the issue of bypassing General Grant.[12]

Following the Christmas holiday, congressional impeachment activities had accelerated, focusing on Johnson's alleged abuse in the issuing of Confederate pardons, his reversal of Freedmen's Bureau acquisition of confiscated property, and his vetoing congressional Reconstruction legislation. One such veto was the Washington, DC, suffrage bill, which Congress overrode on January 8, giving Black men the right to vote, at least in municipal if not federal elections. The door to Black suffrage had opened just a crack.[13]

A week later, Boutwell pushed the door still wider when he introduced an amendment requiring Nebraska's territorial legislature to disavow, as a condition of statehood, a previous constitution restricting suffrage to whites. Calling suffrage without regard to color "a fundamental principle of republican government," Boutwell's amendment, opposed by moderates such as John Bingham, who felt it impinged on states' rights, was praised as "clear, distinct, precise, and effective" by fellow representative and *New York Times* editor Henry Raymond. President Johnson vetoed the bill incorporating Boutwell's amendment, but Congress brushed it aside and Nebraska was admitted as the country's thirty-seventh state on March 1, 1867.[14]

With his dual commitment to suffrage and education, Boutwell also assisted James Garfield of Ohio in creating a Department of Education to promote public schooling at the state and local levels, particularly in the South, as a means of strengthening citizen engagement with democracy. Andrew Johnson signed the bill into law, but members of Congress who saw the measure as "designed to enforce unwelcome measures" on state and local authorities were successful in gradually reducing its funding and effectiveness.[15]

Most significant of all, Congress began developing a Military Reconstruction Act to deprive the president of the unilateral power to reorganize the southern state governments, which were continuing to block ratification of the Fourteenth Amendment. Likewise passed in early March, the Reconstruction Act abolished the existing white state governments and divided the South into five military districts, giving the US Army authority to counteract the Black Codes that were restoring white supremacy. Black men would now be allowed to vote for, and serve as, delegates to state constitutional conventions that in turn would establish more representative state governments that could act on the Fourteenth Amendment and apply for representation in Congress.[16]

Republicans also moved to protect Secretary of War Edwin Stanton by drawing up the Tenure of Office Act, stipulating that the president would have to confer with the Senate before dismissing a cabinet member. Most likely unconstitutional, the bill passed Congress on February 18. It was vetoed by Johnson on March 2, the same day he signed the military appropriations bill, but was overridden by Congress later that afternoon and became law. Pending a Supreme Court decision on its legality, a president who violated its terms would be committing "high misdemeanors." The trap had been set by which Andrew Johnson might be impeached if he sought to unilaterally dismiss Stanton.[17]

BY THE SPRING of 1867, the impending constitutional struggle between the Radical Republicans and President Johnson seemed a boil ready to burst. Boutwell, hard at work on drawing up possible articles of impeachment, eagerly investigated any and all accusations against the president, from the serious (Johnson's possible involvement in treasonous plots during the war with Jefferson Davis) to the trivial (whether Johnson had issued presidential commissions in the correct manner). When nothing of substance had materialized by June, the Judiciary Committee voted 5–4 not to recommend articles of impeachment. One of the no votes was cast by Representative John Churchill from upstate New York, a political moderate who lived in Boutwell's boarding house on Twelfth Street; the two men often walked together to Capitol Hill.

Boutwell was also preoccupied during this period—his critics said obsessed—with investigating the role played by Jefferson Davis and other Confederate officials in the Lincoln assassination conspiracy and whether that conspiracy extended to Andrew Johnson. Like a bloodhound roused by a scent, Boutwell received congressional authority to conduct an intensive review of captured Confederate archives and interview witnesses.[18]

There had been an earlier investigation of such a Confederate conspiracy, led by the army's judge advocate general, Joseph Holt, following Lincoln's murder. When Jefferson Davis was captured in May 1865 in Georgia, disguised in his wife's clothing, Judge Holt accelerated the investigation. But a year later, Holt was saying there were no solid grounds on which to bring Davis and others to trial.[19]

Boutwell felt otherwise, suspicious because President Johnson was refusing to share evidence with the Judiciary Committee. Boutwell and others criticized the government's failure to arrest Booth conspirator John Surratt, who had escaped through Canada but was known to be living in England. Boutwell hinted that perhaps Johnson's government had helped Surratt escape to hide its involvement in the conspiracy to kill Abraham Lincoln so that Johnson could become president. In truth, Surratt needed no such help, given the well-established network of Confederate agents and sympathizers in Canada that was active throughout the war.[20]

Despite Boutwell's best efforts, even his case against Jefferson Davis was weak. Much of the testimony and evidence regarding the involvement of high Confederate officials in Lincoln's assassination—collected after the executions of four Booth co-conspirators in July 1865—was either perjured or flimsy. Even Edwin Stanton thought so, saying the files should not be released to the Judiciary Committee. As for John Surratt, the president's motive in not actively pursuing him in Europe could well have been that Johnson was being criticized at the time for a "rush to judgment" to execute Surratt's mother, Mary, for involvement in the Booth conspiracy. It's likely that the president was content to let "Surratt lose himself on the continent."[21]

None of this deterred Boutwell. He was convinced that Johnson was blocking congressional Reconstruction and investigations of Confederate involvement in Lincoln's assassination so that white rule could be restored in the South as a means of winning the presidency in 1868. Critics at the time ridiculed Boutwell for "brooding over trunks-full of rebel archives" and entertaining "wild stories of double spies, cipher correspondence, traitor's pardons, revocations of rewards, winkings at escapes, Jeff Davis' long impunity." Fearful that Johnson would release Davis from imprisonment at Fort Monroe, Virginia, Boutwell engineered a House resolution to keep Davis in prison.[22]

Boutwell was so determined to uncover evidence of a conspiracy that he impetuously blocked a Democratic colleague, Andrew Rogers, from examining the subcommittee's files. Accusing Rogers of leaking sensitive information to the press and of hiring a stenographer who had been "in the rebel service" during the war, Boutwell at one point grabbed the committee papers out of Rogers's hands and locked them in a trunk.[23]

THE SUMMARY REPORT on the assassination that Boutwell presented to the House consisted mainly of circumstantial evidence that Jefferson Davis and Confederate authorities had provided assistance to Booth and his conspirators with money and other resources. Killing Lincoln instead of the original plan of kidnapping the president was Booth's decision alone. Believing that evidence was still out there, Boutwell demanded that Davis remain at Fort Monroe while additional investigations were made.[24]

But Boutwell had come up empty. The war had been over for fifteen months and the press and public were tiring of conspiracy talk; The Nation magazine pointed out that the Boutwell report "contains . . . almost nothing that is new . . . direct proof is wanting."[25]

One tantalizing loose thread did remain. Boutwell would later describe "a quantity of papers, affidavits, letters and memoranda" that were sealed in a package and deposited with the clerk of the House of Representatives. While the papers "had no value as evidence," he wrote, preserving them was a mistake and "they should have been destroyed"; it was "not in the public interest" that their contents should ever become known.[26]

These missing papers would germinate, a century later, into renewed conspiracy theories about the assassination and unproven charges of a massive coverup that focused on Edwin Stanton, George Boutwell, and other Radical Republican leaders. This theory posited that it was Stanton and Boutwell, anxious that Lincoln would be too soft on the South, who wanted Lincoln dead and replaced by the more vengeful Andrew Johnson. A book published in the 1950s accused Boutwell of doing "his best to smother the stench" of a coverup when he blocked Andrew Rogers from seeing the box of evidence that Boutwell wrote "should have been destroyed." Another fanciful book in the 1970s was made into a movie that exonerated Andrew Johnson and placed the blame for a coverup squarely on Boutwell, who kept insisting that "John Wilkes Booth shot the President, and some dirty Rebs, including Jeff Davis, helped him do it. Nobody else! So far as I'm concerned, this case is closed!"[27]

Few words better grab the attention of the American public than "Lincoln" and "conspiracy." But among the loose ends and unanswered questions remaining from Lincoln's assassination, one of them will always be: What was in the box of congressional documents that George Boutwell guarded so secretively, warning that the public should never see them?[28]

WHILE GEORGE BOUTWELL investigated the Lincoln assassination conspiracy, the president was directing his attorney general to begin blocking provisions of the Military Reconstruction Act, especially those allowing Union commanders to remove local and state officials who were spreading a new kind of slavery through the Black Codes. Johnson also undermined the effectiveness of the Freedmen's Bureau by replacing officials and seeking to starve the Bureau of resources.[29]

In response, Congress passed two additional Military Reconstruction Acts which were vetoed by Johnson and promptly enacted with congressional overrides. Then, while Congress was in recess in August 1867, the president upped the ante by suspending Edwin Stanton as secretary of war and replacing him on an interim basis with a reluctant General Grant. Boutwell, incensed by Johnson's action, wrote confidentially to Grant that "the suspension of Stanton has awakened the most serious apprehensions," pledging his support to Grant "in the discharge of the difficult duties that are before you." Just weeks earlier, Boutwell had been asking Grant while taking the general's testimony on Capitol Hill whether the president had been making comments about the "illegality" of Congress with the intent of replacing it.[30]

By suspending and not firing Stanton, Johnson avoided violating the Tenure of Office Act; a formal replacement of the war secretary would have to wait for December when the Senate reconvened. But Grant, acquiescing to a presidential order, was not happy, and he became even less so when Johnson removed two of the generals commanding southern military districts, the popular Philip Sheridan (Texas and Louisiana) and Daniel Sickles (North and South Carolina), replacing them with generals who would do his bidding. Although Grant did not yet support growing calls to impeach the president, and told Boutwell so, he became increasingly vocal about the need for federal protection of Black rights in the South. Boutwell knew that Grant supported congressional Reconstruction and that the commanding general had told Sheridan and the other commanders of the southern military districts to "study what the framers of the reconstruction laws wanted to express . . . and to execute the law accordingly."[31]

In the country at large, Radical Republican fury with the president was blunted by a public that was getting tired of the controversy and largely believed that whites should remain in control of the government. In autumn local elections, Democratic candidates did surprisingly well, including in Ohio where they took control of the legislature, giving them the power to deny the later reelection of Republican senator Ben Wade in 1868. Referenda to grant Black suffrage were defeated in Connecticut, Ohio, and Minnesota. Even leading Republicans such as the Speaker of the House, Schuyler Colfax, rejected the concept of Black equality. For the moment, Andrew Johnson felt vindicated, expressing his confidence in the people: "they have come . . . our Republic will be saved."[32]

But Boutwell, with the bit between his teeth, charged on regardless. He again supported an impeachment resolution in the House Judiciary Committee, and this time it passed by a vote of 5–4 on November 25, clearing the way for consideration by the full House. It was John Churchill who switched his previous "no" vote, convinced to do so because of Johnson's most recent vetoes, the sacking of Sheridan and Sickles, and the suspension of Stanton.[33]

WHEN GEORGE BOUTWELL rose to his feet on November 25 to report the impeachment resolution, it was the first time in American history that Congress had debated articles of impeachment against a sitting president. On that day, at least, the occasion fizzled. There was confusion on the floor as numerous congressmen interrupted, unsure how the House should proceed. With gavel in hand, the Speaker ordered the clerk to read out: "Resolved: That Andrew Johnson, President of the United States, be impeached of high crimes and misdemeanors." In the upper gallery, white spectators hissed while Blacks applauded, and the hearing was delayed a week, until December 4.[34]

Boutwell knew that the resolution was likely to fail; his own Judiciary Committee chairman, James Wilson of Iowa, opposed it, asserting that impeachment must rest on criminal offenses, otherwise a majority in Congress could remove a president merely for policy disagreements. It should be left to the voters at the next election, not Congress, to remove him. Thaddeus Stevens, hobbled by illness, came to the House hoping to energize the pro-impeachment forces. At the other end of Pennsylvania Avenue, Andrew Johnson was unrepentant; his annual message to Congress warned that, "Of all the dangers which our nation has yet encountered, none are equal to those which must result from the success of the effort . . . to Africanize the [southern] half of our country."[35]

Boutwell again was chosen to present the impeachment case to the full House. In a speech lasting several hours over two days, he checked off a long list of Johnson's subversions of congressional authority and misuse of presidential power. He cited precedents from English common law and the 1787 Constitutional Convention debates to make a strong legal argument that impeachment did not have to rest on overtly illegal acts. He quoted Alexander Hamilton in the *Federalist Papers* as saying that the "misconduct of public men or abuse of the public trust" should be sufficient for impeachment. How, Boutwell pleaded, could the House and the Senate not respond when a president refused to acknowledge the "lawful and constitutional existence and authority . . . of Congress."[36]

A packed House gallery listened intently as Boutwell delivered what one historian has described as "the clearest, most eloquent, and most convincing argument" needed for a "broad interpretation" of impeachment powers, one that should include violations of the public trust and failure to execute the office of the president. Boutwell himself admitted that, if impeachment was valid only for indictable crimes, then the resolution must fail. What was at stake, however, was the integrity of the national government, which the president was subverting by blocking congressional prerogatives such as the Freedmen's Bureau, by unilaterally pardoning former rebels, and by supporting southern state governments comprised of officials who were ineligible to take the loyalty oath because of their participation in the Confederate rebellion. The president had campaigned against the Fourteenth Amendment and declared that Black freedmen had no right to vote. All of these, Boutwell maintained, were part of the president's campaign to restore "the rebels to power . . . in the Government of the country." Declaring that Congress had the primary authority to determine how the former Confederate states would rejoin the Union, Boutwell concluded that any attempt by the president to do so "must be treated as an act of usurpation."[37]

In rebuttal, Judiciary chairman Wilson argued that Boutwell was guilty of constitutional overreach. The president might deserve "censure and condemnation" for his policies, but impeachment was not the answer. What if Democrats took control of Congress and Republicans found themselves at the wrong end of the impeachment gun barrel? Wilson asserted that "political unfitness and incapacity must be tried at the ballot box, not in the high court of impeachment."[38]

Wilson's argument was enough to keep even some Radical Republicans from stepping into the unknown; the resolution was defeated by 108 to 57. If evidence of criminality was needed to impeach the president, Boutwell himself acknowledged that "it may not be possible, by specific charge, to arraign [the president] for this great crime."[39]

PERHAPS THE COUNTRY breathed a sigh of relief at dodging the impeachment bullet, but the battle between Congress and the president continued unabated. Under the protection of the US military, Blacks were registered to vote, and conventions were held to devise constitutions that would protect voting and other rights prior to holding elections for new state governments. Fighting back, Johnson fired two more commanders of the southern military districts, replacing them with more pliant subordinates. In doing so, the president butted heads with Ulysses Grant, who was able to countermand some of the president's directives.[40]

With Congress back in session, Johnson continued to stew over the problem of Edwin Stanton and the Tenure of Office Act. The president hoped that Grant, still the acting secretary of war as well as general-in-chief, would take the job on a permanent basis. But Grant, tired of being manipulated by Johnson, refused, physically surrendering the office in mid-January after the Senate restored Stanton as secretary.

Implacable and prickly, Edwin Stanton was a formidable opponent. He quickly took possession of his office at the War Department and remained holed up there for the next several weeks, having his meals delivered. The president, exasperated beyond belief as he looked for a solution to his problem, asking Gen. William Tecumseh Sherman to fill the position but being rejected by him, finally fired Stanton in the third week of February.[41]

Stanton responded by barricading himself in his office to prevent Johnson's designee, Adj. Gen. Lorenzo Thomas (whom Stanton detested), from taking over. Stanton supporters on Capitol Hill flooded the war secretary with expressions of support; Boutwell sent a note encouraging Stanton to "hold the office yielding only to force actual and present." For the next several days, Stanton refused to leave his office, with General Grant providing a military guard and Lorenzo Thomas making a weak show of trying to assume the position of secretary.[42]

Believing the president had stepped into the tenure of office trap set by Thaddeus Stevens, the House of Representatives held a special session on Saturday, February 22, George Washington's birthday. Crowds made their way along snow-lined streets to Capitol Hill early in the morning. Mark Twain was among those watching from the crowded, noisy gallery, reporting on the event for a Nevada newspaper, writing how an audible gasp greeted George Boutwell when he appeared on the House floor, followed by Thaddeus Stevens. Both men would soon be selected by their House colleagues to serve on the seven-man House impeachment committee. Boutwell was then chosen by his fellow managers as committee chair, but caring more for results than the spotlight, he diplomatically stepped aside to placate the moderate John Bingham, who felt slighted after having received the most House votes in the selection process.[43]

Boutwell and Stevens had been the two most forceful advocates for impeaching the president, so it was fitting that Boutwell handed the impeachment papers to the ailing Stevens that morning to be presented to the full House. As Twain wrote, Stevens "was a corpse that was ready for the shroud," but "there was a soul in his sunken eyes." Following lengthy discussion that extended until midnight, with raucous spectators applauding from the galleries, the House agreed to continue the debate on Monday morning.[44]

It was dark and snowy when the House reconvened on February 24, the galleries full once again. House Republicans rose to denounce the president, both for indictable crimes like violating the Tenure of Office Act and for misuse of presidential power in enabling ex-Confederates to take power in the South. Although Democrats argued, justifiably, that the tenure act was likely unconstitutional, that was a moot point; a president would still be bound by its provisions until the Act was ruled on by the Supreme Court. Plus, sentiment against Johnson had gone far beyond his firing of Edwin Stanton. It was the end of a long winter's day when the impeachment resolution passed by a vote of 126 to 47. Shortly before adjournment, Boutwell was accorded the honor of chairing the drafting committee that would write up and declare the articles of impeachment against the president.[45]

THE NEXT MORNING, Thaddeus Stevens and John Bingham walked the impeachment articles over to the Senate where they were received by its presiding officer, Benjamin Wade of Ohio, the very man who would become president if a Senate trial convicted Andrew Johnson. Because Andrew Johnson had no vice president, the radical and intemperate Ben Wade was next in the line of succession, a prospect that caused no little anxiety for some moderate Republicans.[46]

The House impeachment committee began its work, with a subcommittee of Boutwell, Stevens, Bingham, and James Wilson of Iowa drafting the indictment by which the president would be arraigned. Meeting in the House Judiciary Committee chamber, the four men represented a balance of Radical Republican thinking that emphasized Johnson's broad usurpation of presidential power (Boutwell and Stevens) and the moderate Republican focus on the criminally indictable offense of Johnson's having violated the Tenure of Office Act (Bingham and Wilson).[47]

The ten impeachment articles presented by Boutwell to the full House on February 29 reflected more the thinking of Bingham and Wilson than of Boutwell and Stevens. Having failed to make their case the previous December that Johnson had "usurped" power by blocking Congress, Boutwell and Stevens reluctantly agreed that the impeachment articles should rest on the "painfully narrow and obscurely legalistic" consequences of Johnson's firing of Edwin Stanton. Of the ten articles, the first nine were a tangle of confusing iterations of the president's having violated either the Constitution, or the

Tenure of Office Act, or the federal conspiracy law, or having illegally distributed military funds, with many of the articles making the same charges in
different ways. The tenth article was completely extraneous to Johnson's firing
of Stanton and was but a poor plea for why the president should be removed
from office.[48]

After the House clerk had read out the ten, lengthy articles, Boutwell was
given the floor for fifteen minutes to try and make sense of it all. It was not
one of his finest moments, but perhaps no one could have done a good job of
clearly stating why the country was taking the historic step of removing a sitting president. Since May 1865, Boutwell and his colleagues had been savaging
the president for overturning the results of the Civil War, restoring the white
power structure in the South, and endangering the lives and liberties of newly
freed Blacks and their white Unionist supporters. Now, the enormity of Johnson's crimes was being reduced to the splitting of legal hairs on issues where
the president had the advantage.

Among his detractors, Boutwell's penchant for getting lost in convoluted
speeches had earned him the nickname "Steady Wind Blowing Aft," and he
lived up to that billing on this occasion. With only fifteen minutes to clarify a complicated case, Boutwell's summation of the charges was dense and
confusing. Unlike the previous December, when he was presenting his own
case for impeachment, based on his conviction that Johnson was usurping
the powers of Congress, he now was a spokesman for a case cobbled together
by committee.

In response, the Democrat Albert Burr of Illinois rose and artfully
exposed the two major weaknesses of the Republican impeachment case.
Decrying how "the accumulated wrath of radicalism" was being "poured out
upon the head of the Chief Executive of this nation," Burr got to the heart
of his argument. First, he lampooned what was plain to see: "[T]en articles have been presented, or rather ten specifications of one article." Boutwell and his impeachment committee colleagues were trying to dress up
one questionable and likely unconstitutional legal charge in ten different
ways. Second, Burr exposed the political Achilles' heel of impeachment by
playing on the fears of many moderate Republicans that Ben Wade would
become president if Johnson were removed from office. Noting that Wade
had "never received the vote of the people" (senators were chosen by their
state legislatures at the time), Burr asked how it was that such a man should
become president "without public sanction, without public consent." If the

Republicans were unhappy with Johnson as president, they should vote him out of office at the next election. As the impeachment trial proceeded in the Senate over the next three months, these would be the two main arguments by which even moderate Republican senators would justify the acquittal of Andrew Johnson.[49]

Struggling to improve their case, Boutwell, Stevens, and Bingham proceeded to delete, add, and change the articles, finally settling on eleven of them. When these were delivered to the Senate on March 4, one of the new articles was the brainchild of Boutwell's colleague from Massachusetts, the freshman congressman and extremely polarizing figure, Benjamin Franklin Butler.[50]

Although respected and feared as a devilishly clever criminal lawyer, Butler was an unfortunate addition to the impeachment committee given his abrasive personality. Known as "The Beast" for his heavy-handed command of occupied New Orleans in 1862, Butler also earned the nickname "Spoons" for allegedly abetting widespread theft (such as precious silverware) and extortion of local residents. In fairness, Butler had an extremely difficult mission which he did well, overseeing affairs in the South's largest city, now occupied by federal troops, with an ethnically diverse population of 170,000 augmented by thousands of formerly enslaved Blacks seeking refuge. The Crescent City was a combustible mix of Confederate loyalists, white supremacist Union supporters, and a proud free Black/Creole community, which Butler managed with an iron fist. Having been a Democrat, like Boutwell, in Massachusetts in the 1850s, Butler switched to the Republican Party after his war service as a political general and was elected to Congress in 1866, parlaying his headstrong personality into a top leadership role. Cross-eyed, balding, and with a "stout, shapeless body," Butler was easily caricatured by the nation's political cartoonists, and often was.[51]

The flamboyant Butler was especially detested by the spare, rather proper John Bingham, regarded by his colleagues as having one of the sharpest legal minds in Congress. When House Speaker Schuyler Colfax read off the names of Stevens and Butler at the top of the list of committee members, seemingly implying roles for them as chair and vice chair, respectively, Bingham threw a hissy fit, declaring, "I'll be damned if I serve under Butler." Irritated by Butler's ego-driven showmanship, Bingham still resented Butler's having called him a "woman-killer" for Bingham's role in the military tribunal that sentenced Mary Surratt to death following the Lincoln assassination trial. Bingham's ego was assuaged when the full House put his name at the top, but he again complained when the managers themselves chose Boutwell as their chairman. Bingham threatened to resign, but Boutwell quickly moved to smooth things over. He voluntarily gave way to Bingham as chair, knowing how important a role the moderate Bingham would play in convincing wavering senators to convict the president.[52]

WHEN THE SENATE PROCEEDINGS began on March 30, Boutwell and his colleagues were more united in their desire to see the president convicted than on which legal arguments to emphasize. Hoping for a speedy trial to capitalize on the decidedly anti-Johnson mood throughout the country, the process was, fatally for those backing the impeachment effort, tedious, unfocused, and replete with speeches and posturing. George Boutwell remained in the background for much of the first three weeks, leaving the spotlight to the fiery Ben Butler, who assumed the role of lead prosecutor.

On April 22, Boutwell opened the final phase of the trial by promising Chief Justice Salmon Chase and those present that they could "now anticipate the speedy conclusion of your arduous labors." Sadly, this was not to be. For three hours extending over two days, Boutwell labored through the details of the impeachment charges in a densely argued speech that consumed fifty pages of the official impeachment transcript. Although rich in historical and literary allusion, and fueled by deep passion, the speech fell flat, doing little to persuade those senators who might be undecided.[53]

As he droned on, Boutwell sought to spark some levity with a quote from *Hamlet*. Portraying Johnson's cabinet members as nothing more than servile yes-men for acquiescing in the president's assault on Congress, Boutwell likened them to the obsequious Polonius, father of Ophelia, who all too readily agrees when Hamlet compares clouds in the sky, first to camels, then weasels, but no, maybe whales.

Returning to his theme, Boutwell sought to reconcile the contradictory arguments that impeachment need not rest on indictable offenses while maintaining that Johnson had indeed violated the provisions of the Tenure of Office Act.[54]

Boutwell complicated matters when he then accused the president of contemplating a coup d'état against Congress, using an unfortunate celestial analogy that would come back to haunt him. Waxing eloquent, Boutwell described for his listeners a magical "hole in the sky," a region of the heavens near the Southern Cross constellation, "where the eye of man, [even] with the aid of the powers of the telescope, has been unable to discover nebulae, or asteroid, or comet, or planet, or star, or sun." Having painted this picture of a giant black hole, Boutwell hoped that "justice and virtue" would "project this enemy [Andrew Johnson] . . . into that vast region, there forever to exist in a solitude eternal as life." With many in the Chamber suppressing a grin, one of the president's defense lawyers, William Evarts, muttered, "I'll put Boutwell into that hole in the sky so that he'll never get out again."[55]

Which is precisely what Evarts did. In his closing argument, Evarts allowed as to how George Boutwell might have found "an astronomical fact which many professors of that science are wholly ignorant of." Twisting his rhetorical knife, Evarts addressed Boutwell as "the honorable and astronomical manager," adding that "if the learned manager can only get over the obstacles of the laws of nature, the Constitution will not stand in his way." Longtime Washington journalist Ben Perley Poore noted that, although visibly disturbed by Evarts's criticism, "Boutwell bore it well."[56]

For Frederick Douglass and America's Black community, however, the issues being discussed were deadly serious. On the day the trial opened, March 30, a white Unionist politician, George Ashburn, had been brazenly assassinated by the Ku Klux Klan in Columbus, Georgia, shortly after addressing a Republican rally. Citing that and other examples of terrorist violence, Douglass accused the president of responsibility for the deaths of scores of African Americans throughout the South. Douglass dismissed the Tenure of Office Act as a legal triviality, saying it was only necessary to fully expose Andrew Johnson's criminal conduct. For its part, the African American newspaper, *The Christian Recorder* of Philadelphia, lauded Boutwell's speech for its strong moral convictions, predicting that it would sway doubtful senators and that Johnson would indeed be found guilty.[57]

IT WAS NOT TO BE. Andrew Johnson was acquitted by a vote of 35–19, one shy of the two-thirds needed for conviction. The key votes supporting Johnson were cast by seven moderate Republicans, who were motivated by doubts about using the Tenure of Office Act as a legal basis for impeachment as well as the promise of political favors from the president and his friends. There was also political expediency. Andrew Johnson had less than a year remaining in office, and his removal would elevate the abrasive Benjamin Wade to the presidency.

Known as the *Recusants*, these seven Republican senators included Senator Edmund Ross of Kansas, later extolled by John F. Kennedy in *Profiles in*

Courage for putting conscience above party in what Kennedy described as "the most heroic act in American history." The reality was more mundane, as Edmund Ross was involved with numerous individuals—known as "the Kansas cabal"—who were actively soliciting bribes and favors for the president's acquittal.[58]

In Boston, a prominent Republican lawyer criticized his party for having devised an overly complex impeachment strategy born of "the malevolence of Stevens, the ambition of Butler, the theories of Boutwell, & the folly of an unthinking crowd of party followers." The "theories" of Boutwell is an interesting reference, acknowledging Boutwell's emphasis that impeachment and conviction should not have to rely on technical violations of the law. Despite Johnson's acquittal, Boutwell would continue to believe that, as impeachment is more a political than a legal act, "the President of the United States [should be] liable to impeachment and removal from office for acts and conduct that do not subject him to the process of indictment and trial in the criminal courts." It's a concept much more commonly accepted today.[59]

Five days after the first impeachment vote, the Republican convention in Chicago nominated Ulysses S. Grant for president. The party was coalescing behind a national hero as their candidate, the general who with Abraham Lincoln had won the Civil War. That Grant was seen as a political moderate and friendly to business interests, one who seemingly would not push a Radical agenda, made him even more attractive.

AS FOR ANDREW JOHNSON, he wooed the Democratic Party but was considered damaged goods. At the party's convention in New York in July, Johnson finished well behind Horatio Seymour as the Democratic nominee for president.

As a lame duck president, Johnson could do little to block congressional Reconstruction through the end of his term. Congress brushed aside a Johnson veto in June, granting congressional representation to seven southern states that promised to permit Black suffrage and ratify the Fourteenth Amendment. When Georgia ratified in late July, the Fourteenth Amendment became law. Congress then overrode the president's veto of a bill to extend the Freedmen's Bureau.[60]

Although Johnson was less of a threat to Reconstruction in the final months of his presidency, the fact that he remained in office energized white supremacists in the South and Democrats throughout the country. Reconstruction opponents took heart from the fact that Evarts and other members of Johnson's defense team had "put Boutwell in the cloud and Butler in the gutter" during the impeachment trial. Southern newspapers gleefully predicted a Republican disaster in the November election while white vigilantes intensified their violence. US troops in the South, now led by officers appointed by Johnson, largely stood by and did little.[61]

Frederick Douglass summarized the feelings of many Black Americans who despised Johnson for "feeding the rebel imagination with a prospect of regaining through politics what they lost by the sword." Douglass was furious that Johnson was escaping responsibility for inciting widespread violence against Blacks.[62]

WITH CONGRESS IN RECESS, Boutwell returned to Groton. His farm had grown to three hundred acres, and although well-tended by his farm manager, the summer crop of grains and vegetables would soon need harvesting. He also needed to tend to his reelection campaign for Congress that coming November.

Reflecting on the grueling impeachment process that he and the country had just endured, Boutwell might have engaged in what has become one of the great parlor games of American history: Would things have been different had Abraham Lincoln lived? Andrew Johnson claimed he was implementing Lincoln's plan of conciliatory Reconstruction, but in truth, Lincoln had no definite strategy when he died. The slain president had only an "experimental, pragmatic approach" to the complex problem of restoring the "proper practical relations" of the seceded and defeated states to a Union now fundamentally changed with a more powerful national government. Tragically, what the country received instead was the stubborn inflexibility of Andrew Johnson wanting to restore the South on its terms, but to a Union that was fundamentally different from that which existed in 1860.[63]

George Boutwell didn't leave any thoughts on how Reconstruction might have been different had Lincoln lived. The reality now was that most Americans, South and North, had to be convinced of the necessity of Black equality. For Boutwell, Lincoln's importance was that "through his agency the Constitution of the United States had been brought into harmony with the Declaration of Independence." But work was still needed if Jefferson's goals of "life, liberty, and the pursuit of happiness" for all Americans were to be fully realized through the safeguards of the Constitution.[64]

Soon, Johnson would be gone and Ulysses Grant would be the next president. Boutwell and Grant were coming to know each other better; Boutwell was confident that Grant as president would support the objectives of congressional Reconstruction. Yet the politics of racial equality were as vicious as ever. There was no guarantee, even with Ulysses Grant seeking to bring the country together, that Americans would respond to "the better angels of our nature."

The Fifteenth Amendment
and the 1868 Election

George Boutwell stood before the cheering crowd on the steps of the Grant residence on I Street in Washington, waving his hand for silence as he introduced the man next to him, "the next President, the General of the armies." Earlier, the US Marine Band had led a throng of well-wishers up New Jersey Avenue to congratulate Ulysses Grant on winning the Republican nomination for president at the Chicago convention the previous day. From inside the house, Boutwell appeared with Grant at his side to "prolonged and enthusiastic cheering." Boutwell told the crowd that Grant would give the country "the same patriotism . . . and the same faithfulness" that the general had demonstrated at "the battles of Shiloh, the Wilderness, and Richmond."[1]

Turning to Grant, Boutwell spoke of the "unanimous effort" with which the Republican Party would sustain him, especially as the general would be "opposed by the same men who opposed you in the rebellion." (A voice from the crowd cried out, *"That's so!"*) Grant, thanking his supporters in a low gravelly voice, promised he would, if elected, discharge the duties of president "impartially and for the welfare of the country." As he turned back into the house, Grant murmured to Boutwell that he wasn't sure if the crowd had heard him or not.

Grant had been nominated on the first ballot in Chicago, with Speaker of the House Schuyler Colfax of Indiana chosen as his running mate. The party platform consisting of fourteen principles, perhaps a symbolic nod to the Fourteenth Amendment, praised the Reconstruction policy of Congress as

helping to secure "equal civil and political rights to all." Grant's message to
the country during the forthcoming campaign would be, "let us have peace."

THE DEMOCRATIC PARTY motto for the 1868 presidential campaign was, "This
is a white man's country, let white men rule." Presidential candidate Horatio
Seymour, governor of New York, called for an end to federal intervention in
the South and for the states of the former Confederacy to set their own suffrage rules. The vice presidential candidate, Frank Blair, a decorated Union
general during the war but now a fierce critic of Reconstruction, was the party's attack dog. The son of Francis Preston Blair Sr., owner of the slave woman
whom George Boutwell had met during his first trip to Washington, DC, in
1839, Frank Blair vowed that Democrats "would prevent the people of our
race . . . from being driven out of the country or trodden under foot by an
inferior and semi-barbarous race."[2]

Despite the gains of the three Military Reconstruction Acts and the Fourteenth Amendment in providing for Black suffrage and office holding, Republicans were nonetheless worried about losing the election. Yes, Black men in
the South could now vote, and by the thousands they attended public meetings to listen to speakers from the Freedmen's Bureau and the Republican
Party explain their new franchise to them. For George Boutwell, "the privilege
of the elective franchise . . . without distinction of race or color," would be the
final, crowning achievement of the Civil War.[3]

But with the Black vote came the white backlash. The Ku Klux Klan, the
Knights of the White Camelia, and other night riders were murdering and terrorizing Blacks and their white Republican allies from the Carolinas to Texas.
White employers threatened Blacks with losing their jobs and credit if they
voted Republican, or if they voted at all. Southern poll watchers continued to
turn away Blacks who showed up to vote.[4]

In the border states and throughout the North, there was widespread hostility to the prospect of Black suffrage. Black males had unrestricted suffrage in
five New England states, but elsewhere, their ability to vote was either severely
restricted by literacy and property tests, or banned altogether.

Grant and the Republicans won the 1868 election, but not handily. His
popular vote margin of 300,000 was made possible by the votes of 500,000
Black votes in the southern states. Most of the country's white voters voted
for Seymour. Grant won the Electoral College 214 to 80, but here again Blacks
supplied the crucial edge in winning the electoral votes of North and South

Carolina, Alabama, and Florida. Conversely, Grant's margin of victory in white, northern and western states such as Connecticut, Indiana, and California, was slim. In Congress, the Democrats gained twenty seats in the House of Representatives.[5]

The election results were a troubling indicator of white fatigue with Reconstruction. The Republicans might be in control, but with Grant a political newcomer, federal government support for Reconstruction was uncertain in a country wanting to get back to business as usual.

Grant's victory margin would likely have been greater, of course, had Blacks been allowed to vote in the border states of Delaware, Maryland, and Kentucky, which he lost. Having remained in the Union, these states were not covered by the Reconstruction Acts and maintained their bans on Black suffrage, even for free Blacks. In Georgia and Louisiana, which Grant also lost, there was widespread suppression of the Black vote through violence and intimidation.

Republican candidates had largely skirted the issue of Black suffrage during the campaign. Fearful that, as one Democrat sneered, "any party with an abolition head and a nigger tail will soon find itself with nothing left but the head and the tail," Republicans tried to have it both ways on Black voting rights: supporting federal intervention in the South while giving northern and western states a free hand to devise their own rules. Within the party, Thaddeus Stevens was furious, calling the party platform "tame and cowardly" shortly before dying of intestinal disease in August. Equally distressed, the Colored Men's Border State Convention in Baltimore demanded national suffrage as "the crowning right of citizenship" as contained in the Fourteenth Amendment.[6]

With the election over and Grant's victory secured, Republicans did begin to find their courage. Referenda to allow Black suffrage were enacted in Iowa and Minnesota, and Republican newspapers began to advocate for constitutional guarantees to settle the issue nationally. Without the fiery leadership of Stevens and with House colleague James Ashley having lost his bid for reelection, it was up to Boutwell, Ben Butler, and Representative George Julian of Indiana to rally the party. Knowing the electoral importance of protecting the Black vote in the South while extending it to Blacks in the North, George Boutwell took the lead in formulating a positive guarantee of universal male suffrage that would become the Fifteenth Amendment to the Constitution.[7]

EASILY REELECTED TO his House seat in November, Boutwell was in Groton preparing to return to Washington when he gave a provocative interview to the *New York Daily Herald* that he knew would be widely reprinted in newspapers across the country. First, he called for "more stringent measures of reconstruction" to protect civil rights in the three states not yet readmitted to the Union: Virginia, Mississippi, and Texas. Next, he stirred up the states' rights hornet's nest by saying that Congress must decide who could vote, not only in *national* elections for president and Congress, but perhaps in *state* elections as well.[8]

Backlash to Boutwell's challenge was immediate. The *Charleston Daily News* had duly warned that, if Grant were elected, then Congress might seek "the power of controlling absolutely and without limitation the elective franchise in every State in the Union." Now that Boutwell and the Radical Republicans had imposed the "African carnival" of "negro suffrage" on the South, the paper noted with "grim satisfaction" that the rest of the country was in for similar treatment. The *San Francisco Daily Examiner*, ridiculing Boutwell as "the discoverer of the famous 'hole in the sky,'" warned that Boutwell and Congress might seek to confer both "negro suffrage and Chinese suffrage" in the coming months. Northern newspapers wrote of Boutwell and the national government doing the same with the Irish and other immigrants.[9]

True to his word, Boutwell introduced a bill on the first day of Congress a week later "providing that all male citizens of the United States not under 21 years of age shall be entitled to vote for electors for President and Vice-President and Representatives in Congress." Although the language would change in the coming months, this was the first official formulation of what would become the Fifteenth Amendment to the Constitution guaranteeing a national right to vote.[10]

In the new Congress, Boutwell replaced the deceased Stevens as chair of the House Select Committee on Reconstruction (the Senate created its own committee to continue the work of the Joint Committee). In the weeks following, he and his colleagues argued that national citizenship conferred by the Fourteenth Amendment (except for Native Americans) demanded a uniform, national standard of suffrage, unimpaired by different restrictions imposed by different states. Early in the new year, in support of his goal of "universal suffrage to all adult male citizens," Boutwell introduced two different measures. The first was a bill (H.R. 1667) to enact a law protecting such rights in both national elections and for state legislatures. The second (H.R. 402) would enshrine such rights in a constitutional amendment.[11]

Boutwell was transparent about his dual strategy. He explained that H.R.

1667 would extend suffrage to an additional 150,000 Black voters in the North. Then, once his constitutional amendment (H.R. 402) had passed Congress with the necessary two-thirds majority, these new Black voters in the North would help pressure their state legislatures to ratify what would become the Fifteenth Amendment. As had been necessary with the Fourteenth Amendment, once the Fifteenth was added to the Constitution, no future Congress could tamper with it.[12]

Some of his colleagues, future president James A. Garfield among them, criticized Boutwell's strategy and voiced doubts about the constitutionality of having Congress legislate over voting rights that were the preserve of the states. One New York newspaper warned Boutwell "not to whet a knife that might someday cut his and the Negro's throat," which is what could happen if the amendment failed and a future Congress overturned any bill that might be enacted now.[13]

Boutwell yielded to his critics, asking the House to shelve the proposed bill and focus on the more difficult task of enacting a constitutional amendment. He and others supporting full voting rights had learned a lesson; northern support for Black suffrage would go only so far, and it would take the more difficult process of enacting a constitutional amendment to achieve it.[14]

Boutwell introduced that amendment in the House on January 28, with William Stewart of Nevada introducing a similar bill in the Senate. The next several weeks were filled with legislative wrangling in both chambers. Wording changes were proposed, altered, and abandoned. Political coalitions formed and dissolved, positions were staked out and cast aside.[15]

WHILE DEBATING THE Fifteenth Amendment, the US Senate also considered a measure to reform the Electoral College, with Charles Buckalew of Pennsylvania arguing that voters and not their state legislatures should choose the electors who vote for president and vice president. In eliminating the power of state legislatures "to meddle with or molest" the rights of voters, Buckalew declared that Congress and not the states should determine the manner and timing of national elections.

With Buckalew having opened the door of Electoral College reform, Charles Sumner of Massachusetts strode right through it. Declaring the Electoral College "a sham," Sumner argued for "a much more radical change," that of electing the president "by the people directly, without the intervention of the Electoral College." Doing so would put the power of electing the president and vice president where it belonged, in the hands of the people, not the states. Sumner argued that the Buckalew amendment would only "prop up" an "*effete* system," leaving open the danger, as expressed by another senator, that "at any time a candidate with a minority" of the popular vote could nonetheless become president by winning the Electoral College.

Sumner's proposal for direct election of the president was a bridge too far; even Buckalew's more modest amendment went nowhere. In the House, a disappointed Boutwell had supported Electoral College reform. Decades later, when individual voters did select presidential electors, he would criticize the "winner take all" system that awarded all of a state's electoral votes to a candidate who might have won only 51 percent of the vote. Believing such a system to be fundamentally undemocratic, Boutwell was ahead of his time in proposing a proportional system of dividing a state's electoral votes. What he recommended was that electoral votes be awarded to the candidate who won each of a particular state's congressional districts. Today, only two states, Maine and Nebraska, allow for such splitting of their electoral votes and a more equitable representation of the support received by candidates in their states. The "winner take all" system remains in the other forty-eight states, and the American president is still not elected directly by the people.[16]

GEORGE BOUTWELL'S LEADERSHIP in the House to enact the Fifteenth Amendment took all the negotiating skills he could command. Since his days in the Massachusetts legislature, he had been a staunch advocate of eliminating all restrictions on voting, be these poll taxes, literacy tests, or property requirements. The one exception had been the educational requirement in Massachusetts law, which he argued was acceptable because Massachusetts had *mandatory* public education; Boutwell had always believed that suffrage and education were inextricably linked and reinforced each other. It was hardly fair, accordingly, for the southern states to impose literacy requirements for formerly enslaved Blacks who were totally denied any opportunity for education. Moreover, Boutwell was seeking to expand public education in the South, for whites and Blacks, through his support of James Garfield's bill to create the Department of Education.[17]

In promoting the Fifteenth Amendment, however, Boutwell found he had to abandon his opposition to poll taxes and literacy tests as qualifications for voting. Despite the support of colleagues such as Henry Wilson in the Senate who advocated unfettered universal suffrage, many other Republicans wanted to maintain such restrictions so they could limit the Irish Catholic vote in the North and the Chinese vote in the West. Even some of his southern Republican colleagues were nervous about supporting suffrage with no restrictions, as this might sweep away the loyalty oaths required of former Confederates to regain the franchise. Given these demands, it was up to Boutwell to craft the "compromise language" needed for the Fifteenth Amendment to be enacted.[18]

It was a job made more difficult by the impending deadline of the current congressional session and President Grant's being inaugurated on March 4. Working with Senator Stewart of Nevada, Boutwell produced a watered-down amendment that switched from a positive guarantee of voting rights to a negative prohibition on states denying the vote to males over the age of twenty-one "on account of race, color, or previous condition of servitude." Boutwell admitted that it was a lowest common denominator bill, as it also did not prohibit literacy tests and poll taxes and had no guarantees of Black office holding.[19]

An outraged Charles Sumner vigorously opposed the bill, arguing that it did not go far enough in protecting Black suffrage from unfair poll taxes and literacy tests and that it didn't guarantee "the right to hold office." Boutwell countered that the right to vote implied the right to hold office. If Sumner insisted on that provision, and on positive voting rights guarantees, Boutwell warned, he would jeopardize ratification in states such as Ohio, Indiana, and Illinois.[20]

In his memoirs, Boutwell tells the dramatic story of how the bill to create the Fifteenth Amendment was likely saved by the intervention of revered abolitionist Wendell Phillips. Writing in the *National Anti-Slavery Standard*, Phillips had put his full support behind Boutwell's House version of the bill, calling on Sumner and Senate Republicans to "be a little more *politicians* and a little less reformers" in voting for it. Later, Boutwell thanked Phillips for his intervention, believing that "your voice saved the Fifteenth Amendment."[21]

The House of Representatives approved Boutwell's draft amendment with the necessary two-thirds majority on February 25, and the Senate followed suit the next day. Sumner withheld his support from the bill but was unable to influence his fellow senators; according to biographer David Donald, it was "more than ever clear that Sumner had no significant following in the Senate on domestic political issues." As ultimately enacted, the amendment's first section stated that "The right of citizens of the United States to vote shall not be denied or abridged by the United States or by any State on account of race, color, or previous condition of servitude," with a second section giving Congress the power "to enforce this article by appropriate legislation."[22]

Over time, it became apparent that a fatal weakness of the Fifteenth Amendment was the misguided thinking that, because states were prohibited from using race-based obstacles to prevent voting, then measures such as poll taxes and literacy tests wouldn't be imposed at all. After all, any limitations on voting imposed by the states would now have to be applied to whites as well as Blacks. George Boutwell himself fell prey to this thinking, saying shortly after the amendment's passage that "my own conviction is that no such qualification will ever be imposed."[23]

Such hopes were dangerously misplaced. Quite quickly, white supremacist governments in the South found creative ways of imposing such obstacles selectively on Black voters. One such was the "grandfather clause," giving exemptions to voters who couldn't pay a poll tax or pass a literary test if they could prove that their grandfathers had voted. With most Blacks having had slaves as grandfathers, they of course didn't qualify. In the North and West, state governments would give the same treatment to their Irish and Chinese citizens. Moreover, many white southern politicians had few qualms about imposing obstacles on poor whites as well as on Blacks. Boutwell and other Republican leaders frankly did not anticipate that "the South's political leaders would not mind—or might even welcome—the fact that significant numbers of poorer whites would lose the right to vote because of such laws."[24]

CONSPICUOUSLY ABSENT IN the Fifteenth Amendment was any mention of female suffrage. For years, advocates for Black civil rights and women's suffrage had sought to make common cause, but with difficulty. Frederick Douglass, despite having supported women's suffrage since the inaugural women's rights convention in Seneca Falls, New York, in 1848, believed that Black political capital had to be spent on Black male suffrage. During the Johnson impeachment trial (which Douglass chose not to attend, fearing that his presence would be racially exploited to torpedo Radical Republican support for Black equality), he attended a women's suffrage meeting in New York City. Tensions between the two movements burst into the open when Douglass, challenged on the issue of women's suffrage, answered that the vote for the Black man must come first.[25]

The main reason for no action on female suffrage, of course, was that even progressive male politicians such as George Boutwell had no interest in supporting it. America at the time was still locked in a social mentality in which husbands were the heads of households and even those few women allowed to get an education were still expected to content themselves with domestic pursuits or teaching. Later, during his years in the Senate, Boutwell voted against female suffrage in the Dakota Territory, despite women having the right to vote in the adjacent Wyoming Territory. Although his daughter Georgianna was a vocal advocate of women's suffrage and was appointed to various state boards in Massachusetts, it was only years later that her father committed himself to extending the vote to women.[26]

FOLLOWING CONGRESSIONAL PASSAGE of the Fifteenth Amendment, ratification by the states was achieved within a year, though not without hiccups. President Grant, in stark contrast to Andrew Johnson's attempts to undermine the Fourteenth Amendment, put his full weight behind ratification, lobbying individual governors on its behalf. Congress enacted new Reconstruction laws in the spring and summer, mandating ratification by those remaining southern states—Virginia, Mississippi, and Texas—which had not yet qualified for House and Senate representation. The same was required of Georgia, which had been readmitted to the Union in 1868 but then was tossed out when its legislature refused to seat Black members. In Ohio and Indiana, the ratification votes were close calls. By February 1870, the required twenty-eight states had approved ratification and on March 30, President Ulysses Grant officially confirmed the Fifteenth Amendment as incorporated into the US Constitution.

Parades and joyous celebrations were held across the country. In New York, more than 7,000 Black military veterans marched from the Bowery to Broadway in front of crowds that included another 15,000 Black citizens. The parade ended and the speeches began at the Cooper Institute, site of Abraham Lincoln's famous speech of February 1860 that helped launch his candidacy for the presidency. In Boston, thousands marched from Boston Common to Faneuil Hall to hear Black speakers such as Charles Lenox Remond proclaim it to be "the proudest day in all his experience." An even larger celebration took place in Baltimore on May 19, despite the Maryland state legislature's having refused to ratify the amendment. A Maryland crowd of twenty thousand listened to their native son Frederick Douglass proclaim it "the day of all days." As the news spread more slowly across the South, Blacks gathered in town squares and village commons to express their joy.[27]

The Fifteenth Amendment seemed to promise a revolution in promoting equality between Blacks and whites. The president used a special message to Congress to praise it as "a measure of grander importance" than any since the founding of the republic. William Lloyd Garrison praised the "transformation of four millions of human beings from . . . the auction-block to the ballot box." Northern states that just a few years before had greatly restricted Black suffrage were now committed to allowing Black men to vote on an equal basis with whites, albeit with obstacles such as poll taxes and literacy tests remaining. For those who believed, like George Boutwell, that the ballot would open the way for greater civil and social equality for Blacks, the Fifteenth Amendment represented a major step on the road to institutionalizing racial democracy.[28]

Black leaders like Frederick Douglass weren't so sure. Although he shared the joy of the New York and Baltimore celebrations, he cautioned that Black voting rights needed to be guaranteed with additional legislation to prevent states and individuals, South and North, from continuing to interfere with suffrage. What Douglass feared was the attitude typified by the *Richmond Dispatch*, which criticized any such enforcement measures as "a monstrous Federal cancer, sending its roots deep into the States." Even with Ulysses Grant in the White House, Douglass knew that the struggle was far from won.[29]

AS FOR GEORGE BOUTWELL, in the weeks prior to the Grant inauguration he had an additional task needing his personal attention. Shortly before Christmas, he had received a letter from Mary Todd Lincoln, postmarked from the Hôtel d'Angleterre in Frankfurt, Germany. "Will you not," Mary wrote pleadingly, "as the true friend of my beloved husband, exert your influence & have Congress give me an appropriation *as soon as* possible of at least $3000 a year—whilst I am in such infirm health . . . I feel that I am writing to a noble man—one whom my idolized husband respected & loved most truly."[30]

The widow of Abraham Lincoln was in Europe with her son, Tad, now fifteen years old, and not doing well. She had received a one-time stipend of $22,000 from Congress in December 1865, but those funds had long since run out. She now "was more painfully conscious of her limited means than ever before" as she and Tad were forced into modest hotels, compelled to take dinner alone in their rooms to escape the constant stare of strangers. Reaching out first to Charles Sumner, who had formed a special bond with Lincoln during the war, she now wrote to Boutwell to ask him to support a House version of the bill for pension relief that Sumner had introduced in the Senate. "Emboldened by distance, spurred by a spark of hope," the unfortunate Mary Lincoln, still disliked by many in Congress for her imperious behavior and overspending while in the White House, was sending pleas for help from across the Atlantic.[31]

On January 14, Boutwell supported the joint resolution seeking a pension of $5,000 a year "in consideration that her husband, Commander-in-Chief of the army and the navy, had been killed in wartime by enemies of the republic, and that his widow was entitled to a pension 'upon the same principles and for the like reasons with any other officer who fell in the war.'" Sadly, in what would be a long, drawn-out affair that reflected little credit on Congress, the initial request was rejected and a pension for Mary was only finally approved in July 1870 at the reduced amount of $3,000 a year.[32]

Mary and Tad returned from Europe in May 1871, with Tad dying two months later of tuberculosis at the age of eighteen, the third Lincoln son to die before reaching the age of twenty. Mary descended into a depression that led to her institutionalization in 1875. She died of a stroke in 1882 at the age of sixty-three.[33]

Boutwell had given Mary's request what help he could while still in Congress, in memory of the president with whom he had worked closely and forged a special bond. He had done so while fully engaged in drafting what would become the Fifteenth Amendment and preparing for the inauguration of a new president who he knew would, if the country yet didn't, fully support political and civil equality for Blacks. What Boutwell himself didn't yet know was that his days in Congress were numbered and he would soon find himself a member of Ulysses Grant's cabinet. In that role, he would forge an even more special relationship with a sitting president than he had had with Abraham Lincoln. It would be the beginning of a political partnership to defend the gains of Reconstruction from northern whites as well as former southern Confederates. It would also be the deepening of a friendship that would extend to both their families and continue for the next several decades.

PART FOUR

ULYSSES GRANT AND AMERICA'S TROUBLED REBIRTH, 1868–1885

Managing America's Economy

The country wasn't quite sure what to make of its eighteenth president when Ulysses Grant took the oath of office on a blustery cold day in March 1869. Known as the "American Sphinx" and "Grant the Silent," the president was uncomfortable with the small talk common among politicians. Most Americans knew Grant as the war hero, the general who brought a battering ram to the Confederacy in stark contrast to the indecisiveness and self-promoting preening of the other Union generals. They had heard the reports about his drinking and failed businesses, but knew little of Grant the individual.

Such was not true of George Boutwell, who had come to know Grant quite well during the tumultuous years of Andrew Johnson's presidency. From questioning the general during congressional hearings to conferring with Grant and Edwin Stanton about President Johnson's attempts to interfere with congressional Reconstruction in the South, Boutwell knew that Grant was committed to equality of rights and opportunity for all Americans, Black and white.

Boutwell also came to appreciate, as those close to Grant already knew, that the general had a sensitive side, despite his gruff exterior, especially where women and family were concerned. Although Grant sought to avoid conflict in personal relationships, and often retired into his "silent" mode in group settings, he could be a relaxed conversationalist "with habitual companions and trusted friends." The problem, Boutwell added, was that Grant "disliked controversy even in conversation," and thus his silence was often mistaken for agreement with what was being said.[1]

Grant's electoral slogan of "let us have peace" had great appeal precisely because different sections of the country could interpret it as they wished. To whites in the North and West, the phrase meant moving on from the bitterness of the Johnson impeachment and getting back to the business of the country. White southerners hoped "peace" meant a withdrawal of federal troops and "bayonets" from their homeland so they could regain political power. And for the Black freedmen, Grant was the general who had dismantled slavery and who now, they hoped, would don Lincoln's mantle and help them achieve equality.

IN HIS MARCH 4 inaugural speech, Ulysses Grant surprised many by forcefully promising support for both Black suffrage and Native American citizenship. In a "soft, almost inaudible voice," Grant spoke to the thousands gathered at the Capitol about the need to deal with the country's troubles "calmly, without prejudice, hate or sectional pride." Grant called for ratification of the Fifteenth Amendment, declaring that the issue of Black voting rights "should be settled now." Boutwell was sitting nearby on the Capitol's east portico, knowing the president's support would be decisive.[2]

Following his well-received address, Grant stumbled politically in putting together his cabinet, thus confirming for many his image as a political neophyte. In the months between election day and the inauguration, Grant had kept his cabinet thoughts to himself, not even sharing them with his wife, Julia. He abhorred office seekers and supplicants and seemed to enjoy keeping everybody guessing; one newspaper described those seeking Grant's favors as "hounds which have lost the trail; they do much smelling and no small yelping, but all to little purpose."[3]

Grant's secretiveness about his cabinet choices only fueled speculation and political gossip about who was in and who was out. Boutwell's name appeared often in the newspapers, variously described as a shoo-in for the Treasury Department, or a shoo-in not for Treasury but perhaps Interior, or off the list altogether. In fact, Boutwell had already declined Grant's offer of the Interior Department, saying his services to the administration would be more valuable if he remained in Congress. Boutwell also took the opportunity at that meeting with Grant to dissuade the president-elect from choosing former Massachusetts governor John Clifford to be attorney general, thinking Clifford too conservative and not supportive of Reconstruction. Boutwell proposed instead Judge Ebenezer Rockwood Hoar of the Massachusetts Supreme Court, whom

Grant selected. In giving this advice, Boutwell knew that he was lessening his own chances of gaining a cabinet position, given the custom at the time of not having two men from the same state serving in the cabinet.[4]

When the president did submit his cabinet choices to the Senate, matters unraveled quickly. For secretary of state, Grant selected his longtime political mentor, Elihu Washburne, but Washburne was in ill health and resigned after eleven days so he could take the job he really wanted, minister to France. Grant then turned to a former New York senator and governor, the patrician lawyer Hamilton Fish, who would serve the president well for eight years.[5]

At the War Department, Grant acquiesced in granting a favor to his long-time army colleague and friend, John Rawlins, who very much wanted to be secretary but was already ill with the tuberculosis that would kill him within six months.

For the all-important position of treasury secretary, Grant picked wealthy New York businessman Alexander T. Stewart. Here again, controversy ensued. Back in November following the election, Stewart had bought Grant's residence on I Street in Washington for twice its value and bestowed it on William Tecumseh Sherman, who was replacing Grant as general-of-the-army. Such favors were not unknown at the time, nor illegal, but it meant that Grant would be starting his presidency with the taint of cronyism.[6]

Stewart certainly had the credentials for the Treasury job and was confirmed by the Senate, even though his low tariff views rankled many Republicans. Yet before he could be sworn in, Charles Sumner discovered a 1789 statute crafted by Alexander Hamilton barring anyone from becoming treasury secretary who had obvious conflicts of interest in "trade or commerce." Owner of the largest luxury department store in the world, Stewart offered to put his business interests in a blind trust, but Sumner and the Senate, wanting to assert congressional prerogatives in the wake of struggles with Andrew Johnson, refused. Anxious to put the embarrassing affair behind him, the president turned to Boutwell for help.[7]

But Boutwell for his part was fully expecting to remain in Congress. With the death of Thaddeus Stevens, he was now chairman of the House Select Committee on Reconstruction and would take the lead in protecting Black civil rights and securing ratification of the Fifteenth Amendment. He might even become Speaker of the House now that the former Speaker, Schuyler Colfax, was Grant's vice president.

Grant, however, now desperately needed Boutwell as his treasury secretary.

In a cabinet of mostly conservative Republicans, Boutwell as a Radical Republican would bring political balance and his congressional connections to Grant's administration. Plus, his protectionist views were more in line with dominant Republican thinking. As the country's first internal revenue commissioner and a former Massachusetts governor, he had clear budgetary and administrative skills. Lauded in the press for his "high and unimpeachable integrity," Boutwell was quickly confirmed by the Senate. He and Hamilton Fish would turn out to be Grant's two best cabinet selections, helping the president recover his political footing in the administration's early months.[8]

Even so, Boutwell accepted the president's offer reluctantly. He had become accustomed, as a member of Congress, to being in Washington for only a few months each year. From late spring through the autumn, he could be with his family in Groton, overseeing his farm and business interests. But with Stewart's resignation, Boutwell broke the news to Sarah that neither had expected, writing to her that "Gen. Grant has become involved in difficulties in consequence of the inability of Mr. Stewart to take the office of Secretary of the Treasury . . . neither Gen. Grant nor his friends see any way out . . . but for me to take the place. . . . I know you will be disappointed as I am myself, but there seems to be no alternative unless I leave Gen. Grant to new difficulties."[9]

AS GRANT'S TREASURY SECRETARY, Boutwell and the president would forge a close working relationship that deepened into lasting friendship. Even before the inauguration, in fact, there had been a telling incident that symbolized how well the two men would work together to advance their common goals.

On February 25, the same day that he submitted his conference committee's version of the Fifteenth Amendment to a House vote, Boutwell introduced a resolution to strip Georgia of its statehood and return it to military rule, given that the Georgia legislature had recently expelled thirty-three of its Black members and that Blacks were being systematically terrorized by local sheriffs and white vigilantes. Georgia's congressmen were furious, complaining to the president-elect that "Boutwell from Massachusetts" was seeking to return Georgia "to a military despotism." Not wanting to begin his presidency in the midst of a political firestorm, Grant went up to Capitol Hill and, meeting privately with Boutwell, asked him to withdraw the measure and carry it over to the next session of Congress.[10]

When Boutwell did so, southern congressmen were delighted, thinking that Boutwell had received his comeuppance and that the new president would bring the Radical Republicans to heel in dealing with the South. Democrats lauded Grant for telling Boutwell "to let the state of Georgia alone," saying that the new president would do his duty, "whether the same is pleasing to congress or not."[11]

The reality was quite different. Grant the tactician was seeking a more favorable field of battle, wanting to wait until he was sworn in as president before showing his hand. Days later in his inaugural address, he proclaimed his support for the Fifteenth Amendment and for protecting the rights of the Freedmen. Soon after, Boutwell's resolution was reintroduced, and Georgia was stripped of its congressional representation and returned to the jurisdiction of the US military. The country now knew what Boutwell knew, that Ulysses Grant would be a staunch ally in promoting Reconstruction reforms in the South.[12]

BOUTWELL WAS CONFIRMED as treasury secretary on March 11, along with fellow cabinet members Hamilton Fish and John Rawlins. He met with the president that night at the White House, resigned his seat in the House the following day, and returned to the Treasury Building where he had worked during the war as Lincoln's revenue commissioner. Now, instead of toiling in a ground floor office, Boutwell could look out over the lawn to the White House from the secretary's expansive suite of offices. Along the broad sweep of Pennsylvania Avenue, the Treasury Building's new north wing was just being completed under the direction of Supervising Architect Alfred B. Mullett.[13]

A week earlier, on March 4, the president's inaugural ball had been held in the Treasury Building. It was a disaster. On a snowy evening, more than 2,000 guests arrived to celebrate in the building's two-story, balconied Cash Room, the eponymous location where citizens could walk in from the street, redeem gold and silver certificates, and transact other government business. Beset by a combination of poor planning, a lack of heat, and construction dust, many guests trying to leave were unable to find their coats and hats to brave the raging blizzard outside. Washington wags would later comment that the ball was but a premonition of Grant administration troubles to come.[14]

At the time, the magnificent Treasury Building, with an interior space equivalent to ten acres, was the largest office building in the world. More than 3,000 Treasury employees passed through its doors every day: accountants, assessors, bureau chiefs, and clerks, many of them women. Boutwell's suite of offices, decorated in marble and with lavish chandeliers, was on the building's west side and just a few minutes' walk to the White House. The new secretary would have known that his bête noire, Andrew Johnson, had used these offices for several weeks after Lincoln's assassination to allow a grieving Mary Todd Lincoln to remain in the White House.[15]

IN 1869, THE AMERICAN economy was well on its way to recovering from the ravages of the Civil War. Manufacturing was expanding from home-based and small businesses to companies and factories with dozens and hundreds of employees. The rise of a national banking system provided the capital necessary for groups of investors to pool their resources to help grow the nation's railroads, oil and coal industries, and manufacturing. Businessmen formed corporations, at little expense and largely unregulated, to maximize their profits and reduce their personal liabilities. As described by Charles Francis Adams Jr., older brother of Henry Adams, the corporation was "a new power, for which our language contains no name. We know what aristocracy, autocracy, democracy are, but we have no word to express government by moneyed corporations."[16]

Having been governor and revenue commissioner, Boutwell was well schooled in issues involving the nation's banking system, its gold and currency reserves, and domestic and foreign credit markets—all essential to fueling the growth of American capitalism. His challenge would be that of managing the country's economy at a time when, as Adams described it, "our great corporations are fast emancipating themselves from the State, or rather subjecting the State to their own control." Government regulation of industry and financial markets was practically unknown, as Boutwell would find out soon enough.

As secretary, Boutwell had broad discretion in running the Treasury Department. Akin to Grant's military decision-making during the war, the president "treated Boutwell as he would have treated a proven army commander like Sherman or Sheridan and gave him abundant latitude." Although this management style proved troublesome when the president was taken advantage of by trusted colleagues and family members, it worked well with Boutwell, who of all his cabinet "stood closest to the business interests of the country." On the other hand, given his farm upbringing and Democratic Party roots, Boutwell was also mindful of working-class and agricultural interests.[17]

Boutwell viewed his Treasury position as a delicate "balance wheel" among competing economic interests. This meant navigating a difficult middle course between "hard" and "soft" money policies, the former being an early return to the redemption in gold of the surplus greenback dollars that helped fund the

George Sewall Boutwell, born January 28, 1818, in Brookline, Massachusetts. (*Groton Historical Society*)

Sarah Adelia (Thayer) Boutwell, born October 16, 1813, in Hancock, New Hampshire. (*Groton Historical Society*)

The Boutwell House on Main Street in Groton, Massachusetts, built 1851, now The Groton History Center. (*Groton Historical Society*)

George Boutwell, youngest-ever governor of Massachusetts, elected 1851. *(Alpha Stock / Alamy Stock Photo)*

Auction poster following the death in 1841 of Henry Woods, co-owner of the dry goods store with George Boutwell. *(Groton Historical Society)*

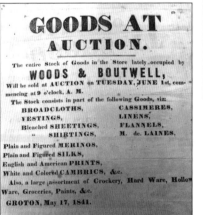

Engraving depicting "Operations of the Fugitive Slave Law" in the 1850s. *(The Miriam and Ira D. Wallach Division of Art, Prints and Photographs: Picture Collection, New York Public Library)*

Abraham Lincoln, sixteenth president of the United States, 1861–1865. *(Library of Congress)*

Cover of *Harper's Weekly* magazine showing the Great War Meeting held on the east portico of the US Capitol Building, August 6, 1862. *(Collection of the US House of Representatives)*

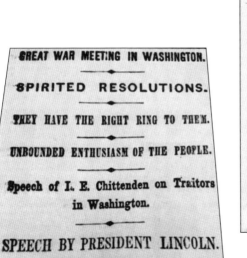

Coverage of the Great War Meeting in the *New York Daily Tribune*, August 7, 1862.

Andrew Johnson, seventeenth president of the United States, 1865–1869. *(Library of Congress)*

Managers of the impeachment of Andrew Johnson in the House of Representatives: (left to right) Benjamin F. Butler, James F. Wilson, Thaddeus Stevens, George S. Boutwell, Thomas Williams, John A. Logan, John A. Bingham. *(National Portrait Gallery, Smithsonian Institution)*

The House impeachment managers in Shakespearean garb, with George Boutwell standing on the left next to a crouching Thaddeus Stevens, with Benjamin Butler as Falstaff and Andrew Johnson on the far right, by Thomas Worth. *(Arts Department, Boston Public Library)*

"SPOONS" AS FALSTAFF—MUSTERING THE IMPEACHMENT MANAGERS.

Ulysses S. Grant, eighteenth president of the United States, 1869–1877. *(Library of Congress)*

Jim Fisk and Jay Gould's attempt to corner the gold market was blocked by President Grant and Treasury Secretary Boutwell on Black Friday, September 24, 1869. *(Currier and Ives, Library of Congress)*

THE "BOY OF THE PERIOD" STIRRING UP THE ANIMALS.

Political cartoon depicting President Grant as Boutwell's puppet in managing the country's finances. *(New York Public Library Digital Collections)*

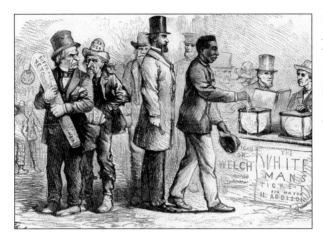

Illustration in *Harper's Weekly*, "The Negro at the Ballot Box," Andrew Johnson is to the left, March 16, 1867. *(Library of Congress)*

William Monroe Trotter organized the Great Emancipation Meeting with George Boutwell as lead speaker in Boston in 1903. *(Alchetron, The Free Social Encyclopedia)*

Frederick Douglass spoke in Boutwell's hometown of Groton, Massachusetts, three times in the early 1840s. *(Onondaga Historical Association)*

New York City.
January 3d 1885.

My Dear Miss Boutwell:

Many thanks for your New Year welcome, just received. There is no family that I have ever known who friendship I prize more highly than that of your father. I wish for him and his family many returns of new years, and that all of them may find him and his in the enjoyment of good health and peace of mind.

Very Truly Yours,
U. S. Grant

Thank-you note from Ulysses S. Grant to Georgianna Boutwell, January 3, 1885. *(Groton Historical Society)*

Funeral procession of U. S. Grant in New York City, August 8, 1885. George Boutwell and John Logan are riding in the second carriage on the right. *(Library of Congress)*

Georgianna Adelia Boutwell, born May 18, 1843. *(Groton Historical Society)*

President McKinley declaring "The flag must stay put" in the Philippines as George Boutwell and other anti-imperialists throw proclamations at his feet, J. S. Pughe, *Puck*, June 4, 1902. *(Library of Congress)*

George S. Boutwell in his eighties. *(Groton Historical Society)*

Last known photograph of George Boutwell, reviewing troops with Henry Cabot Lodge (far left), in Boston, August 16, 1904. *(Groton Historical Society)*

Union war effort, and the latter being the continued circulation of greenbacks so that farmers and small business owners could more easily pay off their debts. Too quick a return to requiring "specie" (gold) payments when redeeming greenbacks would take such paper dollars out of circulation and tighten the money supply, hurting farmers and labor. Yet continued circulation of too many greenbacks would risk inflation and damage both the country's exports and its creditworthiness overseas. Thus, Boutwell pursued a middle course of not resuming greenback redemption in gold too quickly while managing a slow but steady reduction of the government's Civil War debt, all in the service of growing the economy.[18]

To help him manage the sprawling Treasury Department, Boutwell brought in a colleague from Massachusetts, Judge William A. Richardson, to serve as assistant secretary. Richardson took the job reluctantly and was initially overwhelmed by his duties; he wrote of working long hours each day, "with twenty-eight hundred clerks in this building alone, obliged to read, construe, decide and act upon laws which I never before read, surrounded by subordinates whose loyalty is at least suspected." Richardson was referring to the hundreds of holdovers from the Andrew Johnson administration who likely resented Boutwell for having led the impeachment crusade against Johnson. Richardson even took out his frustrations on his boss, seeking to resign several times in the first few months and complaining that he was doing his job "without the least suggestion, direction or instruction from Mr. Boutwell," who likewise was swamped with work. The two soon developed an effective partnership, however, with Richardson managing the sale of US bonds overseas to help reduce the country's Civil War debt.[19]

ONE OF BOUTWELL'S most immediate tasks was bringing greater efficiency and transparency to the complex array of Treasury Department operations needed for managing an increasingly robust American economy. Created in 1789 with Alexander Hamilton as its first secretary, the Treasury Department oversaw the country's fiscal and monetary policies while collecting the diverse range of taxes, duties, and other sources of revenue with which to fund the federal government. Key to these endeavors was the printing and coinage of the nation's money supply through the Bureau of Engraving and Printing (paper currency) and the US Mint (gold and silver coin). Equally important was keeping widespread counterfeit bills out of circulation through the efforts of the US Secret Service, created in 1865 and housed in Treasury until 2003.[20]

Treasury was also home to the US Revenue Marine Service, created in 1790 to oversee oceangoing revenue cutters, lifesaving stations, and lighthouse services, all of which were merged into the modern US Coast Guard in 1915. Treasury had responsibility as well for such issues as public health, illegal narcotics, and management of the budget that only later would be transferred to other agencies and departments. The complexity of Treasury's responsibilities was well illustrated in Boutwell's first Annual Report as secretary in 1869, containing as it did the separate reports of two commissioners (internal revenue and customs), three comptrollers, six auditors, two superintendents (US Coast Survey and Standard Weights and Measures), the director of the Mint, the supervising architect, the lighthouse board, and others. On March 8, George Boutwell had been a member of Congress with no office or staff. Three days later, he was overseeing a federal government department with more than 9,000 employees, an organization that dwarfed all but a few of the nation's largest industrial enterprises.[21]

Meticulous and hardworking, George Boutwell could be opinionated and dismissive of the talents of others, one of his less endearing traits. Finding conditions at the Treasury Department less than ideal when he took over, he blamed them on the "constitutional infirmities" of his two predecessors, Salmon Chase and Hugh McCulloch, both of whom he categorized as "phlegmatic in temperament, lacking in versatility, and lacking in facility for labor and business." In truth, both Chase and McCulloch had performed extremely well under difficult conditions, Chase during the chaos of the Civil War and McCulloch amid the dysfunction between Andrew Johnson and the Republican-controlled Congress.[22]

Still, the Treasury Department in 1869 was beset by inefficiencies, widespread patronage "no shows" on the payrolls, and endemic fraud perpetrated by collectors of customs and internal revenue. This was especially the case with whiskey tax revenue losses of up to $30 million a year. Though Boutwell was successful in stanching this lower-level fraud when he first took office, it would later reappear in the Whiskey Ring conspiracy, one of the major stains on the Grant presidency.

In his first few months, Boutwell began overhauling the department's personnel, replacing up to 30 percent of the country's revenue collectors. Praised as "a pioneer in the advancement of personnel administration who oversaw the first competitive examination of the U.S. civil service" beginning in the early 1870s, Boutwell also emphasized factors such as race and Union army service.

Even his predecessor Hugh McCulloch, an Andrew Johnson ally who differed greatly with Boutwell on monetary policy, was satisfied that, unlike the practice elsewhere in Washington, Boutwell did not engage in the widespread "dismissal [of] those who had the smell of Johnson upon their garments."[23]

To be sure, Boutwell as a committed Republican believed in rewarding party loyalty, but not to the extent of hiring no-shows and incompetents. This didn't stop liberal reformers such as Henry Adams and E. L. Godkin, editor of *The Nation* magazine, from roundly criticizing the administration for adhering to the patronage system that each president implemented upon taking office. Adams, hoping for but denied a plum political job in the Grant administration, took his revenge on Boutwell as the worst offender among Grant's cabinet officers, one who led an "inquisition" that purged the unfaithful at Treasury akin to the "Jacobins of the reign of terror" during the French Revolution. A century later, the civil service historian Ari Hoogenboom would dismiss such criticism as nonsense, writing that "historians relying on such partisan sources as *The Nation* have overlooked Boutwell's reform activities" in trying to portray what was "an enlightened regime" as a "blatant example of the spoils system."[24]

Civil service reform would remain a controversial issue through the eight years of Grant's presidency. Even though the president and Boutwell did much to implement merit-based hiring, it was only in 1883 that Congress finally enacted the Civil Service Reform Act. The political sensitivity of the issue was such that, some fifteen years after having left Treasury, Boutwell in 1888 was front page news when Joseph Pulitzer's *New York World* claimed to have found the equivalent of an "enemies list" compiled by Boutwell in 1869 to sweep the Treasury clean of Democrats, southern sympathizers, and anyone of doubtful loyalty to the Republican Party.[25]

There was one well-deserved case of Republican patronage early in Boutwell's tenure, that of Charles Remond Douglass, the youngest son of Frederick Douglass. About to lose his job at the Freedmen's Bureau because of staff reductions, the young Douglass wrote to Boutwell seeking a clerkship at Treasury. Charles noted that, even with his prominent name, "great prejudice . . . exists against employing colored men in respectable positions." As a veteran of the Fifty-Fourth Massachusetts Regiment, Charles asked Boutwell "to give me a trial." Several weeks later, on April 21, Douglass began work at the Treasury Department, where he remained for several years.[26]

In mentioning the Douglass story, it is worth noting that Blacks were not supporters of civil service reform, an attitude that Boutwell and Grant appreciated. With the handicap of having had little to no education as slaves, few Blacks could hope to pass civil service examinations. A former slave from Mississippi applying to become a lighthouse keeper noted the irony of being told "that all the honors of the nation are open to us, yet you exclude us by [exams] that none of us can pass."[27]

SEEKING GREATER EFFICIENCY, Boutwell also moved to implement common bookkeeping and accounting standards, as he had done previously as revenue commissioner. He focused especially on controls for the printing of paper currency, Treasury securities, and revenue stamps to prevent fraud and counterfeiting. His Annual Report for 1869 detailed new arrangements for the printing of a special paper by the firm of Wilcox & Co. near Philadelphia, with Treasury officials continually on site to oversee the transfer of the paper to where it would be manufactured into banknotes. At each of these three plants, separate engraving plates were made "for every issue of currency or other obligation" under the supervision of Treasury agents, who reported daily by telegram or letter to the department in Washington. In toto, these and other measures helped Boutwell increase public debt repayments from $30 million to $100 million a year without "any additional sources of revenue."[28]

His first report as treasury secretary also highlighted his concern with the "moiety custom" of supplementing the salaries of the department's revenue collectors, appraisers, and examiners with a share of Treasury fines and forfeitures imposed on individuals and businesses. Boutwell hated moieties, believing the practice encouraged corruption by department officials and the use of paid informers to unearth tax cheats, legitimate or not. He convinced Grant to include a call for eliminating such payments in the president's annual message to Congress in December 1869 while also advocating higher salaries for mid- and senior-level department executives as a way of attracting and retaining qualified, and honest, individuals. Most of all, he deplored the practice of the secretary's being given a lump sum to distribute as bonuses, in lieu of appropriate salaries, calling it "an unpleasant duty" and one that "cannot be performed without producing jealousies and discontents among the officers of the department."[29]

GOLD AND GREENBACKS were the major economic issue facing the country in 1869. To help pay for the war, the Lincoln administration had issued hundreds of millions of dollars in new paper currency that was not redeemable in gold. This helped equip the Union army with the troops and weapons it needed to win the war, but it also fueled inflation. As the war ended, too many greenbacks in circulation were chasing too few goods and driving up prices. By the late 1860s, it took three times as many greenbacks to buy the same amount of gold as a few years earlier. For merchants needing to exchange greenbacks into gold to conduct business or sell their goods overseas, the falling value of greenbacks was a substantial penalty.

The question was, how quickly should the vast quantity of excess greenbacks be taken out of circulation? There was broad agreement about the wisdom of returning to the gold standard, where all paper currency including greenbacks would be made redeemable in gold coin. Before that could happen, however, the supply of paper currency had to be substantially reduced through the sale of government bonds (purchased with greenbacks and redeemable in fifteen or twenty years for gold, with interest also paid in gold). Not doing so would risk continuing the wartime inflation that was no longer tolerable.

While in Congress, Boutwell gave an indication of the policies he would implement as secretary. Hugh McCulloch had been a staunch "hard money" advocate who wanted to take the greenbacks out of circulation as quickly as possible. Doing so and returning to the gold standard would benefit eastern banking, mercantile, and export interests by keeping inflation in check and stabilizing the country's balance of payments abroad. But such a policy would hurt the farmers and small businesses who were in debt to these same banking and financial interests by squeezing the money supply and choking off credit.

In April 1866, McCulloch helped engineer passage of the Contraction Act, getting only some of what he wanted. Congress was worried that tight money would exacerbate the economic downturn the country was experiencing following the war, so it restricted McCulloch to taking $10 million in greenbacks out of circulation in the first six-month period, and $4 million per month thereafter. For Boutwell, mindful of how contraction might boost unemployment among laborers and tighten credit for the farmers of central Massachusetts, even this was too much. He described the bill as giving the treasury secretary the "power to make every man from Texas to Maine weep or laugh at his pleasure." Joining forces with Thaddeus Stevens and Senator John Sherman of Ohio, Boutwell helped repeal the act in 1868.[30]

A related issue was how the sale of government bonds to finance the Civil War had ballooned the national debt, from $65 million in 1860 to $2.5 billion by 1869. It was a point of honor and economic orthodoxy that this debt must be retired as soon as possible. Fortunately, Boutwell and the Grant administration were well positioned to deal with the debt. The country in the late 1860s was economically robust, with abundant natural resources, healthy commodity and crop prices, and a westward expansion fueled by the railroads (the golden spike completing the transcontinental railroad was driven into the railbed at Promontory Summit, Utah, on May 10, 1869). Moreover, the debt consisted largely of war bonds purchased by individual northerners, not financial institutions, so its repayment was seen as a patriotic trust that could not be shunned. Also, any prospect of having to assume the Confederate debt had been laid to rest with ratification of the Fourteenth Amendment in 1868.[31]

For these reasons, government debt was as much a political as it was an economic issue, harped on by Liberal Republicans who wanted the country to quickly balance its books and return to the gold standard. Critics, including Adams, Godkin, and Senator Carl Schurz, kept up a steady drumbeat of criticism of Boutwell and the Grant administration for not accepting their "enlightened" hard money economic agenda.[32]

Also, during this first year, Boutwell and Grant were criticized for not acting more quickly to reduce America's tariffs on imported goods and raw materials. Here again a balancing act was necessary, to reduce admittedly high tariffs only gradually so that sufficient revenues on imports could permit a simultaneous reduction of income taxes while protecting the steady growth of American industry. Opponents in Congress tried to force Grant to reappoint a supporter of low tariffs, David A. Wells, a special revenue commissioner and holdover from the Johnson years. But Boutwell would have none of it and Wells was let go. Thus, by the end of the congressional session in June 1870, the president and his treasury secretary had succeeded in reducing tariffs and domestic taxes while refinancing the government's debt at lower levels without jeopardizing economic growth or risking inflation.[33]

A KEY PART of this strategy was implemented a few days after Grant's inauguration when Congress passed the Public Credit Act, by which the government promised, eventually, to repay its bonds and other obligations with gold coin (hard money). In providing this reassurance that the country was committed to the gold standard, the pledge helped stabilize markets and bring down interest rates. It made possible George Boutwell's strategy of retiring high-interest Civil War bonds through the sale of new long-term bonds paying lower interest, but redeemable in gold. Boutwell could thus retire expensive previous debt while offering investors a solid return on their money in the new bond issues, what the *New York Times* called "permanent and profitable investments." This pleased the "hard money" advocates among eastern bankers and large business owners while avoiding a contraction of the money supply (taking too many greenbacks out of circulation) that would injure the interests of farmers and small businessmen by limiting the availability of credit.[34]

As part of this regular, methodical approach to reducing the supply of greenbacks and lowering government debt, Boutwell also established a "sinking fund," allocating 1 percent of all customs duties for future payment of the national debt. In similar fashion, he began selling Treasury gold on a regular, well-publicized basis (compared to McCulloch's sporadic sales), which both soaked up surplus greenbacks and stabilized their price relative to gold. In announcing these sales through the press, Boutwell was trying to minimize the risk of speculators manipulating the price of gold. In approving the practice, the *New York Times* applauded the transparency and regularity of the secretary's policy, but only so long as the government maintained a healthy enough gold reserve so that, "at a critical moment," the secretary could "hold the speculators in check." Boutwell's policies even satisfied critics such as Godkin, who commended the treasury secretary in the pages of *The Nation* magazine for his "intelligible business-like purpose" and for policies "frankly announced in advance and faithfully adhered to."[35]

Boutwell's strategy has been described as that of "growing up to specie," whereby the natural processes of an expanding population, increased economic activity, and more favorable trade balances with Europe would increase the value of paper currency relative to gold, rather than artificially taking it out of circulation too quickly. For Liberal Republicans, who were also criticizing the Grant administration for moving too slowly on issues like civil service reform, Boutwell's policy of measured steps and letting the "country grow into its monetary skin" smacked of inertia and simplemindedness. Indulging in his usual "dripping condescension," Henry Adams criticized Boutwell for trusting "in ledgers and cash books but not Adam Smith or [John Stuart] Mill."[36]

Boutwell's policy received wide support at the time and from future economic historians. Writing to President Grant from Paris, Minister Washburne noted the confidence that the policy inspired in America's European trading partners, adding "how splendidly Boutwell has sustained your policy and wishes . . . his success is my vindication and my excuse for so constantly thrusting him before you." Ninety years later, Irwin Unger in his classic *The Greenback Era* would write that Boutwell's policy of letting the economy dictate the pace of returning to the gold standard made "good sense" and avoided the "remorseless greenback destruction" called for by the reformers.[37]

THE EXPANSION OF Treasury Department operations in the years after the Civil War reflected an America bursting at the seams industrially, economically, and geographically. Alaska had been purchased from Russia in 1867, railroads were pushing west, and settlement in the western Plains was intensifying conflict with Native Americans. The country's population had tripled from 1830 to 1870, reaching 38 million, and would grow to 50 million by 1880. American economic growth in the coming decades would double, and double again, positioning the country for its entry onto the world stage in the twentieth century.

Managing this growth was a Treasury bureaucracy encompassing a wide variety of activities that Boutwell as secretary had to get up to speed on quickly. In doing so, he came to know and work with four remarkable men who helped shape a growing and modernizing America.

First was A. B. Mullett, the brilliant but prickly supervising architect for the government whose buildings include the San Francisco Mint, the St. Louis Customhouse and Post Office, and the State, War, and Navy Building next to the White House. With an ego almost as expansive as the French Second Empire buildings he designed, Mullett irritated many in Washington, especially in Congress. Resigning in 1875 over differences with a new treasury secretary, Benjamin Bristow, Mullett later hired George Boutwell to represent him in a suit against the federal government for unpaid compensation, which ended up in the Supreme Court.[38]

Second was the famed naturalist Henry Wood Elliott, who was hired by Boutwell in the spring of 1870 to help the government manage natural resources in the new territory of Alaska. This included Klondike gold, of course, but in 1869 the richest resource was that of northern fur seals inhabiting the Aleutian Islands, the trade in which amounted to millions of dollars a year. After Congress enacted the first federal program in our nation's history to protect a vulnerable animal species, Boutwell hired Elliott to devise a plan for sustainably harvesting and protecting the seal population so the country could continue to profit from the lucrative fur trade, which soon paid off the $7 million purchase price for all of Alaska.[39]

Third was Sumner Increase Kimball, a thirty-six-year-old native of Maine whom Boutwell appointed in 1871 as the new chief of the Revenue Marine Service, responsible for oceangoing revenue cutters, coastal lifesaving services, and lighthouses. Seeking "a man of character to reform the bureau," with coastal lifesaving stations having atrophied and the cutters having become "little more than the pleasure yachts of public men," Boutwell hired Kimball, promising that he would prevent congressional meddling with Kimball's plans to modernize the service. Kimball stayed for forty-four years until the Revenue Marine Service was folded into the modern US Coast Guard in 1915.[40]

BY FAR THE MOST colorful of Boutwell's associates at Treasury was Hiram Coombs Whitley, director of the US Secret Service. With a checkered past that included business fraud, slave catching in the Kansas Territory, and serving as a spy in New Orleans during the Civil War, Whitley used his connections with Benjamin Butler to wrangle a sixty-day temporary appointment as a special agent with the Internal Revenue bureau, where he was when Boutwell became secretary in 1869.[41]

The main job of the Secret Service at the time was preventing the widespread counterfeiting of banknotes. As revenue commissioner in 1862 when greenbacks were first introduced, Boutwell knew full well the scope of the problem. Bogus currency was easy to print and easy to get into circulation, and those receiving or being paid in counterfeit bills were more likely to pass them on to the next unsuspecting victim than to report them.

On taking office, Boutwell fired Secret Service director William Wood, accused of tolerating kickbacks and extortion by his agents, and replaced him with Whitley, who standardized procedures for dealing with informers, catalogued seized equipment, and greatly improved organizational pride. Whitley would often bring accomplished counterfeiters to Boutwell's office so the secretary could witness the tricks of their trade.[42]

A few months into the job, Whitley convinced Boutwell to relocate the service's headquarters to New York, the hub of counterfeiting activity. Although it made sense for Whitley to be in the nation's counterfeiting capital, being removed from Washington gave the freewheeling Whitley the opportunity to indulge in questionable sting operations, such as the famous Miner case involving William "Boss" Tweed and Tammany Hall, that would get the Grant administration into trouble.[43]

WHITLEY WAS NOTHING if not energetic, expanding the service's operations from counterfeiting, smuggling, and pension fraud to mail robbery, illegal voting practices, and even infiltrating the Ku Klux Klan and other white supremacist groups in the South. When the Department of Justice was created in July 1870 with its offices in the Treasury Building, Whitley would report on Klan and other activities to both Boutwell and Attorney Gen. Amos T. Akerman. By 1871, Whitley and his agents in the South were showing impressive results in disrupting the Klan and other white supremacist groups.[44]

In doing so, Whitley made a special enemy of a Kentucky representative and fiery opponent of Reconstruction, James B. Beck. On the House floor, Beck never lost an opportunity to criticize Whitley and Boutwell, referring to the Secret Service as nothing but "gangs of spies and informers." In February 1873, Beck sought to rein in Whitley by demanding greater oversight of the service's budget of $125,000. It took the intervention of Boutwell as treasury secretary and House Appropriations Committee chair (and future president) James A. Garfield to kill the bill.[45]

As for Whitley, he was never able to shed his penchant for intrigue and double-dealing. In June 1874 he became involved in a local cabal involving the Washington DC Board of Public Works that resulted in a Watergate-style, hilariously botched burglary and a political scandal involving Orville Babcock, President Grant's personal secretary. Whitley was fired and the episode became one of many that would tarnish the Grant administration with the stain of corruption. Boutwell was no longer treasury secretary at this point, having left in March 1873 to become a senator from Massachusetts.[46]

What did survive from Boutwell and Whitley's relationship was the continued use of the Secret Service to break up white terrorist and vigilante groups in the South. Led by Attorney General Akerman and then Benjamin Bristow, who took over as treasury secretary in 1874, Secret Service agents were successful in helping bring about hundreds of successful prosecutions.[47]

Amos Akerman was one of Ulysses Grant's most remarkable cabinet choices, having served in the Confederate army during the war but having become committed to protecting Black civil rights and enforcing the Fourteenth and Fifteenth Amendments. Until Republican Party politics forced his resignation in December 1871, he and Boutwell led the administration's Reconstruction policy. On another front, however, the country first had to survive the financial meltdown of the Gold Panic of September 24, 1869, known as Black Friday.[48]

The General and the Governor

Arising on a beautiful June morning, Ulysses Grant felt he hadn't slept so well in months. He looked out the window of the second-story bedroom of the Boutwell house on Main Street in Groton and could see the train station where he and George had arrived from Boston the night before. A refreshing breeze was ruffling the leaves of the elm and linden trees in the center of town. He might have been reminded of some famous lines from a James Russell Lowell poem, "what is so rare as a day in June? / Then, if ever, come perfect days."[1]

The president and Boutwell, accompanied by sixteen-year-old Ulysses Jr. and Ralph Waldo Emerson, had taken the train out from Boston after a long day of music and speeches at the National Peace Jubilee, a three-day extravaganza commemorating the Union victory in the Civil War. Grant and Emerson sat together, discussing the state of American education until Waldo got off at Concord. The other travelers were peering out through the darkening June night as the train rolled by the "Middlesex villages and farms" made famous by Longfellow in his "The Midnight Ride of Paul Revere." On arriving in Groton, the president's group was met by a throng of local citizens and serenaded by the Groton Cornet Band on their short walk to the Boutwell home.[2]

Grant and Boutwell had traveled up from New York to Boston by steamship and rail several days earlier. After hosting a morning reception for the president at the Massachusetts State House, the two men walked across Boston Common to the specially constructed Boston Coliseum, where they were the guests of honor among a crowd of 35,000 people. The Jubilee program that day included massive choral works by Handel, Mendelssohn, and Haydn. When asked after the performances which of the works he liked best, the president did himself little favor with Henry Adams and other of his intellectual critics when he responded, "the cannons!" In truth, Grant was most likely serious. From an early age, the president enjoyed the literature of Washington Irving and James Fenimore Cooper, but as biographer Ronald C. White has written, "Ulysses had no ear for music," not even "military bands or Methodist hymn sings."[3]

Following a celebratory dinner at the Revere Hotel, the entourage departed for Groton. More than a few "proper" Bostonians were insulted that the president would travel to the boondocks of Groton and sleep "anywhere but under the shadow of the state house [on Beacon Hill]." Grant had two good reasons for doing so. One was accepting the hospitality of his treasury secretary. The other was to travel through Middlesex County and "pay honor to the region which, on the opening of the rebellion, sent the first soldiers to defend the capital of the nation." These were the men of the "Old Sixth" Massachusetts regiment, many from Groton, Acton, and surrounding towns, five of whom died in the Baltimore riots of April 19, 1861. Eight decades earlier on that April morn, colonial Minutemen of Middlesex County had been the first to fall at Lexington and Concord.

The next morning, after showing Ulysses his farm and cattle, Boutwell hosted a reception at the house, where over 3,000 citizens came through to shake the president's hand. In the early afternoon, Boutwell and Grant were hosted at a reception in nearby Worcester prior to the president traveling on to New York and Boutwell returning to Groton. As Boutwell and Grant went their separate ways, the General (as many continued to call Grant) and the governor little knew of the financial plot being hatched—literally under their noses—that would rock Wall Street and the country in a few short months.[4]

IN THE LATE 1860s, Jay Gould and "Diamond Jim" Fisk were the Butch Cassidy and Sundance Kid of Wall Street finance. Having wrested control of the Erie Railroad from rival Cornelius Vanderbilt, they joined forces with "Boss" Tweed of Tammany Hall to influence legislation, control judges, and seek to monopolize whatever economic activity they could lay their hands on.[5]

The story of "Black Friday" has been told many times, but the essence is this: In early 1869, Jay Gould devised a scheme to drive up the price of gold on Wall Street, corner the market, and make a fortune selling it before anyone was the wiser. September would be the prime month for doing so, as heightened economic activity during the autumn harvest season would tighten credit and lead to a shortage of gold coin (specie) that was needed to buy and transport grain and foodstuffs to the east coast and Europe.[6]

That spring, Gould tested his plan by buying moderate amounts of gold at the Gold Room on Wall Street next to the New York Stock Exchange. Satisfied that his scheme would work, he later boasted that "a man with $100,000 of money and with credit can transact a business of $20,000,000." The only major flaw in his plan was the regular and well publicized sale of Treasury gold by Secretary Boutwell. With government gold reserves on the order of $100 million, Boutwell could release enough into the market at any time to stabilize prices. If only Gould could find a way to get the treasury secretary to suspend such sales, at least for a month or two. To succeed, he would have to convince the president that a higher price for gold in the autumn benefited everyone: farmers seeking to sell their crops, middlemen arranging sales to Europe, railroads transporting the grain (including, of course, his own, the Erie), and the administration politically. Calling it his "crop theory," he set to work.[7]

Working with Jim Fisk, a larger-than-life New Yorker with a penchant for opera houses and showgirls (Fisk would be shot to death in 1872 in a love triangle), Gould reached out to Abel Rathbone Corbin, who at age sixty-one had recently married Grant's thirty-seven-year-old sister, Jennie. Convincing Corbin that their "crop theory" would work, Gould and Fisk enticed the president's brother-in-law to join them with a gold account worth $1.5 million.

The president often stayed with Corbin and Jennie in New York, as he did that June on the way up to Boston for the National Peace Jubilee. Leaving New York, Grant and Boutwell traveled on the Fisk-owned steamship the SS *Providence*. They had dinner with Fisk and Gould, listening to the latter's theory of how higher prices for gold would benefit farmers, the railroads, the American economy, and by extension, the Grant administration itself. The president said little, and it is unlikely that Gould and Fisk thought they were making much headway. Nonetheless, on returning to New York the pair pushed ahead with plans to get Boutwell to suspend his regular sales of Treasury gold. To help, they brought into their scheme Daniel Butterfield, a Civil War colleague of Grant's who had just taken over as assistant US treasurer in New York.[8]

THAT SUMMER, Gould and Fisk began buying up steady amounts of gold, pushing the price above $140. They spread the word that the Grant administration favored a rising price for gold and would delay Treasury sales by planting a story to that effect in the *New York Times*. Then, Jay Gould brazenly sent a letter to Secretary Boutwell himself, asking if the general contours of the *Times* article "correctly reflects your financial policy during the next three or four months." Boutwell was noncommittal in his reply, but now his guard was up.[9]

In September, Grant appeared to have swallowed the "crop theory" when he told Boutwell that it would be "undesirable to force down the price of gold," while leaving the final decision to his treasury secretary. In fact, the president was only making an economically sound decision to neither force down nor push up the price of gold but let market forces determine its price to avoid disrupting the movement of crops to market. Accordingly, Boutwell decided not to increase the amount of Treasury gold to be sold in September but to continue with the previously announced sales. Gould, however, took this as affirmation that the administration was playing along by letting gold rise.

Soon after, while vacationing in western Pennsylvania, Grant became suspicious that his brother-in-law was scheming with Gould and Fisk and jeopardizing both his administration and his sister's reputation. Meanwhile, Boutwell was in Washington and similarly smelling a rat, particularly Jay Gould's Tenth National Bank, which was certifying checks for gold brokers worth more than what was due them.[10]

Gold prices kept rising that month as Gould and Fisk kept buying, often through third parties. At one point Gould, becoming nervous that Boutwell's Treasury sales would continue, began anonymously selling some of his gold to cut his losses, not telling Jim Fisk, who continued buying. All hell was breaking loose in the Gold Room as speculators, whose contracts Gould held, and short sellers (those who bet on gold falling) faced devastation. One witness to it all was a young Thomas Alva Edison, working the stock tickers in the balcony above the Gold Room, who described scenes of "sober-suited men behaving like a pack of howling coyotes."[11]

As the frenzy mounted on Thursday, September 23, Boutwell dispatched Treasury accountants to New York to examine the books of the undercapitalized Tenth National Bank, and then shut it down. On Friday morning at around 10:30, Boutwell hurried over to the White House to meet with the president, just back from Pennsylvania. The price of gold in New York was now $145 but within hours had reached $160. As noted by the congressional committee that investigated Black Friday, gold prices fluctuated so wildly that telegraph operators could barely keep pace with the news: "[B]usinessmen everywhere, from Boston to San Francisco, read disaster in every bulletin."[12]

As for the president, Grant was furious over the duplicity of his brother-in-law and agreed that Treasury gold sales must resume. Boutwell proposed $3 million, the president countered with $5 million, and they settled on $4 million. At 11:32 a.m., Boutwell sent a telegraph to New York announcing that a Treasury order for the sale of $4 million in gold would be executed the next day. That was enough to break the fever. Prices quickly dropped back into the $130s, but serious damage had been done. Lack of investor confidence had spread to the stock market, where shares dropped some 20 percent. Sadly, the farmers who were supposed to benefit from Jay Gould's "crop theory" saw the value of their corn and wheat shipments drop by as much as 50 percent given the disruption in the amount of gold available to get their products to market.

While Jay Gould and Jim Fisk broke no laws in manipulating the price of gold, their bribes of government officials and the drawing of funds from the undercapitalized Tenth National Bank were another matter. According to a later congressional investigation, Gould and Fisk had converted the bank "into a manufactory of certified checks to be used as cash at their pleasure." But neither of them ever served a day in jail thanks to the political protection provided by Boss Tweed and his Tammany Hall circle of sympathetic judges and lawyers. And neither suffered much in the way of financial loss. Gould's selling of gold at the end of the panic limited his losses, and Fisk was able to hide behind corrupt judges in voiding his contracts with other speculators. As for the two other main actors, Daniel Butterfield was forced to resign his assistant treasurer position in October while Abel Corbin never again enjoyed the full confidence of the president.[13]

The Black Friday gold panic caused widespread economic pain throughout the country. Opponents ripped the president and his treasury secretary for not acting sooner. The complicity of Butterfield and Corbin led to charges of cronyism against the president that would dog his administration for the next eight years. In fairness to Grant and Boutwell, the ethos of the time was decidedly anti-regulation. Boutwell correctly described his role as secretary as being "in no part . . . to regulate affairs in Wall State [and to refrain from] forcing up or forcing down the price of gold." In its report, Congress concluded that the gold conspiracy was a product of the failings of the country's "present financial machinery" where two currencies were in circulation, stimulating speculation in fluctuating rates between them, thus making "the national government a dealer in gold" and giving the treasury secretary in particular "most delicate and difficult duties."[14]

In the weeks leading up to Black Friday, Boutwell had been besieged with letters and telegrams imploring him to act, many from short sellers who would be ruined unless gold prices were driven down. The depth of the pain was most graphically expressed in a handwritten note he received two weeks after the affair. Written in red ink, the message was stark: "If gold does not sell at 150 within 15 days, I am a ruined man. You will be the cause of my ruin! Your life will be in Danger. (signed) Wilkes Booth." Attempts by New York police and the Secret Service to identify the author of the note were unsuccessful.[15]

CRONYISM IN THE Grant administration also appeared in the person of Gen. Alfred Pleasonton, a Civil War cavalry hero appointed by the president to Boutwell's old job, commissioner of internal revenue. Boutwell was doubtful from the start both of Pleasonton's capabilities for the job and his ties to big business. Learning that Pleasonton was involved with Washington's premier lobbyist, Samuel Ward, in seeking an illegal refund of a $60,000 cotton tax, Boutwell demanded and ultimately prevailed in having the president fire him.[16]

Then there was Julia Grant's brother, "Judge" Lewis Dent, promoted by conservative Republicans in Mississippi for that state's gubernatorial nomination. Boutwell vigorously opposed the nomination in cabinet discussions, saying the Dents in Missouri had been slave owners prior to the war and were not fully reconciled to the new social order. When Dent showed up at Boutwell's office in the Treasury Building to plead his case, the secretary brusquely dismissed him, telling the "Judge" to go "mind his own business."[17]

Boutwell was never hesitant about speaking his mind to the president, or to railroad barons such as Thomas Scott, president of the Union Pacific Railroad, whose chief lobbyist in Washington called Boutwell "cross and malignant" for "threatening Scott's interests." Partisan critics such as James Gordon Bennett of the *New York Herald* branded Boutwell a "negative, feeble man, without ideas or generous vision, who sits upon the neck of the President like the Old Man of the Sea." But the president often said, as he did in a letter to House Speaker Schuyler Colfax, that "there is no man in or out of the Cabinet who has more fully my confidence." In lighter moments, Grant would tell friends that his treasury secretary was so strict about keeping government bond sales secret that the president himself, had he known about one such sale, would have made a nice profit.[18]

AS BOUTWELL'S FRIENDSHIP with the president deepened, so did the relationship between their two families. Georgie Boutwell, now in her twenties and a frequent social companion for her father, was not at all shy about becoming better acquainted with the general. Even before Grant became president, Georgie had a delightful encounter in the spring of 1867 with the man she and many others called "the Sphinx." Two young lady friends of hers were visiting from Boston and were dying to meet the hero of the Civil War. On "an unusually stormy day," the three of them paid a call on the general at his office at the War Department. Grant was not in, so they waited. Upon his return, Georgie remembers that the general, "evidently unaccustomed to being called upon by young ladies . . . felt it incumbent to be as entertaining as possible." He regaled them with war stories. Georgie and her friends "were delighted with our visit" and went away with a new appreciation of a man who "was a ready and interesting talker with the right people."[19]

Another story that endeared Georgie to the president involved Julia Dent Grant, whom Georgie and her mother often accompanied at the First Lady's official White House functions. Georgie and Julia were out riding in a four-horse carriage when they passed the president and New York senator Roscoe Conkling driving a modest, one-horse buggy. Back at the White House, Julia, whose eyesight was poor, apologized to her husband for not having recognized him driving through the park. Ulysses said, that was all right, there were many people in Washington who failed to recognize those, like him, "who only drove one horse."[20]

Given the pecking order in Washington, feeling comfortable among the nation's political elite was not always easy for George Boutwell's wife Sarah, who was less outgoing than her daughter. Despite the growing friendship between the two families, Julia Dent Grant was still the First Lady, and was wont to remind everyone of that. Following a luncheon in January 1872 for "the ladies of the Cabinet," Julia Grant would recycle a story of Sarah's embarrassment on discovering that the other ladies present had noticed how Sarah's skirt "had felt the deadly pressure of an iron."[21]

In addition to regular dinners at the homes of Salmon Chase and Hamilton Fish, one of Boutwell's frequent companions was William Tecumseh Sherman, now general-of-the-army. Sherman and Boutwell were an odd pairing, the hard-charging, blunt spoken general and the close-to-the-vest New

Englander. They also differed politically, with Sherman growing increasingly critical of congressional Reconstruction that relied upon the US Army to protect Black political rights. What brought them together, George remembers, was "a like love for the game of billiards." Boutwell enjoyed Sherman for his "genial nature and vivacity of spirit," while daughter Georgie found Sherman "always interesting. He was approachable, a great talker and the kindest of men to his family and friends."[22]

DURING HIS FIRST YEAR at Treasury, Boutwell worked closely with William Tecumseh's brother, Senator John Sherman of Ohio, chairman of the Senate Finance Committee. Following enactment of the Public Credit Act in March 1869, which committed the nation to an eventual return to the gold standard, Boutwell and John Sherman helped ensure congressional passage of the Currency Act of 1870 that both stabilized the currency and provided for a modest increase of $45 million in banknotes to meet the needs of midwestern farmers. This was paired with the Funding Act of 1870, which retired higher-interest, short-term bonds with longer-term bonds with a lower rate of interest but that were guaranteed to be paid in gold. Along with these steps, Boutwell continued his sales of Treasury gold for greenbacks that were then used to slowly retire the country's Civil War debt.

Together, these measures greatly enhanced America's credit with its trading partners abroad, an essential part of George Boutwell's strategy for sustaining the country's postwar economic expansion. Applauding Boutwell's efforts, Elihu Washburne wrote to the president from Paris that "Europe is more and more amazed at the achievements of your administration in reducing the debt." Domestically, approval for Boutwell's economic policy helped offset criticism of Grant administration corruption, at least temporarily.[23]

IN DUE COURSE, though, the scent of political corruption caught the noses of Liberal Republicans such as Senator Carl Schurz and East Coast intellectuals such as Henry Adams. The two biggest scandals were those of Crédit Mobilier and the Whiskey Ring. Both would become defining signatures of Grant's presidency for years to come, even though both had been gestating well before Grant moved into the White House.

The fraudulent Crédit Mobilier construction and finance company was created by Union Pacific railroad executives to inflate profits in building the transcontinental railroad. Like many of the railroads multiplying across the country, the Union Pacific was a shining example of how to make money, "not by running railroads but by gathering subsidies, insider construction contracts, and financial manipulation." At the heart of the Union Pacific scheme was Massachusetts congressman Oakes Ames, also a company director, who liberally distributed shares of company stock to House and Senate colleagues in exchange for their support of relevant Union Pacific legislation.[24]

When the New York *Sun* broke news of the scandal in September 1872, Boutwell was one of many prominent names exposed for all to see. Others accused included Vice President Schuyler Colfax, House Speaker James Blaine, future president and Ohio representative James A. Garfield, and Senators Henry Wilson and Roscoe Conkling. Over the next several months, the Crédit Mobilier saga played out as Congress tried to untangle truth from hearsay, legitimate gifts from bribes, and honest from perjured testimony. Anti-Grant newspapers such as the *New York World* had a field day, trumpeting headlines such as "Is Boutwell a Bribe Taker?," openly questioning whether the treasury secretary could be trusted as the fiduciary steward of the nation's resources.[25]

Soon after that year's election, the congressional committee investigating the scandal cleared George Boutwell of any involvement. Oakes Ames admitted he had approached Boutwell, offering to "carry" the stock for him so Boutwell could collect dividends prior to having to buy the stock himself. But Boutwell adamantly refused, telling Ames he wasn't interested in having anyone "carry stock for me that I don't pay for."[26]

Numerous congressmen were implicated in the Crédit Mobilier scandal, but only Oakes Ames and one other congressman were censured by the House. These mere slaps on the wrist outraged the public as much as the corruption itself. To this day, Crédit Mobilier continues to be a watchword for Gilded Age corruption, though the scandal involved Congress and not Grant's administration.

The same cannot be said of the Whiskey Ring conspiracy, for which Ulysses Grant would be justly criticized. As for Boutwell, his sins would be more of omission than commission.

COLLUSION BETWEEN WHISKEY distillers and revenue agents to defraud the government has a long and colorful history in America. After the Civil War, with the accelerated westward push of railroads and settlers, it became more and more difficult to police the production of liquor and the proper payment of whiskey excise taxes. Such criminal activity certainly existed during the Andrew Johnson presidency and continued when Grant became president in March 1869.

By 1870, the "Whiskey Ring" in St. Louis, with counterparts in Chicago, Milwaukee, Louisville, and other Midwest cities, was a multilayered affair, involving distillers, gaugers, storekeepers, revenue agents, and US Treasury clerks. By clandestinely producing whiskey at night and not reporting the production figures, distillers could sell their alcohol at below cost, make a profit, and then split the seventy-cents-a-gallon tax they withheld with distributers, storekeepers, and revenue agents.

In 1871, this illegal activity took on a distinctly political hue when Republican Party operatives in Missouri and other western states began to divert whiskey excise taxes into political slush funds and to finance partisan newspapers in advance of Grant's reelection campaign in 1872.[27]

The political situation in St. Louis was especially sensitive given that Missouri senator Carl Schurz, attacking Grant's seeming lack of support for civil service reform, was leading a faction that hoped to deny Grant the party's 1872 presidential nomination. To shore up his political support in Missouri, the president was persuaded to appoint a Civil War general, John McDonald, as supervisor of internal revenue in St. Louis. McDonald, who ultimately would be sentenced to three years in prison, helped siphon off more than a million dollars a year in government tax revenues as the Whiskey Ring transitioned from a political slush fund to an overtly criminal enterprise in 1873 and beyond. Not until 1875 was decisive action taken to dismantle the Whiskey Ring amid allegations that President Grant's private secretary, Col. Orville Babcock, had directed the conspiracy from within the White House. Refusing to believe strong evidence of Babcock's complicity, Grant took the unusual step of providing an oral deposition that likely helped Babcock escape a conviction and jail sentence. Although the president probably had no direct knowledge of McDonald's activities, the Whiskey Ring scandal would taint his administration for decades to come.[28]

As for George Boutwell, did he know anything of the cabal, and if so, when did he know it? While never accused of any involvement with the Whiskey Ring, it is odd that such a hands-on administrator would have had no inkling of whiskey tax revenues being siphoned off. Boutwell makes no mention of the Whiskey Ring in his memoirs, despite devoting more than 130 pages to his tenure as treasury secretary and the Grant presidency. True, the scandal broke in 1875, two years after Boutwell left Treasury, but when it did it was front page news, resulting in 238 indictments and 110 convictions.[29]

A MAJOR POLITICAL HEADACHE for Grant from the beginning of his administration, with Boutwell caught in the middle, was the president's contemptuous relationship with Senator Charles Sumner. With the incoming president considered a political novice, Sumner took it for granted that Grant would defer to "the father of the Senate" on major policy issues. As chair of the Senate Foreign Relations Committee, for example, Sumner quickly sought to control negotiations with the British regarding restitution for the UK having provided sanctuaries and support for the CSS *Alabama* and other Confederate commerce raiders during the Civil War. Initially, Grant tried to conciliate the vainglorious Sumner, appointing a close Sumner friend, John Lothrop Motley, to be the new US minister to the Court of St. James's. This was the same Motley whom Boutwell had hoisted on "his own dunghill" during the education funding debate in the Massachusetts legislature in the 1840s.[30]

Whatever truce Grant hoped to effect by appointing Motley didn't last long. Boutwell, closer to the two men than perhaps anyone else in Washington, acknowledged how Sumner never believed "in General Grant's fitness for the office of President," while Grant never considered Sumner to be "a wise and safe leader in the business of government."[31]

Boutwell and Sumner, with a relationship dating to the 1850 coalition in Massachusetts that elected Boutwell governor and sent Sumner to the Senate, were, in the words of Sumner biographer David Donald, "in habits of daily and most friendly intercourse." Boutwell, writing that Sumner never "acquired the church-going habit" while his own was "spasmodic rather than systematic," remembered paying Sunday visits to Sumner's home near Lafayette Square. During their long relationship, the only implacable issue that arose between them was Ulysses Grant.[32]

The prime example of this arose from the president's desire to acquire the Caribbean territory known as Santo Domingo (the present-day Dominican Republic), adjacent to Haiti on the island of Hispaniola. Increasingly in 1869, Grant became convinced that acquiring Santo Domingo would provide economic and trade benefits as well as a strategic naval outpost to counter English and Spanish influence in the region. Grant also sincerely believed that abolishing slavery there and demonstrating the superiority of free labor would both hasten the demise of slavery in nearby Cuba and provide economic leverage and perhaps a voluntary refuge for America's Black citizens. By the autumn of 1869, the president was eager to sign a draft treaty and consummate the deal. From his perch on Capitol Hill, Charles Sumner made it very clear that any such treaty would have to go through him.[33]

In the hope of enlisting Sumner's support for the treaty, Grant took a famous evening stroll from the White House across Lafayette Park to visit Sumner at his home on Vermont Avenue, believing that a show of presidential deference might smooth relations between the two. It was New Year's weekend and Boutwell had just arrived to call on Sumner, who was already dining with two journalists. Then the president arrived. Grant made a pitch for the treaty, adding that he would have the relevant papers brought to Sumner the next morning. Sumner said he would examine them, adding that, according to Boutwell, "I expect, Mr. President, to support the measures of your administration."[34]

The president returned to the White House believing he had Sumner's support; Boutwell would later say that Grant "most naturally" believed "that Mr. Sumner was with him." For his part, Sumner claimed he had only been talking in general terms. In the coming weeks, Sumner and the Foreign Relations Committee bottled up the treaty before voting to oppose it. The president, feeling betrayed, soldiered on in what ultimately was a lost cause, even appointing a Santo Domingo commission with Frederick Douglass as its secretary to report back on the pros and cons of US annexation.[35]

AS THE SANTO DOMINGO treaty was going down to defeat in the summer of 1870, Grant became even more furious with Sumner over the ongoing *Alabama* claims negotiations. In London, Minister Motley was exceeding his instructions, pushing Sumner's hard line with the British rather than the more conciliatory posture favored by Grant and Hamilton Fish. In addition to Motley's insubordination, Grant had never taken to Sumner's protégé, commenting snidely that "the fact that the minister wore a monocle and parted his hair in the middle was simply outward evidence that he was unmanly and not wholly American." Just days after the Senate killed the Santo Domingo treaty, Grant made it known he'd be firing Motley.[36]

Sumner was personally insulted by Motley's recall. Fully believing that "the policies of the Republican administration were determined on his side of Lafayette Square, not on Grant's," the senator's ego was sorely bruised. Caught in the middle and not wanting to lose Sumner's friendship, Boutwell felt compelled to issue an ultimatum. At Sumner's house one day, Boutwell quietly but firmly declared, "Senator, if you ever mention General Grant's name in my presence, I will never again cross your threshold." Sumner promptly replied, "Agreed." Boutwell remembers that "there the matter ended, and the promise was kept."[37]

But Sumner continued publicly attacking the president. Grant and Fish, worried that Sumner might block ratification of any prospective *Alabama* claims agreement with Britain, sought ways to reduce his influence. One option was to get him out of Washington by appointing him as minister to the Court of St. James's in place of the departing Motley. When asked what he thought of the idea, Boutwell had the good sense to say no, "the President should not put himself in Sumner's power by making the offer [only] to be refused and have it thrown up at him." Eventually, even Republican senators realized how damaging Sumner was to party unity and helped engineer his ouster as chair of the Foreign Relations Committee in the spring of 1871.[38]

The Grant-Sumner feud marked a "turning point in Grant's administration and in Sumner's career as well." A split was weakening the Republican Party that could prove disastrous ahead of the 1872 presidential election. Newspapers trumpeted administration corruption as Liberal Republicans threatened to desert Grant and support Horace Greeley as the party's presidential nominee. Northern fatigue with Reconstruction, and the failure to curb continued violence against Blacks in the South, were undermining Grant's 1868 promise to "let us have peace." Incensed by continued KKK night-riding, however, the president would soon have one of his finest hours, with Boutwell at his side, in meeting this threat to American democracy.[39]

13

A Most Trusted Cabinet Member

I t was sunny and mild as George Boutwell took his usual brisk walk from his Twelfth Street residence to the Treasury Building six blocks away. The azalea bushes were beginning to bloom as he strode past historic St. John's Church on Lafayette Square, across from the White House. St. John's, an elegantly understated, yellow-hued house of worship built in 1815, already known as "the Church of the Presidents," was being readied for the premier event of the social season. Nettie Chase, youngest daughter of Supreme Court Justice Salmon Chase, would be wed that afternoon in March 1871 to William Hoyt, member of one of New York's wealthiest families.[1]

Boutwell's daughter Georgianna would be at St. John's for the service; her father would join her afterward for the lavish reception being held at the mansion of Kate Chase Sprague, Nettie's older sister and the acknowledged "belle" of Washington, married to Senator William Sprague of Rhode Island. Boutwell looked forward to congratulating the father of the bride, a man whose presidential ambitions he distrusted, but whose commitment to country he never doubted.

Before he could enjoy the afternoon reception, the secretary faced a full morning of office work. Little did he know that, in a few hours, he would be making an unplanned trip to Capitol Hill with the president, the consequences of which have reached into the twenty-first century.

BOUTWELL ARRIVED AT the secretary's suite of offices, wished his staff a good morning, and settled down to work. From his desk, he enjoyed looking across the shady expanse of lawn to the Executive Mansion with its porticoed entry and semicircular drive.

While thumbing through his papers, Boutwell looked up when an aide announced that a note had just arrived from Orville Babcock, the president's chief of staff. Boutwell was not a particular fan of Babcock, believing the presidential aide often skirted the edge of propriety in carrying out his duties. Such thoughts were pushed aside when he read the note, whose importance he well understood: "The President desires me to say that he will visit the Capitol today at twelve o'clock and will be pleased to have you call here and ride up with him in his carriage."[2]

At the time, Congress was debating whether and how to strengthen federal enforcement of the Fourteenth Amendment guaranteeing civil and political rights for the four million Black freedmen in the South. White supremacist violence terrorizing Blacks and their white supporters was again on the rise across the region. Just the day before, Boutwell had met in his office with a revenue tax assessor who had to flee Mississippi after being whipped by members of the Ku Klux Klan, which was operating so blatantly that it published open letters in local newspapers bragging of its campaign of terror and intimidation.[3]

From modest origins in Tennessee in 1866, the KKK (derived from the Greek *kuklos*, meaning "circle" or "band") had been transformed by former Confederate general Nathan Bedford Forrest into a paramilitary organization that brought terror to Black homes, schools, and churches from the Carolinas to Texas. In the 1870 midterm elections, voter suppression by the Klan and other white paramilitary groups had resulted in substantial gains by Democrats, especially in the House but also in the Senate.[4]

Boutwell knew that the president was determined to respond, forcefully. Congress's First Enforcement Act in May 1870 gave Grant the authority to deploy the US Army to block the Klan, but more stringent measures were needed. In February 1871 a Second Enforcement Act became law, allowing for federal regulation of state elections, but that wasn't enough. The president urged Congress to convene again in March and not wait for its next regular session in December. When it did, the Senate passed a bill for a Third Enforcement Act that allowed for suspending the writ of habeas corpus if needed to stem the violence, but the bill got bogged down, stymied by moderate Republicans joining Democrats in decrying what they considered "military despotism" on the part of the president.[5]

This was the situation when Boutwell hurried over to the White House in response to the president's call. The two men spoke briefly in Grant's office, and then climbed into the presidential carriage for the twenty-minute ride up Pennsylvania Avenue, newly paved with wooden blocks, to the Capitol. The carriage had no sooner left the White House grounds than Boutwell became worried. Despite his faith in the president's conviction, Boutwell sensed that Grant was wavering. Nationally, public support for Reconstruction protections was weakening. Carl Schurz, a vocal critic of the enforcement acts, was scheming on how to deny Grant the 1872 Republican presidential nomination. Boutwell listened intently as Grant expressed concern that "the public mind is already disturbed by the charge that I am exercising despotic powers in the South."[6]

On reaching the Capitol, Boutwell implored the president to stay the course as a vigorous discussion ensued with a group including Attorney General Akerman and Congressman Benjamin Butler, Boutwell's successor as chair of the House Reconstruction Committee and initial author of the House enforcement legislation. Finally, Boutwell noted with relief, Grant stood firm. The president composed his message on the spot, declaring that further legislation was needed to "secure life, liberty and property, and the enforcement of law, in all parts of the United States." It was delivered to the Senate floor during an already contentious debate over a separate resolution describing violence in Kentucky arising from "bands of lawless and desperate men, mainly composed of soldiers of the late rebel armies."[7]

The president was not exaggerating when he described the desperate "condition of affairs" throughout the South. In early March, a white vigilante mob had gone on a rampage in and around Meridian, Mississippi, chasing down and killing thirty Black men following a shooting at the local court house. The outburst of violence was so effective in terrorizing Blacks and forcing white Republicans to flee the area that the "Meridian riot" became a template for how Democrats would reestablish white supremacist control in towns and municipalities throughout Mississippi. In South Carolina, the Republican governor was urging the president to issue a proclamation ordering all "combinations of armed men" organized by the Klan and other paramilitary groups to disperse within twenty days.[8]

Congress acted swiftly following Grant and Boutwell's visit to Capitol Hill. Known as the "Ku Klux Klan Act," the House version was introduced in late March, returned with amendments from the Senate in mid-April, and agreed to by the full Congress and signed by President Grant on April 20. Seeking to provide real teeth to enforcing the Fourteenth Amendment, the KKK Act permitted federal prosecution of individuals who engaged in conspiracies to "deprive citizens of the right to vote, hold office, serve on juries, and enjoy the equal protection of the laws." It also criminalized the use of "force, intimidation, or threat" against government officials and officeholders who sought to carry out the duties of their office, especially in the holding of elections. Its most far-reaching provision, and the one most worrisome for those who criticized this "crowning act of centralization," was the law enabling the president to deploy US soldiers to restore civil order and to suspend the writ of habeas corpus.[9]

Critics maintained that giving Grant the authority to order the detention of citizens without having to provide arrest warrants or proof of suspected crimes struck at the heart of America's constitutional freedoms. Suspending habeas corpus had been controversial enough when invoked by President Lincoln for a brief period during the Civil War, but Grant was seeking this authority in peacetime, unleashing a storm of protest across the country, not only in the South. Despite its being a temporary measure, valid only through the end of the next session of Congress, the KKK Act was derided as little more than a "military despotism bill," with *The Cincinnati Enquirer* pronouncing that "no country without the writ of *habeas corpus* is worthy . . . of being called free."[10]

In sum, the KKK Act was seen by states' rights proponents as giving far too much power to the federal government. It was bad enough that the initial Reconstruction protections for Blacks sought to prevent *state governments* from passing laws and regulations denying essential freedoms. Now, the federal government was seeking to usurp state power in seeking jurisdiction when *private citizens* were accused of using violence and intimidation to deny such freedoms. Democrats and Liberal Republicans alike blasted the Act as heavy-handed and unconstitutional. Yet for Radical Republicans like Boutwell and Black leaders such as Frederick Douglass, the equation was simple: "[T]he law on the side of freedom is of great advantage only where there is power to make that law respected." If state and local governments in the South wouldn't prosecute individuals for violating the law, the federal government would do so.[11]

Following their successful intervention with Congress, Grant and Boutwell rode back down Pennsylvania Avenue to join the elite of Washington society at the Chase family wedding reception. Arriving at the ornate Sprague mansion at Sixth and E Streets, they could hear the strains of the Marine Band

serenading Chase's Supreme Court colleagues, members of Congress, and foreign diplomats as the bride and groom prepared to depart for New York on
their honeymoon.[12]

IN THE SHORT TERM, the KKK Act was successful in giving the federal government the tools it needed to launch a legal counterattack against the Klan and
other white supremacist groups in the South. Led by Attorney General Akerman, the government successfully prosecuted and jailed a modest number of
Klan leaders. At the president's cabinet meetings, Akerman and Boutwell continued to press the Klan issue so vigorously that Secretary of State Hamilton
Fish complained that it was "a bore to listen twice a week to this thing."[13]

Undeterred, the president pressed the issue vigorously, returning early from
his summer vacation home in Long Branch, New Jersey, in late August to direct
the campaign. He suspended the writ of habeas corpus only once, in nine South
Carolina counties in October, but it had the desired result of putting hundreds
of Klansmen on trial and sending hundreds more fleeing to other states. Akerman and Boutwell oversaw the efforts of Hiram Whitley in North Carolina
as the Secret Service infiltrated Klan groupings in the Tar Heel state. Agents
would gain the confidence of local Klan members by posing as traveling merchants selling cheap bootleg tobacco on which no federal excise tax had been
paid. One of Whitley's star agents, Joseph G. Hester, foiled a murder by the
Klan of a white Union supporter in North Carolina, and later tracked down a
Klan leader in Canada and brought him back to the US for trial.[14]

Members of a congressional committee were traveling through the South
at this time, interviewing victims of and witnesses to Klan violence. The committee published its findings in February 1872 in a report of more than six
hundred pages, with twelve volumes of accompanying testimony. Predictably,
support around the country for the committee's findings split along partisan
lines, with Democratic papers both South and North blaming the violence on
"negro militias" and "Republican oppression."[15]

By the time the report appeared, however, Akerman was gone. The president dismissed him in December 1871 due to internal party politics and criticism from railroad barons Collis Huntington and Jay Gould over the attorney
general's rulings on land grant issues involving the Union Pacific. Grant
bowed to the pressure, but replaced Akerman with an equally zealous foe of
white terrorism, Judge George H. Williams, who as a senator from Oregon

had worked closely with Boutwell on both the Andrew Johnson impeachment committee and the Joint Committee on Reconstruction.[16]

Williams and Boutwell, along with Secretary William Belknap of the War Department, coordinated federal operations in the South and were able to increase the number of prosecutions. But they did so in an atmosphere of rising northern impatience where even Republican newspapers began referring to Grant as a "military despot" and "Kaiser Grant." Grant's old comrade, Gen. William Tecumseh Sherman, openly criticized the president for using the US Army to put down the Klan. As Grant prepared for the 1872 elections, opposition to Reconstruction from within his own party would be a major factor in whether he would serve a second term.[17]

THE NATION'S ECONOMY would be the other major campaign issue. Wall Street gold traders and financial houses had suffered greatly from Black Friday in 1869, with many going bankrupt. American farmers and exporters, both dependent on a stable price for gold, were also hit hard. Wheat and corn prices dropped by 40 percent, American goods piled up waiting to be shipped overseas, and credit from banks would be tight for several years. Nonetheless, Grant and Boutwell did help prevent an even worse financial catastrophe, and the treasury secretary returned to maintaining a stable balance between greenbacks and gold while reducing the country's debt and improving its creditworthiness overseas.

This was not an easy task. There was no Federal Reserve Bank at the time able to adjust the volume of paper currency in circulation. This was particularly important each autumn, as Jay Gould had correctly said, when the harvesting and transport of crops soaked up available greenbacks and gold and reduced the money available for lending by banks. Boutwell himself, pointing to the example of the Bank of England, predicted that the federal government would need something like a Federal Reserve Bank to help provide "seasonal elasticity" in the money supply. Illustrating this in his 1872 Treasury report, he emphasized the importance of increasing the money supply in the autumn to help move crops to the Atlantic seaboard, but also of reducing the money supply in November and December to control inflation and resume the gradual process of redeeming all paper currency in gold.[18]

The other major economic issue of the time was the constitutionality of the greenbacks themselves. There had been continuing controversy over the

legality of issuing paper currency not backed by gold from the first days of
the Legal Tender Act of 1862, when Boutwell was internal revenue commissioner and Salmon Chase was secretary of the treasury. Chase had come to
believe that the Legal Tender Act was only permissible as a wartime measure
to suppress the rebellion of the southern states. With the war over, he helped
rekindle the debate over whether the implied powers of the Constitution gave
Congress the authority to continue to print greenbacks not redeemable by the
"full faith and credit of the U.S. government," i.e., in gold. More than $400
million in greenbacks had been printed and were in circulation; the problem
of making them "as good as gold" had become "the largest single financial
problem facing the United States after 1861."[19]

As chief justice of the Supreme Court, Chase now had the power to decide
the issue. Opposing him was the man holding Chase's former job as treasury
secretary, George Boutwell, who very much believed in the constitutionality of greenbacks. Although Congress had tried to resolve the issue with the
Contraction Act of 1866, specifying a firm date for mandatory redemption of
greenbacks into gold, that provision was rescinded when it was seen that the
increased debt burden caused by tightening the money supply fell disproportionately on farmers and small businesses. By the time of Grant's election in
1868, pressure was again building to test the constitutionality of paper currency not backed by gold.

Salmon Chase initially had his way when the Supreme Court ruled in February 1870 (*Hepburn v. Griswold*) that greenbacks were unconstitutional, at
least for those debts incurred prior to the 1862 Legal Tender Act. His victory
was short-lived, however. A year later, Chase was in the minority when the
court ruled in *Knox v. Lee* that "paper money was a constitutional means of
carrying out other specific powers of Congress."[20]

As with many Supreme Court decisions, the politics of the *Hepburn* decision were just as important as the constitutional principles involved. Salmon
Chase was speaking for hard money advocates in ruling the act unconstitutional, while those favoring soft money worried that the decision would
"prove disastrous to the business of the country" if individuals and businesses
were now forced to pay their mortgages, loans, and other obligations "in gold
and silver."[21]

In any event, Grant and Boutwell were soon able to overturn the decision.
The very day that *Hepburn* was announced in February 1870, the president
was nominating two new justices, one to fill an open seat and the other to

create a ninth justice as authorized by Congress. In May 1871, the case of *Knox v. Lee* reestablished greenbacks as legal tender.[22]

Now in the minority, Salmon Chase was furious with Boutwell for supporting Grant's decision to appoint new judges "to overrule me." With his health beginning to suffer, Chase was coming to the end of a long and distinguished, if frustrating, political career. Lukewarm about Liberal Republicans seeking to nominate him for another presidential run in 1872, Chase suffered a final disappointment when his fellow justices voted the next year to overturn key protections of the Fourteenth Amendment in the *Slaughter-House Cases*, yet another signal that Reconstruction was dying.[23]

THE OTHER MAJOR economic issue at the time was the status of the national income tax that Boutwell had helped introduce in 1862. In advance of the 1872 election, "the great moneyed interests" of the eastern business establishment were pressuring Grant to abolish the tax, even though it was levied on no more than 10 percent of the population. Without knowing it, Grant was undermined on the issue by his own secretary of state, Hamilton Fish, himself a product of that "moneyed" establishment. In a highly questionable move, Fish quietly asked "a friend to have some test cases started in the courts" to have the income tax ruled unconstitutional. For his part, Boutwell warned that abolition of the income tax would place an unfair burden on farmers and laborers who already paid the lion's share of the tariffs and duties imposed via increased prices on sugar, coffee, and alcohol.[24]

In the spring of 1871, as time was running short for Congress to act on the issue, Boutwell played a wily game of cat-and-mouse. Knowing that robust government revenues would make eliminating the income tax more politically feasible, Boutwell stalled on giving Fish and the cabinet his most up-to-date Treasury report. When he finally relented, he admitted that the state of the nation's finances would probably support "a repeal of the income tax, if there were time for Congress to act, but there is not." Fish would have to wait until 1872 for Congress to eliminate the tax. Forty years later, in 1913, the country's income tax was reinstated with ratification of the Sixteenth Amendment.[25]

ULYSSES GRANT WAS in good shape politically heading into that year's election, despite carping by Liberal Republicans regarding administration corruption, civil service reform, and federal interference in the South. The president did support a civil service commission to introduce competitive examinations and jobs based on merit, but this wasn't enough for critics such as Godkin of *The Nation* magazine; he and others could point to continuing corruption at the Interior Department and its Bureau of Indian Affairs in making civil service reform a centerpiece of their good government campaign.[26]

In foreign affairs, the president's dogged obsession with annexing Santo Domingo was offset by the high praise he won for successfully concluding the contentious *Alabama* claims issue with Great Britain. In what would become a model of settling disputes through international arbitration, the United States received more than $15 million in damages from Britain. The amount wasn't anywhere close to the unrealistic $2 billion that Charles Sumner had originally sought, nor did Britain give up Canada as Boutwell and others had thought possible. Nonetheless, the Treaty of Washington was a decided victory for Grant and Fish, establishing clear precedents for protecting the rights of neutral parties in times of conflict that would benefit the United States in the future given its singular dependence on maritime commerce.[27]

As for the two major issues of the campaign, the economy was healthy and the federal government was actively trying to safeguard civil liberties in the South, much to the satisfaction of Frederick Douglass and the country's new Black voters. Above all, Ulysses Grant had won respect, as expressed by *The Times* of London, for "the firmness and moderation with which order has been restored" following the chaos of the Andrew Johnson years.[28]

Nonetheless, Liberal Republicans led by Schurz and Charles Francis Adams challenged Grant, hoping to create a new political party. Supported by eastern intellectuals such as Godkin and the poet, abolitionist, and editor of *The Atlantic Monthly*, James Russell Lowell, Liberal Republicans espoused issues that would today be considered "conservative": limited government, reduced tariffs and free trade, noninterference by the federal government in the affairs of states, and unfettered individual liberty.

At their renegade convention in Cincinnati in May 1872, Liberal Republicans did themselves no favors by nominating Horace Greeley for president—the *New York Tribune* editor described as having "a large ego in a slender body." Two months later, the Democrats nominated Greeley at their convention in Baltimore, marking the only time a major American political party has chosen a candidate from a third party. Greeley was a marvelous stump speaker, always good for a memorable quote, such as his most famous one, "Go West, Young Man." But he was also mercurial, took highly inconsistent positions, and had turned against Reconstruction protections for Black Americans in the South.

During the autumn campaign, the Greeley forces launched an all-out attack on corruption in the Grant administration, with George Boutwell squarely in the bull's-eye. In August, the *New York World* published what it trumpeted as a major exposé under the headlines, "Unparalleled Frauds, Treasury Plundered of Millions." In three columns spread across the front page, the paper reprinted what it claimed were Treasury Department reports contradicting Boutwell's claims of reducing the public debt. Dozens of newspapers across the country, all supporters of Greeley, reprinted the story from the *World* with headlines such as "Overwhelming Proofs of Robbery from Boutwell's Own Statements."[29]

There was similar mudslinging over Reconstruction, with Greeley supporters accusing Boutwell and the Radical Republicans of waving the "bloody shirt" and needlessly antagonizing southern whites. Seeking to exploit the voters' fatigue with discord, Greeley promised reconciliation, declaring that the country instead should "clasp hands over the bloody chasm" dividing it. Boutwell responded by ridiculing Greeley for believing that sectional and racial divisions could be wished away by clasping hands; what was needed was strong federal protection of voting rights, educational opportunities, and equal access to jobs.[30]

Boutwell stumped for Grant and local Republican candidates from Maine to North Carolina that summer and fall. In mid-July, he gave rousing campaign speeches in Greensboro and Charlotte that derided Greeley's simplistic notion of "clasping hands over the bloody chasm." Two weeks later, the Republican governor of the Tar Heel state was reelected by the slimmest of margins, thus blunting the momentum of "the combined forces of Ku Klux Conservatives, Democracy, and Greeley" heading into the presidential election that November.[31]

During his campaign swing, Boutwell was constantly criticized by opposition newspapers, as when the *Buffalo Weekly Courier* referenced the 1868 impeachment proceedings by predicting that perhaps the "famous *hole in the sky*, which Secretary Boutwell was so anxious to consign Andrew Johnson to, may possibly be the destiny in store for Grant after all." Democrats accused him of giving "incendiary speeches" with the aim of stoking "ceaseless enmity between the negroes and whites," describing southern Blacks as "degraded, ignorant and intolerant." Boutwell responded by criticizing Greeley and the Democrats for advocating policies that "promote disorder and place upon the blacks the yoke of white tyranny."[32]

Come November, Boutwell's famous "hole in the sky" was Greeley's destiny, not Grant's. (Sadly, Greeley's wife had died just days before the election, and he died of poor health several weeks later, even before the presidential electoral votes were counted.) Douglass and other Black leaders stood by the president, mobilizing Black voters across the country, and giving Grant a much-needed cushion to offset the defection of white Republicans to Greeley. In the South, African Americans elected 320 Black state and federal legislators, a record that wouldn't be surpassed for 120 years.[33]

For its part, the eastern business establishment was well pleased with George Boutwell's management of the nation's finances. During the campaign, even longtime critic James Gordon Bennett of the *New York Herald* applauded the treasury secretary for once again blocking the "gambling propensity and grasping cupidity" of Jay Gould, who was orchestrating a speculation scheme involving "the purchase of three millions of bonds." Most important of all was the electorate's desire to keep a reassuring presence in the White House. Grant won 56 percent of the popular vote and swamped Greeley in the Electoral College, 286 to 66. Liberal Republican hopes for building a separate political party evaporated more quickly than those of the Free Soil and Know-Nothing Parties of earlier decades.[34]

His solid victory notwithstanding, Ulysses Grant knew there were serious headwinds coming in his second term, especially on Reconstruction issues. In a meeting with African American leaders in the White House following his reelection, Grant promised to maintain federal government support for Black political and civil rights, even though such support was declining in his own party. What the president didn't know was that an economic storm was coming, and that he wouldn't have his valued treasury secretary with him to navigate the turbulence.[35]

ULYSSES GRANT'S RUNNING MATE in the November 1872 election was Henry Wilson, US senator from Massachusetts and longtime Boutwell colleague from the days of the Democrat–Free Soil coalition in 1850. If Grant won the White House, as was likely, then Wilson's Senate seat would become vacant in March 1873. Boutwell, tiring of the administrative burdens of running the most complex department in the federal government and wanting to support Grant's agenda in Congress, began politicking for Wilson's Senate seat.

Shortly before Christmas, Boutwell declared his candidacy in a letter to members of the Massachusetts Senate, which would be selecting Wilson's replacement in January. Agitation over Boutwell's successor at Treasury roiled the New York financial community when the news became public. The *New York Times* reported "considerable excitement" as "bankers, brokers, and merchants" gathered at the Fifth Avenue Hotel shortly after Christmas to discuss both Boutwell's departure and who would replace him. Those in the running included several New York financiers and Columbus Delano, revenue commissioner under Boutwell and the current secretary of the interior. The prospect of Delano as treasury secretary horrified Boutwell and Hamilton Fish because of scandals at the Interior Department and Delano's chummy relationship with the questionably honest Orville Babcock. Assistant Secretary William Richardson did get the job, largely by default, but was never to have the confidence of the business community that Boutwell enjoyed. Plus, just months into the job, Richardson was complaining to Boutwell that, "whether Babcock can succeed in undermining me remains to be seen."[36]

Back in Boston, Boutwell's only serious opponent for the Senate seat was Henry L. Dawes, a Massachusetts congressman from Pittsfield in the western part of the state. With a reputation tarnished by having accepted Union Pacific stock in the Crédit Mobilier scandal, Dawes's candidacy suffered further when it became known that, as chair of the House Appropriations Committee, he had blocked an attempt by Boutwell as treasury secretary in 1871 to end the sweetheart deal by which the Union Pacific deferred interest payments on its government bonds while profiting handsomely from transporting US Army troops and carrying the mail.[37]

The one blemish on Boutwell's successful campaign for Senate was his association with the ever-controversial Ben Butler, manipulator of a formidable political machine back in Massachusetts. Though entirely different in style and temperament, Boutwell and Butler were seen as allies; *The Nation* labeled them "thick as two thieves." In truth, theirs was an alliance of convenience which would come to haunt Boutwell four years later in his 1876 reelection campaign.[38]

Once his Senate election was confirmed by the Massachusetts legislature, Boutwell resigned as treasury secretary, thanking the president for his "full confidence and support" during their four years together. Grant responded in kind, assuring Boutwell "of my desire to continue the warm personal relations that have existed between us during the whole of our official connection." When sworn in, Boutwell was touched that Charles Sumner, Massachusetts's senior senator, made a point of standing by his side, even though the infirm senator had been housebound for months with the angina pectoris that would kill him within a year.[39]

ONE OF BOUTWELL'S final acts as treasury secretary, little noticed at the time, would become highly controversial a few years later and would greatly affect American politics for the rest of the century. The affair, concerning silver and its role in the US monetary system, came to be known as the "Crime of 1873."

Since 1792, the country had been on a bimetallic system of hard currency, with both gold and silver being legal tender. Prior to the Civil War, silver began to fall out of favor as gold was discovered in California. The greenbacks issued in 1862 were a free-floating currency, not backed by either gold or silver. After the war, Treasury Secretary McCulloch (quickly) and then Boutwell (more slowly) began to bring the country back to what most people referred to as the "gold standard" (allowing for the automatic redemption of greenbacks for gold coin) but which technically remained a "gold-silver" standard, even though silver wasn't much in use. That changed in the late 1860s, when increased silver production in Nevada, particularly from the Comstock Lode, lowered the cost of minting silver and threatened to drive gold from circulation. For Boutwell, who wanted the United States to join England and Germany on a unilateral gold standard to boost America's foreign trade and creditworthiness, a return to full bimetallism would be a disaster, unless fully agreed to by its major European trading partners.[40]

In his Secretary's Report in December 1872, Boutwell made clear his desire to "prohibit the coinage of silver for circulation in this country." He and Senator John Sherman, chair of the Senate Finance Committee, oversaw the drafting of the Coinage Act of 1873 to eliminate domestic use of the silver dollar, leaving only what would become known as the "China trade dollar," needed for trade with Asia, that they hoped would replace silver dollars minted in Mexico. Signed by President Grant in February 1873, the Coinage Act meant that silver could no longer be struck into coin and would only be redeemable in greenbacks for a few more years.[41]

Politicians and the press paid little attention to the Coinage Act at the time. Only the *New York Daily Herald* correctly observed how the new Act would prove "of more importance to the 'plain people' than all the political investigations and buncombe upon which the high-priced people's servants have spent their valuable time." Even so, it was not until several years later, when the country was feeling the full pain of the recession caused by the Panic of 1873, that critics of the Coinage Act, accusing Boutwell and others of misleading the country on the future role of silver, would begin referring to the Coinage Act as the "Crime of 1873."[42]

A major player in the issue was Nevada senator William M. Stewart, who had worked with Boutwell in framing the Fifteenth Amendment. Even though Stewart had a financial interest in the Comstock Lode, he had voted for the Coinage Act, knowing full well that it would demonetize silver. His reason for doing so was that he, banker William Ralston, and Henry Lindemann, long-time head of the Philadelphia Mint, had pulled off one of the great sleights of hand in American financial history.[43]

Lindemann was the principal author of the Coinage Act of 1873, with over-all guidance provided by Boutwell and Sherman. Although the bill served Boutwell's purpose in moving the country away from silver to a single gold standard, it also protected the silver interests of Stewart and Ralston in two ways. First, by eliminating the American silver dollar from domestic use, it prevented European silver producers from dumping their lower-priced silver by selling it to the US Mint. Second, it gave producers like those of the Comstock Lode an inside advantage in selling silver to the nearby San Francisco Mint for production of the "China trade dollar." For crafting legislation that admirably served the needs of the silver interests, Linderman was paid hand-somely by William Ralston.[44]

As for William Stewart, known as the "Silver Senator," he ended up having his cake and eating it, too. Politically, he could claim to be representing the interests of western farmers and miners by attacking the Coinage Act as the "Crime of 1873." Financially, his Comstock Lode interests helped him amass a fortune of $25 million, and the financial support he received from William Ralston for his political campaigns kept him in the US Senate, off and on, until 1905.

The Coinage Act wasn't criticized until silver had seriously depreciated a few years later when the country was suffering the depression caused by the Panic of 1873. Only then did Stewart, who voted for the law, begin attacking the Act for eliminating an effective way of pumping more money into the American economy during a painful recession.[45]

By 1876, the politics of the issue were inflammatory enough that a govern-mental Silver Commission recommended reintroducing $2 million a month of silver coin as legal tender. The lone dissenting voice on the commission was George Boutwell, by then the senior senator from Massachusetts, who argued that only with "the concurrence of the commercial nations of the world" should the US return to bimetallism.[46]

The politics of gold and silver would divide the country until well into the twenty-first century. Domestically, they pitted the Republican financial and corporate preference for gold (a tight money supply and high interest rates) against the silver interests of Democratic farmers and laborers (a loose money supply and easy credit). The controversy would peak in the 1896 presidential election when Democratic candidate William Jennings Bryan admonished the country for crucifying American farmers and workers upon the tight money policy of a "cross of gold."[47]

Evaluating the "Crime of 1873" one hundred years later, economists Milton Friedman and Anna Schwartz absolved Boutwell and Sherman of trying to mask their intentions in the Coinage Act, as critics maintained at the time. Far from committing subterfuge, Boutwell had been quite open about omitting the silver dollar from domestic circulation given the realities of international adherence to the gold standard. That belief was likely correct; Friedman and Schwartz wrote that "an early commitment to gold would have been preferable to the uneasy compromise" of continuing to allow silver coinage for the next twenty years. At the time, however, such reasoning was hard to come by; the currency issue was so politicized that the debate "brought out the same kind of emotions as gun control, abortion, and immigration today."[48]

ASSESSING HIS LEGACY as treasury secretary, there is no gainsaying that George Boutwell was a fortunate recipient of the postwar economic recovery gathering steam in 1869. Industry in the North was again expanding, the South was beginning to rebuild, and settlers were moving west to establish farms and build communities. Railroads were connecting the country and facilitating American exports to Europe. Resisting calls for a faster repayment of the Civil War debt, Boutwell managed to balance a stable money supply and continued reduction of the war debt while improving the country's creditworthiness abroad. Liberal Republicans might criticize Boutwell's policy as too passive, but it was showing results in gradually allowing the redemption of greenbacks in gold while avoiding tight money and a credit squeeze.

Yet just below the surface, the American economy was resting on a financial house of cards. There was no Federal Reserve Bank to respond quickly to changes in the money supply and no governmental regulatory system to impose restraints on financial speculators like Jay Gould and Jim Fisk or commercial cartels like the Union Pacific and Crédit Mobilier.

In his final act as treasury secretary, pulling one of the few levers he could control, Boutwell introduced competition into the sale of government securities. In January 1873, he split a $300 million issue of new 5 percent bonds between Jay Cooke, who previously had a monopoly on such sales, and the financiers Pierpont Morgan and Anthony Drexel. As applauded by the *New York Times*, the treasury secretary had "rendered an additional service to the Public Credit" by improving the prospects of a future planned sale of 4.5 percent bonds that would further reduce the national debt and hasten a return to the gold standard.[49]

At least that was the goal as Ulysses Grant began his second term and George Boutwell moved to the Senate. Sadly, the bond issue turned out to be a bust. A slowdown in the nation's economy and the overextension of credit to the nation's railroads had all but eliminated the demand for the government bonds needed to fuel continued railroad expansion. It would not be apparent for several more months, but the overproduction of crops, steel, and manufactured goods in a climate of falling demand was setting the stage for a serious recession, the Panic of 1873, that would devastate the country for years.[50]

14

Reconstruction Dying

In January 1873, George Boutwell was riding a wave of good fortune far beyond what he could have imagined growing up as a store clerk in Groton, Massachusetts. He was finishing a successful four-year tenure as secretary of the treasury, one of President Grant's most trusted cabinet members. On New Year's Day, with his wife Sarah and daughter Georgie, who was dressed in "a pale-blue silk dress trimmed with black lace," the family enjoyed the president's reception at the White House. Soon, Boutwell would be taking his seat as the junior senator from Massachusetts, joining Charles Sumner in defending Black civil rights. A former governor and congressman and a veteran of the Lincoln and Grant administrations, he was only fifty-five, with possibly even greater accomplishments ahead.[1]

Yet, just days before the anticipated celebration of Grant's second inauguration, the public mood was soured by yet another case of political malfeasance. Newspaper headlines screamed "Salary Grab" in reporting that Congress, in a bill promoted by Ben Butler, had voted itself a pay raise, retroactive to two years earlier. Salary increases were also provided for the president and the Supreme Court, but these were less controversial. Given the uproar, Congress rescinded the pay raises for its members, but the damage was done. Boutwell and the president were not in any way involved, but it was yet another example of what the public viewed as widespread corruption in Washington.[2]

Inauguration Day dawned bitterly cold as Ulysses S. Grant prepared to be sworn in for a second term. Georgianna Boutwell had the honor of being an official escort for Julia Dent Grant, sitting near the president on the east portico of the Capitol. Recalling how "nothing is so thrilling as the cheers of a vast concourse of people" (the crowd for the Inauguration was estimated at 40,000), Georgie felt fortunate to be part of this honored ritual of American democracy, "at once so simple and so impressive."[3]

Standing nearby with his cabinet colleagues, George Boutwell was pleased that Grant's inaugural address forcefully defended the need to protect the citizenship rights of Black Americans. Declaring the denial of such rights as "wrong, and should be corrected," the president voiced support for equal access to schools and public transportation that "would advance the social status of the colored man." Grant also spoke of the "wrong already inflicted" on Native Americans and the need for the country to take a "moral view" when addressing the Indian question.[4]

A Grant trait that Boutwell had always appreciated was the president's willingness to change course when dictated by circumstances. Describing the inner workings of cabinet meetings, Boutwell admired how Grant "often yielded to the suggestions or arguments of others" and that it "was not a humiliation to acknowledge a change in opinion, or to admit an error in policy or purpose." The president brought this same flexibility to his inaugural address, acknowledging how his Santo Domingo policy had been "rejected constitutionally, and therefore the subject was never brought up again by me."[5]

As daughter Georgie would remember decades later, few in the crowd could even hear the president's speech. Blustery winds ripped flags from their stanchions and blinding dust made it difficult to see amid bone-chilling temperatures of sixteen degrees. The inaugural ball festivities held that night in a cavernous temporary hall constructed in Judiciary Square were a disaster. Musicians were unable to play their frozen instruments, guests tried to dance while keeping their coats on, and canaries in cages strung from the roof froze to death and fell on the guests below. Still, the thousand or so guests did their best to enjoy themselves, consuming vast quantities of fried, scalloped, and pickled oysters and turkeys, capons, and mutton. Ulysses and Julia Grant didn't arrive until 11:30 p.m. and were reported to have left thirty minutes later, unable to stand the cold.[6]

BOUTWELL RESIGNED AS secretary and was sworn in as senator two weeks later, flanked by Charles Sumner and Benjamin Butler, with Vice President Henry Wilson administering the oath of office. The four of them standing together presented quite a tableau. Boutwell, Sumner, and Wilson had been part of the grand coalition in Massachusetts twenty years earlier that elected

Boutwell governor and sent Sumner to the US Senate. Benjamin Butler was now a three-term Massachusetts congressman, both loved and hated, who was building a formidable political machine in the Bay State.

If the four men standing together were supposed to represent political harmony, the image fooled no one. The patrician Sumner and scheming Butler had been at odds for years, with Boutwell, as was often the case, caught in the middle. For the swearing-in, Butler had rushed over from the House at the last minute, as newspapers reported, arriving "as a kind of dramatic accessory" that gave "a theatrical air to what would otherwise have been a very simple and pleasant ceremony." Butler intended for his presence to irritate Sumner while reminding Boutwell that it was he, Butler, who now controlled political power back in Massachusetts.[7]

The current bad blood between Sumner and Butler had to do with the so-called battle-flags controversy. In December 1872, Sumner had consciously antagonized the president by introducing a motion in Congress to delete the names of all Civil War battles from the government's official Army Register honoring those who have served their country. Sumner innocently portrayed the move as reflecting a desire that only battles fought in foreign conflicts should be so listed. Doing so, he piously maintained, would promote reconciliation with the South. But beyond its intention of being an insult to Ulysses Grant, the former commanding general of the Union armies, Sumner's action denigrated the service of hundreds of thousands of Union army veterans. In Massachusetts, his opponents in the legislature—many of them Butler supporters—were furious. They took the extraordinary move of passing a censure resolution of their state's senior senator in Washington, calling Sumner's battle-flags resolution "an insult to the loyal soldiery of the nation."

During the controversy, according to Sumner biographer David Donald, "Butler made a tacit deal with Boutwell." If Boutwell's friends in the Massachusetts House would support Sumner's censure, Butler allies would help elect Boutwell to the US Senate. Sumner was indeed censured, and Boutwell was elected, though the link between the two remains unclear. Greatly offended by the censure, Sumner didn't hold it against Boutwell. Despite being severely ill with angina, Sumner insisted on presenting the Senate credentials for Boutwell that day. As for Butler, his presence conveyed the image he desired of being "the past and future of Massachusetts politics" to the outside world.[8]

AS SPRING RETURNED to the nation's capital, Grant's second term otherwise appeared to be off to a good start. Judge Richardson replaced Boutwell as treasury secretary, deciding not to go into private banking. The president felt that Richardson, with four years of experience as assistant secretary, would provide "continuity" and "no departure . . . from Boutwell's successful financial stewardship." In May, Richardson sent Boutwell a note, reassuring his old boss that "everything is going on here smoothly and pleasantly."[9]

Overseas, though, trouble was brewing in central Europe. Germany and Austria were only slowly recovering from the crash of the Austrian stock market following the 1871 Franco-Prussian War. Economic tremors spread to England, where nervous bankers began raising their interest rates, which affected British investment in American railroads, which themselves were vulnerable because of undercapitalized loan obligations to investors such as Jay Cooke. Within a few short months, Europe's economic troubles would cross the Atlantic to New York, Chicago, and the American West.

With more than 30,000 miles of new track having been laid since the end of the Civil War, US railroads had become the country's largest nonagricultural employer and Wall Street's hottest investment. Jay Cooke and Company, having been instrumental in selling Civil War bonds to finance the Union war effort, now became the primary agent in arranging government financing for postwar railroad construction. Capitalizing on public euphoria following completion of the country's first transcontinental link in Utah between the Central Pacific and Union Pacific railroads, Cooke began pushing bonds to develop a second route, the Northern Pacific Railroad from the Great Lakes to Puget Sound.[10]

As dire economic news arrived from overseas, Jay Cooke became increasing alarmed, given that his company raised much of its capital in Europe. Moreover, Cooke and the owners of the Northern Pacific had greatly underestimated construction costs in the forbidding forests and wilderness of present-day Montana and Idaho. With the European market for his bonds drying up, the House of Cooke found itself dangerously overextended, and on September 18, his banking firm collapsed. Only days before, Grant had been staying at Cooke's mansion outside Philadelphia, further adding to perceptions of cronyism enveloping his administration.[11]

The extent of the financial rot on Wall Street and in the rail industry revealed itself quickly as banks began calling in loans and businesses collapsed.

Railroad companies lost 60 percent of their value and within two years more than 125 of them had defaulted on their loans. Iron foundries and construction businesses dependent on the railroads suffered greatly, as did America's farmers, who faced shrinking profit margins from the higher transport rates from those railroads still in business. Most wrenching of all was the widespread unemployment suffered by the country's laborers. Not only did millions find themselves out of work, but the social dislocation, broken families, and ruined communities that spread across the country would be dominant features of "the long depression of the late nineteenth century" that lasted into the 1890s.[12]

Politically, the Panic of 1873 slammed headlong into Grant and the Republicans. As late as August, Secretary Richardson had been reassuring troubled markets and nervous investors that he was "very much pleased at the . . . condition of the commerce of the country." When the shock wave came, critics charged that Richardson "was completely paralyzed and rendered powerless" on how to respond. For the remainder of his term, Grant would lose support from both the "hard money" eastern business establishment and "soft money" midwestern farmers, one result of which was the disastrous Republican Party showing in the 1874 midterm elections.[13]

Admittedly, Grant and Richardson had few fiscal and monetary policies at their command, and no Federal Reserve Bank as a lender of last resort, with which to meet the crisis. Richardson had the option of selling Treasury gold to stabilize the currency, but little else. There was no effective regulation of Wall Street and few tools for constraining financial speculators, limiting the sale of undercapitalized bonds, or stanching the endemic corruption that characterized Gilded Age business and politics. Not until the 1930s and FDR's New Deal would the federal government be given the tools to moderate the bull and bear cycles that were a natural consequence of unbridled capitalist free enterprise taking advantage of tremendously cheap resources in land (western expansion) and labor (immigration) coupled with leapfrogging developments in technology. Until then, the only real option available was regulating the supply of gold and paper currency in the economy, debates over which dominated American politics into the twentieth century.

EVEN SO, as one historian has described it, Secretary Richardson "knew that a crisis was coming, but only in the dim way of a man who might dismiss a tidal wave as a high tide." Declaring tendentiously that confidence was to be restored only "by the slow process of gaining better knowledge of true values," he authorized the release of $26 million in greenbacks to prop up commercial activity. It was far too modest a response. Six months later, as bankruptcies rose and employment plummeted, Congress authorized an increase of up to $100 million to meet the demands of western farmers, factory workers, and those hit hardest by falling wages and crop prices. Opposing the measure were the tight money advocates of Wall Street and American business who argued that the increased inflation resulting from expanding the money supply would damage US government credit and devalue the greenbacks.[14]

Following events from his home in Groton during the Senate recess, George Boutwell wrote several letters to Grant offering advice. The former treasury secretary approved of the president's measured response to the unfolding panic, even indulging in some schadenfreude at Wall Street's expense by noting how "Wall Street always disturbs the country whenever their gambling brings its proper reward." Although concerned that financial distress in Europe might continue to roil the American economy, Boutwell also greatly misjudged the extent of the coming pain, writing that "I think the crisis is over for this country. . . . By December I trust we shall be on a smooth sea."[15]

By December, the initial tremors had subsided, though the crisis was far from over. Business owners and railroad men were bombarding Congress with pleas for loosening credit and expanding the money supply, while bankers called for fiscal restraint. In the spring of 1874, Congress sent to the president a politically popular bill authorizing the release of an additional $44 million in greenbacks into the economy. Most everybody expected the president to sign it.

Despite knowing that he would face "a storm of denunciation," Grant vetoed the bill. As a member of the Senate Finance Committee, Boutwell supported Grant's veto, believing that "inflation of the local currency" as well as railroad overextension had led to the Panic of 1873. Grant's policy might exacerbate economic pain in the short term, but Boutwell, as always, believed it imperative to restore European confidence and investments in American industry and railroads.[16]

Republicans suffered badly in the midterm elections of November 1874, with Democrats taking control of the House and trimming the Republican majority in the Senate. Economic woes were the chief cause, but tales of continuing insider corruption and scandal didn't help. Just months before the election, William Richardson was forced out of Treasury because of the

"Sanborn Incident," a tax fraud scheme orchestrated by John Sanborn, a distinguished Civil War general hired by Richardson to help the Revenue Bureau
collect unpaid taxes while keeping 50 percent of the proceeds, as allowed by
law. Boutwell had eliminated the moiety system at Treasury during his tenure, but Ben Butler in Congress had helped to restore it. This allowed Sanborn
to pocket legitimate moieties from tax delinquents such as railroad companies, but also to pad his books with what he claimed were delinquent taxes
that were in fact already scheduled for payment. Sanborn's agents, known col-
orfully as "tax ferrets," collected hundreds of thousands of dollars, some of
which Sanborn likely shared with Butler. Secretary Richardson didn't personally profit but was certainly guilty of lax oversight of Sanborn's operations and
was forced by Grant to resign. Once again, the president was tarnished by a
scandal involving a Civil War colleague, Sanborn having fought in the Vicksburg campaign. The one positive result was that Grant convinced Congress to
pass the Anti-Moiety Acts in June 1874, finally abolishing the system of financial reward that Boutwell so detested.[17]

THE PANIC OF 1873 and the resulting economic depression profoundly
impacted American society for years to come. Politically, the Panic further
weakened northern support for Reconstruction, given the public's necessary
preoccupation with economic recovery. Financially, it was the final nail in the
coffin of the Freedman's Bank, which had already been hemorrhaging money
through mismanagement and which even Frederick Douglass as its newly
installed president couldn't save. When it closed its doors in July 1874, what
began as a noble experiment to increase the economic power of the country's
new Black citizens was just one more of the Panic's many victims. Despite
the opinion of historian William McFeely, not even George Boutwell with
his Treasury expertise and commitment to Black equality could have saved
the Bank.[18]

The major issues now occupying the country were those of gold versus silver and the relationship of both to paper currency. From his perch on the
Senate Finance Committee, Boutwell helped pass the Specie Resumption
Payment Act in January 1875 with the goal of restoring US credit with overseas investors. With a target date of 1879 for mandating the redemption of all
greenbacks in gold coin, the Act sought to bring greenbacks up to par with
gold so that specie payments could resume without jeopardizing the gold standard. As such, it firmly established Republicans as the party of tight money,

based on the gold standard, thus ensuring that American farmers and laborers would continue to gravitate to the Democrats.[19]

Yet the status of silver remained unresolved. In 1876, Boutwell was one of three senators appointed to the United States Monetary Commission, tasked with making recommendations for the long-term future of silver in the American economy. A majority of its members advocated restoring silver as legal tender, reversing the action taken by Treasury Secretary Boutwell in what many still denounced as the "Crime of 1873." Boutwell disagreed, believing that restoring silver would be premature without international bimetallism agreements reached with major trading partners such as England, Germany, and Japan. The only other commission member to agree with Boutwell was Francis Bowen, the Harvard professor involved twenty years earlier in the Harvard reorganization controversy. The commission's recommendations became law in 1878, when the Bland-Allison Act authorized the coinage of two to four million silver dollars per month, thus restoring the full redemption of greenbacks in silver. Gold versus silver now fully pitted Republicans versus Democrats and would continue to do so up to the famous "Cross of Gold" election in 1896 between William Jennings Bryan and William McKinley.[20]

THE EARLY MONTHS of 1875 were gloomy ones for the Grant administration. Democrats in the upcoming 44th Congress would command a substantial 180 to 103 seat advantage in the House of Representatives. Republicans were weakened enough that rumors of Ulysses Grant considering a run in 1876 for a third term were met with derision. In the Senate, Boutwell was working with colleagues on the finance committee to stanch the economic bleeding from the Panic of 1873 while watching with growing concern the mounting white supremacist violence against Blacks in the South.

Despite the initial success of the KKK Act, violence and night-riding by the Klan and other white supremacist groups had returned with a vengeance. Federal troops were slowly being withdrawn from the South. Thousands of Black southerners and their white Republican allies had been whipped, maimed, and murdered from Virginia and North Carolina to Arkansas and Texas, the most barbaric incident being the massacre of some 150 Blacks in Colfax, Louisiana, in April 1873.[21]

In what would be the final major attempt to salvage Reconstruction in the waning days of the lame duck, Republican-controlled Forty-Third Congress, George Boutwell joined Ben Butler and others in passing the Civil Rights Act of 1875. As originally proposed by Charles Sumner, who died before it became law, the legislation began as an ambitious attempt to promote equality in civil society, outlawing racial segregation in schools, transportation, public accommodations, and juries. As it worked its way through the House and the Senate in 1874, however, it was weakened considerably by both Democratic opponents and moderate Republicans who felt it went too far in "legislating" social equality between Blacks and whites.[22]

Symbolic of the contentious debate regarding the bill was a famous exchange on the floor of the House between the aging and infirm Georgia congressman Alexander Stephens, former vice president of the Confederacy and the consummate defender of white supremacy, and a young Black congressman from South Carolina, Robert Brown Elliott. Stephens claimed to believe in equality before the law but objected to any role for government in promoting social equality. He used the occasion to espouse an early version of the "separate but equal" doctrine that the Supreme Court would enshrine in its *Plessy v. Ferguson* decision in 1896, remarking that a colored man who buys a first-class ticket is entitled to a seat "of equal comfort" with whites who purchase a similar ticket, "but that does not entitle him . . . to a seat in the same car with the white man."[23]

It was the end of a long day in the House and Stephens was permitted to speak for an hour rather than the allotted twenty minutes, but only on the condition that Elliott was allowed the same. Craftily, Boutwell's colleague from Massachusetts, George Frisbie Hoar, asked for an adjournment as Stephens was finishing so that Elliott could start fresh in the morning. Hoar did so, knowing that he and Elliott could pack the gallery with a large and enthusiastic crowd of Black supporters. The next morning, Elliott's speech didn't disappoint. The urbane young congressman told Stephens that, although "the dark hue of my skin" might suggest personal motives for what he had to say, "my advocacy of this great measure of national justice . . . is restricted by no such narrow boundary but is as broad as your Constitution."[24]

True to form, Boutwell focused on strengthening the education component of the Civil Rights Act as it was debated and revised in the Senate. He knew he faced an uphill battle in promoting integrated public schools, given that the issue aroused more opposition from whites throughout the country than any other section of the legislation. Even Ulysses Grant was reluctant to throw his support behind school integration given the intense racial animosities it generated.[25]

Despite opposition, Boutwell continued to press for integrated schools in the South to avoid the development of the "separate but unequal" school facilities that ultimately did arise under Jim Crow. He also emphasized the value of "diversity" in educating Blacks and whites together, a concept little known at the time. In proposing his amendment for mandating integrated public schools, Boutwell argued that "equal facilities . . . in different schools" would diminish the quality of public education by depriving whites and Blacks of the opportunity to assimilate the values of a multiracial society.[26]

Boutwell made the argument that public school integration was necessary for fostering a greater sense of community among whites and Blacks that would strengthen the bonds of democracy. In a last-ditch effort to save the education component of the Civil Rights Act, Boutwell invoked the dream that Martin Luther King Jr. would conjure on the steps of the Lincoln Memorial almost one hundred years later. Speaking on the Senate floor on February 17, 1875, Boutwell declared that "when the children of the white people and the black people are compelled to go into the same schools, sit upon the same forms [classroom groupings], accept the same teachers, study the same books, become rivals in education and in the pursuits of life, you will have a community that will believe practically in human equality."[27]

Sitting down, Boutwell knew that his remarks would prove "more disagreeable than anything I have said." No sooner had he finished than Senator John W. Stevenson of Kentucky rose to attack "that sectional hatred which is still lurking in the breasts of some of the fanatics in Massachusetts." Other opponents of school integration raised the specter of miscegenation and the dilution of white racial purity. In the House, Representative Atkins of Tennessee, asserting that God had "stamped the fiat of his condemnation" upon mixed marriages, bringing "decay and death," asked "why have not the states the power to keep the races apart in the schools and elsewhere?"[28]

Southern Blacks considered public funding of integrated schools the "most important feature" of the proposed Civil Rights Act. Frederick Douglass had said that Blacks could only make progress in the South if there was "a schoolhouse at every crossroad . . . and a bayonet between every ballot box." As historian Eric Foner has written, however, "only Boutwell among prominent Republicans forthrightly defended school integration as a way of eroding racial prejudices." The education amendment was defeated in the Senate by a vote of forty-two to five. A weakened Civil Rights Act was passed shortly thereafter, but within a year, states such as Louisiana and Georgia were instituting mandatory state constitutional provisions for separate educational facilities for Blacks and whites. The Civil Rights Act was declared unconstitutional by the Supreme Court in 1883 when it ruled that the equal protection clause of the Fourteenth Amendment applied only to state actions, not to those of private citizens, or companies such as bus lines and places of business. By the time of the *Plessy v. Ferguson* decision in 1896, ironically just a year after the death of Frederick Douglass, the rout of Reconstruction was complete and the "separate but equal" doctrine endorsed by the court "merely gave sanction to a long-established situation that had been generally accepted for a generation." George Boutwell's belief that whites and Blacks could eventually be "made one in the fundamental ideal of human equality" wouldn't even begin to be possible until 1954 when the court's decision in *Brown v. Board of Education* finally overturned the "separate but equal" doctrine.[29]

WEAKENED LEGAL PROTECTIONS and reduced numbers of US troops resulted in new waves of violence across the South. In Mississippi, the Democratic Party was formulating what it called the Mississippi Plan, using blatant voter suppression and ballot stuffing to defeat Republican white and Black officeholders (Blacks at the time held about one-third of the thirty-six seats in the state legislature). In the August 1874 elections in Vicksburg, white militias terrorized Blacks into not voting, then went on a rampage several months later, killing as many as three hundred. In his annual message to Congress on December 7, the president vowed to enforce the Constitution and declared, "Treat the negro as a citizen and a voter, as he is and must remain." That very day, racial violence in Vicksburg killed more than a dozen Black citizens, prompting Grant to send Gen. Philip Sheridan with troops.[30]

Just weeks later, in January, the struggle over Reconstruction came to a head in Louisiana when US Army soldiers entered the state legislature with fixed bayonets after the Democrats attempted a takeover supported by white supremacist militias. The president defended Sheridan's action in a strongly worded message to the Senate, denouncing the "lawlessness, turbulence, and bloodshed" blocking Reconstruction efforts and the "butchery of citizens" that had occurred in Colfax and elsewhere in the South. Yet members of his own cabinet criticized sending troops into a government building to break up a legislative session, and much of the country felt the same. In Boston's Faneuil Hall a few days later, "highly respectable citizens" gathered to pass resolutions demanding Sheridan's removal and favorably comparing Louisiana's "White

League" to Sam Adams and the colonial patriots as defenders of republican freedom. Nonetheless, Grant's urging had been enough to ensure passage of the Civil Rights Act.[31]

In Mississippi, as the November 1875 elections approached, the Democrats were organizing "Red Shirt" and "White Line" paramilitary units operating with the support of local businesses and newspapers. Unionists (white Republicans) were coerced through economic pressure to vote Democratic, while Black citizens were beaten and intimidated. In early September, several thousand Blacks and their white Republican allies gathered in Clinton, ten miles west of the state capital of Jackson, for a day of picnicking and political speeches. Drunken whites opened fire on the crowd, killing several. The fuse was lit; rumors spread of a Black insurrection and several hundred white vigilantes descended on the town and went on a killing spree, murdering between thirty-five and fifty Black men over the next several days.[32]

The state's governor, Adelbert Ames, had been a major general in the Union army, serving with distinction at the battles of Chancellorsville and Gettysburg. Appointed by Grant in 1868 as both military commander of the Mississippi-Arkansas district and provisional governor of Mississippi, he was elected senator from Mississippi in 1870 and then won the governorship in 1873. Ames was considered, even by Democratic opponents, to be an honest, if somewhat indecisive, administrator. He and his wife, Blanche, the daughter of Ben Butler, had a complicated relationship with Boutwell stemming from the cut and thrust of Massachusetts politics. In her memoirs, Blanche tells of her husband and Boutwell's passion for billiards while living in Washington in the early 1870s, remarking that "Mr. Secretary's whole soul is wrapped up in the game." But, intensely loyal to her father, Blanche Butler often derided Boutwell, writing in her journal that Boutwell "does not look like a statesman . . . his head is far too narrow, his eyes too weasely for grand thoughts and schemes."[33]

Following the Clinton killings, Governor Ames appealed for federal troops and assistance. The president, knowing that support for continued federal intervention was ebbing, equivocated, replying that "the whole public are tired out with these annual, autumnal outbreaks in the South." Grant's sense of duty favored sending troops, but his willingness to do so was intentionally undermined by his less than candid attorney general, Edwards Pierrepont, who claimed that Governor Ames could handle the situation. Shortly thereafter, the president departed for a lengthy trip out west, leaving behind officials who had little desire for strong federal intervention in the South.[34]

The November 1875 state and county elections in Mississippi were a travesty. Through fraud, intimidation, and violence, white militias and vigilante squads terrorized Republican supporters while stealing votes and stuffing ballot boxes for Democrats. The Mississippi Democratic Party won 80 percent of the seats in the state legislature and five of six House congressional seats. A few months later, the state legislature impeached and removed from office the Black lieutenant governor, Alexander Davis, preventing him from becoming governor when the legislature then forced Ames to resign under threat of impeachment. Ames and his wife soon left the state, moving to Minnesota. The victory of Mississippi "Redemption" was complete, and with it, in Ames's words, "a *revolution* has taken place—by force of arms—and a race are disenfranchised—they are to be returned to a condition of serfdom—an era of second slavery."[35]

A similar dynamic was happening in the North, where many Republicans were retreating from efforts to safeguard Black political rights. The *New York Post* compared federal intervention and military protection to "political quack medicines," while the semi-official Republican Party newspaper, the *National Republican*, could only despair that "Northern people have lost all interest in the welfare of colored Southern Republicans."[36]

Frederick Douglass was outraged at this shift in public opinion. In an open letter published by the *National Republican*, Douglass described the "peace" that would come from the end of federal intervention in the South as one where "the heels of one class are on the necks of another." Speaking in New England shortly thereafter, Douglass charged Democrats with hypocrisy for having supported federal intervention in the past on behalf of slave owners and the Fugitive Slave Act, but not now for upholding the Fourteenth and Fifteenth Amendments.[37]

George Boutwell had first felt the power of Frederick Douglass's oratory as a young man attending antislavery meetings in Groton in the early 1840s. Thirty years later, on a spring day in Washington, Boutwell was sitting nearby when Douglass delivered one of the most powerful speeches of his career.

The occasion was the dedication of the Emancipation Memorial statue, several blocks east of the US Capitol Building, on the eleventh anniversary of Lincoln's assassination. Flags flew at half-mast on this April 14 as a crowd of many thousands, including three companies of Black militia troops, formed a procession that wound around the White House and up Capitol Hill to Lincoln Park. President Grant was the guest of honor, accompanied by George

Boutwell and other US senators, cabinet members, Supreme Court justices, and former Union army generals. Following a reading of the Emancipation Proclamation and the unveiling of the statue by President Grant, Frederick Douglass stepped to the podium.[38]

The Emancipation statue, carved by noted sculptor Thomas Ball, depicts a newly freed slave clutching a broken chain and rising beneath a standing Abraham Lincoln, whose outstretched hand holds a copy of the Emancipation Proclamation. The symbolism of the tableau is both profound and ambiguous. Has the newly freed slave (modeled after Archer Alexander, an enslaved Black who escaped to Union lines in Missouri in 1863) broken the chains of bondage himself, or is Lincoln's Emancipation Proclamation primarily responsible?[39]

For Frederick Douglass, the larger question was, "if *war* among the whites brought peace and liberty to the blacks, what will *peace* among the whites bring?" While praising Lincoln, Douglass averred how, "in his habits of thought, and in his prejudices, he was a white man." In an early formulation of the concept of Black agency, Douglass declared that Blacks had been largely responsible for their own emancipation through their contribution to the war effort as soldiers, laborers, and disruptors of southern life. A few days after the speech, Douglass would write that "what I want to see before I die is a monument representing the negro, not couchant on his knees like a four-footed animal, but erect on his feet like a man."[40]

As he sat on the platform that day, Boutwell shared Douglass's apprehension over the implications of "peace" for America's Blacks. Boutwell told Douglass that he was so impressed with the speech that he read it aloud to his family. But, as Boutwell well knew, just weeks earlier, the US Supreme Court, some of whose justices were sitting on the same platform as Douglass, had overturned the murder convictions of whites tried for the Colfax massacre. In Congress, the Democratic majority in the House was seeking to weaken the recently enacted Civil Rights Bill of 1875 and kill the Freedman's Bank, of which Douglass had been president in 1874. About the only remaining lever of Republican power was a Senate Select Committee, created on March 31 and chaired by George Boutwell, charged with investigating white vigilante terrorism in Mississippi during the previous year's state elections.[41]

KNOWN INFORMALLY AS the Boutwell Committee, its five senators met on April 4 with a mandate set by the Republican majority in the Senate "to inquire into alleged frauds in the recent election in Mississippi." Senator Oliver

Morton of Indiana had proposed the creation of such a committee the previous December, citing widespread reports of voter fraud, intimidation, ballot-stuffing, and violence that he claimed doubled the statewide Democratic vote to 96,000 while shrinking Republican votes in some counties from 1,000 to fewer than twenty. Consisting of Republicans Samuel McMillan (Minnesota) and Angus Cameron (Wisconsin), and Democrats Thomas Bayard (Delaware) and Joseph McDonald (Indiana), the Boutwell committee began its work. Predictably, southern newspapers accused Morton, Boutwell, and the Radical Republicans of seeking "to restore the black carnival of corruption" throughout the region "at the cost of destroying the constitution of [the] country."[42]

The committee met from early April through the end of July, holding twenty-five meetings and interviewing some 150 witnesses in Washington, DC. In June, Boutwell took the committee to Mississippi to hold hearings in Jackson and Aberdeen. Its report, *Mississippi in 1875*, some 2,000 pages of detailed testimony and documentary evidence, was published in August. Summarizing it, Boutwell noted that Democratic committee members, while agreeing that violence had been pervasive during the Mississippi campaign, piously insisted that "these outrages had *no* political significance, that they were due to personal quarrels, and to uprisings of negroes for the purposes of murdering the whites."[43]

Committee hearings began with three days of testimony from former governor Ames. Interviewed by the *New York Times*, Ames emphasized that the core problem was southern white "hostility to the negro as citizen. The South cares for no other question." He provided examples of how the Democratic victory in the November 1875 elections had been "due wholly to fraud, violence, and murder to such an extent and degree that the Northern mind seems incapable of comprehending it." A special object of Ames's scorn was Mississippi congressman Lucius Quintus Cincinnatus Lamar, whom Ames charged with voicing support for Black equality in Washington while working to support the "supremacy of the unconquered and unconquerable Saxon race" back home in Mississippi.[44]

During the hearings, Boutwell introduced into the record hundreds of state Democratic Party telegrams, many of them to and from party chairman J. Z. George, that showed a coordinated effort to suppress and steal the votes of Blacks and Republicans. Many were brief and perfunctory, emphasizing that party officials should maintain peace and order to minimize any chance of intervention by federal troops. Others were sent to Attorney General

Pierrepont in Washington, protesting any possible interference by the US Army. By late October, the "white line" campaign of intimidation and voter suppression had been effective enough that Democrats were already congratulating themselves on how they would sweep the statewide elections. Still other telegrams called for demonstrations of force, as typified by one to Chairman George pleading, "Can you send us cannon, good size, for display at Lexington? Want it Friday night. Answer quick." George's reply on October 29 was brief: "We telegraph to N.O. [New Orleans] to have cannon sent you, paying transportation both ways. You must provide ammunition."[45]

On election day, Democratic Party officials telegraphed to Chairman George that "all [is] quiet; election progressing finely; radicals and negroes refusing to vote." Wasting no time, J. Z. George telegrammed news of the impending Democratic victory to newspapers around the country, including the *New York Tribune*, writing that "the State has been redeemed by a large majority."[46]

Two telegrams in particular revealed how J. Z. George intervened on election day to save the life of the chair of the Republican state committee, General A. Warner. Chairman George had cautioned his subordinates that, "If Warner goes to Madison [near Jackson], see by all means that he is not hurt. We are nearly through now and are sure to win. Don't let us have any trouble of that sort." A reply sent to George the day after the election read simply, "Your telegram of last night saved A. Warner."[47]

Having successfully suppressed or stolen the Black vote—five counties with large Black majorities registered only a handful of Black votes each—the Mississippi Plan resulted in a swing of some sixty thousand votes to the Democrats from 1874 to 1875. Among the victories was Lucius Lamar's reelection in Mississippi's First District, encompassing Oxford and Tupelo in the northwest part of the state. In addition to condoning the intimidation of Black voters, Lamar had admitted that his famous 1874 eulogy for Charles Sumner, a plea for reconciliation that brought him much acclaim, was nothing more than "a political necessity, to give the South a hearing in the North." In 1956, Senator John F. Kennedy of Massachusetts would cite Lamar's Sumner eulogy as a reason for including the Mississippi senator as an example of political integrity in *Profiles in Courage*, written in part to boost Kennedy's national political ambitions.[48]

DURING THEIR STAY of several weeks in Jackson and Aberdeen, Boutwell and the committee faced open hostility from local whites. Shortly after arriving in the Mississippi capital, one Jackson paper noted smugly that the firebrand

Boutwell, having given a "quite moderate speech to townspeople the previous Saturday," was perhaps "afraid of being *ku kluxed*, and did not like the idea of becoming a martyr for the Republican party."[49]

Given the volatile atmosphere, many local Blacks and white Republicans refused to testify in full view of their neighbors. One anonymous Black man wrote to the committee that "a great many colored are intimidated & fear . . . that they would be shot down if it was known they were going to testify." Similarly, a white Republican by the name of E. Stafford from Macon, Mississippi, refused to appear, saying he had been "*ku-kluxed*" defending Reconstruction, "and I still . . . see my bitter political enemies walk off with the rewards."[50]

Those who did testify included J. W. Lee, a former captain in the Third Texas Regiment of the Confederate army who moved to Mississippi at the end of the war to become mayor of Aberdeen and sheriff of Monroe County. Lee told the committee about gangs of armed whites, both on horseback and on foot, intimidating hundreds of Blacks from voting. For himself, "I am satisfied that if I had attempted to vote . . . I should have been killed."[51]

Less fortunate was a young Black man, Square Hodge, who was murdered along with one hundred other Blacks during the Mississippi election season. His eighteen-year-old widow, Ann Hodge, testified that her husband had returned home from the Clinton political rally in early September when ten white men arrived on horseback, took him into the woods, shot him, and left his body in the swamp.[52]

In his recounting of the Clinton massacre, the venerable Judge George T. Swann, born in Virginia and a resident of Mississippi for forty years, admitted how drunken young whites were to blame for heckling and shouting down the Republican speaker and then pulling pistols. He might have regretted that Blacks had been killed, but the judge seemed more concerned with the "excessive injury that the reputation of Clinton would sustain by the doings of the day."[53]

Local newspapers blamed outside agitators for the violence, writing that Radical Republicans were seeking, "by precipitating a war of races, to procure the interference of United States troops." Democratic committee members Bayard and McDonald accused Governor Ames and elected Black officials of constituting an illegitimate government that wasted taxpayers' money and trampled on local rights. They also repeated the fiction that white Mississippians only armed themselves in fear of the "negro militia" being raised by the Ames government. Boutwell corrected them, noting that the governor's efforts to organize a state militia had failed and were broken off entirely when Ames received assurances from J. Z. George that there would be "a peaceful election and the full and free enjoyment of the elective franchise by every citizen," a promise that Boutwell concluded "was systematically disregarded by the Democrats in the larger portion of the State."[54]

The Boutwell report also confronted the widespread rumors that Blacks were "organizing themselves into [informal] military bands for the destruction of the white race," noting how such reports were used to conjure up white fears of slave revolts that had been common prior to the Civil War. Compared to the white population, Boutwell concluded, "negroes were not armed generally; that those who had weapons were furnished with inferior and second-hand weapons, and that their leaders, both religious and political, had discounted a resort to force."[55]

What was beyond question, the report noted, were systematic efforts by white employers to intimidate their employees into voting for Democrats or not at all. There were provisions in labor contracts "that they should be void in case the negroes voted the republican ticket."[56] Whites also targeted those Blacks who had the temerity to own farms and small businesses. One such farmer, Lewis McGee of Bolton, wrote to the governor of being holed up in Jackson, as white vigilantes were "looking for me on ever[y] train and have got men on ever[y] road watching for me. They have sworn to take my life." Adding that he had cotton and corn that needed harvesting and no one to tend to it, McGee pleaded, "tell me what to doe [sic] if you please."[57]

In minute detail, the Boutwell report illustrated how the Mississippi Plan successfully returned white Democrats to power in the 1875 state elections. As was common elsewhere in the South, the campaign to "redeem" Mississippi stopped dead in its tracks the progress that had been made toward Black civil and political equality. Especially chilling was Boutwell's conclusion that the violence surrounding the 1875 election was fomented, not just by Confederate army veterans seeking revenge, but also by "the young men of the State, especially those who reached manhood during the war, or who have arrived at that condition since the war." If the Lost Cause banner of white supremacy in Mississippi in 1875 was being hoisted most violently by young men who had not even fought in the Civil War, then the prospects for Reconstruction and racial reconciliation were indeed doomed for generations to come.[58]

BOUTWELL FULLY EXPECTED a hostile response when he presented his committee's report to the US Senate in August 1876. Even the usually sympathetic *New York Times* called him "obtuse" for misreading the mood of both the country and his own party. Noting how the end of Republican Reconstruction had "restored to the South its forfeited rights, and to the whole people, white and Black, control of their affairs," the paper lauded "the conciliatory tone" of that year's Republican presidential candidate Rutherford B. Hayes as reflecting "the prevailing spirit of the party." Democratic papers like the *New York Herald* criticized Boutwell for "arbitrary interference" in questioning the validity of Mississippi's electoral votes in the upcoming 1876 election should widespread voter suppression continue to exist.[59]

Even Boutwell's hometown newspapers criticized him. Writing that the Senate report was guilty of "violent partisanship as to make it comparatively worthless," the *Boston Daily Globe* nonetheless admitted that "intimidation and coercion . . . were undoubtedly exercised . . . and that lawless combinations in many localities controlled the election." In a brazen display of northern racist paternalism, the paper excused such violence on the grounds that Mississippi has "such a mass of ignorant voters . . . led by unscrupulous demagogues . . . against which the minority [a code word for white supremacists] is disposed to use violence or any other desperate means that promise success." Not to be outdone, the *Boston Post* termed it "the fantastic and malignant Boutwell report," adding piously that reports from the South were that "the negroes are contented, happy and secure in their rights . . . this is the testimony of businessmen, planters, and cotton dealers."[60]

Equally caustic was *The Nation*, a frequent critic of Boutwell and the Grant administration, calling the committee recommendations "wicked and imbecile" and Boutwell a "rabid partisan . . . with little mental balance or judicial faculty." Editor Godkin downplayed the widespread violence in Mississippi and dismissed the report as little more than a vehicle for Republican election-year politicking. He concluded his editorial with the astonishingly naïve observation that violence only seemed to occur in states such as Mississippi and South Carolina, "where the negroes and their friends have a decided majority. How is it that peace and order reign in the [Southern] States in which whites are in a majority?"[61]

Just weeks before, the infamous Hamburg massacre in South Carolina had produced national headlines when a white rifle club, the "Red Shirts," had attacked thirty Black servicemen of the state militia in Hamburg, a Black majority town. During Fourth of July celebrations, six Blacks were murdered, and others were tortured. Ninety-four whites were indicted for murder, but none was ever prosecuted. Even as Boutwell was presenting his report on election violence in Mississippi, the US Senate was hotly debating the "Hamburg Massacre" that very same week.[62]

IT WAS 1876. America was celebrating its one hundredth birthday. It was eleven years since the war had ended; the country welcomed the opportunity to enjoy the Centennial celebrations and was tired of being reminded of how "life, liberty and the pursuit of happiness" were not universally applied throughout the country. President Grant had helped kick off America's birthday party the previous spring by opening the six-month-long 1876 Centennial Exhibition in Philadelphia. With cavernous halls showcasing the latest in American industry, agriculture, technology, law, medicine, and the arts, well over eight million people would visit the Exhibition.

The Centennial year provided an opportunity for Americans to celebrate Manifest Destiny, the new industrial age, and a burgeoning American power that would soon make its presence felt on the world stage. Marginal players in American society—Blacks and Native Americans especially—were not part of the narrative. Except, of course, when they proved troublesome, as the Lakota Sioux did when they wiped out Custer's Seventh Cavalry at the Little Big Horn while the Philadelphia Centennial Exhibition was in full swing.

Reconstruction efforts had already suffered another blow in March 1876 when the Supreme Court gutted the ability of the federal government to apply the equal protection and due process clauses of the Fourteenth Amendment to all Americans. By overturning the convictions of three whites in the Colfax, Louisiana, massacre case (*U.S. v. Cruikshank*), the court decreed that only those actions by state governments to deprive individuals of "equal protection of the laws," not acts committed by private citizens, were covered by the Fourteenth Amendment. Once more, white southerners knew they had carte blanche to violate Black civil and political rights, given that such cases could only be tried in state courts, in front of white juries, where Blacks could not testify.

Nonetheless, in the autumn of 1876 Ulysses Grant was still seeking to protect Black rights and ensure free elections throughout the South, despite public fatigue and opposition from within his own party. In the wake of the Hamburg massacre, the president ordered federal troops to South Carolina prior to the election, at the request of Governor Daniel Henry Chamberlain, to prevent the suppression of Black voters that had characterized the 1875 Mississippi state elections. For his efforts, Grant received death threats signed by the KKK.[63]

As the fall election campaign gathered momentum, Ulysses Grant was a lame duck president and Boutwell one of the few supporters of Reconstruction remaining in Congress. Charles Sumner had died in March 1874, followed in November 1875 by Vice President Henry Wilson, the third part of the Massachusetts triumvirate dating to 1850. The Republican presidential candidate, Governor Rutherford B. Hayes of Ohio, tried to appeal to different constituencies by promising to protect Black rights while promoting "honest and capable local self-government" in the South.[64]

Throughout the 1876 campaign, Boutwell continued to warn that the rights of Blacks would be in jeopardy should the Democrats be returned to power. Despite being criticized for waving the "bloody shirt," Boutwell asserted that "the country cannot have peace or security in its business and financial interests until justice, absolute political justice, is secured for the negro."[65]

To keep his Senate seat, Boutwell would have to defeat George Frisbie Hoar, a Massachusetts congressman for the previous eight years. The Hoars were an illustrious family from Concord, Massachusetts, whom Boutwell knew well; older brother Ebenezer Rockwood Hoar had been Grant's first attorney general. George Frisbie was Harvard-educated and a firm proponent of Black rights in the South. But he was supported by the likes of Godkin and the Adams family, who would be delighted to send Boutwell into early retirement. In addition to facing the well-regarded Hoar, Boutwell knew that his reelection prospects would depend on the shifting sands of Massachusetts politics back home, and on the tempestuous Ben Butler in particular.[66]

15

With Grant to the End

Georgi Boutwell was with friends and supporters on January 19, 1877, at Boston's Parker House Hotel when he learned of his surprising Senate defeat. A telegram arrived with results of the voting by Massachusetts legislators in the nearby State House, stating simply, "Hoar elected one forty six votes, Boutwell forty nine." Just a month before, his reelection had seemed assured. He was a well-respected incumbent who had been a mainstay of Massachusetts politics for twenty-five years. Even his opponent thought Boutwell would be reelected; Hoar confided to his wife that such an outcome was all "for the best."[1]

Boutwell, however, had suspected that two issues might prevent his reelection. The first was his steadfast loyalty to Ulysses Grant and his "guilt by association" with Grant administration corruption. Massachusetts Republicans were tiring of the Grant wing of the party and supporting more independent Liberal Republicans such as Hoar. Boutwell's second problem was his association, fairly or not, with the bare-knuckle, political machine tactics of Benjamin Butler.[2]

Evaluating Boutwell's defeat, the *New York Times* complimented Boutwell for his "conscience, sensitiveness, and an honest record" but noted that it was Boutwell's "unhappy fate" to be tainted with Butlerism. This was ironic, given that the two had quarreled and still not reconciled over the nomination of a Butler candidate, William Simmons, for the patronage-rich position of collector of customs for the port of Boston. At the time, Butler had stormed into Boutwell's room, threatening to "spend half a million dollars to defeat" his reelection; Butler's wife Sarah called Boutwell "a rat" who owed everything to her husband. Despite this and other differences between them, Boutwell and

Butler remained linked in the public mind as Grant men and supporters of
Reconstruction.[3]

Family friend Peter Pineo sought to console Boutwell by saying that Hoar's
victory was one of "money, aristocracy and organization" over genuine Republicanism. The reality, however, was that Boutwell's brand of Radical Republicanism was no longer in vogue. Liberal Republicans such as Hoar were
emphasizing big business, the economy, and honest government. In Massachusetts, the party was falling under the sway of the Boston elite who had
disdained Boutwell for decades. With a jab at Boutwell, Hoar's Harvard classmate, Charles Eliot Norton, declaimed, "We look to you [Hoar] to maintain
Puritan traditions of uprightness & intelligence."[4]

DOWN IN WASHINGTON, a far more important political drama was playing
out that would determine the next president of the United States. The contest between Republican Rutherford B. Hayes and the Democratic governor
of New York, Samuel J. Tilden, had turned into the most contentious election in American history. Following the November voting, Tilden had a sizable popular vote advantage and was leading in electoral votes by 184 to 165.
But the electoral votes of four states—South Carolina, Florida, Louisiana, and
Oregon—were being disputed, largely over allegations of white Democratic
suppression of the Black vote; it's estimated the Republicans were denied as
many as 250,000 votes throughout the South. When it came time to count the
electoral votes in December, there were two sets of competing electors from
the four states with no prescribed mechanism for deciding whether these tal-
lies should be Republican for Hayes or Democratic for Tilden.[5]

Violence seemed certain as the controversy mounted. White rifle clubs
mobilized in South Carolina, and federal troops were called out to protect
state legislatures. Newspapers and party leaders spread rumors of possible coups and assassination attempts against Grant himself. During one of
the biggest challenges ever to American democracy, Ulysses Grant provided
firm, steady, impartial leadership. Finally, in mid-January, Congress approved
a fifteen-member electoral commission to examine the competing claims
of the electoral slates from the three southern states, plus Oregon, to decide
the presidency.[6]

Through February and into March, the country was on edge as the commission weighed testimony on Capitol Hill while Hayes and Tilden emissaries

circulated in and out of the White House. Finally, in a straight-line partisan vote (there were eight Republicans on the commission and seven Democrats), all twenty electoral votes were given to Hayes, providing a 185–184 Electoral College victory. To the dismay of Democrats, many of whom derided him as "Your Fraudulency," Hayes joined John Quincy Adams as the only candidate, up to that time, to win the presidency while losing the popular vote.[7]

George Boutwell was back in Washington by this time, a lame duck senator. Georgie was with him in their house on Twelfth Street; each heard the rumors of possible armed attempts to disrupt the inauguration ceremony on Monday, March 5, at the Capitol. Georgie would write of Ulysses Grant arranging for Hayes to take the oath of office in a private ceremony at the White House on Saturday, March 3, "lest trouble might arise and there would be a question as to who had the legal right to act as President," given that March 4 was the official inauguration day but had been delayed because it fell on a Sunday. On Monday at the Capitol, hundreds of soldiers provided security as Hayes was publicly sworn in; Georgie recalled with pride "the stability of the American people and their devotion to constitutional methods in solving questions."[8]

In what historian C. Vann Woodward called the "Compromise of 1877," Hayes gained the presidency by promising Democrats that he would curtail federal intervention and promote railroads and industrial development in the South, while believing naïvely that southern state governments would live up to their promises to protect Black rights. Whatever the exact contours of any such deal, it was clear that the Hayes administration would give the South a much freer hand in disposing of the rights of America's four million new Black citizens.[9]

RETURNING TO GROTON after the inauguration, Boutwell found himself a private citizen for the first time since the outbreak of the Civil War. He could focus on his family, his law practice, and managing his farm with its three hundred head of Ayrshire cattle. But in less than two weeks, he was called back to Washington. President Hayes asked Boutwell to take on the task of compiling an authoritative revision of the entire US legal code, a massive job that would take a year. Georgie would again accompany her father, continuing her own work in the nation's capital, which included serving as a trustee of the Miner Normal School for Colored Girls, founded in 1851 by the abolitionist educator Myrtilla Miner, with help from Frederick Douglass and Harriet Beecher Stowe.[10]

Dividing his time between Washington and Boston, Boutwell set to work updating the Revised Statutes of the United States, known today as the United States Code. An earlier attempt at revision had been rejected by Congress in 1873 as sloppy and incomplete. Prior to the Civil War, there had been no official record of the laws of Congress and of Supreme Court decisions that judges, lawyers, and legislators could easily consult. With neither a college nor a law degree, Boutwell had the responsibility of compiling the government's Revised Statutes, which remained the standard text, with only minor revisions, until 1926 when Congress formally adopted the revamped United States Code. In 1895, Boutwell published a stand-alone volume, *The Constitution of the United States at the End of the First Century*, a 430-page, fully annotated and cross-referenced compendium that was favorably reviewed by the *Yale Law Journal* and *Harvard Law Review*. In it, Boutwell again asserted his belief in the primacy of national over state citizenship, that the rights and liberties of Americans should be protected by the federal government and not left to the whims of state governments.[11]

Given his acknowledged expertise in constitutional law, Boutwell was a suitable candidate for the US Supreme Court, or at least his daughter Georgie thought so. When there was a vacancy in the fall of 1881, Georgie wrote to her father, "why don't you tell [President Chester A.] Arthur that your family think you are consummately fitted for a judge. [At least] do all you can to prevent Judge Gray from having it." Georgie knew that her father and Arthur had worked together to clean up corruption at the New York Customs House in 1872 when Boutwell was treasury secretary and Arthur was collector at the New York port. She was hoping that Arthur might select her father rather than Horace Gray, chief justice of the Massachusetts Supreme Judicial Court, whom Arthur did nominate and who served for twenty years.[12]

Boutwell didn't make it to the Supreme Court, but President Arthur did offer him a second stint as secretary of the treasury in 1884, and then the office of secretary of the navy, both of which Boutwell declined.[13]

CHESTER ARTHUR HAD BECOME the country's twenty-first president because of the assassin's bullet and resulting infection that killed President James A. Garfield in September 1881. As chair of the New York state Republican Party, Arthur had joined Garfield on the Republican ticket following the deadlocked

1880 convention between James Blaine, then senator from Maine, and Ulysses Grant, controversially seeking an unprecedented third term as president.[14]

When Garfield won the party nomination, he turned to the Grant forces for his vice presidential candidate. Boutwell was a Grant campaign manager at the convention and was one of several names considered, recalling that the "Vice-Presidency was placed in the hands of the friends of General Grant. The nomination was offered to me." It is unclear whether Boutwell really was seriously considered, but it is plausible. What certainly weighed in Arthur's favor was New York's thirty-five electoral votes compared to thirteen from Massachusetts.[15]

BY THE EARLY 1880s, Boutwell had successfully rebuilt his law practice. He was lead counsel in several high-profile military courts-martial, two of them involving US Navy officers serving in China and Brazil. He was also appointed to the prestigious French and American Claims Commission, established by the two countries in 1880 to adjudicate claims by French citizens for damages suffered during the Civil War. Most of the hundreds of cases decided were minor, involving French citizens living in Louisiana and elsewhere in the South during the Civil War. One of them, though, involved "Champagne Charlie" Heidsieck, family member of one of the world's foremost champagne brands. Heidsieck was seeking damages for having been imprisoned in New Orleans by none other than Ben Butler, which damages Boutwell helped to successfully deny.[16]

Boutwell father and daughter were fixtures on the Washington social scene during these years. One newspaper columnist wrote that Boutwell "arrays himself in claw-hammer coat and with his accomplished daughter beards the social lion," while another described George as "a man of polished manners and gaiters, of diffuse and divergent eyebrows, and concentrated speech." Back home in Massachusetts, as Boutwell wrote to Hamilton Fish, "I'm dividing my labors, doing something in law, a little in politics, managing the affairs of a railroad in embryo, and looking after the farm." The "railroad in embryo" was the Massachusetts Central Railroad Company, which recruited Boutwell to be its president. Similar to many railroad ventures during those turbulent economic times, this one did not have a happy ending. The company had overextended itself before Boutwell came on board and would soon run out of capital.[17]

Around this time the Boutwell family and Groton were welcoming to town Robert Heberton Terrell, whose father Harrison, born into slavery, was Ulysses

Grant's trusted valet and friend. Robert attended Lawrence Academy, possibly on Boutwell's advice, becoming the school's first Black graduate in 1880. He then earned degrees from Harvard and Howard Universities before being appointed the first Black judge on the District of Columbia's Municipal Court.[18]

In 1884 Boutwell was hired by the government of Haiti to help with a fascinating legal case which he called "the last of the ocean slave traders," involving the criminal undertakings of ship captain Antonio Pelletier on the eve of the Civil War. Pelletier was a notorious slave trader plying the waters of the Caribbean; he was arrested along with a cargo of enslaved persons by Haitian authorities just days before Fort Sumter was bombarded. Pelletier managed to escape to the United States where, many years later, he had the audacity to lodge a claim with the US State Department seeking restitution in the amount of $2.5 million from Haiti for wrongful conviction and imprisonment. The case languished until 1884, when the Haitian and US governments referred it for international arbitration.[19]

In June 1885, Pelletier died of unknown causes in a New York hotel room as the commission was beginning its work; all but one of his claims were dismissed shortly thereafter. Boutwell appealed even that ruling to President Grover Cleveland and won, thus relieving Haiti of having to pay any claims.[20]

In doing so, Boutwell scored a double victory. Not only did he block any restitution for slave trading, but he tweaked the nose of a Supreme Court justice who had undermined many of the Reconstruction protections for Blacks that Boutwell had helped enact. Justice William Strong, whose decision it was to award some damages to Pelletier's family that Boutwell helped overturn, was the man who wrote the majority opinion in *Blyew v. United States* in 1871 that overturned a key provision of the Civil Rights Act of 1866 regarding the rights of Blacks to sit on juries and give testimony against whites.[21]

ON JULY 23, 1885, Ulysses Grant succumbed to throat cancer just days after finishing his memoirs at the Drexel cottage on Mount McGregor north of Albany, New York. His illness and courageous battle to finish the memoirs, justly regarded as among the finest in American letters, had been front page news for months. With publishing help from Mark Twain, the two-volume memoirs were an instant best seller, providing the financial security for his family that helped motivate Grant to finish them before he died.[22]

Having forged a family friendship over two decades, the Boutwells and Grants stayed in close touch during the final months of the general's illness.

Of the many notes and letters expressing this relationship, none is so poignant as the one Grant sent in response to an 1885 New Year's greeting that he had received from Georgie. "My Dear Miss Boutwell," it began, "There is no family that I have ever known whose friendship I prize more highly than that of your father." George Boutwell regarded the note as "a precious souvenir of my acquaintance and service with a man who was great and good above any estimate that the world has placed upon him."[23]

One of Georgianna Boutwell's fondest memories of the general dated to October 1876, when she and her mother were having dinner with the Grants at the White House. Her father was delayed at the Senate that evening, so the president offered to walk the two women home. They strolled through Lafayette Park in the gathering dusk and approached McPherson Square, where construction was almost finished on the statue, still standing today, of Gen. James B. McPherson, killed in the Battle of Atlanta during Sherman's march through Georgia. "Huge timbers were in the pathway," Georgie recalls. "Gen. Grant remarked that we could turn back, but he had always objected to doing that and he hoped that we would go over." As was the case so many times during the Civil War, most crucially after the battles of The Wilderness and Spotsylvania Court House during the campaign to take Richmond, Grant was determined to press on, no matter the odds. The president assisted the two ladies over the timbers and through the construction site and delivered them to their door. As Georgie knew, "every man has some superstitions and possibly Gen. Grant's objection to retracing his steps even in the most trivial of affairs was his superstition."[24]

In the spring of 1885 as Grant's condition worsened, both father and daughter paid visits to the Grant brownstone on East Sixty-Sixth Street in Manhattan. Georgie visited on April 24, three days before Grant celebrated his sixty-third and final birthday with visits from William Tecumseh Sherman and Mark Twain. Georgie was the lone visitor that Friday evening, spending two hours with the Grant family. She had been passing through New York, "between trains in the evening . . . and drove to the house to enquire for him." The Grant family was at dinner, the general upstairs, seemingly too ill to come down to say hello. Nonetheless, he descended the stairs and Georgie "expressed [her] surprise at seeing him. He replied that he was afraid that I would get away without his seeing me. He was utterly changed in looks and bearing and it was difficult to understand him when speaking."

Georgie stayed that evening for as long as the general's stamina allowed, noting how "his interest and thoughtfulness for his friends was unabated." Recalling how she stayed in close touch with the Grant family up until the general's death in July, Georgie penned her own eulogy for the man revered as a Civil War hero and a courageous president: "[T]hose of us who knew those last days feel that they were his best and the crowning glory of his life."[25]

GEORGE BOUTWELL WAS one of twelve pallbearers when Ulysses S. Grant was laid to rest on August 8 in Riverside Park in New York City. The funeral procession, one of the grandest spectacles in American history, was viewed by more than a million and a half people who crowded city streets to see Grant's hearse at the head of a parade that stretched for seven miles and included 30,000 soldiers, 10,000 civilians, and dignitaries from all over the world. The day began with a low cloud cover, but as noted by one poetic reporter, "now and then the whole landscape was lit up with a flash of gold as the August sun shook off the floating masses of fleece that were fain to shield his face."[26]

Boutwell assembled with the other pallbearers, a total of six civilians and six military officers, early that morning at the Fifth Avenue Hotel at West Twenth-Fourth Street to await the start of the procession. His billiards partner William Tecumseh Sherman was there, along with Philip Sheridan and Confederate generals Joseph E. Johnston and Simon Bolivar Buchner, the latter two having been especially close friends of Grant's from before the Civil War. Wearing "broad silken sashes of black and white," the twelve pallbearers paired off two-by-two to ride in the carriages following Grant's hearse. Boutwell rode with a longtime Grant friend, John Logan of Illinois, while Generals Sherman and Johnston, and Sheridan and Buckner, rode together in a show of Union-Confederate reconciliation. The procession took three hours to make its way from lower Manhattan up Broadway to Riverside Park, arriving at the site marked for Grant's Tomb shortly after noon. When the tail of the procession arrived around 4 p.m., George Boutwell and his fellow pallbearers escorted the president's coffin into the temporary tomb, where it would remain until the permanent tomb was completed twelve years later.[27]

In the years following, Georgie remained close to Julia Dent Grant and the family, and was often invited to come stay at the Grant summer cottage in Elberon, New Jersey, part of the Long Branch seaside resort which the Grants had been visiting since 1867. Georgie also stayed in touch for many years afterward with Ida Honoré Grant, wife of eldest son Col. Frederick Dent Grant, having first met them in Washington in the 1870s.[28]

When Grant's Tomb was dedicated on April 27, 1897, in Riverside Park, more than one million people again turned out to honor the famed general and president. Boutwell was one of the invited VIPs but was unable to attend when his invitation and ticket were sent by mistake to Washington. In a letter to Georgie a few days later, Ida Grant regretted that the general's "old and valued friend" hadn't been with them in New York, but she looked forward to continuing the warm friendship between the two families.[29]

Dating back to their first meeting at the reception hosted by Lincoln at the White House in March 1864, Grant and Boutwell had come to recognize how much they had in common, from their modest upbringings to their disdain for affectation, their reliance on common sense, their love of family, and their devotion to fairness and equality in American life. They had worked closely together to advance and protect the Reconstruction goals of political and civil equality for Black Americans. They had sought, not always successfully, to organize an efficient government and manage the American economy for the benefit of farmer, laborer, and business owner alike. Each represented what was best in the term *public servant*. With Grant's death, George Boutwell—now in his late sixties—would press on for another two decades.

FOLLOWING GRANT'S FUNERAL in 1885, Boutwell resumed his law work in Washington and Boston. Georgie no longer came with him to Washington each year during the "winter season," choosing to remain in Groton to care for her ailing mother. When Boutwell was finished with work for the day at his law office on New York Avenue, he would take long walks through the neighborhood of the Treasury Building and the President's House. One reporter noted how, even having celebrated his seventieth birthday, Boutwell was "a man who has grown so old so gracefully that it would reconcile me to advancing years if I might follow his example."[30]

Early in 1886, Boutwell took on a most unusual client, the Church of Jesus Christ of Latter-day Saints. The Mormons were fighting proposed legislation that, by adding new prohibitions and fines to the Edmunds Anti-Polygamy Act of 1882, could possibly destroy the church. Seeking some additional legal firepower, they hired the former senator and Grant cabinet member to protest a provision of the bill that would compel husbands and wives to testify against each other, thus making convictions easier.[31]

Testifying before the House Judiciary Committee in May, Boutwell warned of the dangers of government policy being driven by public opinion, noting how the Constitution, in guaranteeing the free exercise of religion, prohibited Congress from having "any judgment as to what a religion is." More ominously, he felt that the whole intent of the Edmunds Act and supplemental legislation was "not so much to eradicate the social evil . . . as to seek the destruction of the Mormon Church as a religious organization."[32]

At that time in America, the anti-Mormon campaign had taken on the trappings of a moral crusade. Amos A. Lawrence, the longtime Boutwell colleague who had been so important in funding antislavery activists in Kansas in the 1850s, was now supporting the Utah Emigrant Aid Company to "fill Utah with Christian citizens and to free the Territory from the [Mormon] curse." The effort went nowhere. Lawrence realized that the Mormons were already too well entrenched in Utah and that "moral enthusiasm" for such a venture was wanting.[33]

Still, the anti-Mormon fervor of the period was such that Boutwell's acceptance of the case was described as "a shock his moral Massachusetts friends will never recover from." True to form, Boutwell believed fundamental principles were at stake, from the constitutional guarantee of "the free exercise of religion" to the legal safeguard of not compelling wives to testify against their husbands. His efforts notwithstanding, the Tucker-Edmunds Act was signed into law in March 1887 and upheld by the US Supreme Court in 1890. Bowing to the inevitable, the Mormon leadership banned polygamy among its followers, which facilitated statehood for Utah in 1896 and allowed the Mormons to regain their political status.[34]

BOUTWELL ALSO HAD battles to fight back home in Groton. In the spring of 1891, he made a special trip from Washington to attend a town meeting that would decide the fate of his beloved Groton Public Library, which he and others had established in 1854. By the 1890s, having outgrown its library, the town needed to decide whether to accept the generous offer of Mrs. Charlotte Sibley, widow of a former librarian of Harvard College, to give the town $4,000 and a prime plot of land on Main Street, provided the town would agree to commit $15,000 for a new building.

A spirited public debate ensued at that year's April town meeting, worthy of a Norman Rockwell painting. Long a champion of public education, Boutwell spoke in favor of accepting the Sibley proposal and was joined by the Reverend Endicott Peabody, headmaster of the newly established and already prestigious Groton School. Opposing were members of Groton's most prominent family, the Lawrences, who argued that what Groton needed most were improvements to its physical infrastructure, especially the paving of roads. In response, Boutwell emphasized the importance of the town's social infrastructure and intellectual capital, arguing that assets like a modern library would attract new residents who would improve Groton's cultural life and business activity, thus attracting more residents, which in turn would improve its property tax base. As judged by one onlooker, Boutwell's speech "was excellent . . . cheers upon cheers." The Sibley offer was approved by a vote of 120 to 53. Eighteen months later, Boutwell spoke at the dedication of the library's new building, designed pro bono by famed Boston architect Arthur Rotch, a member of the Lawrence family which had opposed the project.[35]

WHETHER IN WASHINGTON or at home in Groton, George Boutwell was always writing. In 1886 he became a columnist for the *Boston Globe*, writing more than forty articles and opinion pieces for the paper's Sunday edition through the early 1890s. He wrote widely on such topics as the latest advances in agricultural practices and technology, civil service reform, military history, and foreign affairs. One such article, "China and the Western Nations," predicted that the West would find it difficult to "withstand the free and continuous competition of the Chinese."[36]

Another column urged reform of the Electoral College. Although Boutwell preferred direct election of the president by popular vote, he insisted that the country should at least do away with the "winner take all" system used to allocate electors from each state. What kind of democracy was it, he argued, where a presidential candidate winning 49 percent of the vote in a particular state would receive none of that state's electoral votes?[37]

More and more, Boutwell began focusing on international affairs. In 1889 he wrote a provocative article about US options for annexing Canada, still a long-held dream of many in American government. The Irish troubles were a frequent subject; his ironclad support for Home Rule and representative government in Ireland naturally played well in Irish Boston. He also wrote articles on Marxian economics, global free trade, and German and Italian unification. A constant theme was the folly of America acquiring physical control of overseas possessions and the dangers of the country's embarking on empire-building. It was an issue that would soon fire his passion in one last great cause.[38]

PART FIVE

THEODORE ROOSEVELT AND AMERICA ABROAD, 1886–1905

Annexation of Hawaii and the Spanish-American War

If there was one area of disagreement between George Boutwell and Ulysses Grant, it was the wisdom of America acquiring overseas territories. Boutwell had been uneasy with Grant's desire to annex Santo Domingo, emphasizing in cabinet discussions that America could reap all the economic and commercial benefits it desired without formally annexing foreign territory. If the US did plant its flag on foreign lands, then annexation *must* ensure a path to statehood and full citizenship; otherwise, America would be betraying its faith in republican government and its commitment to the principle of "consent of the governed."

In New York in the 1880s, there was a young state assemblyman, soon to be a rising star in the Republican Party, who would surpass Grant in seeking to expand American influence over foreign territories. Theodore Roosevelt was living in the Dakota Territory, running a cattle ranch, and seeking an emotional refuge from the tragedy of losing his wife, Alice, in childbirth, just hours after his mother had died, both on Valentine's Day in 1884. Returning east, he reentered politics, married Edith Carrow, and began his ascent to national prominence. When he became assistant secretary of the navy in 1898, Roosevelt took advantage of the country's lightning victory in the Spanish-American War to begin implementing his vision of extending American power overseas, which brought him into conflict with George Boutwell over the aims and means of American imperialism.[1]

IN ADDITION TO his work on the French and Haitian international commissions, Boutwell was hired as legal counsel by the Kingdom of Hawaii in 1886 to oppose attempts by American sugar producers, mainly in Louisiana, to abrogate a ten-year-old agreement allowing duty-free Hawaiian sugar into the country.[2]

At the time, Hawaii was ruled by King David Kalākaua, a member of the Kamehameha family that first established the monarchy in the 1790s. As a senator in 1875, Boutwell had voted in favor of the Reciprocity Treaty, a free trade agreement which eliminated duties on Hawaiian sugar and rice exports to the US and on American goods exported to Hawaii. The agreement also gave the US initial rights to developing the port facilities around Pearl Harbor to help facilitate American trade across the Pacific. A few years earlier, Boutwell as treasury secretary had urged expanding the country's merchant marine capabilities to take advantage of new trade opportunities in the Far East. Later, in 1882, he told the House Foreign Affairs Committee how important Hawaii was as "a depot of commerce, a depot for the navy." The one thing he opposed was American physical and governmental control of the islands.[3]

Now, as counsel for Hawaii, Boutwell was seeking to protect the political independence of the kingdom while maintaining mutually advantageous economic relations between the islands and the US. Yet events in Hawaii were moving in another direction. In July 1887, American business elites led by Sanford Dole imposed the "Bayonet Constitution" on King Kalākaua, stripping him of authority and disenfranchising most local Hawaiians and Asian immigrant laborers of the right to vote. A few months later, the Reciprocity Treaty was renewed, but with a major addition: the United States was given *exclusive* use of Pearl Harbor as a "coaling and repair station for the use of vessels of the United States." In 1893, Queen Lili'uokalani, Hawaii's last monarch, was overthrown by white business elites, supported by a detachment of US Marines.[4]

Hawaii for George Boutwell symbolized America's growing appetite for acquiring overseas possessions. He warned of Britain's troubles in India and South Africa as examples of how the US might get sucked into foreign entanglements that were not in the country's best interests. In 1895, when President Grover Cleveland threatened Great Britain over a boundary dispute taking place in Venezuela, Boutwell witnessed how easy it was for the American press, led by the Hearst newspapers, to whip up war fever. A few years later, the same dynamic would play out with a different adversary, Spain, over a different issue, Cuba, but with a far different outcome.[5]

IN DOMESTIC POLITICS, Americans in 1896 were fixated on the election campaign between Republican William McKinley and Democrat William Jennings Bryan. The country was still suffering a depression following the Panic of 1893, when bank failures led to business closures, millions being thrown out of work, and violent labor unrest. Grassroots populist movements among farmers and workers were directing their anger at a Republican Party increasingly identified with industrialists and the eastern business establishment. A mesmerizing speaker, Bryan capitalized on this discontent with his attacks on the hard money/tight credit policies emanating from Washington and by proposing government relief for debt-burdened farmers and laborers.

A vivid symbol of the national discontent was Coxey's Army, a mass of unemployed workers led by businessman Jason Coxey, which marched on Washington in the spring of 1894 to make their case directly to Congress. Boutwell was in the city as the army approached, having been hired by the government of Chile to assist an international claims commission that was adjudicating claims arising from Chile's war with Peru the previous decade. With Washington bracing for violence, Boutwell described in letters home how "the coming of the Coxey army disturbs the powers that be." Heavily infiltrated by Pinkerton detectives and confronted by soldiers, Coxey's Army approached Capitol Hill, but the unfolding drama fizzled when Coxey was promptly arrested as he stepped onto the grounds of the US Capitol, and his supporters dispersed.[6]

Boutwell joined the national debate on how the government's monetary policy could help extricate the country from the Panic of 1893. To increase liquidity in the American economy, he relented and supported allowing silver to be used as domestic currency, though he continued to insist that "gold must be used for all international exchanges." Opposing Bryan's call to establish parity between gold and silver, Boutwell stated, as he had since his Treasury days, that America's economic growth was tied to her main trading partners in Europe and thus depended on the primacy of gold.[7]

In one of the great political speeches in American history, Bryan electrified the country when he proclaimed at the 1896 Democratic national convention in Chicago, "you shall not crucify mankind upon a cross of gold." A return to full bimetallism was needed, Bryan insisted, to relieve the debt pressure on America's farmers and workers and bring the country out of the "long depression" that he traced back to the "Crime of 1873." He was referring, of course, to the Act supported by Boutwell and others that removed silver from the domestic economy. Long before Ronald Reagan, Bryan made "trickle-down economics" a major campaign theme by attacking the Republican Party for believing that, by enriching the well-to-do, "their prosperity will leak through to those below." As for McKinley, his political strategist Mark Hanna raised millions of dollars from Standard Oil and other American businesses in what's been described as the first modern political campaign fueled by money.[8]

It was a close contest right up until election day, with just 20,000 votes spread over six states giving McKinley the Electoral College victory. Boutwell may have been relieved that Bryan and the Democrats would not be bringing their "free silver" policies to Washington. Yet he knew that the Democratic Party of the 1890s better represented many of his values, at least those relating to economic fairness, than did the Republican Party, which had increasingly become beholden to corporate interests and big business. While he vehemently protested as white Democrats in the South implemented Jim Crow laws, he also knew that the Republicans were no longer the party of Lincoln and Grant and were content to let Blacks fend for themselves. The Republican Party of that era was grooming younger, more dynamic personalities such as Theodore Roosevelt and Henry Cabot Lodge, who would soon be promoting American adventurism abroad, which Boutwell was convinced struck at the very heart of American democracy.[9]

McKINLEY HAD BEEN in office for a year when George Boutwell celebrated his eightieth birthday on January 28, 1898. It was cold, with enough snow on the ground for well-to-do Bostonians to race their horse-drawn sleighs along city streets. In Groton, with his wife bedridden, Boutwell was joined by his sisters Olive and Abby from nearby Fitchburg in receiving well-wishers at the Main Street home. Lauding the ex-governor's "well-known mental virility and his genial personality," the *Boston Daily Globe* reported that "Gov. Boutwell received his guests with that charming grace so characteristic of him and had a cheery word for each one who clasped his hand." Massachusetts senators George Frisbie Hoar and Henry Cabot Lodge sent birthday greetings from Washington.[10]

Three days earlier the American battle cruiser USS *Maine* had arrived peacefully in Havana harbor from Key West, dropping anchor beneath the iconic Morro Castle, built by the Spanish in 1589 to protect Havana from foreign intrusions. Heavily armored and 325 feet long, the *Maine* had a crew of 355 officers, sailors, and marines. She had been dispatched by President McKinley to "protect American interests" as the decades-long Cuban rebellion against Spanish rule flared up once more. Observing diplomatic protocol, the ship was received with official courtesies by the Spanish authorities.

In Washington, Henry Cabot Lodge was one of several influential figures itching for the US to go to war with Spain. Elected to the Senate in 1892 and a descendant of not one but two eminent New England families, Lodge was making a name for himself by promoting American political and economic expansionism overseas. In doing so, he worked closely and conferred often with longtime friend Theodore Roosevelt, whom Lodge helped install as McKinley's assistant secretary of the navy.[11]

Allies of both were the naval officer and historian, Alfred Thayer Mahan, and the publisher William Randolph Hearst of the increasingly influential *New York Journal*. Mahan's book, *The Influence of Sea Power Upon History, 1660–1783*, would help define the critical role to be played by the US Navy in extending American influence abroad. As for Hearst, he had long ago decided that America at war would be good for the newspaper business.[12]

As street fighting between Spanish troops and Cuban nationalists intensified in January 1898, Hearst's "yellow press" swung into action, printing stories about "atrocities in Cuba" that critics charged were largely "fabricated by writers and illustrators who had never been there." Americans were already in the grip of war fever when Boutwell was given a festive birthday dinner in early February at the Massachusetts Club in Boston's financial district. Commenting on the situation in Cuba, Boutwell once again cautioned about America seeking overseas territories.[13]

Days later, on a warm Havana evening, a tremendous blast ripped through the *Maine*'s forward ammunition magazine, sinking the ship in minutes. Some 260 seamen and marines were killed. Roosevelt, Hearst, and others immediately blamed the Spanish for sinking the *Maine* with a naval mine (the cause was most likely a buildup of methane gas in the ship's ammunition magazine). Newspapers owned by Hearst and rival Joseph Pulitzer began the drumbeat for war, urging Americans to "Remember the *Maine*" and "To Hell with Spain."[14]

IN THE WEEKS FOLLOWING, President McKinley, whose inaugural address had sounded a note of caution about "the temptation of territorial aggression," was hard put to resist increasingly shrill calls for American retaliation. Having served as a sergeant in the Ohio Twenty-Third Infantry in the Civil War, and witnessing the horrors of 20,000 Union and Confederate casualties at Antietam, McKinley sought to deflect Roosevelt's charges of "dirty treachery" by Spain and delayed asking Congress for a declaration of war. By the end of the month, however, Roosevelt was ordering the US Asiatic squadron to set sail for the Philippines and to be battle ready against the Spanish fleet in Manila Bay.[15]

With war fever mounting, Boutwell contacted former Senate colleague Justin Morrill of Vermont, acknowledging that the *Maine* disaster was "deplorable . . . whatever the cause," but urging arbitration with Spain rather than war. By April, McKinley could no longer resist the pressure and now demanded that Spain cease all hostilities against Cuban independence fighters, or else. When Spain responded on April 24 by declaring war on the United States, Congress returned the favor but went one better, making its declaration retroactive to April 21. In the immortal phrase of John Hay, Abraham Lincoln's former secretary and soon-to-be secretary of state, America's "splendid little war" was on.[16]

And in a matter of months, it was over. On May 1, Admiral Dewey's flotilla sank the antiquated Spanish fleet in Manila Bay. In July, having resigned as assistant secretary of the navy, Teddy Roosevelt led his Rough Riders up San Juan Hill to help force the surrender of Spanish forces in Cuba. By mid-August, American soldiers had routed Spain in the jungles of the Philippines. Returning from Cuba, Roosevelt boasted that "we have had a bully fight. I feel as big and strong as a bull moose." Lodge was equally exultant; "what a wonderful war it has been. Nothing but victory, and at such a small cost."

George Boutwell was not so sure. On Memorial Day weekend near where the Pilgrims landed in Plymouth, he recognized the duty of every American to support a war legitimately declared by Congress but cautioned that "wars for the conquest of mere territory cannot be defended." He rejected those who took refuge in the lofty goals of spreading American democracy and the benefits of Christianity, countering that "ideas are not disseminated by force."[17]

WITH THE WAR OVER, the country was jubilant. The US military had made short work of decrepit Spanish forces and thrust American influence into the nearby Caribbean Sea and to the far reaches of the Pacific Ocean, acquiring five island territories with eleven million inhabitants. As George Boutwell feared, Henry Cabot Lodge boasted that "we must on no account let the islands go . . . we hold the other side of the Pacific and the value to this country is almost beyond imagination." In addition to the military and strategic benefits of establishing naval bases in the Far East, Lodge was salivating that the Philippines and "its ten million inhabitants . . . would have to buy our goods."[18]

Taking advantage of the country's imperialist fervor, the US Senate passed a bill annexing Hawaii, which the president signed the next day. A few weeks later, US troops dislodged the Spanish in Puerto Rico and McKinley signed a "protocol of peace" in mid-August bringing the island under US control. Little was said of the fact that Puerto Ricans had themselves installed an elected government under a far-reaching autonomy agreement with Spain. As for Guam, that little known (at least until World War II) volcanic island, with 50,000 inhabitants, had been seized by the US Navy on June 20. Located in the western Pacific, Guam was seen as a valuable strategic asset, just 1,600 miles south of Japan and 1,500 miles east of the Philippines, where Spain had sued for peace when Manila fell on August 13.[19]

While America was congratulating itself on its triumphs over Spain, prominent political figures gathered at Boston's Faneuil Hall to protest what they viewed as the emerging imperialist designs of the McKinley administration. Calling themselves the Anti-Imperialist Committee of Correspondence (with a nod to the Committees of Correspondence of the American Revolution), they reached out for support to political, religious, business, labor, and civic groups across the country. For his part, Boutwell hoped McKinley would promote self-government for the new territories when the war was over. Writing to Navy Secretary John Long, Boutwell acknowledged that, while the conduct of US military forces had been "admirable and the terms of peace . . . altogether reasonable," the acquisition and military occupation of the Philippines and other territories would impose intolerable financial and political burdens on the country.[20]

As Teddy Roosevelt and Henry Cabot Lodge continued to emphasize the strategic and economic benefits of annexing the Philippines while downgrading humanitarian concerns, a second gathering of anti-imperialists took place in Saratoga, New York, among them former president Benjamin Harrison, the industrialist Andrew Carnegie, the Liberal Republican Carl Schurz, and Democrat William Jennings Bryan. Boutwell was unable to attend that meeting, but agreed with the question posed by Carnegie, "must the millions of the Philippines who have been asserting their God-given right to govern themselves be the first victims of Americans?"[21]

In refuting claims that American annexation of the Philippines would mag-
ically open the door to trade with China and Asia, Carnegie the steel baron
sniffed that, "trade does not follow the flag; it scents the lowest price current."
Carnegie also pointed out how just one-tenth of the expense of occupying the
Philippines would greatly expand America's transportation and commercial
infrastructure, with far more benefits to the American economy.

Having a conservative industrialist of Carnegie's stature join the anti-
imperialist opposition helped greatly in giving it credibility in American
business and financial circles. Soon, other national figures joining the movement included the labor leader Samuel Gompers, philosopher William James,
businessman and inventor Edward Atkinson, and diplomat Charles Francis
Adams Jr. Each would contribute by reaching out to their respective constituencies, but it was George Boutwell who crystallized their opposition to
McKinley administration policies with a speech in early October in Boston
entitled "Problems Raised by the War."[22]

BOUTWELL BEGAN HIS ADDRESS that autumn evening by noting the diverse
motives feeding annexationist desires regarding the Philippines, Cuba, Puerto
Rico, and the other islands: "[T]he injustice and brutality of Spanish rule in
Cuba . . . a wish to enlarge the American markets . . . the belief that a new
and fruitful missionary ground would be opened . . . a purpose to enlarge the
scope of republican institutions . . . and the wish to secure coaling stations in
the Caribbean Sea."

Whatever the arguments advanced for annexation, Boutwell's fundamental question was, "Shall we treat Hawaii, Porto Rico, Cuba, and the Philippines
as prospective states, or shall we deal with them as perpetual colonies?" If
prospective states, then the peoples living there deserved the same rights as
Americans, including citizenship, local self-government, and the freedom to
travel, sign labor contracts, and engage in business in any part of the country.
"Without hesitation I say give them territorial governments upon the American basis, with the largest opportunity for progress and for statehood in the
American Union."

Boutwell did admit that Cuba was a special case. Throughout their long
struggle to throw off Spanish domination, Cuban nationalists, inspired by the
poet Jose Martí, had organized, and raised funds, in the United States. Given
this history, Boutwell believed that America had a special responsibility to
assist the island in becoming fully self-governing.[23]

Regarding the Philippines, Boutwell proposed simply that the US government "abandon the Spanish islands of the Pacific without controversy, debate or negotiations with anyone." Whether Filipinos were ready for self-governance or not, it was up to them to decide their country's future, not a United States that was more than eight thousand miles away.

And then there was Puerto Rico, the poor relation of the three island siblings. Its proximity and sugar exports to the US gave it a slightly higher profile than the Philippines, but its economic importance and political connections were dwarfed by those of Cuba. For the moment, Boutwell had little to say about Puerto Rico as he and other critics of American imperialism focused on building a movement to oppose McKinley administration policies.

THE ANTI-IMPERIALIST LEAGUE (AIL), with George Boutwell as president, came into being on November 19 at a small meeting in the Boston offices of the millionaire industrialist and longtime abolitionist, Edward Atkinson. In addition to the politicians and businessmen already involved, it would come to include Black educators and intellectuals such as W. E. B. Du Bois and Booker T. Washington, social reformers such as Jane Addams, and America's most prominent celebrity, Mark Twain.[24]

The challenge facing the anti-imperialist movement had been made clear just a few days before when McKinley's Republican Party capitalized on American prowar sentiment with victories in the midterm elections. Henry Cabot Lodge now led an increased Republican majority in the Senate, and Theodore Roosevelt had been elected governor of New York. In December, Spain signed a peace treaty with the US that relinquished its sovereignty over Cuba and ceded the Philippines, Puerto Rico, and Guam for the modest sum of $20 million. Americans rejoiced at the spoils that awaited from winning the "splendid little war."

In addition to bucking public opinion, the leaders of the anti-imperialist cause, most in their sixties or older, were easily caricatured by Roosevelt as "men of a bygone age having to deal with the facts of the present." Then, they selected George Boutwell, now eighty, to be their president. There might be good reasons for doing so, such as his lifelong commitment to democratic governance and republican principles, as well as his unceasing energy and passion for the cause. But he was, after all, eighty years old.[25]

Drawing on his long experience of fighting for Black civil rights in America, Boutwell questioned why the country was seeking to deny those same benefits to the peoples of Cuba, the Philippines, and Puerto Rico, all newly freed from Spanish oppression. He made common cause with leaders of America's Black community, such as Du Bois, Washington, the journalist Ida B. Wells, and the sociologist Kelly Miller, who denounced US annexation as a "revival of racial arrogance." For Du Bois, American colonization efforts abroad were but an extension of Jim Crow and the denial of both Black and Native American rights at home; "Negro and Filipino, Indian and Porto Rican, Cuban and Hawaiian, all must stand united under the stars and stripes for an America that knows no color line in the freedom of its opportunities." Booker T. Washington, sharing a stage with President McKinley in Chicago, condemned American victories overseas that diverted attention from the failure to achieve racial justice at home. Washington, usually criticized for being more moderate than Du Bois in attacking racism, on this occasion spoke of it as "a cancer gnawing at the heart of this Republic" that "shall one day prove as dangerous [as] an attack from an army."[26]

At the time, McKinley was taking a victory lap around the country, basking in the glow of America's military success. His "war tour" included the Tuskegee Normal and Industrial Institute, Booker Washington's home turf in Alabama. To the largely Black audience, McKinley avoided talking about the war, instead dwelling paternalistically on the virtues of "patience, moderation, self-control, knowledge, [and] character" that the Tuskegee students would need to be successful. The president had a very different message a few days later in Montgomery, the former capital of the Confederacy, when he told the Alabama General Assembly how proud he was of southern and northern soldiers fighting together, thus helping to heal the divisions of the Civil War. Consciously or not, McKinley was capitalizing on the wave of American patriotism generated by the war to help advance the South's rehabilitation and the "Lost Cause" narrative of Confederate redemption. Left unsaid by the president was any criticism of spreading Jim Crow segregation or the horrific public displays of Blacks being lynched that were being publicized by Ida B. Wells.[27]

FOR GEORGE BOUTWELL, the racism of those proclaiming white, Anglo-Saxon superiority as a justification for subjugating the peoples of the Philippines was but a replay of the Reconstruction struggle in the 1860s and 1870s. Accusing the McKinley administration of "making war for the establishment of a system of slavery in Asia," he pointed to the constant use of the word *nigger* by American soldiers in the Philippines and in Cuba that appeared regularly in the press. In a pamphlet directed at America's Black citizens, coauthored with Thomas Wentworth Higginson and William Lloyd Garrison Jr., Boutwell wrote of how "young American soldiers" in the Philippines were being trained to the "habit of thinking that the white man, as such, is the rightful ruler of all other men."[28]

Despite America's peace treaty with Spain, fighting broke out in Manila in early 1899 between Filipino insurgents and US troops. As the conflict intensified that spring, Boutwell equated US policy with British colonial rule in India and South Africa, where the second Boer War was about to erupt. Appealing to the American ideal of "the consent of the governed," Boutwell challenged the McKinley administration to "*redeem* the promises you made in April last [with the declaration of war on Spain]. Allow the inhabitants of Cuba, Porto [*sic*] Rico, and the Philippines to enter at once upon the work of self-government."[29]

With 30,000 American soldiers now fighting a guerrilla war in the Philippines, the public began to lose its enthusiasm for the conflict taking place on the other side of the Pacific. The US Army was conducting "scorched earth" operations to separate Filipino fighters from the civilian population through the creation of "protection zones," as would happen later in Vietnam with the "strategic hamlet program." Herded together in tightly packed, unsanitary enclaves, an estimated 150,000 to 200,000 civilians died from a raging cholera epidemic, producing a "demographic catastrophe" that affected Filipino society for decades.[30]

The more vicious the fighting became, the more overtly racist was the language of American political and military leaders. Filipinos needed to be "good Indians" or were called the N-word. In Cuba, Gen. Leonard Wood denigrated Cuban campesinos as "only partially civilized" and beset by a "spirit of savagery."[31]

Boutwell constantly attacked these white superiority rationales for US imperialism. He had no time for benign justifications of a "civilizing mission" being propagated by the likes of Rudyard Kipling in his poem, "The White Man's Burden." Few remember today that Kipling was addressing the American people with his poem, telling them to "send forth the best ye breed" to help lift up "your new caught, sullen peoples" in the Philippines, akin to British colonial subjects in India.[32]

Yet Boutwell's problem in making these arguments was that many prominent anti-imperialists were equally racist, given their distaste for the prospect of America taking control over millions of nonwhite inhabitants of the Philippines, Cuba, and Puerto Rico. Samuel Gompers, president of the American Federation of Labor, raised the specter of hundreds of thousands of "Chinese, Negritos and the Malays" using the Philippines as a springboard for "swarming into the United States, engulfing our people and our civilization." *The Nation* magazine was anti-imperialist for reasons of Anglo-Saxon superiority and fears of colored immigration. The South Carolina senator "Pitchfork" Ben Tillman was proudly racist in describing Filipinos as "barbarians of the lowest type." Sadly, the more that the superiority of the white race became part of the imperialist argument, as C. Vann Woodward noted, the more it legitimized the dominance of white supremacy in American domestic life, South and North.[33]

DESPITE ATTEMPTS AT military censorship, the public grew increasingly uneasy as reports circulated of ever greater numbers of US troop deaths and injuries in the jungles of the Filipino archipelago. Membership in the anti-imperialist movement numbered in the hundreds of thousands, fueled by "scores of mass meetings, hundreds of speeches, thousands of articles, and tens of thousands of pamphlets, leaflets, and broadsides." New converts included members of the eastern establishment such as Henry Adams, who, despite being a close friend of Lodge and Roosevelt, wondered why "we must slaughter a million or two foolish Malays in order to give them the comforts of flannel petticoats and electric railways."[34]

Seeking to capitalize on rising public discontent, George Boutwell organized a protest meeting in April 1899 at a site which, like Faneuil Hall, had deep associations with abolitionist and other social reform movements. The venue was Tremont Temple Baptist Church overlooking Boston Common. In his speech, Boutwell despaired of how the brutal application of US military force was "transforming eight or ten million Filipinos . . . who were our friends . . . into enemies." Moreover, the war was both expensive and it undermined American economic interests in the region. He charged that President McKinley had abdicated his constitutional duty as commander-in-chief by giving unfettered authority to army generals in the Philippines and Cuba, resulting in torture and atrocities committed by US troops. For Boutwell, the most simple and humane solution, and one in the best interests of America, was to suspend hostilities while helping to organize a Filipino government agreeable to its people.[35]

In Chicago, meanwhile, the anti-imperialists held a large gathering featuring the social reformer and women's suffrage advocate Jane Addams. Women had been joining chapters of the League around the country, admittedly only as "women's auxiliaries." When Addams signed on as a vice president, she hoped to provide the movement with heightened visibility. Given the status of American women at the time, her involvement provoked gender derision and ridicule. The annexationists, proud of embodying Teddy Roosevelt's "essential manliness of the American character," took delight in criticizing Addams, Boutwell, and the anti-imperialists as being "feminine and illogical to the last degree."[36]

For all their bravado, McKinley, Roosevelt, and Lodge were becoming, by the fall of 1899, alarmed at the loss of public support for the Filipino anti-insurgency campaign. The administration's position in Cuba was more favorable, having established a military government with the promise of eventual independence for the island. But 1900 would be an election year. Many Americans were coming to share the sentiment that, as expressed by a journalist in this spoof of Kipling's "White Man's Burden": "We've taken up the white man's burden, of ebony and brown / Now will you tell us, Rudyard, how we may put it down?"[37]

17

Republic or Empire?

Republic or empire? That was the challenge George Boutwell issued to his audience in January 1900 in Washington's Masonic Hall, on Sixteenth Street just blocks from the White House. Public opposition to the Philippines conflict was growing as the election year began, and Boutwell and the anti-imperialists were seeking to stoke it. Belying his eighty-two years, Boutwell stridently warned of the dangers of "an unjust and criminal greed for empire and power." Once the nation had established control over a foreign territory, wouldn't future presidents find it difficult to relinquish it? (Which would prove true for the Philippines, which didn't achieve full independence until after World War II.)[1]

Boutwell also appealed to the American worker, warning in nativist undertones that the subjugation of the Philippines and its eight million people would subject the country "to a direct and never-ending competition with the underpaid and half-clad laborers of Asia." The country would be much better off strengthening its trade and economic ties to an independent Philippines, he said, rather than seeking to subjugate its peoples and then allowing them to compete with the American worker.

His third theme challenged the notion of the "white man's burden" when he declared that Filipinos, Cubans, Puerto Ricans, and other newly freed peoples must be allowed to find their own way to self-government. With a dig at Rudyard Kipling, Boutwell demanded that the United States must be free "from the suspicion that we are to cooperate with England in an attempt to subjugate the weaker states of the world to the domination of the Anglo-Saxon race."

DESPITE PUBLIC OPINION swinging behind them, the anti-imperialists faced two major problems in opposing McKinley prior to the November presidential election. One was the difficulty of criticizing a war in which American soldiers were dying, and which the US military was losing, or at least not winning. Lodge questioned the patriotism of the anti-imperialists, saying debates over the Philippines must wait until the fighting was over; this was no time to be undermining our troops in the field. It was a difficult argument to counter.

The bigger problem had to do with election strategy. Boutwell and the anti-imperialists faced the difficult choice of whether to support William Jennings Bryan, once again the Democratic candidate. Although an avowed anti-imperialist, Bryan had angered Boutwell and others when he pulled a last-minute switch and came out in favor of the Treaty of Paris, which formally ended the Spanish-American War. Bryan justified his change of heart by saying it was better to ratify the treaty and oppose McKinley's occupation policy afterward, rather than renegotiate the agreement. Because the treaty only survived by one vote, Boutwell and his colleagues were incensed, believing that voting down the treaty would have been the best way to crystallize public opposition to McKinley's policies.[2]

The more fundamental problem with Bryan, of course, was the Nebraskan's continued support for silver on an equal basis with gold in the nation's monetary system. It was one thing to ask Republicans to oppose their president on Filipino annexation, but quite another to ask them to embrace the domestic economic policies of Bryan and the Democrats.[3]

There was a third option, considered briefly and then discarded, of mounting an independent challenge to McKinley and Bryan. Andrew Carnegie favored this approach, offering to bankroll a third-party effort. The steel baron quickly withdrew his offer, however, when told by J. P. Morgan and other industrialists that, should he go ahead, they would abandon Carnegie's plans for a steel cartel that could dominate the market. Carnegie might believe in anti-imperialism, but business was business.[4]

Boutwell, for his part, was trying to keep his options open, declaring that "we shall rejoice in the triumph of any party that shall secure justice to individual men and the full enjoyment of the right of self-government." That strategy dissolved when Teddy Roosevelt was selected as McKinley's running mate at the Republican convention in Philadelphia. Any hope of convincing McKinley to support independence for the Philippines in his second term was illusory with Roosevelt as vice president.[5]

WITH ROOSEVELT AND LODGE consolidating power within the Republican Party, Boutwell broke openly with the party he had helped create five decades earlier. In May 1900 at Cooper Union in New York, famous as the locale for having helped launch Lincoln's bid for the presidency in February 1860, Boutwell called for defeating McKinley in November so that the Republican Party "might be cleansed of evil influences." When the anti-imperialists met in Indianapolis later that summer, he came out in full support of Bryan, believing that "the question [of imperialism] is one of life or death for the Republic."[6]

This was a remarkable turnabout for a man who, since before the Civil War, had believed that the survival of the American republic depended on the success of the Republican Party. The Democrats, after all, were the party of inflationary monetary policies in the North and white supremacy in the South. But now, on the fortieth anniversary of having helped elect Abraham Lincoln as president, Boutwell was willing to abandon the Republican Party over the issue of annexing an island nation more than 8,000 miles away.

True to form, Boutwell was putting principle over party. As he explained it, in 1854 he "turned aside and left the old Democratic party when it surrendered itself to slavery. I leave the Republican party . . . now that it has surrendered itself to imperialism and tyranny . . . I helped to create the Republican party because I believed it was a party of justice and liberty and honesty. I now believe that it is a party of injustice and despotism, and I will help to destroy it."[7]

A BRIGHT SPOT for the anti-imperialists during the election campaign of 1900 was the return of Mark Twain and his family from an extended stay in Europe. Twain had been criticizing Filipino annexation from abroad, calling the war "a quagmire." Arriving in New York, Twain told a throng of reporters while coming down the gangplank of the SS *Minnehaha*, "I have seen that we do not intend to free, but to subjugate the people of the Philippines. We have gone there to conquer, not to redeem." Yet for all his criticism of Roosevelt and Lodge, Twain couldn't bring himself to support Bryan, who was "all wrong on the money question."[8]

Most Americans felt the same. On election day, McKinley defeated Bryan even more decisively than in 1896. With Bryan now out of the equation,

Boutwell and the anti-imperialists focused all their attention on McKinley and Roosevelt without having to justify supporting the Democrats. Even Twain was energized by the result, agreeing to become a vice president of the Anti-Imperialist League and soon publishing "To the Person Sitting in Darkness," a scathing indictment of the country's "treacherous" and "evil" subjugation of the Filipino people. Andrew Carnegie called it "the new Gospel of Saint Mark" and subsidized the distribution of 125,000 copies around the country.[9]

WHILE PUBLIC ATTENTION remained focused on the Philippines, where American soldiers were fighting and dying, the situation in Cuba was stabilizing, given US promises not to annex the island and to consider its eventual independence. Leading up to the election, McKinley had even promised to withdraw American troops from Cuba within nine months.[10]

Such promises evaporated once McKinley was reelected. Fears that an independent Cuba would become another "slave republic like Haiti" crystallized opposition for granting autonomy to the island, while Cuban nationalist leaders espousing "independent" policies were seen as undermining American economic and political interests. McKinley supported the army commander in Havana, who said the US should "bind Cuba, hand and foot, and put her destinies absolutely within our control." In early 1901, that policy crystallized in the Platt Amendment, enacted by Congress, which circumscribed the freedom of future Cuban governments for the benefit of American economic, political, and military interests. Then, two years later, local authorities in Cuba "offered" a perpetual lease to the United States for the Guantanamo naval base, where the American military remains to this day.

McKinley's change of heart regarding Cuba gave Boutwell and the anti-imperialists a new opportunity to rekindle public opposition to American annexationism. In a meeting at Faneuil Hall with Boutwell as the lead speaker, a letter was read from the journalist Richard Harding Davis accusing McKinley of "breaking faith with Cuba." Davis was America's first great war correspondent and a good friend of Theodore Roosevelt; his stories had spread the fame of Roosevelt's Rough Riders. Now, Davis was criticizing America's double-dealing with the Cubans, describing how "I saw the men of Cuba shot against stone walls because they had dared to fight for their freedom . . . the United States shall not take that right from them."[11]

Nonetheless, the McKinley administration installed the Republic of Cuba's first president and pressured a Cuban constitutional convention into

accepting the Platt Amendment. For the next six decades, a nominally independent Cuba remained a client state of the US until revolutionaries led by
Fidel Castro overthrew the dictatorship of Fulgencio Batista in 1959.

In the Philippines, meanwhile, US forces in March 1901 captured Emilio
Aguinaldo, the leader of the Filipino insurgency. The daring mission carried
out by Gen. Frederick Funston in the Filipino jungle broke the back of the
insurrection, which the US declared formally at an end in July 1902, although
sporadic fighting continued for several years. The McKinley administration
sought to capitalize on Funston's celebrity by bringing the general home in the
summer of 1901 for a speaking tour, which Mark Twain promptly ridiculed by
congratulating America on the "Funstonian boom" of American imperialist
fervor that was sweeping the country.[12]

THE CAPTURE OF Aguinaldo took the air out of the anti-imperialist cause. Future
president William Howard Taft shortly thereafter installed a civilian government in the Philippines and U.S. soldiers began to come home. Undaunted,
Boutwell used a July Fourth speech to assert that "the rights secured by our
Constitution" should apply to *any* territory under American control. A recent
US Supreme Court decision, however, had declared otherwise. In the first of the
Insular Cases, the court ruled that territories under US jurisdiction could be
treated differently, depending on whether Congress had granted them "incorporated" or "unincorporated" status. Only Hawaii had been granted "incorporated" status, thus constitutional protections would apply. This was not the
case with the "unincorporated" status of the Philippines, Puerto Rico, and the
other island territories (Guam, the US Virgin Islands, American Samoa, and
the Northern Mariana Islands) acquired after the Spanish-American War.
Cuba, having been granted autonomy, was a different case, although Cuban
independence was severely constrained by the Platt Amendment.[13]

The court's decision represented all that Boutwell opposed about American
annexationism. That August, in the *North American Review*, he argued that
the Constitution should always follow the flag; that any territory "acquired in
conformity to the law of nations will be under the jurisdiction of the Constitution," whether in terms of tariffs or citizenship rights. By denying constitutional protections such as trial by jury and the writ of habeas corpus to those
living under American control, the country was violating the Fourteenth
Amendment principles of "due process" and "equal protection under the law"
that he had helped bring into being.[14]

Boutwell also criticized the racism underlying the *Insular* cases. In denying the application of full constitutional rights to the territories (except Hawaii), Justice Edward Douglass White had written that "alien races" could not be deemed suitable for "the administration of government and justice, according to Anglo-Saxon principles." (Hawaii with its white governing elite was considered special and thus eligible for eventual statehood.) Pointedly, Boutwell accused Justice White of replicating the racism of *Plessy v. Ferguson* in consigning the peoples of the territories to second-class status.[15]

As he had in *Plessy*, Justice John Marshall Harlan dissented from the *Insular Cases* decision. The failure to extend constitutional rights to territories acquired by the US, Harlan wrote, would result in the nation's passing "from the era of constitutional liberty guarded and protected by a written constitution into an era of legislative absolutism." Harlan's opinion was reprinted and published by the anti-imperialists under the title, "The Supremacy of the Constitution."[16]

FOR BOUTWELL, the notion of establishing different [racial] classes of citizenship, whether domestically in terms of Jim Crow or in the Philippines under American occupation, went to the core of his opposition to segregation at home and American imperialism abroad. As he knew all too well, however, he had to confront this same racism within the anti-imperialist camp, not only with Liberal Republicans and southern segregationists, but with academics such as David Starr Jordan, president of Stanford University.

Like Louis Agassiz, who had lectured at Boutwell's teacher training workshops in the 1850s, Jordan was a proponent of polygenesis, the theory that races evolved separately from different origins. He was one of the earliest supporters of eugenics (literally, "good birth"), the pseudoscience that sought to improve breeding and the human gene pool, a popular concept at the turn of the century. Calling for racial segregation and racial purity, through enforced sterilization if necessary, Jordan thought Black suffrage an "evil" that would eventually become "a festering sore in the body politic."[17]

Jordan took both a racist and a social Darwinist position against the conflict in the Philippines, arguing that America shouldn't be sending "its best and most healthy citizens" to die fighting Filipino rebels. He also joined Samuel Gompers in warning that US annexation of the Philippines would open the door to waves of "inferior" people flooding the country and competing for jobs with white laborers. Jordan and Gompers were fervent supporters, as were many in the country, of increasingly restrictive US immigration policies that would continue for the next several decades.[18]

AS MENTIONED, America's conflict in the Philippines also provided momentum to the growing reconciliation back home between North and South. Newspaper reports of northern and southern soldiers fighting and dying together in the Philippines and Cuba allowed Teddy Roosevelt and others to praise the patriotic "unity it brought about between the sons of the men who wore the blue and those who wore the gray."[19]

Such reconciliation did not, to be sure, extend to America's nine million Black citizens. The irony of Blacks being lynched and segregated in America while Black soldiers died in the Philippines was noted by the African American lawyer and activist Archibald Grimke, among others, in saying that true reconciliation between North and South would require Black Americans receiving "free and equal treatment and opportunities in the rivalry of life."[20]

By the summer of 1901, anti-imperialism was a spent force, undone by the onset of civilian rule in the Philippines, the *Insular* cases decision, and McKinley's promise of self-government for Cuba, hollow as it was. There was the occasional public outcry over continuing US troop casualties and reports that American soldiers were shooting unarmed Filipino prisoners. But McKinley and Roosevelt were able to put a positive spin on political developments in the territories and the anticipated benefits to the American economy of new markets in the Pacific and Caribbean. Others emphasized the civilizing mission of America; Senator John L. McLaurin of South Carolina celebrated America's Fourth of July by proclaiming that "our Nation, with its free government and its aggressive Christian civilization . . . with our wealth and commerce and Anglo-Saxon love of liberty . . . is in a position to march forward and convert the world."[21]

Simply put, Roosevelt and Lodge portrayed themselves as young, dynamic, and forward-thinking in terms of America becoming a global power, while Boutwell and his colleagues were seen as seeking to deny the United States its "manifest destiny" on the world stage. Lodge would dismiss them collectively with the quip, "Poor old Boutwell is not of much consequence, and his violence is the violence of age, I think."[22]

Moreover, in criticizing imperialism on humanitarian, social, economic, legal, and moral grounds, the anti-imperialist message was often confusing and contradictory. This was compounded by the outright hypocrisy of some anti-imperialists who used white superiority and anti-immigrant language that was little different from that of the annexationists. Boutwell's appeal to constitutional principles and human rights might resonate with many, but it was not enough to counter the flag-waving pronouncements of Roosevelt and others about the economic, military, and political benefits to be had by projecting American power abroad.[23]

AT THE OPENING OF the twentieth century, there was no question that America was poised for greatness. In Buffalo, the celebratory Pan American Exposition was under way, showcasing the promises of technology—including the X-ray machine and electric lighting using power generated by Niagara Falls—that heralded a new era. Teddy Roosevelt officiated at its opening, beaming as he led reporters among the Greek classical and French Beaux-Arts exhibit halls. No one was yet calling it "the American century," but they soon would be.

That September, Roosevelt was vacationing in the Adirondacks when President McKinley traveled to Buffalo for his first appearance at the Exhibition. After touring Niagara Falls on the morning of September 6, McKinley was greeting hundreds of spectators when one of them, the anarchist Leon Czolgosz, shot him twice with a concealed .32 caliber pistol. Czolgosz had lost his steelworker's job in the Panic of 1893 and was reportedly angry with the president for "outrages committed by the American government in the Philippines Islands." Only one wound in the abdomen seemed serious; McKinley might have survived if anyone had known how to use the X-ray machine on display nearby. But infection spread and McKinley died a few days later.[24]

With Theodore Roosevelt sworn in as the country's twenty-sixth president, the projection of American power abroad truly gathered steam. When Henry Cabot Lodge returned from a European trip, the two consulted almost daily regarding America's global ambitions. One important piece fell into place when the Senate ratified the Hay-Pauncefote Treaty with Great Britain, making possible Roosevelt's dream of building the Panama Canal.[25]

Boutwell and his colleagues had one last burst of anti-imperialist fervor when newspapers reported that American soldiers were torturing Filipino combatants and civilians. The Senate began an investigation, but it was tightly controlled by Lodge, who made sure that no Filipinos or members of the Anti-Imperialist League would be called to testify.

In July 1902, Congress enacted the Philippine Organic Act, which provided the legal structure for indefinite US governance of the archipelago. On the

Fourth of July, Roosevelt issued a presidential proclamation declaring the Philippines war at an end and praising the American military for its "self-control, patience and magnanimity" in a conflict that killed more than 4,000 American soldiers, 20,000 Filipino combatants, and more than 200,000 Filipino civilians.[26] The Philippines did not achieve full independence until 1946.

Mark Twain chose to celebrate his holiday by writing a blistering satire of a Fourth of July parade that consisted of floats bedecked with 12,000 newly acquired Filipino islands marked "Boodle" and bodies of slaughtered Filipino patriots tagged as "rebels." A few months later, George Boutwell spoke at the Twentieth Century Club in Boston. In what was a benediction for a lost cause, he could offer few constructive options for opposing Roosevelt and the Republican Party in the 1902 midterm election, despite his warnings that the party he had so long supported had become infected with "the missionary spirit, the mercenary spirit, and the vindictive spirit." Soon thereafter, Boutwell appeared in Boston with Democratic Party candidates for governor and Congress. Signaling his complete break from the Republican Party, Boutwell said he would only support candidates who pledged themselves to "an immediate promise of independence . . . to the Filipinos."[27]

The efforts of Twain, Boutwell, Carnegie, and others had amounted to little. In the midterm elections, Republicans maintained a comfortable majority in the House while adding to their two-to-one margin in the Senate. In Massachusetts, the Boutwell-backed Democrats lost both the governorship and ten out of fourteen House seats.

Roosevelt and Lodge could now look forward to two years of Republican dominance on Capitol Hill and a free hand in shaping policy for the Philippines, Puerto Rico, the territories, and Cuba. For Boutwell and the anti-imperialists, some serious stock-taking was in order.

CHRISTMAS THAT YEAR was not especially cheerful at the Boutwell home in Groton. George would soon celebrate his eighty-fifth birthday. Although he remained vigorous and in good health, his wife Sarah's health was failing rapidly. Bedridden with heart and respiratory ailments for the past decade, she would die within three months. Georgie was her mother's principal caregiver, but the daily care and attention she was providing took a toll, which her father knew all too well. That summer, the two went for a drive in the countryside around Groton. Stopping their buggy on the edge of a field, George climbed down to pick some of Georgie's favorite wildflowers. With "the hot sun pouring down on him," as Georgie remembered, she was embarrassed to be sitting comfortably in the buggy while her octogenarian father was stooping low to gather flowers. When she admonished him, he replied, Nonsense, she deserved some attention for having cared so long for her mother.[28]

Sarah's death in March 1903 took from George the partner and friend who had shared his triumphs and disappointments for more than sixty years. Others were gone as well. His closest friend in Groton, Col. Daniel Needham, George's partner in purchasing Liberty Hall in the 1840s to host local antislavery meetings, and later Boutwell's senior aide as governor, had died in 1895. The Reverend Joshua Young, another of Boutwell's links to the antislavery days from before the Civil War, had moved away from Groton and would die within the year. Among his political colleagues, George Frisbie Hoar's death in September 1904 would take one of the few remaining members of Boutwell's political generation. Hoar's replacement as Massachusetts senator, Winthrop Crane, typified the evolution of a Republican Party far different from that which Boutwell helped create. Having made his fortune with the stationery company bearing his name, Crane would become a mentor to President Calvin Coolidge, forever associated with the phrase, "the business of America is business."

Boutwell's own business affairs, moreover, were not faring well. No longer able to maintain his law practice full time, he started remortgaging and then selling off acreage from his Groton farm. One transaction was especially poignant, the sale of 153 acres to Lawrence Brooks of Medford, Massachusetts, a descendant of the same Peter Chardon Brooks (a relative of Henry Adams) who in 1815 had given George's father, Sewell, his first big break as a farm manager outside of Boston. In the search for additional income, Boutwell invested in various gold mining ventures out west that didn't pan out; he also bought land in San Diego at the start of a building boom that would come too late to help him financially.[29]

Fortunately, Groton neighbors and colleagues from the anti-imperialist campaign, from which he had received no salary, stepped in to help. In 1903, Boutwell sent heartfelt thanks to acknowledge the receipt of $3,000 in gold notes from George Augustus King of Concord, Massachusetts, a former law colleague and longtime family friend. Groton resident William F. Wharton, a relative of the writer Edith Wharton, teamed up with the Reverend Endicott Peabody of Groton School to provide a yearly annuity, given that "the Governor and Miss Boutwell are in danger of being turned out of their home."[30]

As if to banish these personal setbacks, George Boutwell drove himself even harder in carrying on the anti-imperialist struggle. He devoured the news coming from the Philippines and Cuba, kept a diary of significant foreign policy events, wrote a steady stream of letters and articles seeking support for the cause, and accepted numerous speaking engagements. On New Year's Day in 1903, in a remarkable speech to a packed audience of white and Black Bostonians in Faneuil Hall, Boutwell made clear his devotion to equality and civil rights both at home and abroad, which was an apotheosis of his sixty years in public life.

18

A "New" Emancipation Proclamation

Temperatures neared fifty degrees as the crowds began streaming from all over Boston toward Faneuil Hall. Described as "almost balmy" for the first of January, the weather helped bring out an overflow crowd for the "Great Emancipation Meeting" that would celebrate the fortieth anniversary of Abraham Lincoln signing the Emancipation Proclamation. Many in the crowd came from the city's Black neighborhoods in the South End, Roxbury, and Hyde Park. Whites in equal numbers came from Charlestown, Beacon Hill, and Cambridge, while speakers and special guests were arriving by horse carriage and rail from Lexington, Concord, and Groton.

The crowds converging on Faneuil Hall passed the vegetable stalls of nearby Quincy Market, where seventy years before a young George Boutwell and his father had made the trek from their farm in Lunenburg to sell vegetables before returning with a herd of cattle. Now eighty-five, Boutwell stepped off the train from Groton to give the keynote speech, in the building reverently referred to as "the cradle of Liberty," in which he would call for America to live up to its principles of equal citizenship and republican government.

Like the colonial revolutionaries Sam Adams and John Hancock in the 1770s, and the abolitionists William Lloyd Garrison and Frederick Douglass in the 1850s, George Boutwell was an integral part of Faneuil Hall's history. Originally built in 1743 and destroyed by fire in 1806, the building was redesigned and rebuilt by the famed American architect Charles Bulfinch. What most of the audience that day, half of them Black, didn't know was that the venerable building was named for an early Boston slave trader, Peter Faneuil.[1]

The Great Emancipation Meeting, organized by business and religious leaders from Boston's Black community, continued a long tradition of Blacks celebrating emancipation throughout America. From small southern towns to the cities of the North, the abolition of slavery had been joyously observed with music, parades, and speeches for years following the Civil War. Yet as time passed and "Jim Crow" entrenched itself, both South and North, there was little reason for Blacks to celebrate what they had considered their "holiday." The Boston event would be the first in twenty-five years. It was hoped that the daylong celebration, consisting of three separate programs of speakers, special guests, and music, would help rekindle a sense of pride and empowerment in Boston's Black community.[2]

William Monroe Trotter, a Phi Beta Kappa graduate of Harvard and the owner and editor of the recently established African American newspaper, the Boston *Guardian*, oversaw the day's events. Assisting him were several notable local Black clergymen, including the Reverend William H. Scott of Woburn and the Reverend Johnson W. Hill of Boston. Trotter hoped that the Great Emancipation Meeting would be not only a day of celebration, but a means of solidifying the voice of his *Guardian* newspaper in the politics of Black America. In the contest between Booker T. Washington and W. E. B. Du Bois for leadership of the Black community, Boutwell's speech that day, directly connecting Filipino freedoms thousands of miles away with Black civil rights at home, would fit perfectly with the more radical "race first" emphasis favored by Trotter and Du Bois as opposed to the accommodationist policies of Washington.[3]

As latecomers noisily took their seats, the morning session began with a Black gospel quartet singing "America," followed by an invocation read by the chaplain of the famed Fifty-Fourth Massachusetts Regiment, whose muster George Boutwell had supported as a Massachusetts congressman in 1863. Later that day, there would be a recitation of the poet Paul Lawrence Dunbar's "Negro Soldier," the renowned Peerless Quartet would sing "John Brown's Body," and the Reverend William Scott would recite the "Oration on Toussaint L'Ouverture." With participants clapping and singing, the atmosphere inside the hall began to take on the trappings of a tent revival meeting.

As noon approached, Boutwell's Groton neighbor and good friend, the Reverend Joshua Young, took the podium. Age eighty-three with "a patriarchal white beard," the Reverend Young was a decades-long participant in the fight for Black emancipation and equal rights. In 1859 he presided over the burying of John Brown's body when no other minister would do so, traveling from his home in northern Vermont to upstate New York, across frozen Lake Champlain in the middle of winter. Widespread revulsion of Brown for his failed attack on Harper's Ferry, followed by his hanging for treason, was pervasive throughout the country. A dummy coffin had to be used as a decoy in Philadelphia so the abolitionist's body wouldn't be hijacked en route to the Brown family home in North Elba near Lake Placid. Following the burial, the Reverend Young was banished from his church in Vermont and then ostracized for years before finding refuge in Groton in 1875 as minister of the First Parish Church. He and George Boutwell became close friends over the next quarter century.[4]

Reverend Young was just finishing his story of lowering John Brown's body into the frozen ground when "Ex-Governor Boutwell entered the hall and was given an enthusiastic ovation." Slightly stooped but firmly gripping the lectern, Boutwell gave the standing-room-only crowd a detailed history of America's struggle with slavery. He began with how slavery was embedded in the American Constitution and recounted the travails of the nation moving through abolitionism, the Civil War and emancipation, and the Thirteenth, Fourteenth, and Fifteenth civil rights amendments. He described President Grant's efforts to safeguard Reconstruction-era protections from southern violence and northern apathy. He asserted how the Emancipation Proclamation was second only to the Declaration of Independence in historic importance and that, despite all the setbacks, America still "leads the world in recognizing equality of rights in men [and] equality of opportunity."[5]

Warming to his topic, Boutwell exhorted his listeners to think of the parallels between the evils of slavery and racial discrimination at home and imperialism abroad. He attacked the Republican Party of McKinley and Roosevelt for establishing American control over Hawaii, the Philippines, and Puerto Rico, "not different from that which existed in the slave States prior to 1863." Speaking directly to the Black members of the audience, the ex-governor asserted that "unless the freedom of the Philippine Islands shall be secured, there can be neither power nor justice for you in America." One reporter noted the tepid response of the crowd, writing that Boutwell's "audience, though cordially attentive, did not show particular enthusiasm." There was a similar lack of enthusiasm when Boutwell declared that perhaps "the Emancipation Proclamation was a mistake," if the United States was now seeking to subjugate eight million Filipinos.[6]

The crowd may have lost the thread of Boutwell's logic, yet his conclusions dovetailed nicely with the purposes of William Monroe Trotter and the "race first" strategy of Blacks supporting selected Democratic candidates to put pressure on the Republicans. Boutwell felt the same, telling his audience that your "race is being used simply for vote-getting purposes" by the Republicans and that they should "assert Negro power" through strategic voting for Democrats throughout the northern states.[7]

Boutwell spelled out how this would work, counting off the numbers, state by state, where the Black vote could be leveraged most effectively. In Pennsylvania there were 30,000 Black voters; in Ohio and New York, 20,000 each. Continuing, he listed 15,000 in New Jersey, 13,000 in Illinois, 12,000 in Indiana, and 3,000 in Connecticut. Because Black voters represented the "balance of power" between Republicans and Democrats in many of these states, they could influence "the electoral vote and the congressional vote" across the North. Not only could this electoral strength help change Roosevelt's policy in the Philippines, it could also impress upon "the white population of every State in the Union" that they could not afford "to alienate a tenth part of the population of the country."[8]

Trotter had made the same argument a few months earlier, just prior to the national midterm elections. In a *Guardian* editorial headlined, "No Republican Congress without Black Votes," Trotter criticized Teddy Roosevelt for sacrificing Black aims on the altar of white supremacy. He asked whether "a million and a half colored people throughout the North" had not already been "cast overboard from the Republican ship as a barrel to amuse the Southern whale, while the imperialistic craft proceeds on her journey."[9]

Each in their own way, Trotter and Boutwell were calling for a "new emancipation proclamation" whereby Black voters would declare their independence from a Republican Party that was no longer protecting their interests. For Boutwell, this would have the added benefit of enlisting Black support in opposing Roosevelt's imperialism.

PRESS AND PUBLIC reaction to Boutwell's speech was decidedly mixed. Despite his impeccable civil rights credentials, the ex-governor was chided for advising Blacks to switch their allegiance to a Democratic Party controlled by white supremacists in the South. Most newspapers advised Black voters to "repudiate" Boutwell's advice that they "desert the Republican party and vote with the Democrats." Boutwell was accused of being fixated on a failed anti-imperialism campaign. "We do not question the sincerity of Mr. Boutwell's belief, but he is in error . . . in Boston one hears ten times as much about anti-imperialism . . . as in Washington . . . anti-imperialism is played out."[10]

In the nation's capital, that's certainly what Theodore Roosevelt thought. As he greeted 7,000 well-wishers at a New Year's Day reception at the White House, the president had a quite different fixation: acquiring the treaty rights with which to build the Panama Canal.[11]

In domestic politics, Roosevelt was taking heat for having appointed fewer Blacks to federal positions than McKinley. Yet, having hosted Booker T. Washington at the White House despite widespread criticism, he still enjoyed much goodwill in the Black community; many Blacks called Teddy "our president" and compared him favorably to Lincoln. Also, Roosevelt was standing firm on some controversial Black nominations he had made for federal government positions. One such, William H. Lewis as assistant district attorney in Boston, was a speaker at the Great Emancipation Meeting. A resolution passed at the gathering commended Roosevelt for his "manly personal stand against lynching and 'lilywhiteism' (a polite expression for white supremacy)."[12]

Boutwell's advice that Blacks desert Roosevelt and vote for the Democrats, the party of southern white supremacy, was considered heresy by many of his Republican friends and colleagues, who likely agreed with Lodge about "the violence of old age." It was one thing to believe that Blacks were being abandoned by the Republican Party, but that shouldn't translate into supporting Democrats. A good friend of Boutwell's agreed that, yes, "the colored people are compelled to choose between the Democratic party, which is cheating and lynching them, and the Republican, which is doing little better." But "while your advice to them on the whole is probably sound, I cannot be surprised if in this alternative they *take to the woods* [refusing to support either party]." Despite the advice of Trotter and Du Bois that Blacks vote race first and party second, Roosevelt could likely continue to count on their allegiance so long as Democrats were viewed as the protectors of southern white supremacy and northern race-based segregation.[13]

GEORGE BOUTWELL TURNED eighty-five a few weeks after the Great Emancipation Meeting, celebrating his birthday with family and friends at home in Groton. Not one to slow down, he took the train to New York two weeks later to be one of the main speakers at a Lincoln Birthday celebration at Delmonico's restaurant on Fifth Avenue. Sitting next to him at the speakers table was the writer and journalist Ida Tarbell, author of the recently published biography

The Life of Lincoln. When it was Boutwell's turn to speak, "the venerable Massachusetts statesman" echoed Lincoln but also wove an "anti-imperialist utterance" into his remarks, declaring that "neither in the nineteenth nor in the twentieth century can a nation live half-slave and half-free . . . the nation which tries to do so is doomed."[14]

Boutwell returned to Groton the next day. The following morning, as reported in the papers, he "made his usual trip to his Boston office and plunged into business, not at all fatigued by his journey." At home, Sarah's health was failing. She lost consciousness on Saturday morning, March 7, and died the next day, aged eighty-nine. Services were held at the home a few days later with Joshua Young presiding. Among the many tributes sent to the house was a wreath of white roses "from the colored citizens of Boston . . . in memory of the helpmate of our friend."[15]

Whether it was his Yankee discipline, a distraction from losing his wife of sixty-two years, or both, George Boutwell persevered with his anti-imperialist crusade. A week after Sarah's death, he took the train into Boston to join others in protesting that Lodge's Senate hearings on the Philippines were "suppressing information and refusing to hear testimony." Boutwell and Boston colleague Moorfield Storey conducted a "mock" hearing of their own, taking eyewitness testimony from US Army soldiers regarding the shooting of unarmed Filipinos, including a Catholic priest. Boutwell was outraged that Lodge left unchallenged the invidious comparisons made by southern senators, that perhaps outrages had been committed, but so too had Union troops in the Civil War been "as brutal, as cruel and as unjust as the army in the Philippines."[16]

Boutwell continued to speak out, opposing US policy in the Philippines through the remainder of 1903. Looking ahead to the 1904 election, defeating Roosevelt was the only option remaining for the anti-imperialists and a diminishing one at that. To many, Boutwell resembled King Lear, thundering against forces beyond his control for violating what he held most dear, his cherished notions of American equality and democracy.

IN THE SPRING of 1904, chance threw Theodore Roosevelt and George Boutwell together in a most unusual setting. It was Prize Day at Groton School, already one of the most elite private schools in the country. With two of his sons as students, Roosevelt was the featured speaker. Boutwell, as the town of Groton's most distinguished citizen, was invited to attend the ceremonies and the luncheon afterward. One can imagine his thoughts, knowing he would see the president on his home turf.

The president's train arrived at 9 a.m., within sight of the Boutwell house. George might have watched Roosevelt from his second-floor study as the president climbed into his carriage for the ten-minute ride to the school. Boutwell drove out later that morning to join the several hundred guests as they walked around the school's stately Georgian buildings and luxuriant grounds, designed by famed American landscape architect Frederick Law Olmsted.

Boutwell was in the audience as the president spoke to the students about the importance of personal character and perseverance. Slapping his hands together for emphasis, Roosevelt exhorted the boys to remember that "the only life worth leading . . . is the life of effort, the life of effort to attain." Whatever faults Roosevelt might have, Boutwell would agree that TR, although born to privilege, had known the value of hard work.[17]

A splendid lunch on the lawn followed, after which, it was noted, "the President, while cordial, did not appear to prefer the society of the mothers." Rather, he would seize "upon a man who broke through the group of femininity about him" to converse and laugh. Roosevelt then walked about the school grounds with his two sons, Theodore Jr. and Kermit. "By 4 o'clock," the *Boston Post* reported, "the crowd had thinned out considerably and following the lead that ex-Governor Boutwell and others set, the President prepared to depart."[18]

It's not known if Boutwell and Roosevelt exchanged even perfunctory pleasantries that day. If so, Boutwell would have shaken the hand of a man who had every reason to believe that it was he who fully embodied the America that was striding into the twentieth century. The Philippines was being pacified and was no longer of public interest. A few weeks earlier, US Army engineers had begun work in the newly acquired Panama Canal Zone on the engineering marvel that would fulfill Roosevelt's dream of projecting American maritime power to the furthest reaches of the world's oceans.

AS GEORGE BOUTWELL returned to the family home on Main Street, the anti-imperialism campaign, to which he had given body and soul in the remaining years of his life, was ending, not with a bang but with a whimper. Conflict in the Philippines had died down to sporadic guerrilla outbursts, and the United States was consolidating its economic and political control over Cuba, Puerto Rico, and Hawaii. The country's first mass mobilization against US military action abroad was dying, not to be rekindled until the Vietnam conflict in the 1960s.

In November, Roosevelt swept to victory in the presidential election by a margin of more than two and a half million votes. The Republican Party was now fully his, and Roosevelt could advance American interests abroad while implementing his progressive agenda of antitrust and labor reform at home. Ominously for the future of American politics, the 1904 election marked the dominance of the racially conservative "solid South" voting bloc of white Democrats that would institutionalize Jim Crow segregation policies for decades to come. These were the very Democrats that George Boutwell was asking Black Americans to support.

TWO WEEKS AFTER the election, Boutwell presided over what one colleague called "a cheery sort of funeral" when the Anti-Imperialist League held its sixth annual meeting on a chilly day at the Twentieth Century Club on Beacon Hill. Its officers were gathering two days after Thanksgiving, but they had little to be thankful for. In what would be Boutwell's final annual meeting, one colleague proposed that, given Roosevelt's reelection, the League might well be advised "to wind up its business, close its doors, and burn its records." In good Yankee fashion, though, the prevailing mood was to press on.[19]

William Lloyd Garrison Jr., son of the famed abolitionist and now sixty-six years old, urged his colleagues to continue "the struggle against the swelling pride of Anglo-Saxon self-consciousness, its lust of power and greed." Others were more realistic, acknowledging that "Theodore Roosevelt represents today the temper and point of view of the American people, as to armies, navies, world power, Panama republics, and American police duty on [sic] the Western hemisphere. That is as undeniable as the rising of the sun." Sharing this sentiment was the philosopher William James, who likened Roosevelt and the annexationists to "the party of red blood . . . the party of animal instinct, jingoism, fun, excitement, bigness." By contrast, he and his fellow anti-imperialists were a "pale reflection . . . of reason, forecast, order." James concluded that all of them were likely seen by the American public as "priggish" and a "bloodless bore . . . [our] only audience posterity."[20]

Two months shy of his eighty-seventh birthday, Boutwell urged his colleagues onward. Describing the struggle as worthy of continuing, he invoked Lincoln's Gettysburg Address in declaring that independence and self-rule for the Philippines would constitute a "new birth of freedom" for Americans just as much as for Filipinos. Quoting Shakespeare, "out of this nettle, danger, we pluck this flower, safety," he still believed, devoid of evidence or realism, that independence for the Philippines might be achieved. He argued that Roosevelt's impressive electoral victory was more about the president's magnetic personality than his policies. Recalling that the US had initially promised independence to the Filipinos, Boutwell said that Roosevelt should be held to account to "perform this signal act of justice . . . to elevate eight million human beings from involuntary servitude to personal freedom, self-government and statehood among the nations of the earth."[21]

Ever the optimist, Boutwell was determined to press on. Writing to Andrew Carnegie, Boutwell agreed—somewhat—with Carnegie's argument that perhaps Roosevelt could be persuaded that, having won the presidency on his own, he could now bring the troops home and join "Washington and Lincoln in the annals of America . . . and a place in history" if he magnanimously granted independence to eight million Filipinos. This did not happen.[22]

His colleagues reelected Boutwell as president of the Anti-Imperialist League. He remained in good health, and the League still had a formidable array of supporters, including the recently retired commanding general of the US Army, Lt. Gen. Nelson Miles. A Medal of Honor recipient in the Civil War, Miles had become disillusioned with the brutality of the conflict in the Philippines and had signed on as a vice president of the league. Even the addition of a war hero such as Miles, however, could not revive the movement's fortunes. And in less than three months, George Boutwell would be dead.

BOUTWELL DIED OF pneumonia at his home in Groton on Monday, February 27, 1905. He was said to have been "clear-eyed and calm," murmuring "I believe I am going to die" shortly before drawing his last breath. Given his special relationship with Georgie, it's not surprising that those present remember that "as he sank lower and lower and his breathing became fainter, his eyes sought those of his daughter." In his will, he left the Groton house and most of his estate to Georgie, "in consideration of her long and valuable service in my family and especially for her care of her mother."[23]

George's son Francis was also at his bedside, with his wife Caroline. The two had married in 1900, late in life, and had no children. Accordingly, George Boutwell had no grandchildren, and his line of the Boutwell family ended when Georgianna, who never married, died in 1933 at the age of ninety. At her death, she bequeathed the house on Main Street, which had been her home for more than eighty years, to the Groton Historical Society.[24]

That Georgie was able to maintain the house on her own for twenty-eight years was due to her father's foresight in taking advantage, decades before, of connections made during his work on the US-Chilean Claims Commission, connections that didn't pay off until well after his death. Having finished his work for the Commission in 1894, Boutwell signed on to represent the part-ners of Alsop and Company, a silver mining firm, in a claim against Chile for debts dating to the 1870s. A complicated affair, the case was finally settled in 1911 after being submitted to King George V of Great Britain for arbitration. The following year, the US State Department distributed more than $860,000 to the claimants, with more than $35,000 (more than one million in today's dollars) making its way to Boutwell's estate for the benefit of his daughter (son Francis had died in 1910). Fortunately for Georgie and her father's legacy, it was money from the Alsop claim that allowed her to pay off the existing mortgage and other debts and focus on preserving the Boutwell papers and family correspondence.[25]

BOUTWELL'S FUNERAL SERVICE and burial in Groton cemetery took place on Thursday, March 2, a sunny day though with plenty of snow on the ground. Massachusetts governor William L. Douglas led a delegation of more than eighty dignitaries traveling by special train from Boston. General Miles was among them, as was ex-governor John D. Long, whose absence from his office as navy secretary in 1898 had allowed Teddy Roosevelt to set in motion prepa-rations for the Spanish-American War.[26]

Boutwell's body lay in state at the Groton Town Hall, across the street from his home, attended by a bodyguard of twenty-four members of the George S. Boutwell Post 48 of the Grand Army of the Republic. Among the wreaths adorning the casket were floral tributes from the Anti-Imperialist League and one from "the colored citizens of Boston, in commemoration of the notable services rendered to their race by the liberty-loving ex-governor." That same day, a tribute written by T. Thomas Fortune, editor of the African American newspaper *The New York Age*, praised Boutwell for having "to his last days preserved his devotion to the human rights of all races."[27]

Six weeks later, on the 130th anniversary of Paul Revere's ride in April 1775, five hundred people gathered in Faneuil Hall to pay tribute to George Boutwell and his decades of service to the Commonwealth and to the nation. Speakers included General Miles and a young Filipino, Martin P. DeVerya, who praised Boutwell for "fostering . . . the spirit of liberty and independence for the Filipinos." Tributes came in from around the country, including from Andrew Carnegie, who praised Boutwell for having "served the republic in the greatest crisis of its history." *The Nation* magazine, for decades one of Boutwell's severest critics, acknowledged the ex-governor's "intensity of conviction and rugged honesty . . . which gave him for many years a position of almost unparalleled influence in the counsels of the Republican party." His colleagues that day recalled his "absolute absorption in the cause" and "inspiring confidence in the ultimate triumph of the right." More than anything, they praised his unflagging perseverance, even in the months before he died, and his unwillingness to never "barter his convictions for repose."[28]

THE ANTI-IMPERIALISTS may have lost their indefatigable president, but they soldiered on, hoping that an educated public would become more receptive to warnings about the dangers of American adventurism abroad. The League next met in November 1905 at the Twentieth Century Club on Beacon Hill, where Boutwell had spoken so many times. In a resolution moved by Treasurer David Greene Haskins, the only objective left the group was to "assist in educating public opinion . . . patiently and enthusiastically."

Replacing Boutwell as president was his longtime friend and abolitionist colleague Moorfield Storey. It was Storey who had sat with William Evarts during the impeachment trial of Andrew Johnson and passed on for posterity George Boutwell's now well-traveled "hole in the sky" joke. In 1909, Storey would become founding president of the National Association for the Advancement of Colored People (NAACP), serving for twenty years until his death.[29]

The most immediate problem confronting Storey was money; there was less than one hundred dollars in the organization's bank account. Ever hopeful, Garrison Jr. sought to raise morale with a poem referencing Civil War ammunition (the Minié ball) and the Gutenberg printing press: "William McKinley was not Fate, Theodore Roosevelt is not Time; Minié is good, but, spite of change, Gutenberg's gun has the longest range."[30]

For his part, League secretary Erving Winslow, who with Boutwell had been most responsible for keeping the organization going, proclaimed that "the mantle of our Elijah [George Boutwell] has fallen upon a worthy Elisha

[Moorfield Storey]." Taking his reference from the Book of Kings in the Old Testament, Winslow was reminding his colleagues how the Hebrew prophet Elisha was said to have performed twice as many miracles as Elijah, his predecessor. In his heart of hearts, Winslow must have known that nothing short of divine intervention would redeem the promise of the anti-imperialists.[31]

Epilogue

In May 1908, with a New England spring again coming into bloom, several hundred Boutwell friends and colleagues gathered to dedicate a memorial tablet at his grave in the "new" Groton cemetery, laid out in 1847 (the original Old Burying Ground, dating to 1678, was full). Boutwell himself had helped plan the cemetery in the 1840s; it was now adorned with the magnificent beech and maple trees that he had insisted be planted. A five-foot-high "plain tablet of white statutory marble," a gift from Andrew Carnegie and others, was placed at the head of his and Sarah's grave and dedicated with a benediction from the Reverend Endicott Peabody while daughter Georgianna and son Francis looked on.[1]

The main speaker back at Groton Town Hall, to which the several hundred participants retreated because of the threat of impending rain, was Winslow Warren, prominent attorney and a member of the Board of Overseers of Harvard College. Warren remembered Boutwell as a "devoted husband, the fond and loving father, and the exemplary fellow citizen." What opponents derided as fanaticism in defense of a cause, whether Black civil rights or Filipino citizenship, Warren described as "an unconquerable belief in the wisdom and permanency of republican institutions." Most of all, George Boutwell would be remembered for his dedication to the Union, the abolition of slavery, and equality for America's Black citizens: "He deprecated war but was a vigorous and constant upholder of the civil war which meant to him the destruction of African slavery which he thoroughly detested . . . the cost of its removal was as nothing to him compared with the curse of its existence. He knew not the meaning of compromise upon such a subject."[2]

IN WASHINGTON, Theodore Roosevelt, who sent a telegram of remembrance to be read at the ceremony, was pushing full speed ahead with expanding America's global reach. In the Philippines, the United States was instituting civil and educational reforms following the surrender of the insurrectionists, after which there was limited autonomy in 1916, but complete independence for the country wouldn't come for another three decades. In 1906, Roosevelt promised citizenship for the people of Puerto Rico, but the island to this day remains an unincorporated territory and has not attained statehood. General elections were held in Cuba in 1908, but as with Puerto Rico, the island was dominated by American economic interests, at least until Fidel Castro's revolution in 1959.

Also in 1906, President Roosevelt won the Nobel Peace Prize for his efforts in mediating an end to the Russo-Japanese War of 1905, further burnishing America's stature on the world stage. That conflict was the subject of one of George Boutwell's very last diary entries, made a month before his death in almost illegible handwriting, when he noted the fall of Port Arthur to the Japanese Navy, which in the decades ahead would become America's main naval competitor in the Pacific Ocean.[3]

Boutwell would not live to see Teddy Roosevelt's most spectacular display of America's new global reach when, in December 1907, the president launched the "Great White Fleet" on its fourteen-month tour around the world. Comprising sixteen battleships manned by 14,000 sailors, the American armada sailed for fourteen months around Cape Horn into the Pacific and through the Mediterranean back to Hampton Roads, Virginia, making twenty port calls on six different continents. Painted a gleaming white instead of the usual navy gray, the fleet became a public relations spectacular for the world's newest naval power and cemented Roosevelt's reputation as the architect of American empire.

Had he been alive, the "Great White Fleet" for George Boutwell would have symbolized a misguided emphasis on military power rather than America using its economic and political strengths to extend its influence abroad. In the coming decades, but especially after World War II, the type of military intervention Boutwell opposed in the Philippines would replay with disastrous consequences in Vietnam, Iraq, and Afghanistan, costing trillions of dollars and tens of thousands of American lives. More than a century after his death, the nation wrestles with the dilemma posed by the anti-imperialists:

how to project American influence and values abroad without succumbing to the temptation of ill-advised and counterproductive military adventures.

Boutwell would have been equally pained by the arc of America's race relations in the coming decades. In 1912, the growing political power of white southern Democrats would send Woodrow Wilson, progressive in his politics but a white supremacist in his racial views, to the White House. In 1913, at the fiftieth reunion of the Battle of Gettysburg attended by 50,000 veterans, Wilson gave his version of the "Gettysburg Address" that spoke only of reconciliation between Blue and Gray and totally neglected the racial divide between white and Black. As one African American newspaper asked, "A Reunion of whom?"[4]

America's racial divide deepened in the years following. The 200,000 Black soldiers who served in Europe in World War I came home to the violence of the Red Summer of 1919, when white mobs across America killed hundreds of Blacks and made thousands homeless. The lynching of Blacks across the country increased, sometimes of army veterans targeted because they were wearing their uniforms. Over Memorial Day weekend in 1921, the Tulsa Race Massacre burned out thirty-five square blocks of the prosperous Greenwood district of Black-owned businesses and homes and left 6,000 people homeless while killing and wounding hundreds.[5]

The widespread racial and anti-immigrant violence in the 1920s also found a home in Groton, Massachusetts. Georgianna Boutwell was in her early eighties, living in the family home on Main Street, when the Ku Klux Klan held rallies in Groton in 1925 and 1926 as part of a national resurgence that witnessed tens of thousands of Klan members marching down Pennsylvania Avenue in Washington, DC, with the US Capitol in the background.[6]

The nationwide Klan revival, with membership peaking in the millions, was fueled in central Massachusetts primarily by anti-immigrant sentiment, a recurring phenomenon in American politics. Local Klan supporters in Groton organized electoral tickets seeking to take control of town offices. In October 1926, four hundred Klansmen gathered in a Groton meadow and were met by shotgun blasts from outraged residents. There were numerous cross-burnings in town that Georgie certainly knew of and perhaps witnessed. Fifty years earlier, her father had documented in his Senate report the violence and intimidation used by the Klan and white terrorists to help the Democrats steal the 1875 Mississippi state election.[7]

George Boutwell lived in a momentous period of American history. He helped reformulate the concepts of citizenship, voting, and equality before the law as necessary pillars of representative democracy in a multiracial society, whether in America or its overseas possessions. He believed that putting too much power into the hands of state governments had been a fundamental flaw of the original Constitution, a flaw which permitted slavery to grow, igniting the Civil War. Having helped write the Fourteenth Amendment, he emphasized that Americans were "first citizens of the United States and then citizens of the State wherein they reside," and declared, "these words were chosen with care." This was the original intent of the amendment, he believed, that the protections of the US Constitution would be uniformly applied for all citizens, no matter their race, religion, or creed, or in which state they resided. Only by doing so could the ideals of the Declaration of Independence be fully realized for all Americans. That, for Boutwell, was the American promise, a goal worthy of continued struggle.[8]

Acknowledgments

I owe much to all the family members, friends, colleagues, librarians, archivists, and others who helped make this book possible. Thank you.

For well over a century, the Groton Historical Society, the Groton Public Library, and the townspeople of Groton, Massachusetts, have kept alive the legacy of George Boutwell and his family. Special thanks and appreciation go to Kara Fossey and Joshua Vollmar for their extensive research help throughout the project. Other Groton friends who provided help and encouragement include Owen and Stuart Shuman, Nancy Barringer, Michelle Collette, Richard Chilcoat, Kathryn Liebowitz, Carolyn Perkins, Beverly Smith, Bobbie Spiegelman, Brian Bixby, the late Earl Carter, David Gordon, Vanessa Abraham, Becky Pine, Don Black, and so many others, including Deborah Johnson and Russell Harris of *The Groton Herald*.

Felicia Eth, agent and friend, had faith in a book being written "by an unknown author on an unknown subject." Will Murphy performed editorial magic on an unruly manuscript. John Glusman, my editor at W. W. Norton, provided seasoned overall guidance and the perfect home for George's story. Helen Thomaides, assistant editor, responded to my queries almost before I made them and provided professional assistance at every juncture, as did the entire team at Norton, including, but not limited to, Rebecca Homiski, Julia Druskin, Don Rifkin, Rachel Salzman, Amina Washington, Gary Von Euer, Wickliffe Hallos, and WordCo Indexing Services.

Readers of the manuscript included Nancy Ames, Michael Burlingame, Benson Bobrick, Charles Calhoun, Jere Nash, David Stewart, and Peter Swift, with a very special thank-you to Robert Levine for his constant enthusiasm

and support. Authors in the field who provided early and greatly appreci-
ated encouragement were Suzanne Berger, Eric Foner, Kerri Greenidge, Allen
Guelzo, Stephen Kinzer, Charles Lane, Nicholas Lemann, Megan Marshall,
Robert Putnam, Cass Sunstein, Steven Weisman, and Richard White. Joshua
Cohen surprised and delighted me by mentioning George S. Boutwell in his
Pulitzer Prize–winning novel, *The Netanyahus*.

Wonderful hours were spent gathering material from and working with very
special people at the American Antiquarian Society (Dan Boudreau), Boston
Athenaeum (Mary Warnement), Boston Public Library (Jessy Wheeler), Con-
cord Free Public Library (Anke Voss), Houghton Library at Harvard Univer-
sity, Massachusetts Historical Society (Dan Hinchen and Hannah Elder), the
Commonwealth of Massachusetts State Library (Elizabeth Carroll-Horrocks)
and Archives (Susan Greendyke), and the Supreme Judicial Court Archives
(Jennifer Pino). Also, at the Library of Congress (Michelle Krowl), Ulysses S.
Grant Presidential Library (Ryan Semmes), Internal Revenue Service (Miana
Breed), Gilder Lehrman Institute of American History (Allison Kraft),
Abraham Lincoln Presidential Library and Museum (Christopher Schnell),
National Archives and Records Administration (Dorothy Alexander), New
York Public Library (Cara Dellatte), Mississippi Department of Archives and
History (Jere Nash and Brother Rogers), the Benjamin A. Quarles Archive at
Morgan State University (Ida Jones), John Hay Library at Brown University
(Laurie Rossi), The Newberry Library in Chicago, Rutherford B. Hayes Pres-
idential Library (Julie Mayle), the Offices of the Historian of the U.S. House
of Representatives and the U.S. Senate, the U.S. Treasury Department Librarian (Andy Young) and Curator's Office (Luke Leyh), the Treasury Historical Association (Tom O'Malley and Daisy Mullett Smith), the Omni Parker
House Hotel in Boston (John Murtha), and the Virginia Museum of History
and Culture (Matthew Guillen). Above all, I'm lucky that my local Howard
County (Maryland) public library system is one of the best in the country, and
that my cousins, Mary Ann and Rob McFarland, brought a wealth of library
expertise to my research.

Local historical societies in Massachusetts, in the towns of Brookline, Con-
cord, Lunenburg, and Weymouth, provided important information, as did
historians and archivists at Groton School (Doug Brown and Andy Reyes),
Lawrence Academy (Paul Husted), The Country Club in Brookline (Frederick
Waterman), the Evans Memorial Library in Aberdeen, Mississippi (Barbara
Blair and David Uptain), the Lancaster History Museum (Heather Tennies),

the Thaddeus Stevens Society (Ross Hetrick), and the Onondaga (NY) Historical Association (Sarah Kozma and Maria Lore). Thanks as well are due the colleagues and friends newly made at the Abraham Lincoln Association, The Lincoln Forum, The Lincoln Group of DC, and the Ulysses S. Grant Association.

To Buthaina, my love and appreciation for your constant support and for knowing before I did that what started as a long essay would turn into a book. Family members—Roland Boutwell, Barbara Strell, Molly Sperduto, Mary Lou Boutwell, David Boutwell, Sarah Boutwell, Rachael and Casey Seiler, Laura Edwards, Karen Sinclair, Jessica O'Brien, Rob Boutwell, and Charlie Boutwell—have made my life special in countless ways. And to the generation following them—Talia, Ben, Nick, Cole, Erin, Siyah, Jack, Lillian, and Owen—I hope they'll do all they can to redeem America's promise.

Notes

The principal sources for this biography are the letters, essays, speeches, and journal and newspaper articles written by George S. Boutwell and by members of his family (especially his daughter Georgianna), several hundreds of which, many previously unexamined, have been preserved by the Groton Historical Society (GHS) at the Governor Boutwell House in Groton, Massachusetts. Other Boutwell items can be found in the collections of the American Antiquarian Society (AAS), Boston Athenaeum (BA), Boston Public Library (BPL), Houghton Library at Harvard University (HL-HU), Groton Public Library (GPL), the Library of Congress (LC), Massachusetts Historical Society (MHS), Massachusetts State Archives and Libraries (MSAL), Newberry Library in Chicago (NL), New York Public Library (NYPL), and the presidential libraries of Abraham Lincoln (ALPL), Rutherford B. Hayes (RBHPL), and Ulysses S. Grant (USGPL). These locations are cited by their abbreviations in the Notes, as are references to issues of the *Congressional Globe* (*CG*) and *Congressional Record* (*CR*).

The most important published collections of Boutwell's writings are *Reminiscences of Sixty Years in Public Affairs,* vols. 1 and 2 (1902, Greenwood Press, 1968); *Speeches and Papers Relating to the Rebellion and the Overthrow of Slavery* (Little, Brown, 1867); *The Lawyer, the Statesman, and the Soldier* (D. Appleton, 1887); *Why I am a Republican* (W. J. Betts, 1884); *The Constitution of the United States at the End of the First Century* (D.C. Heath, 1895); *Thoughts on Educational Topics and Institutions* (Phillips, Sampson, 1859); *The Crisis of the Republic* (D. Estes, 1900), and *A Manual of the Direct and Excise Tax System of the United States* (Little, Brown, 1863).

Boutwell's daughter Georgianna was a mainstay of her father's life when he was in Washington, DC, and herself a judicious observer of American politics. Her illuminating essays available at the Groton Historical Society include: "Washington City Paper" (1895), "George Sewall Boutwell" (1917), and "Washington" (undated).

There have been three academic treatments of Boutwell's life and career: the unpublished and previously uncited MA thesis of Benjamin Arthur Quarles, "George S. Boutwell: A Radical with Reasons" (University of Wisconsin, 1933); Thomas H. Brown, *George Sewall Boutwell: Human Rights Advocate* (Groton Historical Society, 1989); and Thomas Domer, "The Role of

George S. Boutwell in the Impeachment and Trial of Andrew Johnson," *The New England Quarterly* 4 (December 1976): 4.

Other original documents, personal papers and diaries, and contemporaneous accounts of Boutwell's life and career are cited in the notes, as are the histories, biographies, newspapers, and other secondary sources consulted for this book.

Introduction

1. Orville Babcock to Secretary George S. Boutwell, March 23, 1871, Papers of Ulysses S. Grant, LC, 21:246.

2. Boutwell had sent the president a note that morning regarding some of the hundreds of nominations needed for Internal Revenue tax assessors and collectors. See Geo. S. Boutwell to the President, March 23, 1871, USG Collection, Unpublished Correspondence, S3.B10-1.257, USGPL.

3. George S. Boutwell, *The Lawyer, the Statesman, and the Soldier* (D. Appleton, 1887), 170–71.

4. *The Evening Star* (Washington, DC), March 24, 1871; *Boston Evening Transcript*, March 23, 1871; *New York Herald*, March 24, 1871; Charles W. Calhoun, *The Presidency of Ulysses S. Grant* (University Press of Kansas, 2017), 317–20.

5. The Ku Klux Klan Act of 1871 (42 U.S.C. § 1985(1)), also known as the Third Enforcement Act, allowed injured parties to take their case to federal court. See *Congressional Globe*, 42nd Congress: First Session, p. 18 (April 20, 1871); hereafter noted as *CG*, 42/1, 18 (April 20, 1871).

6. A comprehensive account is Fergus Bordewich, *Klan War: Ulysses S. Grant and the Battle to Save Reconstruction* (Alfred A. Knopf, 2023).

7. The Supreme Court case in 1883 was *United States v. Harris*, 106 U.S. 629. In 2021, the KKK Act became the basis of a lawsuit following the January 6 attack on the US Capitol Building, naming President Donald Trump and others for conspiring to "incite an assembled crowd to march upon and enter the Capitol of the United States for the common purpose of disrupting" congressional certification of the electoral vote count from the November election. See Jeffrey Boutwell, "Trump lawsuit has historical roots," *The Baltimore Sun*, April 18, 2021. This and similar lawsuits remained unresolved as of early 2024.

8. Eric Foner, *The Second Founding: How the Civil War and Reconstruction Remade the Constitution* (W. W. Norton, 2019); Ilan Wurman, *The Second Founding: An Introduction to the Fourteenth Amendment* (Cambridge University Press, 2020); Kermit Roosevelt III, *The Nation That Never Was: Reconstructing America's Story* (University of Chicago Press, 2022). For an excellent discussion of how Washington, Jefferson, Madison, and other Founding Fathers sought to balance slaveholding interests with concepts of individual liberty, see Edward J. Larson, *American Inheritance: Liberty and Slavery in the Birth of a Nation* (W. W. Norton, 2023).

9. In 1859, Boutwell declared slavery to be "the enemy of justice; and therefore it is the enemy of the Union." See George S. Boutwell, "Jefferson: Speech Delivered at Boston, April 13, 1859 at a Festival on the Anniversary of Jefferson's Birthday," in George S. Boutwell, *Speeches and Papers Relating to the Rebellion and the Overthrow of Slavery* (Little, Brown, 1867), 1–8. In August 1876, Boutwell delivered the report of the Senate Select Committee he chaired, *Mississippi in 1875: Report of the Select Committee to Inquire into the Mississippi Election of 1875*, United States Senate, vols. 1 and 2 (US Government Printing Office, 1876).

10. Thomas H. Brown, *George Sewall Boutwell: Human Rights Advocate* (Groton Historical Society, 1989). Good examples are Eric Foner, *Reconstruction: America's Unfinished Revolution, 1863–1877* (1988; HarperPerennial, 2014); Nicholas Lemann, *Redemption: The Last Battle of the Civil War* (Farrar, Straus & Giroux, 2006); Richard White, *The Republic for Which It Stands: The United States During Reconstruction and the Gilded Age, 1865–1896* (Oxford University Press, 2017).

11. Allan Nevins, *Hamilton Fish: The Inner History of the Grant Administration* (Dodd, Mead, 1936), 139. See also Samuel Eliot Morison, "Francis Bowen, an Early Test of Academic Freedom in

Massachusetts," *Massachusetts Historical Society Proceedings*, February 1936, 65; David M. Jordan, *Roscoe Conkling in New York: Voice in the Senate* (Cornell University Press, 1971), 122; John Niven, *Salmon P. Chase, A Biography* (Oxford University Press, 1995), 421.

12. The description is Fawn Brodie's from her superb political biography, *Thaddeus Stevens: Scourge of the South* (1959; W. W. Norton, 1966), 119.

13. Nevins, *Hamilton Fish*, 139.

14. *The Education of Henry Adams*, ed. Ernest Samuels (1918; Houghton Mifflin, 1973), 263. For a detailed description of Radical Republicanism, see Foner, *Reconstruction*, 228–39.

15. See David O. Stewart, *Impeached: The Trial of Andrew Johnson and the Fight for Lincoln's Legacy* (Simon & Schuster, 2009); Brenda Wineapple, *The Impeachers: The Trial of Andrew Johnson and the Dream of a Just Nation* (Random House, 2019); Robert S. Levine, *The Failed Promise: Reconstruction, Frederick Douglass, and the Impeachment of Andrew Johnson* (W. W. Norton, 2021).

16. Quote is from *The Education of Henry Adams*, 265. In addition to Calhoun's definitive *The Presidency of Ulysses S. Grant*, see also Brooks D. Simpson, *Let Us Have Peace: Ulysses S. Grant and the Politics of War & Reconstruction, 1861–1868* (University of North Carolina Press, 1991); Frank J. Scaturro, *President Grant Reconsidered* (Madison Books, 1999); Jean Edward Smith, *Grant* (Simon & Schuster, 2001); Joan Waugh, *U.S. Grant: American Hero, American Myth* (University of North Carolina Press, 2009); H. W. Brands, *The Man Who Saved the Union: Ulysses Grant in War and Peace* (Random House, 2012); Ronald C. White, *American Ulysses: A Life of Ulysses S. Grant* (Random House, 2017); Ron Chernow, *Grant* (Penguin Press, 2017); *The Annotated Memoirs of Ulysses S. Grant*, ed. Elizabeth D. Samet (Liveright, 2019); and the essays in *Grant at 200: Reconsidering the Life and Legacy of Ulysses S. Grant*, ed. Chris Mackowski and Frank J. Scaturro (Savas Beatie, 2023).

17. Stephen Kinzer, *The True Flag: Theodore Roosevelt, Mark Twain, and the Birth of the American Empire* (Henry Holt, 2017).

18. Edward A. Pollard, *The Lost Cause: A New Southern History of the War of the Confederates* (1866; Gramercy Books, 1994); and *The Lost Cause Regained* (G. W. Carleton, 1868), 112–13. See also Caroline E. Janney, *Remembering the Civil War: Reunion and the Limits of Reconstruction* (University of North Carolina Press, 2013), 136–37.

19. John F. Kennedy, *Profiles in Courage* (Harper, 1956), 153. The book received the Pulitzer Prize for biography in 1957.

20. Benjamin B. Kendrick, "The Journal of the Joint Committee of Fifteen on Reconstruction," PhD diss., Columbia University, 1914, 187–90. Kendrick derided Boutwell as "almost entirely self-educated, and like men who attain success largely through their own efforts, his tendency seems to have been to overestimate his own importance." As a Union army soldier, Ambrose Bierce fought in some of the bloodiest battles of the war, including Shiloh, and wrote some of the most enduring Civil War literature; see his "A Bivouac of the Dead," in *Shadows in Blue and Gray: The Civil War Writings of Ambrose Bierce*, ed. Brian M. Thomsen (Forge, 2001), 280.

21. Benjamin Quarles, *Frederick Douglass* (Associated Publishers, 1948). See also Benjamin Quarles, *The Negro in the Civil War* (1953; Da Capo, 1991), and *Lincoln and the Negro* (1962; Da Capo, 1991).

22. Benjamin Arthur Quarles, "George Sewall Boutwell: A Radical with Reasons," unpublished MA thesis, University of Wisconsin, 1933, pp. 39 and 74–75. After my wife Buthaina discovered the largely unknown Quarles thesis, I learned that Quarles's white academic advisors had initially "dissuaded" him from writing about Black subjects; their reasons were the supposed lack of objectivity of a Black academic writing about Black topics and the dearth of reliable historical sources about Black Americans. It was only several years later that one of his professors, William Best Hesseltine, relented, and Quarles was "allowed" to write about Frederick Douglass for his PhD thesis. See David W. Blight, "The Restoration of Black History: Benjamin Quarles and the Paradox of Race," *Reviews in American History*, 17:1:152–53 (March 1989). In his review, Blight highlights Quarles's importance in emphasizing Black "agency"

in the making of America. Blight's own research would lead to his Pulitzer Prize–winning biography, *Frederick Douglass: Prophet of Freedom* (Simon & Schuster, 2018). See also David W. Blight to Prof. Benjamin Quarles, 9 September 1981, *Benjamin Arthur Quarles Archive*, Morgan State University.

23. W. E. B. Du Bois, *Black Reconstruction: An Essay Toward a History of the Part Which Black Folk Played in the Attempt to Reconstruct Democracy in America, 1860–1880, & Other Writings*, ed. Eric Foner and Henry Louis Gates Jr. (1935; The Library of America, 2021); and John Hope Franklin, *Reconstruction: After the Civil War* (University of Chicago Press, 1961).

24. Joshua Cohen, *The Netanyahus* (New York Review Books, 2021), 4.

Chapter 1: Young Mr. Boutwell

1. Robert F. Dalzell Jr., *Enterprising Elite: The Boston Associates and the World They Made* (Harvard University Press, 1987), ch. 1 and 2. Francis Cabot Lowell personified a famous Boston ditty: "And this is to good old Boston, the home of the bean and the cod. Where the Lowells talk to the Cabots, and the Cabots talk only to God." "A Boston Toast" by John Collins Bossidy.

2. Jill Lepore, *These Truths: A History of the United States* (W. W. Norton, 2018), 191–212.

3. The Boutwell name is likely an Americanization of Boutell, Boutelle, Bowtell or other earlier English spellings. The original Boutwells may have been French Huguenots (Boutelle), who fled to England following Catholic persecution of the Protestants that culminated in the St. Bartholomew Day Massacre in 1572, though some family members doubt this; see L. H. Boutell to George S. Boutwell, August 31, 1855, *George S. Boutwell Papers*, AAS. Today there are several thousand Boutwells in the United States, many in the Deep South, the product of a distinct southern line having developed in the 1700s. See Dan C. Boutwell, "The American Boutwell Surname—A Theory" (unpublished memo, January 2023).

4. Family ties do matter. George's father, Sewell, got the Spooner job with the help of a distant relative and one of the wealthiest men in Massachusetts, Peter Chardon Brooks, who made his fortune in the marine insurance business which helped facilitate the transatlantic trade in enslaved Blacks. Brooks was a grandfather of Henry Adams, thus George Boutwell and Henry Adams were distantly related. The foundation of the farmhouse where George was born still exists as part of the clubhouse of The Country Club of Brookline, site of several US Open golf championships. See Georgianna A. Boutwell, "George Sewall Boutwell," unpublished manuscript, April 9, 1917, p. 3, Boutwell Collection, GHS; George S. Boutwell, *Reminiscences of Sixty Years in Public Affairs* (1902; Greenwood Press, 1968), 1:5; Roger B. Tyler and William B. Tyler, "A 300-Year Land History of The Country Club," *The Country Club*, Brookline, Mass., April 1982; personal communication from Frederick Waterman, club historian.

5. *Boston Morning Journal*, September 11, 1897, cited in Samuel A. Green, *Groton Historical Series*, 4:3, 420.

6. Lepore, *These Truths*, 201.

7. Boutwell, *Reminiscences*, vol. 1, ch. 2; Mark Littman, *The Heavens on Fire: The Great Leonid Meteor Storms* (Cambridge University Press, 1998). In the 1930s, the meteor shower became the inspiration for the classic jazz song, "Stars Fell on Alabama."

8. *The Times and Seasons* (Church of Jesus Christ of Latter Day Saints, 1845), 6, 898 (May 15, 1845); Frederick Douglass, *My Bondage and My Freedom* (1855; Penguin Books, 2003), 137.

9. Founded in 1655, Groton took its name from the ancestral family home of Puritan leader John Winthrop near London. Long a trading post situated at the western "frontier" of the Massachusetts Bay Colony, Groton was burned to the ground in March 1676 during King Philip's War with the Nipmuc and Abenaki peoples. The town was rebuilt two years later but would suffer again from conflict with Native Americans in the 1690s and early 1700s. Jeffrey Boutwell, "It All Started with a Move to Groton in 1835," *The Groton Herald*, January 29, 2021.

10. Green, *Groton Historical Series*, 4:2, 374–75.

11. Philip F. Gura, *American Transcendentalism: A History* (Farrar, Straus, and Giroux, 2008); Lawrence Buell, *Emerson* (Harvard University Press, 2003), 23; Megan Marshall, *Margaret Fuller: A New American Life* (Houghton Mifflin Harcourt, 2013), 144.

12. Boutwell, *Reminiscences*, 1:35; Marshall, *Margaret Fuller*, 70; Green, *Groton Historical Series*, 3:6, 218; Albert J. von Frank, "Life as Art in America: The Case of Margaret Fuller," *Studies in the American Renaissance* (1981), 8–9.

13. Marshall, *Margaret Fuller*, 71–127. The books can be seen today in George's study at the Governor Boutwell House, home of the Groton Historical Society.

14. Boutwell, *Reminiscences*, 1:48; Address by the Hon. Winslow Warren, *Commemorative Exercises in Connection with The Erection of a Memorial Tablet for George Sewall Boutwell in Groton Cemetery, May Fifteenth, 1908* (Boston, 1908), 8.

15. George S. Boutwell to William H. Barnham, January 25, 1882, George S. Boutwell Papers, RBHPL.

16. George S. Boutwell, "Commercial Legislation," *Hunt's Merchants' Magazine*, November 1842.

17. Silas Hawley, "Reminiscences of Groton During the Years 1839, 1840, and 1841: A Letter from Silas Hawley to Dr. Green, 25 January 1886, Beaver Dam, Wisconsin," in Samuel Abbott Green, *Groton Historical Series* (Groton, 1899), 11:14. I'm indebted to Joshua Vollmar and his encyclopedic knowledge of Groton history for helping me gather this information.

18. See Frederick Douglass, *Autobiographies: Narrative of the Life of Frederick Douglass, an American Slave* [1845], *My Bondage and My Freedom* [1855], *Life and Times of Frederick Douglass* [1893] (Library of America, 1994); and Blight, *Frederick Douglass*.

19. Wendy Warren, *New England Bound: Slavery and Colonization in Early America* (Liveright, 2016).

20. Hawley, "Reminiscences of Groton," 1–24; *The Liberator*, September 17, 1841. I've found no record of Boutwell attending one of the Douglass meetings in Groton, though he likely did.

21. Blight, *Frederick Douglass*, 116; Joshua Vollmar, "Millerism: The 19th Century Religious Movement That Swept Groton," *The Groton Herald*, February 26, 2021.

22. Sidney E. Ahlstrom, *A Religious History of the American People* (Yale University Press, 1972), 478–81.

23. Frederick Douglass to William Lloyd Garrison, March 6, 1844, *The Frederick Douglass Papers, 1842–1852*, ed. John R. McKivigan (Yale University Press, 2009), 18–22.

24. Edward Adams Richardson, *The Community, Groton, Massachusetts: The Story of a Neighborhood* (Ayer, MA, 1911), 4.

25. Mary Kay Ricks, *Escape on the Pearl: The Heroic Bid for Freedom on the Underground Railroad* (William Morrow, 2007).

26. For an account of his trip to Washington, see Boutwell, *Reminiscences*, 1:50–54.

27. *John Quincy Adams and the Politics of Slavery: Selections from the Diary*, ed. David Waldstreicher and Matthew Mason (Oxford University Press, 2019).

28. Boutwell, *Reminiscences*, 1:54.

29. Chris Myers Asch and George Derek Musgrove, *Chocolate City: A History of Race and Democracy in the Nation's Capital* (University of North Carolina Press, 2017).

30. Jefferson Davis, future president of the Confederacy and a slave owner, described how the "Yellow House" and Robey Tavern slave pens were directly on the path "by which all must go who wish to reach the building of the Smithsonian Institution." See Mark Auslander, "Enslaved Labor and the Smithsonian: Reading the Stones," *Southern Spaces*, December 2012.

31. Bob Arnebeck, *Slave Labor in the Capital: Building Washington's Iconic Federal Landmarks* (The History Press, 2014).

32. Walter Johnson, *Soul by Soul, Life Inside the Antebellum Slave Market* (Harvard University Press, 2001); Steven Deyle, *Carry Me Back: The Domestic Slave Trade in American Life* (Oxford University Press, 2006).

33. *Tudor Place: America's Story Lives Here*, ed. Leslie L. Buhler (The White House Historical Association, 2016).

Chapter 2: Rising Star in Massachusetts Politics

1. *Boston Evening Transcript*, March 10 and 11, 1848.
2. The Congressional delegation ran up a big bar bill, Boutwell remembered, and curious reporters "made vain attempts to ascertain the facts," but his committee was able to keep the matter out of the papers. Boutwell, *Reminiscences*, 1:102–3.
3. Fred Kaplan, *John Quincy Adams: American Visionary* (HarperCollins, 2014), 487–94.
4. *CG*, 25/3, 98–99 (January 7, 1839).
5. Boutwell, *Reminiscences*,1:55.
6. Brown, *George Sewall Boutwell*, 16; Boutwell, *Reminiscences*, 1:59–68.
7. The Reverend Silas Hawley thought George possibly suicidal; see Hawley, "Reminiscences of Groton," in Green, *Groton Historical Series*, no. 1.
8. Boutwell, *Reminiscences*, 1:75–76.
9. *The Liberator*, February 25, 1842; *Boston Post*, February 6, 1843. Massachusetts at the time had separate seating for whites and Blacks in "Jim Crow" railcars, an early use of the phrase. The railway companies themselves ended the practice in late 1843 under pressure from the Massachusetts legislature. See Steve Luxenberg, *Separate: The Story of Plessy v. Ferguson and America's Journey from Slavery to Segregation* (W. W. Norton, 2019), 16–23.
10. Louis Ruchames, "Race, Marriage, and Abolition in Boston," *The Journal of Negro History* 40, no. 3 (July 1955):273; "Vote on the Intermarriage Law," *The Liberator*, March 10, 1843.
11. *Boston Post*, March 18, 1843.
12. Boutwell surveyed tax history from Judaic and Greco-Roman times to the present, with quotes from Alexander Pope thrown in for good measure. See *Boston Post*, March 22 and May 9, 1843; Boutwell, *Reminiscences*, 1:80–81.
13. "The Clergy and the Gallows," *The Liberator*, March 10, 1843; *Boston Post*, February 28, 1843.
14. Boutwell, *Reminiscences*, 1:80–90. Boutwell also lost his bid for a seat in the US House of Representatives, a dual campaign strategy he admitted was a mistake; Brown, *George Sewall Boutwell*, 22.
15. Blight, *Frederick Douglass*, 126; US Supreme Court, *Prigg v. Pennsylvania*, 1842; and George S. Boutwell to Wendell Phillips, March 17, 1843, Special Collections, BPL, describing resolutions that Boutwell was submitting on behalf of the antislavery movement.
16. *The Liberator*, January 22, 1847.
17. Brown, *George Sewall Boutwell*, 24; David M. Potter, *The Impending Crisis: America Before the Civil War, 1848–1861* (1976; HarperPerennial, 2011), 67–69.
18. David Herbert Donald, *Lincoln* (Jonathan Cape, 1995), 134–35; Eric Foner, *The Fiery Trial: Abraham Lincoln and American Slavery* (W. W. Norton, 2010), 53–54.
19. Potter, *The Impending Crisis*, 225–30.
20. George S. Boutwell, "State Debts," *The Merchants Magazine and Commercial Review* 8 (January–June 1843); "Oregon: The Claim of Great Britain," *The Merchants Magazine and Commercial Review* 12 (June 1845).
21. Boutwell, *Reminiscences*, 1:99–100; *The Liberator*, August 18, 1848.
22. George S. Boutwell to Oliver Wendell Holmes, Sr., October 14, 1878, in Oliver Wendell Holmes Sr., *John Lothrop Motley—A Memoir* (Houghton Mifflin, 1881), 56–57.
23. George S. Boutwell, *Thoughts on Educational Topics and Institutions* (Phillips, Sampson, 1859), was favorably reviewed in *North American Review* 89 (July 1859): 184. See also Douglas Alan Frank, *The History of Lawrence Academy at Groton, 1792–1992* (Lawrence Academy, 1992), 84–89.
24. For more on Adams and the "gag rule," see William Lee Miller, *Arguing About Slavery: The Great Battle in the United States Congress* (Knopf, 1996), 465–87.
25. "No Union with Slaveholders!," *The Liberator*, February 22, 1850.
26. The growing disconnect between the free labor economy of the North and the slave-based economy of the South led Senator Timothy Pickering of Massachusetts to predict as early as 1803 that the young country would soon split, and that "the white and the black population will mark the

boundary," which is precisely what happened in 1860. See Thomas J. DiLorenzo, "Yankee Confederates: New England Secession Movements prior to the War between the States," in David Gordon, ed., *Secession, State and Liberty* (Transaction Publishers, 1998).

27. *The Liberator*, March 2, 1849.

28. Fred Harvey Harrington, *Fighting Politician: Major General N. P. Banks* (University of Pennsylvania Press, 1948), 9; William S. Robinson, *"Warrington" Pen-Portraits: A Collection of Personal and Political Reminiscences from 1848 to 1876, from the Writings of William S. Robinson* (Mrs. W. S. Robinson, 1877), 431–32; *New York Daily Herald*, February 21, 1849, and October 30, 1849.

29. Thomas J. Weiss, "U.S. Labor Force Estimates and Economic Growth, 1800–1860," in Robert E. Gallman and John Joseph Wallis, *American Economic Growth and Standards of Living before the Civil War* (University of Chicago Press, 1992), 27–31.

Chapter 3: Governor of Massachusetts

1. Robert V. Remini, *Daniel Webster: The Man and His Time* (W. W. Norton, 1997), 669–81.

2. Michael F. Holt, *The Rise and Fall of the American Whig Party: Jacksonian Politics and the Onset of the Civil War* (Oxford University Press, 1999), 582–83.

3. Ernest A. McKay, "Henry Wilson and the Coalition of 1851," *New England Quarterly* 36 (1963): 341; Ernest A. McKay, *Henry Wilson: Practical Radical* (Kennikat Press, 1971), 62–63.

4. Representing Benjamin Roberts and his five-year-old daughter Sarah, seeking to enroll in an all-white school, Sumner argued that the truly harmful effects of segregation were "psychological and sociological," not just the unequal condition of school facilities and resources. See David Donald, *Charles Sumner and the Coming of the Civil War* (Alfred A. Knopf, 1960), 180–81. In 1896, the US Supreme Court ruled otherwise in *Plessy v. Ferguson*, upholding the validity of "separate but equal" facilities for Blacks and whites, which was then overturned by *Brown v. Board of Education* in 1954. See Leonard W. Levy and Harlan B. Phillips, "The *Roberts* Case: Source of the 'Separate but Equal Doctrine,'" *American Historical Review* 56 (1956): 510–18.

5. Richard H. Abbott, *Cobbler in Congress: The Life of Henry Wilson, 1812–1875* (University Press of Kentucky, 1972), 38–39. Charles Sumner, dubious at first about cooperating with a Democratic Party that was proslavery at the national level, gradually came to support these local coalition-building efforts that ultimately helped send him to the US Senate; see Edward L. Pierce, *Memoir and Letters of Charles Sumner*, 4 vols. (Roberts Brothers, 1877–1894), 3:223–24.

6. *Buffalo Morning Express*, November 7, 1850.

7. Abbott Lawrence to R. C. Winthrop, January 8, 1851, Robert C. Winthrop Papers, vol. 35, MHS. See also William F. Hartford, *Money, Morals, and Politics: Massachusetts in the Age of the Boston Associates* (Northeastern University Press, 2001).

8. Kevin Sweeney, "Rum, Romanism, Representation, and Reform: Coalition Politics in Massachusetts, 1847–1853," *Civil War History* 22, no. 2 (June 1976): 120–21. Boutwell's antislavery credentials were also compromised by his association with Cushing, whom he appointed to the Massachusetts Supreme Judicial Court. Cushing, "hated by thousands of New Englanders as the 'crusher of abolitionists,'" later became attorney general for President Franklin Pierce and worked closely with Jefferson Davis, Pierce's secretary of war and future president of the Confederacy; Allen Nevins, *Ordeal of the Union: A House Dividing, 1852–1857* (Scribner, 1947), 49.

9. John G. Whittier to Henry Wilson, November 18, 1850, in *The Letters of John Greenleaf Whittier*, ed. John B. Pickard (Harvard University Press, 1975), 2:166–67.

10. Samuel Gridley Howe to Horace Mann, February 6, 1851, in Laura E. Richards, ed., *Letters and Journals of Samuel Gridley Howe* (Dana Estes, 1906), 2:337–38. Georgianna Boutwell would later assist Julia Ward Howe, author of *The Battle Hymn of the Republic*, in seeking to establish a women's civic organization in Washington, DC. Boutwell maintained he stayed neutral in the election of Sumner: see Boutwell, *Reminiscences*, 1:119, but a different account has him urging Sumner to step aside: see Moorfield Storey, *American Statesmen: Charles Sumner* (Standard Library, 1900), 83.

11. William S. Robinson, "Election of Charles Sumner," *Lowell American*, April 25, 1851, in Robinson, *"Warrington" Pen Portraits*, 194–95.

12. Adams, *The Education of Henry Adams*, 49; David S. Brown, *The Last American Aristocrat: The Brilliant Life and Improbable Education of Henry Adams* (Scribner, 2020), 34–36. Adams openly admitted his obsession with renewing "the lease of life . . . of the house of Adams" in American politics; quoted in Ari Hoogenboom, "Henry Adams and Politics," in David R. Contosta and Robert Muccigrosso, eds., *Henry Adams and His World* (American Philosophical Association, 1993), 24.

13. "Address by His Excellency George S. Boutwell, January 16, 1851," *Boston Daily Evening Transcript*, January 16, 1851. The phrase "a government of laws, and not of men," is from John Adams's draft of the 1780 Massachusetts Constitution. See Amanda A. Mathews, *"A Government of Laws and Not of Men": John Adams, Attorney, and the Massachusetts Constitution of 1780* (unpublished diss., Boston College, 2008).

14. "Extracts from Gov. Boutwell's Message," *The Liberator*, January 24, 1851. "Doughface" was a common Civil War insult for a northerner supporting southern slavery; J. G. Whittier to Charles Sumner, January 16, 1851, *The Letters of John Greenleaf Whittier*, 2:171–72.

15. Charles Sumner to John Bigelow, May 2, 1851, in Pierce, *Memoir and Letters of Charles Sumner*, 3:247.

16. Massachusetts and other northern states enacted "personal liberty laws" that prohibited state officials from assisting federal authorities in carrying out the Fugitive Slave Act, while also seeking to ensure *habeas corpus* and jury trials for any Blacks, enslaved or free, who were apprehended under the Act; see Stanley W. Campbell, *The Slave Catchers: Enforcement of the Fugitive Slave Law, 1850–1860* (University of North Carolina Press, 1970).

17. Gary Lee Collison, *Shadrach Minkins: From Fugitive Slave to Citizen* (Harvard University Press, 1997), 79–86.

18. *Boston Evening Transcript*, April 12, 1851. Sims escaped slavery during the Civil War, met Ulysses Grant during the Vicksburg campaign, and then returned to Boston. In July 1863, he watched Black soldiers of the Fifty-fourth Massachusetts Regiment march to their ships to deploy for action in South Carolina; see Leonard W. Levy, "Sims' Case: The Fugitive Slave Law in Boston in 1851," *The Journal of Negro History* 35:1 (January 1950).

19. *The Liberator*, April 25, 1851; Ralph Waldo Emerson, "Bad Times, Spring, 1851," journal entry in *Selections from Ralph Waldo Emerson*, ed. Stephen E. Whicher (Houghton Mifflin, 1960), 354. By this time, Douglass supported a more activist role for the antislavery movement, disdaining the "moral suasion" approach of William Lloyd Garrison; see Robert Levine, *The Lives of Frederick Douglass* (Harvard University Press, 2016), 112–16.

20. Quoted in Nell Irvin Painter, *The History of White People* (W. W. Norton, 2010), 174–75. See also Buell, *Emerson*, chap. 6: "Social Thought and Reform: Emerson and Abolition."

21. Barry M. Andrews, "Was Emerson a Racist?," *Transcendentalist Spirituality* blog, August 31, 2018.

22. George S. Boutwell, "Sudbury Monument," in *Reminiscences*, 1:162–83.

23. Jill Lepore, *The Name of War: King Philip's War and the Origins of American Identity* (Alfred A. Knopf, 1999), 5–8; Mary Rowlandson, "The Sovereignty and Goodness of God," reprinted in Alden T. Vaughn & Edward W. Clark, *Puritans Among the Indians: Accounts of Captivity and Redemption, 1676–1724* (Harvard University Press, 1981), 70.

24. Slavery having been legalized in 1641, Massachusetts had more enslaved Native Americans than Blacks by 1700; many would be sold to British plantations in the Caribbean. See Margaret Ellen Newell, *Brethren by Nature: New England Indians, Colonists, and the Origins of American Slavery* (Cornell University Press, 2015); Boutwell, *Reminiscences*, 1:177–81.

25. Anne Kusener Nelsen, "King Philip's War and the Hubbard-Mather Rivalry," *The William and Mary Quarterly* 27, no. 4 (October 1970).

26. Lepore, *The Name of War*, 222; Boutwell, *Reminiscences*, 1:182–83.

27. "Governor's Address," *Boston Evening Transcript*, January 16, 1851.

28. Whig Party leaders stationed supervisors from their factories at polling stations to make sure employees voted "correctly"; see Hartford, *Money, Morals, and Politics*, 175–78.

29. Brown, *George Sewall Boutwell*, 41.

30. "Until after the Civil War . . . the assumption was widespread that a corporate charter" granted by legislatures was to be "for purposes clearly in the public interest"; see Alan Trachtenberg, *The Incorporation of America: Culture and Society in the Gilded Age* (1982; Hill and Wang, 2007), 6. Boutwell's data showed that Harvard's room and tuition cost was twice that of colleges like Brown and that Harvard's student body had remained constant since 1819 despite a doubling of the Commonwealth's population to almost one million. See *Boston Post*, June 19, 1850. Wilson quote in Elias Nason and Thomas Russell, *The Life and Public Services of Henry Wilson* (B. B. Russell, 1876), 109.

31. See Acts and Resolves of Massachusetts, 1851, cap. 224; Harvard University, *Historical Register*, 34. Nine days after the Act became law, Boutwell was awarded an honorary LLD from Harvard, this being a customary honor that Harvard bestowed on each new governor of the Commonwealth; Boutwell, *Reminiscences*, 1:96.

32. Samuel Eliot Morison, "Francis Bowen, an Early Test of Academic Freedom in Massachusetts," *Massachusetts Historical Society Proceedings*, 65:508 (February 1936). Bowen was initially denied tenure by an act that predated Boutwell's becoming governor, but soon was appointed Alford Professor of Moral Philosophy; he and Boutwell would serve together on a national monetary commission in the 1870s.

33. Commonwealth of Massachusetts, *Official Report of the Debates and Proceedings in the State Convention* (White and Potter, 1853), 1:666.

34. Quoted in Michel Brunet, "The Secret Ballot Issue in Massachusetts Politics from 1851 to 1853," *The New England Quarterly* 25, no. 3 (September 1952): 357.

35. *National Aegis* (Worcester, MA), January 19, 1853; *Greenfield Democrat* (MA), March 14, 1853.

36. Boutwell, *Reminiscences*, 1:227; Abbott, *Cobbler in Congress*, 50–51. Boutwell was lucky even to be a delegate, having lost his bid to represent Groton because of his temperance views. Given that delegates were allowed to run in multiple townships, and because Henry Wilson had won both his hometown of Natick (which he wasn't sure he would win) and Berlin, the latter town was able to elect Boutwell.

37. Samuel Shapiro, "The Conservative Dilemma: The Massachusetts Constitutional Convention of 1853," *The New England Quarterly* 33, no. 2 (June 1960): 213.

38. Boutwell, *Reminiscences*, 1:216–35; Charles F. Adams, *Richard Henry Dana* (Houghton, 1890), 243–45.

39. Eli A. Glasser, *Government and the Constitution (1820–1917)*, 4:22, in *Commonwealth History of Massachusetts: Colony, Province and State*, ed. Albert B. Hart (The States History Co., 1930); Boutwell, *Reminiscences*, 1:220.

40. Boutwell, as treasury secretary, would appoint Bryant to design Boston's Post Office and Sub-Treasury Building; Bryant's work in Boston marked the mid-1800s transition from Charles Bulfinch of the colonial era to Henry Hobson Richardson of the Gilded Age. See Roger G. Reed, *Building Victorian Boston: The Architecture of Gridley J. F. Bryant* (University of Massachusetts Press, 2007), 144. Boutwell purchased the Main Street lot on February 19, 1851, for $925 ($35,000 in today's dollars) from the local Bancroft family. See Groton Historical Society, *Images of America: Groton* (Arcadia Publishing, 2009), 71–72; *Middlesex South Registry of Deeds*, Cambridge, MA (Book 603:331, 507, and Book 626:215).

41. Georgianna A. Boutwell, "George Sewall Boutwell: Remarks at the Dedication of the George Sewall Boutwell Elementary School, Groton, Massachusetts, April 7, 1917," 10–11, Boutwell Collection, GHS.

Chapter 4: Birth of the Republican Party

1. Anthony Burns was imprisoned on his return to Richmond at the infamous Lumpkin's Jail, where he likely contracted tuberculosis; see Kristen Green, *The Devil's Half Acre: The Untold Story of How One Woman Liberated the South's Most Notorious Slave Jail* (Seal, 2022). When his freedom was purchased in 1855 by a group of free Blacks, Burns moved to Oberlin, Ohio where he studied theology before moving to Canada. He died an early death from tuberculosis on July 17, 1862. Lawrence quote in Albert J. von Frank, *The Trials of Anthony Burns: Freedom and Slavery in Emerson's Boston* (Harvard University Press, 1999), 207.

2. Ralph Waldo Emerson, "To Oliver Wendell Holmes," March 1856, in *Selections from Ralph Waldo Emerson*, ed. Stephen E. Whicher, 357–58.

3. Potter, *The Impending Crisis*, ch. 10.

4. Tyler Gregory Anbinder, *Nativism and Slavery: The Northern Know Nothings and the Politics of the 1850's* (Oxford University Press, 1992); Abraham Lincoln to Joshua Speed, August 23, 1855, Roy P. Basler, ed., *The Collected Works of Abraham Lincoln [CWAL]*, 8 vols. (Rutgers University Press, 1953), 2:320–23.

5. John R. Mulkern, *The Know-Nothing Party in Massachusetts: The Rise and Fall of a People's Movement* (Northeastern University Press, 1990).

6. *New York Times*, September 8, 1854.

7. James McPherson, *Battle Cry of Freedom: The Civil War Era* (Oxford University Press, 1988), 20–21. For more on Mann, Boutwell, and other pioneers of American public education, see Michael B. Katz, *The Irony of Early School Reform: Educational Innovation in Mid-Nineteenth Century Massachusetts* (Harvard University Press, 1968). Boutwell, *Reminiscences*, 1:257.

8. J. Asbury Pitman, "The Salem Normal School: Past, Present, and Future," *The Elementary School Journal* 30, no. 6 (February 1930): 417; Charlotte Forten, "Life on the Sea Islands," *The Atlantic Monthly* 13 (May 1864). Boutwell referred to Forten in his speech, "Personal Equality and Public Prosperity, Speech Delivered at Baltimore, April 1, 1864," in Boutwell, *Speeches and Papers*, 295–96; see also *The Liberator*, May 13, 1864. In 1878 Charlotte married Francis James Grimke of the famous mixed-race Grimke family; see Kerri K. Greenidge, *The Grimkes: The Legacy of Slavery in an American Family* (Liveright, 2023).

9. "Address by George S. Boutwell," *Account of the Proceedings of the Inauguration of the State Industrial School for Girls, at Lancaster, Aug. 27, 1856* (John Wilson and Son, 1856); the Lancaster school today is part of the National Park Service.

10. George S. Boutwell, "Female Education: An Address before the Newburyport Female High School," in Boutwell, *Thoughts on Educational Topics*, 222–25.

11. Martin B. Duberman, "Some Notes on the Beginnings of the Republican Party in Massachusetts," *The New England Quarterly* 34, no. 3 (September 1961): 364–70; *The Times-Picayune* (New Orleans), August 13, 1855.

12. *Boston Evening Transcript*, August 23, 1855; *Springfield Republican*, August 27, 1855.

13. Joshua Vollmar, "The Paradox of a Moral Millionaire: The Business and Reputation of Abbott Lawrence," unpublished honors undergraduate thesis, University of Massachusetts Lowell, 2022.

14. *The Pittsfield Sun*, August 23 and 30, 1855.

15. *New-York Daily Tribune*, August 25, 1855.

16. George S. Boutwell to Richard H. Dana, September 18, 1855, Dana Family Papers, N-1088, Box. 14, MHS. Having heard that "Gov. Boutwell is not able to attend the Philada. Convention," John Greenleaf Whittier urged Emerson to go; John G. Whittier to Ralph Waldo Emerson, June 13, 1856, *The Letters of John Greenleaf Whittier*, 2:751–52.

17. Nichole Etcheson, *Bleeding Kansas: Contested Liberty in the Civil War Era* (University Press of Kansas, 2004).

18. Notices of land for sale by the firm Bassett & Blackett listed Boutwell's name and title of ex-governor. See *The Kansas Herald of Freedom* (Wakarusa, Kansas), September 11, 18, and 25, 1858; and the *Western Railroad Gazette* (Chicago), September 4, 11, and 18, 1858.

19. Sumner's speech, "The Crime Against Kansas," singled out Senator Andrew Butler of South Carolina, a distant relative of Preston Brooks, for helping to orchestrate the "swindle" of the Kansas-Nebraska Act that tore up the Compromise of 1850 and exposed Kansas to the evils of slavery. It was wildly inflammatory, with Sumner predicting that "the Slave Power . . . will be swept into the charnel-house of defunct tyrannies." Senator Stephen Douglas was heard muttering, "that damn fool will get himself killed." See Donald, *Charles Sumner*, 279–311.

20. A stickler regarding potential conflicts of interest, Boutwell undoubtedly would have resigned his position on the state Board of Education had he been elected to Congress, as he did similarly in 1863, resigning as Lincoln's commissioner of revenue before taking his seat in the House of Representatives, despite advice from Treasury Secretary Salmon Chase to stay on until Congress was officially in session.

21. Boutwell, *Reminiscences*, 1:249. For more on Emerson's role in shaping American political thought, see Buell, *Emerson*.

22. Boutwell aptly described how Emerson "was not an orator in a popular sense, but he had the capacity to make his auditors anxious to hear what he would say in his next sentence, which, not infrequently, was far removed from the preceding sentence." A century later, Emerson biographer Lawrence Buell noted similarly that "much of the excitement of his [Emerson's] writing lies in sentences that jump out of their contexts, *take unexpected turns*, prove on close inspection knottier than they seem." Buell, *Emerson*, 10.

23. George S. Boutwell to Salmon P. Chase, Governor of Ohio, November 24, 1857, Kansas Historical Society. See also Walter Stahr, *Salmon P. Chase: Lincoln's Vital Rival* (Simon & Schuster, 2021), 258–59.

24. Peter S. Canellos, *The Great Dissenter: The Story of John Marshall Harlan, America's Judicial Hero* (Simon & Schuster, 2021), 101–5.

25. Peter Irons, *A People's History of the Supreme Court* (1999, Penguin Books, 2006), 168–77.

26. George S. Boutwell to Amos A. Lawrence, February 23, 1857 and March 27, 1858, A. A. Lawrence Papers, MHS.

27. *Boston Post*, April 14, 1859. Schurz had been a prominent figure in the liberal revolutions in Europe in 1848 before emigrating from Germany to the United States.

28. The *Cleveland Daily Leader*, April 20, 1859, reprinted the letters from Seward, Chase, and Blair, but not Lincoln, he being the least well-known candidate at the time.

29. For a comprehensive account of how Lincoln's debates with Douglas propelled him to the presidency, see Michael Burlingame: *Abraham Lincoln: A Life* (Johns Hopkins University Press, 2008), 1:486–577.

30. George S. Boutwell, "Jefferson: Speech delivered at Boston, April 13, 1859," in Boutwell, *Speeches and Papers*, 1–8.

31. *New York Herald*, April 17, 1859.

32. *Buffalo Courier*, April 19, 1859. Lincoln quote in Abraham Lincoln to Mssrs. Henry Pierce & Others, April 6, 1859, Basler, *CWAL*, 3:374–76. See also *Wisconsin State Journal* (Madison), April 18, 1859.

33. Abraham Lincoln, "Address Before the Wisconsin State Agricultural Society," September 30, 1859; Basler, *CWAL*, 3:471–82; see also Heather Cox Richardson, *To Make Men Free: A History of the Republican Party* (Basic Books, 2014), 14–20.

34. William Seward was one of the first to articulate these themes in the early 1850s; see James Oakes, *Freedom National: The Destruction of Slavery in the United States, 1861–1865* (W. W. Norton, 2013), 29–34.

35. By far the best account is Tony Horwitz, *Midnight Rising: John Brown and the Raid That Sparked the Civil War* (Henry Holt and Company, 2011).

36. Southerners mocked Brown, thanking him for reviving, "with ten-fold strength, the desire for a Southern Confederacy," *Richmond Enquirer*, October 25, 1859.

37. Sidney Blumenthal, *All the Powers of Earth: The Political Life of Abraham Lincoln, 1856–1860* (Simon & Schuster, 2019), 571–97.

38. The massive wooden structure was the pride and joy of Chicago Mayor "Long John" Wentworth, who in 1848 as an Illinois congressman had been Boutwell's companion during the funeral services for John Quincy Adams; P. Orman Ray, *The Convention That Nominated Lincoln* (University of Chicago Press, 1916), 17.

39. Edward Achorn, *The Lincoln Miracle: Inside the Republican Convention That Changed History* (Grove/Atlantic, 2023).

40. McPherson, *Battle Cry of Freedom*, 220.

41. Greeley only decided to attend at the last minute, and the Oregon delegate spot was the only one open. Leslie M. Scott, "Oregon's Nomination of Lincoln," *The Quarterly of the Oregon Historical Society* 17, no. 3 (September 1916): 207. The Kentucky legislature had recently voted to allow importing slaves from abroad, a practice banned by the Constitution since 1808; *New York Times*, February 1, 1860. "National Republican Platform, adopted by the National Republican Convention, Held in Chicago, May 17, 1860" (Press & Tribune Office, Chicago).

42. Achorn, *The Lincoln Miracle*, 283–85.

43. Gustave Koerner, *Memoirs of Gustave Koerner* (The Torch Press, 1909), 2:90; Achorn, *The Lincoln Miracle*, 291. The criticism of Massachusetts that Andrew was objecting to concerned immigrants in the Bay State having to wait for two years after being naturalized before they could vote.

44. Ray, *The Convention That Nominated Lincoln*, 27; Blumenthal, *All the Powers of Earth*, 595.

45. "Mr. Lincoln and the Official Committee," *New York Daily Tribune*, May 25, 1860.

46. Hay wrote that Boutwell "lives kindly in the commencement dinner memories of Brunonians [Brown alumni]," *Lincoln's Journalist: John Hay's Anonymous Writings for the Press, 1860–1864*, ed. Michael Burlingame (Southern Illinois University Press, 1998), 2. For a report of Boutwell's commencement address, see *Providence Journal*, September 14, 1858.

47. See *Conversations with Lincoln*, ed. Charles M. Segal (Putnam, 1961), 29–32.

48. *Chicago Tribune*, May 21, 1860, quoted in Ida M. Tarbell, *The Life of Abraham Lincoln* (McClure, Phillips, 1900), 1:360.

49. *Springfield Republican*, August 30, 1860; Boutwell, *Reminiscences*, 1:252.

50. Bradley P. Dean and Ronald Wesley Hoag, "Thoreau's Lectures after 'Walden': An Annotated Calendar," *Studies in the American Renaissance*, 1:339–47 (1996); Randall Fuller, *The Book That Changed America: How Darwin's Theory of Evolution Ignited a Nation* (Viking, 2017), 190–95.

51. Dean and Hoag, "Thoreau's Lectures after 'Walden,'" 341; Laura Dassow Walls, *Henry David Thoreau: A Life* (University of Chicago Press, 2017), 471. Boutwell was a frequent speaker at agricultural society meetings for more than fifty years; for one of his final speeches, see *Address before the Oxford Agricultural Society, September 21, 1897* (Beacon Press, 1897). Coverage of Thoreau's talk is in the *New York Weekly Tribune*, October 6, 1860. Thoreau was incorporating his essay into a larger work when he became ill with bronchitis and died in May 1862; the essay was eventually published as Henry David Thoreau, *Faith in a Seed: The Dispersion of Seeds and Other Late Natural History Writings* (Island Press, 1993).

52. Fuller, *The Book That Changed America*, x.

Chapter 5: Organizing for War

1. George S. Boutwell to Abraham Lincoln, December 17, 1860, *Abraham Lincoln Papers*, Series 1, General Correspondence, 1833–1916, LC. See also Michael J. Kline, *The Baltimore Plot: The First Conspiracy to Assassinate Abraham Lincoln* (Westholme Publishing, 2008).

2. Doris Kearns Goodwin, *Team of Rivals: The Political Genius of Abraham Lincoln* (Simon & Schuster, 2005), 293–95.

3. Ernest B. Furgurson, *Freedom Rising: Washington in the Civil War* (Alfred A. Knopf, 2004), 28.

4. George S. Boutwell, "Secession: An Address delivered at Charlestown, Mass., on the eve of the Eighth of January 1861," in Boutwell, *Speeches and Papers*, 76; *Hartford Courant*, January 10, 1861.

5. Groton neighbor and antislavery colleague Daniel Needham wrote to Lincoln on Boutwell's behalf; Daniel Needham to Abraham Lincoln, January 8, 1861, Abraham Lincoln Papers, Series 1, General Correspondence, 1833–1916, LC.

6. Furgurson, *Freedom Rising*, 37.

7. "Robert Toombs Speech to the Georgia Legislature, November 13, 1860," in *Secession Debated: Georgia's Showdown in 1860*, ed. Craig M. Simpson and William W. Freehling (Oxford University Press, 1992), 40.

8. Charles Sumner to G. S. Boutwell, February 1, 1861, Gilder-Lehrman Collection, GLC06714. See also Sarah Forbes Hughes, *Letters and Recollections of John Murray Forbes* (Houghton, Mifflin, 1899), 1:188–89. Forbes was a wealthy railroad owner and member of the Massachusetts delegation who was instrumental in coordinating the transport of troops and matériel to Washington, DC once war broke out in April. Andrew quote is in Henry Greenleaf Pearson, *The Life of John A. Andrew, Governor of Massachusetts, 1861–1865*, 2 vols. (Houghton Mifflin, 1904), 1:164.

9. Boutwell's memory is likely faulty when he writes that he helped remove Seddon's political disabilities as called for by the Fourteenth Amendment. Boutwell, *Reminiscences*, 1:269–70. I could find no confirmation of this in official US records or from the Office of the Historian of the House of Representatives. Because Seddon remained a diehard racist and "Lost Cause" supporter, he was an unlikely candidate for Boutwell's help in any event. See Roy W. Curry, "James A. Seddon, A Southern Prototype," *Virginia Magazine of History and Biography* (1955), 63; and Gerald F. J. O'Brien, "James A. Seddon, Statesman of the Old South," unpublished PhD diss. (University of Maryland, 1963). Samuel Eliot Morison believed Boutwell and Seddon to be the two individuals most responsible for the convention's failure: Boutwell by objecting to any conciliation whatsoever and Seddon because he was not interested in compromise and wanted Virginia to secede and join the Confederacy. See "The Peace Convention of February 1861," *Proceedings of the Massachusetts Historical Society*, 1961, 3:73.

10. Furgurson, *Freedom Rising*, 39–40.

11. *New York Daily Herald*, February 19, 1861.

12. "Boutwell, of Massachusetts, made a long and eloquent speech . . . the most elaborate and able yet delivered," *Louisville Daily Courier*, February 22, 1861. George S. Boutwell, "Concession and Compromise: Speech Made in Peace Congress, February 18, 1861," in *Speeches and Papers*, 92–93. Henry Wilson described Boutwell confronting the "imperious Virginian [Seddon]," who had just "uttered his slaveholding demands and the doctrine of State-rights as if the Old Dominion spoke with an authority akin to that of the 'divine right of kings.'" See Henry Wilson, *History of the Rise and Fall of the Slave Power in America* (James R. Osgood, 1877), 3:87–90. David Potter has written that Senator William Seward of New York, soon to become Lincoln's secretary of state, upbraided Boutwell for needlessly antagonizing the South with his "bellicose" speech, and convinced Boutwell to tone down his rhetoric so that the South would ultimately appear the aggressor if conflict broke out. See David M. Potter, *Lincoln and His Party in the Secession Crisis*, 2 vols. (Yale University Press, 1942), 2:21.

13. L. E. Chittenden, *A Report of the Debates and Proceedings in the Secret Sessions of the Conference Convention, for Proposing Amendments to the Constitution of the United States, Held at Washington, DC in February, A.D. 1861* (D. Appleton, 1864), 440–45.

14. Chittenden, *A Report of the Debates*, 450. The report sent by the Massachusetts delegation to Governor John Andrew is on 613–21.

15. Michael Burlingame, ed., *Lincoln's Journalist: John Hay's Anonymous Writings for the Press, 1860–1864* (Southern Illinois University Press, 1998), 51.

16. Goodwin, *Team of Rivals*, 312–15.

17. Brown, *George Sewall Boutwell*, 59–60; Boutwell, *Reminiscences*, 1:277.

18. Quoted in James M. McPherson, *The Struggle for Equality: Abolitionists and the Negro in the Civil War and Reconstruction* (Princeton University Press, 1964), 50. See also Richard H. Abbott,

Cotton & Capital: Boston Businessmen and Antislavery Reform (University of Massachusetts Press, 1991), 72–75.

19. Boutwell, *Reminiscences*, 1:284.

20. M. P. McConnell, *Surgeon of the "Old Sixth": The Life and Times of Dr. Norman Smith and the Civil War's 6th Massachusetts* (Ellen Carson Publishers, 2015), 25–48; Goodwin, *Team of Rivals*, 354.

21. Pearson, *The Life of John Andrew*, 1:201–10.

22. Boutwell wrote later that "it never occurred to me to return the pistol. I discharged the barrels and laid the weapon away, only too glad to have it out of sight." Boutwell, *Reminiscences*, 1:285. Also see George S. Boutwell to Sarah Adelia Boutwell, April 24, 1861, Boutwell Collection, GHS.

23. George S. Boutwell to Governor Andrew, April 28, 1861, in Boutwell, *Reminiscences*, 1:286–88.

24. Boutwell, *Reminiscences*, 1:288.

25. Governor Andrew, the Union's foremost "war governor," had quietly and effectively begun to organize the state's military resources well before the first shot was fired at Fort Sumter; Stephen D. Engle, *In Pursuit of Justice: The Life of John Albion Andrew* (University of Massachusetts Press, 2023), 144–47.

26. *Boston Evening Transcript*, July 18, 1861.

27. George S. Boutwell, "The Conspiracy: Its Purposes and Its Power," Address Before the Phi Beta Kappa Society of Harvard University, July 18, 1861, in Boutwell, *Speeches and Papers*, 94–122.

28. George S. Boutwell to Governor John Andrew, August 17, 1861, John Andrew Papers, reel 8, MHS; Stephen D. Engle, "'Under Full Sail': John Andrew, Abraham Lincoln, and Standing by the Union," *Massachusetts Historical Review* 19 (2017): 59.

29. George S. Boutwell, "Emancipation: Its Justice, Expediency, and Necessity, as the Means of Securing a Speedy and Permanent Peace, December 16, 1861," in Boutwell, *Speeches and Papers*, 123–58. Douglass accepted "with joy" an invitation to join the League as a lecturer, see *The Life and Writings of Frederick Douglass*, 4 vols., ed. Philip S. Foner (1952; International Publishers, 1975), 3:20. Boutwell's "cotton mill" argument was first advanced by prominent businessman Edward Atkinson, who was on the stage that night. Forty years later the two would be key founders of the Anti-Imperialist League opposing US annexation of the Philippines. See Abbott, *Cotton & Capital*, 77–80. See also *The Liberator*, December 20, 1861.

30. White, *American Ulysses*, 156–61.

31. Georgianna A. Boutwell, "George Sewall Boutwell," 21–22.

32. Steve Inskeep, *Imperfect Union: How Jessie and John Frémont Mapped the West, Invented Celebrity, and Helped Cause the Civil War* (Penguin Press, 2020), 345.

33. Salmon P. Chase to Abraham Lincoln, July 3, 1862. Days later, Pennsylvania governor Andrew Curtin sent a telegram to Lincoln secretary John Nicolay, asking for a delay in selecting the new revenue commissioner, likely hoping that Pennsylvania native Joseph Lewis, the candidate earlier preferred by the president, would be selected, but it was too late; Andrew G. Curtin to John G. Nicolay, July 9, 1862; both in Abraham Lincoln Papers: Series 1. General Correspondence, 1833–1916, LC.

34. Charles A. Dana, *Recollections of the Civil War* (D. Appleton, 1898), 11–15; Boutwell, *Reminiscences*, 1:293–95.

35. Boutwell later wrote an article praising Frémont's talents as an explorer and scientist, comparing him to the famed German naturalist Alexander von Humboldt. See George S. Boutwell, "John C. Fremont," *Proceedings of the American Academy of Arts and Sciences* (1891–1892), 27:422–26.

36. *Free at Last: A Documentary History of Slavery, Freedom, and the Civil War*, ed. Ira Berlin et al. (The New Press, 1992), 186; George S. Boutwell to Sarah Adelia Boutwell, July 8, 1862, Boutwell Collection, GHS.

37. George S. Boutwell to Horatio Woodman, July 4, 1862, Horatio Woodman Papers, 1843–1899, MHS. A Boston journalist, Woodman is famous for initiating the Saturday Club in Boston in 1857, a regular gathering of noted writers and intellectuals such as Emerson, Longfellow, Hawthorne, James Russell Lowell, and others, from which emerged *The Atlantic Monthly*.

Chapter 6: Financing the War

1. Roger Lowenstein, *Ways and Means: Lincoln and His Cabinet and the Financing of the Civil War* (Penguin Press, 2022).

2. Quoted in Allen C. Guelzo, *Abraham Lincoln: Redeemer President* (Eerdmanns Publishing, 1999), 379–82; George S. Boutwell to Charles Sumner, January 18, 1862, Sumner Correspondence, Microfilm 24/461–63, HL-HU. See Heather Cox Richardson, *The Greatest Nation of the Earth: Republican Economic Policies during the Civil War* (Harvard University Press, 1997).

3. Thaddeus Stevens, *CG*, 37/1, 247 (July 24, 1861).

4. *Report of the Secretary of the Treasury for the Year 1861* (Washington, 1861), 15.

5. Dozens of lobbyists seeking to protect business interests "swarmed in and about the Capitol" as Congress debated the 119 sections and 315 proposed amendments to The Revenue Act; see Lowenstein, *Ways and Means*, 126–29.

6. Steven R. Weisman, *The Great Tax Wars: Lincoln-Teddy Roosevelt-Wilson: How the Income Tax Transformed America* (Simon & Schuster, 2004), 43.

7. Chase biographer Walter Stahr correctly disputes Boutwell's claim that "Chase was not much involved in these appointments," this being another example of Boutwell's unfortunate tendency to disparage colleagues; see Boutwell, *Reminiscences*, 1:305–7, and Stahr, *Salmon P. Chase*, 403–4. See also *New York Times*, July 21, 1864.

8. "Report of the Commissioner of Internal Revenue, January 13, 1863," reprinted in the *Chicago Daily Tribune*, January 23, 1863; Joseph J. Thorndike Jr., "An Army of Officials: The Civil War Bureau of Internal Revenue," *Tax Notes*, December 24, 2001. Quote is from Philip J. Staudenraus, ed., *Mr. Lincoln's Washington: The Civil War Despatches of Noah Brooks* (Thomas Yoseloff Pub., 1967), 35–36.

9. Boutwell, *Reminiscences*, 1:306.

10. There were three such notices on the front page of the *Boston Evening Transcript*, January 5, 1863.

11. *Chicago Daily Tribune*, October 29, 1862.

12. Chase's diary for Friday, August 15, 1862 notes that he and Boutwell met for breakfast to discuss tax collector appointments in Indiana and Ohio and then did more of the same that night. See *The Salmon P. Chase Papers, Vol. 1, Journals, 1829–1872*, ed. John Niven (Kent State University Press, 1993), 362–64. Quote is from Hugh McCulloch, *Men and Measures of Half a Century: Sketches and Comments* (C. Scribner's Sons, 1888), 185. *IRS Historical Fact Book: A Chronology, 1646–1992* (Department of the Treasury, 1992), 199.

13. Hay described Boutwell as usually taking "the near horse" on their rides (the horse on their left), "John Hay to John G. Nicolay," August 27, 1862, in *At Lincoln's Side: John Hay's Civil ar Correspondence and Selected Writings*, ed., Michael Burlingame (Southern Illinois University Press, 2000); Boutwell, *Reminiscences*, 1:309.

14. Pamela Scott, *Fortress of Finance: The United States Treasury Building* (Treasury Historical Association, 2010), 181–89.

15. Quotes are from Kenneth J. Winkle, *Lincoln's Citadel: The Civil War in Washington* (W. W. Norton, 2013), 121–24; Boutwell, *Reminiscences*, 1:310; Georgianna A. Boutwell, "Washington City Paper" (typed manuscript, 1895), 1, Boutwell Collection, GHS.

16. Georgianna A. Boutwell to Abby Boutwell, January 20, 1864, and Sarah Adelia Boutwell to Abby Boutwell, February 5, 1863, Boutwell Collection, GHS.

17. Sarah Adelia Boutwell to Abby Boutwell, May 18, 1864, Boutwell Collection, GHS.

18. Taxpayers were allowed to deduct "all other national, state, and local taxes" to avoid double taxation; Sidney Ratner, *American Taxation: Its History as a Social Force in Democracy* (W. W. Norton, 1942), 74.

19. Weisman, *The Great Tax Wars*, 44; Lowenstein, *Ways and Means*, 262–63. Boutwell was pleased that "the people of this country have accepted it with cheerfulness, to meet a temporary exigency, and it has excited no serious complaint in its administration." Quoted in Edwin Robert

Anderson Seligman, *The Income Tax: A Study of the History, Theory,and Practice of Income Taxation at Home and Abroad* (Macmillan, 1911), 439.

20. Abraham Lincoln, Executive Order—General Orders No. 94: War Department, November 1, 1861; *Douglass' Monthly*, 5:11, 830 (April 1863).

21. Lowenstein, *Ways and Means*, 68, 286–87.

22. Boutwell, *Reminiscences*, 1:306–7; Ratner, *American Taxation*, 77n43; George S. Boutwell, *A Manual of the Direct and Excise Tax Systems of the United States* (Little, Brown, 1864), 4th ed.

23. George S. Boutwell to Hon. S. P. Chase, Secretary of the Treasury, March 30, 1863, in Boutwell, *A Manual*, p. III.

24. The colleague was John Quincy Adams Griffin, warmly described by Boutwell as "a man of infinite jest," who died at age thirty-nine of consumption in 1866. Boutwell, *Reminiscences*, 1:312, and Green, *Groton Historical Series*, 242–44.

25. Boutwell, *Reminiscences*, 1:304.

26. Goodwin, *Team of Rivals*, 631–35; John Niven and Don E. Fehrenbacher, , "Lincoln and Chase, A Reappraisal [with Comment]," *Journal of the Abraham Lincoln Association* 12 (1991): 1–20. In his assessment of Chase, Fehrenbacher acknowledges that the talented Chase "might have made a very good president" save for "an excessively self-centered view of the political universe," illustrating the English philosopher John Ruskin's quip that, "when a man is wrapped up in himself, he makes a pretty small package," 19–20.

27. Francis P. Blair Sr., to Governor John Andrew, November 19, 1864, in *Conversations with Lincoln*, ed. M. Segal (Putnam, 1961), 361. Quote is in Donald, *Lincoln*, 551–52.

28. Boutwell, *Reminiscences*, 2:28.

29. David M. Silver, *Lincoln's Supreme Court* (University of Illinois Press, 1998), 209.

30. See *Hepburn v. Griswold*, 75 U.S. 603 (1869); the case reinstating greenbacks was *Knox v. Lee*, 79 U.S. 457 (1871). John Hay and John Nicolay found it hard to believe that Chase, "the father of the National Currency should ever disown his own offspring"; quoted in Carl Sandburg, *Abraham Lincoln: The War Years* (Harcourt, Brace, 1939), 3:599. For Chase's rationale, see Salmon P. Chase Papers, Library of Congress, 5:343–49.

31. Jeffrey Boutwell, "When the chief justice himself was the Supreme Court leak," *The Baltimore Sun*, January 29, 2023.

Chapter 7: The Promise of Emancipation

1. Boutwell writes, "during the autumn and winter of 1862–63, I was in the habit of calling at the War Office for news, when I left the Treasury—usually between nine and eleven o'clock [in the evening]. Not infrequently I met Mr. Lincoln on the way or at the department. When the weather was cold he wore a gray shawl, muffled closely around his shoulders." Boutwell, *Reminiscences*, 1:310. With his abiding interest in military history and strategy, Boutwell assembled an impressive collection of Civil War campaign maps that is available online at https://www.digitalcommonwealth.org/search?f%5Bcollection_name_ssim%5D%5B%5D=George+S.+Boutwell+Map+Collection&f%5Binstitution_name_ssi%5D%5B%5D=Groton+Historical+Society. He also wrote perceptively on Union war strategy, advocating in early 1863 "that the success of the Union armies is to be achieved by transferring the war to the Mississippi" rather than focusing on capturing Richmond; see George S. Boutwell, "Suggestions Concerning the Further Prosecution of the War," in Boutwell, *Speeches and Papers*, 189–215. Many years later, he compared the military reputations of Robert E. Lee and Stonewall Jackson, George S. Boutwell, "Gen. Wolseley and Gen. Lee," *Boston Globe*, October 2, 1888.

2. Personal communication from Allen C. Guelzo, April 1, 2021.

3. *National Republican*, August 6, 1862.

4. *New York Herald*, August 7, 1862; the text of Lincoln's brief remarks is "Address to Union Meeting at Washington," August 6, 1862, *CWAL*, ed. Roy P. Basler, 5: 358–59.

5. Doris Kearns Goodwin cites Lincoln's remarks about McClellan and Stanton as a good example of a leader shielding his subordinates from blame while assuming full decision-making responsibility; see her *Leadership in Turbulent Times* (Simon & Schuster, 2018), 221−27. Douglas Wilson writes that Lincoln's brief remarks demonstrate the president's wisdom in knowing when *not* to speak. Wilson describes how the president had "almost a phobia about speaking without a prepared text" and knew that "too much was at stake to run the risk of inadvertently misspeaking." Thus, Lincoln seemed content to joke with the crowd and make way for Boutwell's remarks on slavery. See *National Republican*, August 7, 1862; *Harper's Weekly*, August 23, 1862; Douglas L. Wilson, *Lincoln's Sword: The Presidency and the Power of Words* (Random House, 2006), 166−67.

6. George S. Boutwell, "Treason the Fruit of Slavery, a Speech delivered in the Capitol Grounds, Washington," in Boutwell, *Speeches and Papers*, 175. This reprint is misdated July 1862.

7. Boutwell, "Treason the Fruit of Slavery," 176.

8. Goodwin, *Team of Rivals*, 463−72.

9. *New York Herald*, August 7, 1862.

10. Boutwell, "Treason the Fruit of Slavery," 179.

11. George S. Boutwell to Charles Sumner, August 9, 1862, Charles Sumner Correspondence, Microfilm 26:264−65, HL-HU. A committee member who likely favored Boutwell speaking was Lewis Clephane, a staunch antislavery Republican and editor of the *National Republican* newspaper, who was close to Lincoln; *National Republican*, August 6, 1862; Harold Holzer, *Lincoln and the Power of the Press: The War for Public Opinion* (Simon & Schuster, 2014), 308; Walter C. Clephane, "Lewis Clephane: A Pioneer Washington Republican," *Records of the Columbia Historical Society*, Washington, DC (1918), 21:263−77.

12. Boutwell, "Treason the Fruit of Slavery," 178.

13. Andrew quote in Henry Greenleaf Pearson, *The Life of John Andrew* (Houghton, Mifflin, 1904), 2:4; George S. Boutwell, "Emancipation: Its Justice, Expediency, and Necessity, as the Means of Securing a Speedy and Permanent Peace, December 16, 1861," in Boutwell, *Speeches and Papers*, 123−58.

14. *New York Times*, August 7, 1862; *New York Tribune*, August 7, 1862; *Boston Evening Transcript*, August 13, 1862. The possibility that Boutwell's speech was a testing of the waters for emancipation is reinforced by an article in the *New York Evening Post* that noted how President Lincoln, who "does nothing thoughtlessly," was attending his first "popular meeting" as president, and "when he departs from precedents so far as to take his seat on the platform of a public meeting, we have a right to infer his deep sympathies in the objects of assemblage." The article then gives credit to "Ex-Governor Boutwell . . . who described the real causes of the rebellion, and who showed that it could never be suppressed, and a permanent Union again restored until the causes of separation had been eternally removed." The story was reprinted in the *National Republican*, August 9, 1862.

15. *The Christian Recorder* (Philadelphia), August 16, 1862; Frederick Douglass, "Anti-Slavery Progress" and "The President and His Speeches," *Douglass' Monthly*, 4−5, 706−7 (September 1862).

16. See *The Morning Post* (London), August 21, 1862; *The Leeds Mercury*, August 22, 1862; *Liverpool Mercury*, August 19, 1862. At the time, Britain was pressuring Lincoln to allow $50 million worth of cotton to pass through the Union blockade so its mills could continue to operate. See Matthew Pinsker, *Lincoln's Sanctuary: Abraham Lincoln and the Soldiers' Home* (Oxford University Press, 2003), 47−48.

17. Quoted in Holzer, *Lincoln and the Power of the Press*, xxix. Douglas Wilson has written that "enlisting popular support for a cause was the guiding star of [Lincoln's] political philosophy," in *Lincoln's Sword*, 109.

18. Michael Burlingame, *The Inner World of Abraham Lincoln* (University of Illinois Press, 1994), 20. Boutwell quote is from his essay in Allen Thorndike Rice, ed., *Reminiscences of Abraham Lincoln*, 6th ed. (*North American Review*, 1888), 136, emphasis added by Burlingame.

19. A mob of four hundred whites in Brooklyn had recently attacked Black workers in a factory, incited by false reports of Blacks insulting white women. See *Brooklyn Daily Eagle*, August 5, 1862.

20. Boutwell, "Treason the Fruit of Slavery," 176–77.

21. Guelzo, *Redeeming the Great Emancipator*, 97–98; Elisha Weaver and Henry McNeal Turner, *The Christian Recorder*, August 16, 1862. For more on the resettlement of Blacks within the United States, see Nicholas Guyatt, "An Impossible Idea?: The Curious Career of Internal Colonization," *Journal of the Civil War Era* 4 (2014), 234–63; and Sebastian Page, *Black Resettlement and the American Civil War* (Cambridge University Press, 2021).

22. Boutwell, "Treason the Fruit of Slavery," 179.

23. Boutwell in Rice, *Reminiscences of Abraham Lincoln*, 123.

24. Boutwell, *Reminiscences*, 1:310–11; George Boutwell, *The Lawyer, the Statesman, and the Soldier* (D. Appleton, 1887), 114–15; and George S. Boutwell to Charles Sumner, August 31, 1862, *Sumner Correspondence*, microfilm, 26:335–36, HL-HU.

25. George S. Boutwell to Sarah A. Boutwell, September 5, 1862, Boutwell Collection, GHS.

26. George S. Boutwell to Abby Boutwell, September 18, 1862, Boutwell Collection, GHS. Boutwell noted how the Union's two-to-one advantage in manpower meant that "battles in which the rebels are not victorious are defeats to them" and that maintaining an offensive strategy—like the one pursued by Ulysses Grant in 1864—would ensure victory; see George S. Boutwell to [unidentified family member, either wife Sarah or sister Abby], September 19, 1862, Boutwell Collection, GHS.

27. George S. Boutwell to Sarah A. Boutwell, September 23, 1862, Boutwell Collection, GHS. Boutwell considered the Emancipation Proclamation to be Lincoln's "passport to immortality." See Boutwell in Rice, *Reminiscences of Abraham Lincoln*, 133–34; Guelzo, *Lincoln's Emancipation Proclamation*, 248–49. For different perspectives on Lincoln as the Great Emancipator, a contentious issue in our own time, see Edna Greene Medford, *Lincoln and Emancipation* (Southern Illinois University Press, 2015) and Harold Holzer, Edna Greene Medford, and Frank J. Williams, *The Emancipation Proclamation: Three Views* (Louisiana State University Press, 2006).

28. Quoted in Boutwell, *The Lawyer*, 116–17, and John G. Nicolay and John Hay, *Abraham Lincoln: A History* (American Historical Foundation, 1914), 6:164–65. It's likely that Lincoln wrote the final draft of the Emancipation Proclamation on the Sunday following the battle of Antietam, even though Boutwell had once maintained that Lincoln told him that the Proclamation was completed prior to the battle; see George S. Boutwell to Josiah G. Holland, June 10, 1865, J. G. Holland Papers, NYPL. Boutwell later dropped this assertion in his portrait of Lincoln in *The Lawyer*, 116–17. See Pinsker, *Lincoln's Sanctuary*, 63–65 and 212n32, where Pinsker thanks Allen Guelzo for pointing out the discrepancy in Boutwell's accounts. See also Wilson, *Lincoln's Sword*, 127–28.

29. A month after the defeat, Union general Ambrose Burnside became the latest commander to be replaced by Lincoln. Peter Pineo to Abby Boutwell, December 16, 1862, Boutwell Collection, GHS. Pineo was working at the Douglas Hospital in Washington, located in the former mansion of the recently deceased Senator Stephen Douglas.

30. Boutwell, *Reminiscences*, 2:307.

31. Ron Chernow provides a wonderful snapshot of the evening; see his *Grant*, 339–44. Although both Boutwell and Thaddeus Stevens had voted against the bill reviving the rank of lieutenant general by which Lincoln promoted Grant, Boutwell did so, he explained, less because he doubted Grant's "commitment to emancipation," as Brooks Simpson has written, than that "the war was not yet ended, and such an appointment might create sectional divisions in the army." See Simpson, *Let Us Have Peace*, 208; *CG*, 38/1, 851 (February 26, 1864); *The Weekly Pioneer and Democrat* (St. Paul, MN), February 12, 1864.

32. Georgianna Boutwell, "Washington City Paper," 7–8. The essay provides a marvelous summary of Georgie's experiences in Washington, DC.

33. George S. Boutwell, "The Power of the Government to Suppress the Rebellion, Speech Delivered Before the National Union League Association, Washington, D.C., June 16, 1863," in Boutwell, *Speeches and Papers*, 227; *CG*, 38/1, 605 (February 12, 1864).

34. Frederick Douglass, "Address for the Promotion of Colored Enlistments," speech in Philadelphia, July 6, 1863, quoted in Blight, *Frederick Douglass*, 395. Governor Andrew in Massachusetts provided the crucial leadership in organizing the Fifty-Fourth Regiment and convincing Robert Gould Shaw to become one of its officers; Engle, *In Pursuit of Justice*, 235–41.

35. Younger son Charles Douglass became the first Black American to enroll with the Fifty-Fourth Regiment in February 1863, but poor health prevented him from deploying with his unit in May 1863 to South Carolina. Older brother Lewis rose to the rank of sergeant major, the highest attainable by a Black soldier. See Blight, *Frederick Douglass*, 391–402. George S. Boutwell to John A. Andrew, June 10, 1863, John A. Andrew Papers, vol. 84, Massachusetts State Library. See also Benjamin Quarles, *The Negro in the Civil War* (Da Capo, 1962; repr., 1991) and Douglas R. Egerton, *Thunder at the Gates: The Black Civil War Regiments That Redeemed America* (Basic Books, 2016).

36. Barbara Murray, Deborah E. Johnson, and Jayme Kulesz, eds., *Groton at 350: The History of a Massachusetts Town* (Town of Groton, 2005), 75.

37. Boutwell, "The Power of the Government to Suppress the Rebellion," in Boutwell, *Speeches and Papers*, 227.

38. Quoted in Lorien Foote, *Seeking the One Great Remedy: Francis George Shaw and Nineteenth-Century Reform* (Ohio University Press, 2003), 120. See also Russell Duncan, *Where Death and Glory Meet: Colonel Robert Gould Shaw and the 54th Massachusetts Infantry* (University of Georgia Press, 1999).

39. Donald, *Lincoln*, 471–74; *Inside Lincoln's White House: The Complete Civil War Diary of John Hay*, ed. Michael Burlingame and John R, Turner Ettlinger (Southern Illinois University Press, 1997), 122.

40. *Inside Lincoln's White House*, 217–19. Hay notes that Boutwell was being considered for treasury secretary, Salmon Chase having resigned in June, but Lincoln selected Senator William P. Fessenden of Maine; 212–17, 355n206.

41. Goodwin, *Team of Rivals*, 639–40; Wilson, *History of the Rise and Fall*, 3:371–73.

42. *Bangor Daily Whig and Courier* (Maine), February 17, 1864; Edward L. Pierce, *Memoir and Letters of Charles Sumner, Period 1860 to Death* (Sampson, Low, Marston, 1893), 217n2. Convinced that South Carolina and Georgia were the two states most responsible for embedding slavery in the Constitution in 1787, Boutwell told a House colleague that "South Carolina, as a State and with a name, should never reappear in this Union. Georgia deserves a like fate." *CG*, 38/1, 2102–5 (May 4, 1864).

43. Foner, *The Fiery Trial*, 290–97.

44. Boutwell again put out feelers for a cabinet position, especially Treasury, but that went to Hugh McCulloch, comptroller of the currency since 1863. See *Cincinnati Daily Gazette*, February 25, 1865; John Murray Forbes to Gov. John Andrew, February 26, 1865, in Pearson, *The Life of John Andrew*, 2:191.

45. George S. Boutwell, "Declaration of Opinions" introduced in US House of Representatives, 1864, reprinted in Boutwell, *Reminiscences*, 2:30–32, and quoted in Edward Winslow Martin, *The New Administration: Containing Complete and Authentic Biographies of Grant and His Cabinet* (George S. Wilcox, 1869), 126.

46. Charles M. Blow, "Why We Need a Second Great Migration," The Week in Review, *New York Times*, January 10, 2020; Charles Blow, *The Devil You Know: A Black Power Manifesto* (HarperCollins, 2021).

47. Wilson, *History of the Rise and Fall*, 3:483–87; *CG* 38/2, 1182 (February 28, 1865); Herman Belz, *Abraham Lincoln, Constitutionalism, and Equal Rights in the Civil War Era* (Fordham University Press, 1998), 155.

48. Georgianna Boutwell, "Washington City Paper," 5–6.

49. Quoted in Brenda Wineapple, *The Impeachers: The Trial of Andrew Johnson and the Dream of a Just Nation* (Random House, 2019), 14–15.

50. For the growing friction between Stanton and Andrew Johnson, see Walter Stahr, *Stanton: Lincoln's War Secretary* (Simon & Schuster, 2017), 452–56.

51. George S. Boutwell, "Abraham Lincoln: Eulogy Delivered before the City Council and Citizens of Lowell, at Huntington Hall, April 19, 1865," in Boutwell, *Speeches and Papers*, 356–71.

Chapter 8: Reconstruction and the Fourteenth Amendment

1. For a personal account of experiencing Juneteenth while growing up in Texas, see Annette Gordon-Reed, *On Juneteenth* (Liveright, 2021).

2. Roger L. Ransom, *Conflict and Compromise: The Political Economy of Slavery, Emancipation, and the American Civil War* (Cambridge University Press, 1989); C. Vann Woodward, *The Strange Career of Jim Crow* (1955; Oxford University Press, 2002), 22–25.

3. Peter Pineo to Abby Boutwell, April 16, 1865, Boutwell Collection, GHS. Pineo describes the shattered condition of Charleston at the end of the war, including the extensive use of quicklime to prevent the spread of infection from decaying animals; see Colonel Peter Pineo to Headquarters, Department of the South, Hilton Head, South Carolina, April 7, 1865, *The War of the Rebellion: A Compilation of the Official Records of the Union and Confederate Armies*, series 1, vol. 67, part 3 (US Government Printing Office, 1896), 126–27.

4. Quoted in Livingstone, *History of the Republican Party*, 1:195.

5. See W. E. B. Du Bois, "The Freedmen's Bureau," *The Atlantic Monthly* 87 (March 1901); William S. McFeely, *Yankee Stepfather: General O. O. Howard and the Freedmen* (1968; W. W. Norton, 1992). Howard, founder and first president of Howard University in Washington, DC, commanded US troops against Chief Joseph in the Nez Perce war in the 1870s and was criticized by some for needlessly provoking the conflict. See Daniel J. Sharfstein, *Thunder in the Mountains: Chief Joseph, Oliver Otis Howard, and the Nez Perce War* (W. W. Norton, 2017).

6. Levine, *The Failed Promise*, 49–54.

7. Geo. S. Boutwell to Major General Butler, April 20, 1865, *Private and Official Correspondence of Gen. Benjamin F. Butler*, vol. 5, August 1864–March 1868 (Plimpton Press, 1917), 599.

8. Edward Winslow Martin, *The New Administration Containing Complete and Authentic Biographies of Grant and His Cabinet* (George S. Wilcox, 1869), 125–26; *New York Times*, May 31, 1865.

9. George S. Boutwell, "Johnson's Plot and Motives," *North American Review* 141 (December 1885): 570–71.

10. The Black Codes were extensively detailed in US Congress, 39th Congress, 2nd Session, Senate Executive Document No. 6, *Freedmen's Affairs*, 170–230.

11. Foner, *Reconstruction*, 189–90; Brodie, *Thaddeus Stevens*, 244–46.

12. See "Special Field Orders, No. 15, Headquarters Military Division of the Mississippi, in the Field, Savannah, Georgia, January 16, 1865," in William T. Sherman, *Memoirs*, 2 vols. (D. Appleton, 1889), 2:250–52.

13. Quoted in Wineapple, *The Impeachers*, 34.

14. Quoted in Levine, *The Failed Promise*, 71; for Wilson's speech, see *Boston Evening Transcript*, July 5, 1865.

15. George S. Boutwell, "Reconstruction: Its True Basis, Speech Delivered at Weymouth, Mass., July 4, 1865," in Boutwell, *Speeches and Papers*, 372–407.

16. Boutwell was an original vice president, working with William Barton Rogers, the association's president and one of the founders of the Massachusetts Institute of Technology that same year; *Constitution, Address, and List of Members of the American Association for the Promotion of Social Science* (Wright & Potter, 1866), 5. In its early years, the association struggled to find its footing; see "Playing at Philosophy," *New York Times*, November 24, 1867. Later, it evolved into the National Institute of Social Sciences, which is still active today.

17. Stewart, *Impeached*, 22; Wineapple, *The Impeachers*, 32. The *Nashville Telegraph and Union*, January 13, 1867, listed the pardon for Confederate officer Edmund Winston Pettus, namesake of the Pettus Bridge in Selma, Alabama, site of the infamous beatings of civil rights demonstrators in March 1965 at the start of the march from Selma to Montgomery.

18. Quoted in Wineapple, *The Impeachers*, 85–86.

19. George S. Boutwell, "Equal Suffrage, Speech before the National Equal Suffrage Association of Washington, December 1865," Boutwell, *Speeches and Papers*, 426.

20. Stewart, *Impeached*, 43; quoted in Brodie, *Thaddeus Stevens*, 241; Bruce Levine, *Thaddeus Stevens: Civil War Revolutionary, Fighter for Racial Justice* (Simon & Schuster, 2021), 197–99.

21. *The Buffalo Commercial*, December 14, 1865.

22. Robert J. Cook, *Civil War Senator: William Pitt Fessenden and the Fight to Save the American Republic* (Louisiana State University Press, 2011), 196; Foner, *Reconstruction*, 243–47.

23. Quarles, "George Sewall Boutwell," 65–70. Boutwell's questions focused on whether Blacks would be safe if the US military was withdrawn, and on the extent to which "leagues or secret societies" were being formed "among the secessionists" to terrorize and intimidate Blacks.

24. Bingham sought to protect individual rights from the actions of state governments, given that the Constitution only applied to actions of the federal government. See Gerard N. Magliocca, *American Founding Son: John Bingham and the Invention of the Fourteenth Amendment* (New York University Press, 2013), ch. 7. See also Kendrick, *The Journal of the Joint Committee*, 8–9, and "Journal of the Joint Committee on Reconstruction, Thirty-Ninth Congress, First Session," compiled under the direction of committee cochair Senator William Pitt Fessenden of Maine (US Government Printing Office, 1915).

25. Kendrick, *The Journal of the Joint Committee*, 40–48.

26. The House resolution sending the Thirteenth Amendment to the states for ratification was passed on January 31, 1865, by the slimmest of margins, 119 to 56 with 8 not voting, thus barely meeting the required two-thirds majority. Boutwell was on the floor casting an "aye" vote while crowds in the galleries exploded in applause; *CG*, 38/2, 531 (January 31, 1865).

27. Quoted in Foner, *The Second Founding*, 41.

28. As admitted by a former Confederate general and future Alabama senator, John T. Morgan, the provision would allow southern whites "to consign to bondage blacks convicted of crime"; quoted in Foner, *The Second Founding*, 47. Ava Duvernay's documentary film, *13th*, explores how the modern, mass incarceration of Blacks, increasingly in prisons run for profit, has its roots in the Thirteenth Amendment.

29. Quoted in Brodie, *Thaddeus Stevens*, 273–82. Brodie goes into detail describing the controversy over whether George Boutwell was one of two members of the Joint Committee on Reconstruction who signed a letter sent to local Republicans in New Orleans urging them to hold what the Democrats insisted was an illegal Constitutional Convention, which they tried to blame as the cause of the violence. Given the president's specious allegations that the massacre had "its origin in the radical Congress," Boutwell and others denied any part in sending the letter "to avoid being implicated in the massacre in any way." See Brodie, *Thaddeus Stevens*, 275–76, 281–82, and 405–6n10.

30. Foner, *Reconstruction*, 222–24.

31. Foner, *Reconstruction*, 261–63 and 220.

32. George S. Boutwell, "Suffrage in the District of Columbia, Speech delivered in the House of Representatives, January 18, 1866," in Boutwell, *Speeches and Papers*, 427–41; See also *CG*, 39/1, 308–10 (January 18, 1866).

33. Boutwell, "Suffrage in the District of Columbia," *Speeches and Papers*, 441.

34. *CG*, 39/1, 311 (January 18, 1866).

35. See Levine, *The Failed Promise*, 86–95; Blight, *Frederick Douglass*, 475.

36. Boutwell was selected to chair the Tennessee subcommittee that included Senators Roscoe Conkling and George Williams; see Kendrick, *The Journal of the Joint Committee*, 63–67. Kendrick and Quarles not surprisingly provide differing perspectives on this, as on many JCR issues; see Kendrick, *The Journal of the Joint Committee*, 68–72, and Quarles, *George Sewall Boutwell*, 70–72.

37. George S. Boutwell to Sarah A. Boutwell, undated, 1866, Boutwell Collection, GHS; *CG*, 39/1, 3975–77 (July 20, 1866). Boutwell was joined by Jacob Howard of Michigan in demanding, ultimately unsuccessfully, that the Fourteenth Amendment include voting rights for Black males; see Joseph B. James, *The Framing of the Fourteenth Amendment* (University of Illinois Press, 1956),

75–82. Kendrick ridiculed Boutwell's support for such voting rights as "either the raving of a diseased imagination or the subtle appeal of a wily politician to the laboring classes of the North to support negro suffrage for the South." See Kendrick, *The Journal of the Joint Committee*, 341.

38. George S. Boutwell to Sarah Adelia Boutwell, March 4, 1866, Boutwell Collection, GHS.

39. Foner, *The Second Founding*, ch. 2.

40. Boutwell quote in *Congressional Record* [*CR*], 43/2, 1379 (February 17, 1875); Foner, *The Second Founding*, 73.

41. Irons, *A People's History of the Supreme Court*, 193. For more on how the Fourteenth Amendment has been interpreted differently regarding the protection of individual rights and whether the amendment contains a "right to privacy," see Randy E. Barnett & Evan D. Bernick, *The Original Meaning of the 14th Amendment: Its Letter & Spirit* (Harvard University Press, 2021) and Ilan Wurman, *The Second Founding: An Introduction to the Fourteenth Amendment* (Cambridge University Press, 2020).

42. Boutwell's opinion that Sumner "could not concede small points for the sake of a great result" was shared by many. See Boutwell, *Reminiscences*, 2:42 and 218–19.

43. Franklin Noll, "Repudiation! The Crisis of the United States Civil War Debt, 1865–1870," Graduate Institute of International and Development Studies, Geneva, December 2012.

44. Letter from Frederick Douglass, *National Anti-Slavery Standard*, July 7, 1866; Boutwell, *Reminiscences*, 2:41.

Chapter 9: Impeaching the President

1. William Shakespeare, *Julius Caesar*, 1:2, 194–95.

2. Questioned by Boutwell, Lee stonewalled, repeatedly saying "I do not know" when asked about anti-Union and anti-Black sentiment among his fellow southerners; see *Report of the Joint Committee on Reconstruction of the First Session, Thirty-Ninth Congress* (US Government Printing Office, 1866), 129–36. Lee's elevation to sainthood among his fellow southerners after his death in 1870 was perhaps "the most important factor shaping Confederate efforts to memorialize their cause"; see Caroline E. Janney, *Remembering the Civil War*, 137–40.

3. At eight hundred pages, *The Report of the Joint Committee* contained the committee's conclusions, the resolutions of Congress and the southern states, and the testimony of hundreds of former Confederate officers and officials, white Unionists, and freedmen.

4. Robinson, *"Warrington" Pen-Portraits*, 308–10.

5. The rumors might have originated with the Philadelphia *Ledger* of October 12, 1866; Boutwell noted nonetheless that Johnson spoke "rather approvingly" of the scheme. Boutwell, *Reminiscences*, 2:77–78. See Stewart, *Impeached*, 57–73; Wineapple, *The Impeachers*, 203–19.

6. George S. Boutwell, "The Usurpation," *The Atlantic Monthly* 18 (October 1866), 506–13.

7. Only six states had ratified the Fourteenth Amendment by December 1866, but momentum picked up in early 1867 with ratification by an additional fifteen northern and midwestern states.

8. Stahr, *Stanton*, 482–85.

9. See Andrew K. Diemer, *Vigilance: The Life of William Still, Father of the Underground Railroad* (Alfred A. Knopf, 2022). Still had been a primary organizer of the Underground Railroad while living in Philadelphia, keeping detailed records that have proved invaluable for historians; see William Still, *The Underground Railroad: A Record of Facts, Authentic Narratives, Letters, &c.* (Porter and Coates, 1872). In his Philadelphia talk, Boutwell recounted the story of meeting the elderly enslaved woman on his first trip to Washington, mistakenly saying it was 1838, not 1839; *The Evening Telegraph* (Philadelphia), December 1, 1866. Described by the *National Anti-Slavery Standard*, December 2, 1866, as "one of Andrew Johnson's most zealous foes," Boutwell asked his audience the rhetorical question, if reading and writing tests weren't required during the war for Blacks "to take their places in the national army" and die for their country, why should they be required for voting?

10. *New York Herald*, December 3, 1866.

11. George S. Boutwell to Sarah Adelia Boutwell, December 2, 1866, Boutwell Collection, GHS; George S. Boutwell, "Johnson's Plot and Motives," 570–79; Boutwell, *Reminiscences*, 2:107–9; Military Appropriations Act, chap. 170, *Thirty-Ninth Congress*, Session 2, March 2, 1867 (US Government Printing Office, 1867), 485–87.

12. St. George L. Sioussat, "Notes of Colonel W. G. Moore, Private Secretary to President Johnson, 1866–1868," *The American Historical Review* 19 (1913): 106.

13. Foner notes that, on the crucial issue of providing Blacks with their own land so they could have the opportunity to create wealth free from white control, "Johnson had in effect abrogated the Confiscation Act and unilaterally amended the law creating the Bureau. The idea of a Freedmen's Bureau actively promoting black land ownership had come to an abrupt end." Foner, *Reconstruction*, 161; Levine, *The Failed Promise*, 137.

14. *CG*, 39/2, 472–81 (January 15, 1867): *CG*, 39/2, 1096, 1120–22 (February 8–9, 1867).

15. Boutwell is mentioned in "John Eaton: A Biographical Sketch," by Ethel Osgood Mason, in John Eaton, *Grant, Lincoln, and the Freedmen: Reminiscences of the Civil War with Special Reference to the Work for the Contrabands and Freedmen of the Mississippi Valley* (Longmans, Green, 1907), xx–xxi. Eaton was commissioner of the office from 1870 to 1886; during the war, he was appointed by General Grant to oversee the welfare and employment of thousands of former enslaved Blacks in Mississippi and Tennessee.

16. Hans Louis Trefousse, *The Radical Republicans: Lincoln's Vanguard for Racial Justice* (Knopf, 1969), 357–59.

17. Stewart, *Impeached*, 77.

18. *CG*, 39/1, 1854–55 (April 9, 1866); also see the detailed account of the Boutwell subcommittee in Quarles, "George Sewall Boutwell," 47–62.

19. Elizabeth D. Leonard, *Lincoln's Avengers: Justice, Revenge, and Reunion after the Civil War* (W. W. Norton, 2004); William Hanchett, *The Lincoln Murder Conspiracies* (1983; University of Illinois Press, 1986), 59–89.

20. Julian Sher, *The North Star: Canada and the Civil War Plots Against Lincoln* (Alfred A. Knopf Canada, 2023), 313–25.

21. Hanchett, *The Lincoln Murder Conspiracies*, 77.

22. D. M. Dewitt, *The Impeachment and Trial of Andrew Johnson* (1903; State Historical Society of Wisconsin, 1967), 147; *CG*, 39/1, 1865 (June 11, 1866).

23. *CG*, 39/1, 4018–19 (July 21, 1866).

24. George S. Boutwell, "Assassination of Lincoln," *Committee on the Assassination of Lincoln*, US House of Representatives, 39th Congress, 1st Session, Report No. 104.

25. *The Nation* 3 (August 2, 1866): 81–82.

26. Boutwell, *Reminiscences*, 2:62.

27. Theodore Roscoe, *The Web of Conspiracy: The Complete Story of the Men Who Murdered Abraham Lincoln* (Prentice-Hall, 1959), 494; David Balsiger and Charles E. Sellier Jr., *The Lincoln Conspiracy* (Schick Sunn Classic Books, 1977), 294–95. Boutwell appears in the 1977 movie, *The Lincoln Conspiracy*, but is misidentified as a senator. See also Leonard F. Guttridge and Ray A. Neff, *Dark Union: The Secret Web of Profiteers, Politicians, and Booth Conspirators That Led to Lincoln's Death* (John Wiley & Sons, 2003).

28. With thanks to the National Archives and Records Administration, I accessed the last surviving box of materials, labeled Trial of Jefferson Davis for Treason. There was no additional evidence incriminating Jefferson Davis or Andrew Johnson, but there was a note revealing that someone had looked before with a similar interest. Dated March 14, 1951, it read, "considerable search was made trying to find testimony relating to HR Report 104, 39th Congress, as referenced by 'GSB Reminiscences, Vol. II, p. 62,' but without success." The interested party was not identified. Center for Legislative Archives, National Archives and Records Administration, HR39A-F13.10.

29. I am indebted to Jere Nash of the Mississippi Department of Archives and History for sharing his research on the Reconstruction process in Mississippi.

30. George S. Boutwell to Ulysses S. Grant, August 17, 1867, *PUSG*, 17:499; for Grant testimony on July 18, 1867. see *PUSG*, 17:225–26.
31. Simpson, *Let Us Have Peace*, 192–93 and 199–204.
32. Stewart, *Impeached*, 87–99.
33. John Churchill became—briefly—the most famous man in America; "his name is printed in every newspaper in the land, is telegraphed in all directions and is on millions of lips," *Brooklyn Daily Eagle*, November 27, 1867. Decades later, "Lost Cause" historian William Dunning would falsely accuse Boutwell of illegally influencing Churchill to change his vote. Churchill was very open about what changed his mind, listing specific examples in a letter to the *New York Times* on how the president was subverting the Constitution by thwarting the will of Congress. See William Archibald Dunning, *Essays on the Civil War and Reconstruction and Related Topics* (Macmillan, 1904), 257; Boutwell, *Reminiscences*, 2:44; "Impeachment: Letter from Hon. J. C. Churchill, of New York, in Regard to His Change of Vote in Committee," *New York Times*, December 6, 1867.
34. *CG*, 40/2, 791–92 (November 25, 1867); Stewart, *Impeached*, 103. Confusion broke out on the House floor when Boutwell tried to read his lengthy report, which would have taken hours; it was decided to have it printed with the majority report and two minority reports for later consideration.
35. Andrew Johnson, Third Annual Message, December 3, 1867, in *The American Presidency Project*, ed. Gerhard Peters and John T. Woolley, https://www.presidency.ucsb.edu/node/201999.
36. Wineapple, *The Impeachers*, 228–31.
37. Michael Les Benedict, *The Impeachment and Trial of Andrew Johnson* (W. W. Norton, 1973), 77. Boutwell's speech is at *CG*, 40/2, 54–62, appendix (December 5 and 6, 1867); "usurpation" quote is from Boutwell, *Reminiscences*, 2:112. The *New York Times*, December 6, 1867, thought Boutwell "able, vigorous and eloquent, as he always is, and the calm, dispassionate tone of his speech went far toward convincing many of his desire to divest the case of its partisan aspect." A young journalist from France, Georges Clemenceau (the country's prime minister during World War I), thought otherwise, writing that Boutwell is "too much a fanatic to command the attention of the Senate, but too honest and sincere for his opinions to be ignored by his party." Georges Clemenceau, *American Reconstruction, 1865–1870* (1928; Da Capo Press, 1969), 178.
38. *CG*, 40/2, 61 (December 6, 1867).
39. George S. Boutwell, *Impeachment* (Congressional Globe Office, 1867), 3.
40. Chernow, *Grant*, 593–602; White, *American Ulysses*, 446–53.
41. Stahr, *Stanton*, 501–13.
42. Geo. S. Boutwell to Hon. E. M. Stanton, February 21, 1868, Edwin Stanton Papers, box 34, image 204, LC.
43. Stewart, *Impeached*, 161–62.
44. Wineapple, *The Impeachers*, 253–54.
45. *CG*, 40/2, 1400–402 (February 24, 1868).
46. At that time, the president pro tempore of the Senate was next in the line for the presidency, not the Speaker of the House; that change was made in 1947 with the Presidential Succession Act, revised in 2006.
47. Lottery selections for desks on the House floor had just been made, and Boutwell found himself relegated to #104 on the outside row of what Thaddeus Stevens jokingly called the "African coast" for being as distant as possible from the House Speaker's podium. Moreover, Boutwell was surrounded by Democrats, there not being a seat for him on the Republican half of the House floor. See *Congressional Directory for The Third Session of the Fortieth Congress*, compiled by Ben. Perley Poore (US Government Printing Office, 1869), 110–11; *Boston Journal*, February 11, 1868; *The Telegraph-Forum* (Bucyrus, Ohio), May 17, 1873.
48. Stewart, *Impeached*, 156–60.
49. *CG*, 40/2, 1542–45 (February 29, 1868).

50. Boutwell had defended Butler on the House floor in 1865 from charges of theft while Butler was in command in New Orleans, and the two had had business dealings together, yet they were oil and water when it came to personality and political style. See "Speech of Hon. George S. Boutwell, in Defence of Major-General Benj. F. Butler, In the House of Representatives, January 24, 1865," reprinted in *Speech of Maj.-Gen. Benj. F. Butler, upon the Campaign before Richmond, 1864, Delivered at Lowell, Mass., January 29, 1865* (Wright & Potter, Printers, 1865). Soon after the war, Butler became president and Boutwell was a trustee of the Chemical Gold & Silver Ore Reducing Co., which like many mining enterprises of the time seems not to have prospered. See *The American Mining Gazette, and Geological Magazine*, ed. G. E. Currie, vol. 2, no. 9, September 1865, 521–24.

51. Elizabeth D. Leonard, *Benjamin Franklin Butler: A Noisy, Fearless Life* (University of North Carolina Press, 2022).

52. For Bingham's role in the Lincoln conspiracy trial, and his feud with Butler on the impeachment committee, see Gerard Magliocca, *American Founding Son*, 89–107 and 141–53; Boutwell, *Reminiscences*, 2:119–20.

53. Speech by Hon. George S. Boutwell, *The Trial of Andrew Johnson, President of the United States, before the Senate of the United States, on Impeachment by the House of Representatives for High Crimes and Misdemeanors*, ed. Benjamin Perley Poore, 3 vols. (US Government Printing Office, 1868), 2:67.

54. William Shakespeare, *Hamlet*, 3.2.393–99; Boutwell speech, *The Trial of Andrew Johnson*, 2:82. Johnson wanted to test the constitutionality of the Tenure of Office Act, but time was lacking in the spring of 1868; only in 1926 did the Supreme Court rule that the president has sole authority to remove executive branch officials, including cabinet officers.

55. Boutwell speech, *The Trial of Andrew Johnson*, 2:116–17. Moorfield Storey overheard the Evarts comment; see Mark Antony DeWolfe Howe, *Portrait of an Independent, Moorfield Storey, 1845–1929* (Houghton Mifflin, 1932), 100. Even fellow Radical Republican George Julian felt Boutwell "had lost his wits and completely surrendered himself to the passions of the hour." George Washington Julian, *Political Recollections: 1840 to 1872* (1884; Mnemosyne Publishing, 1969), 314.

56. Speech by William Evarts, Esq., *The Trial of Andrew Johnson*, ed. Poore, 2:297; Benjamin Perley Poore, *Perley's Reminiscences of Sixty Years in the National Metropolis* (Hubbard Brothers, 1886), 234. Boutwell may have been emulating Daniel Webster's famous Seventh of March speech in 1850, in which Webster predicted that mounting violence over slavery would cause "heavenly bodies [to] rush from their spheres, and jostle against each other in the realms of space." *Speech of Hon. Daniel Webster on Mr. Clay's Resolutions*, March 7, 1850 (Gideon, 1850), 58.

57. Levine, *The Failed Promise*, 205–08; Bordewich, *Klan War*, 53–56; *The Christian Recorder*, May 2, 1868.

58. Kennedy, *Profiles in Courage*, 115–38; Wineapple, *The Impeachers*, 393–95; Stewart, *Impeached*, 184–89.

59. Quoted in Wineapple, *The Impeachers*, 395; Boutwell, *Reminiscences*, 2:117; see also Laurence Tribe and Joshua Matz, *To End a Presidency: The Power of Impeachment* (Basic Books, 2018).

60. Evarts may have "quietly passed along assurances that Johnson, if acquitted, would cease his efforts to obstruct Republicans' Southern policy," Foner, *Reconstruction*, 336.

61. *Nashville Union and American*, June 4, 1868; Foner, *Reconstruction*, 341–45; "Boutwell in the cloud" quote is from Henry Stanbery to President Andrew Johnson, July 3, 1868, *The Papers of Andrew Johnson*, ed. Paul Bergeron (University of Tennessee Press, 1997), 14:313. Stanbery had resigned as Johnson's attorney general in March so he could join the impeachment defense team, then was rejected by the Republican-led Senate when Johnson renominated him, and was ultimately succeeded as attorney general by William Evarts in July 1868.

62. Levine, *The Failed Promise*, 209–17.

63. William B. Hesseltine, *Lincoln's Plan of Reconstruction* (Peter Smith, 1963), 139–41. An astute appraisal of the difficulties that even Lincoln would have faced in seeking to reconcile North and

South while promoting Black political and civil equality is Allen C. Guelzo, "What If Lincoln Had Lived?," *The Civil War Monitor* 13 (Fall 2023): 3.

64. George S. Boutwell, "Mr. Lincoln as an Historical Personage: A speech delivered before the La Salle Club, Chicago, February 12, 1889," in Boutwell, *Reminiscences*, 2:312. The concept of a "Second Founding" dates in part to the eloquent argument of Garry Wills that Lincoln's Gettysburg Address gave pride of place to the Declaration of Independence ("life, liberty, and the pursuit of happiness") as America's foundational document rather than the US Constitution with its protection of slavery; Garry Wills, *Lincoln at Gettysburg: The Words That Remade America* (Simon & Schuster, 1992).

Chapter 10: The Fifteenth Amendment and the 1868 Election

1. For a full account of the celebration and the remarks by Boutwell and Grant, see *National Republican*, May 23, 1868.
2. Chernow, *Grant*, 617.
3. Anne C. Bailey, *The Weeping Time: Memory and the Largest Slave Auction in American History* (Cambridge University Press, 2017), 123; George S. Boutwell, *CG*, 40/3, 555 (January 23, 1869).
4. Bordewich, *Klan War*, 119–27.
5. White, *American Ulysses*, 464–69.
6. Quoted in James M. McPherson, *Ordeal by Fire: The Civil War and Reconstruction* (McGraw Hill, 2001), 530. The party platform adopted in Chicago spoke of "equal suffrage to all loyal men in the South . . . while the question of suffrage in all the loyal States [the North] properly belongs to the people of those States." For Thaddeus Stevens quote and "Address of the Colored Men's Border State Convention to the People of the United States, Baltimore, August 5–6, 1868," see *National Anti-Slavery Standard*, January 30, 1869.
7. Foner, *The Second Founding*, 93–98.
8. *New York Daily Herald*, November 28, 1868. Reports of Boutwell's comments began appearing in newspapers all over the country.
9. The *Charleston Daily News*, November 14, 1868; *The San Francisco Daily Examiner*, November 30, 1868.
10. Johnson's allies introduced a resolution to provide reimbursement of $50,000 for "expenses incurred by [the president] in defending himself in the impeachment trial," *CG*, 40/3, 9–10.
11. The Joint Committee on Reconstruction had separated into House and Senate Select Committees in 1867. In 1868 the House approved a resolution introduced by Boutwell to expand the House committee from nine to thirteen members in the subsequent Congress, and in December 1868 Boutwell assumed the committee chairmanship left vacant by the death of Stevens the previous August. "U.S. House of Representatives, Select Committee on Reconstruction, July 3, 1867 to March 2, 1871, Organization Authority Record," National Archives.
12. Boutwell phrased it as putting "into the politics of the country" the mechanism to ensure the amendment's approval; see *CG*, 40/3, 554–61 (January 23, 1869).
13. William Gillette, *The Right to Vote: Politics and the Passage of the Fifteenth Amendment* (Johns Hopkins Press, 1965), 51–54; *The Evening Post* (New York), February 25, 1869.
14. George S. Boutwell, *CG*, 40/3, 686 (January 28, 1869).
15. Gillette, *The Right to Vote*, 46–78.
16. George S. Boutwell, "The Electoral College," *Boston Sunday Globe*, July 3, 1892.
17. C. W. Goodyear, *President Garfield: From Radical to Unifier* (Simon & Schuster, 2023), 170–73.
18. Alexander Keyssar, *The Right to Vote: The Contested History of Democracy in the United States* (2000; Basic Books, 2009), 74–83; Michael A. Bellesiles, *Inventing Inequality: Reconstructing the Constitution in the Aftermath of the Civil War* (St. Martin's Press, 2020), 209–13.
19. Gillette credits passage of the amendment to the "persistent leadership of [William] Stewart and [George] Boutwell." Gillette, *The Right to Vote*, 78.

20. Boutwell, *Reminiscences*, 2:43–54.

21. Wendell Phillips, *National Anti-Slavery Standard*, February 20, 1869; George S. Boutwell to Wendell Phillips, Esq., March 13, 1870, in Boutwell, *Reminiscences*, 2:50. Boutwell added a postscript, "this letter is not for the public use in so far as names are mentioned, and of course, not for publication." Boutwell wanted to avoid antagonizing Charles Sumner and Henry Wilson, both of whom he thought had jeopardized the potential amendment with their insistence on the office-holding provision. See also Irving H. Bartlett, *Wendell Phillips, Brahmin Radical* (Beacon Press, 1961), 312–15.

22. Donald, *Charles Sumner*, 354.

23. *Boston Daily Advertiser*, March 1, 1869. See also *CG*, 40/3, 727 (January 29, 1869).

24. Foner, *The Second Founding*, 106–7.

25. Levine, *The Failed Promise*, 208–9.

26. Boutwell's vote was on a bill establishing the Territory of Pembina (parts of North and South Dakota), see *CR*, 43/1, 4331–45 (May 28, 1874). Georgie became one of the first female board members overseeing reform schools and mental facilities in the Commonwealth of Massachusetts, as well as the first woman to serve on the Town of Groton school committee; see *Boston Globe*, September 22, 1933. Boutwell's conversion to women's suffrage came about in part due to his growing belief following the Spanish-American War that a greater role for women in politics would temper the type of masculine adventurism demonstrated by Roosevelt and Lodge in seeking to annex the Philippines; see Edward Atkinson to George Boutwell, December 10, 1901, Edward Atkinson Papers, 71.277, MHS, and "Edward Atkinson on Suffrage," *The Women's Journal* (Boston), 32:49, 386, December 7, 1901.

27. Racist language was common, with Blacks referred to as "Sambo and Dinah" and "pickaninnies"; see *New York Daily Herald*, April 9, 1870.

28. Grant also fully supported public education so that "all who possess and exercise political rights" could do so for the benefit of the country; see "To Congress, March 30, 1870," *The Papers of USG*, 20:130–31.

29. *Richmond Dispatch*, April 22, 1870.

30. Mary Todd Lincoln to George S. Boutwell, December 4, 1868, in *Mary Todd Lincoln: Her Life and Letters*, ed., Justin G. Turner and Linda Levitt Turner (Knopf, 1972), 491–92.

31. *Mary Todd Lincoln*, 490.

32. *CG*, 39/2, 348 (January 14, 1869).

33. Jennifer L. Bach, "Acts of Remembrance: Mary Todd Lincoln and Her Husband's Memory," *Journal of the Abraham Lincoln Association* 25 (Summer 2004): 25–49.

Chapter 11: Managing America's Economy

1. White, *American Ulysses*, 447–48; Boutwell, *Reminiscences*, 2:250.

2. Boutwell was convinced that, if Grant had "advised its rejection, or . . . been indifferent to its fate, the amendment would have failed." Boutwell, *Reminiscences*, 2:229–30. See Chernow, *Grant*, 630–32.

3. Senator Carl Schurz of Missouri disparaged Grant for having "much to learn" about civil government and "much to unlearn" from his experience of exercising "large, indeed, almost unlimited, military command." *The Reminiscences of Carl Schurz*, ed. Fredric Bancroft and William A. Dunning (McClure, 1908), 3:304–10; *Yorkville Enquirer* (South Carolina), March 4, 1869.

4. *The Wheeling (West Virginia) Daily Intelligencer*, March 10, 1869; Boutwell, *Reminiscences*, 2:204.

5. Calhoun, *The Presidency of Ulysses S. Grant*, 68–75.

6. Chernow, *Grant*, 626–27, 634–35.

7. H. W. Brands, *The Man Who Saved the Union: Ulysses Grant in War and Peace* (Anchor Books, 2012), 430–31.

8. White, *American Ulysses*, 474; *New York Times*, March 12, 1869; *New York Herald*, September 12, 1869.

9. George S. Boutwell to Sarah A. Boutwell, March 7, 1869, Boutwell Collection, GHS. Boutwell also expressed his reservations to Washburne, writing that "should the President decide to appoint me to the Treasury (which I hope he may not), I desire to have an interview with him before any nomination or public declaration is made. I am still anxious that my name should not be used until Judge Hoar has been seen." George S. Boutwell to the Hon. E. B. Washburne, Sec. of State, March 9, 1869, Elihu Washburne Collection, 7:79B, MHS.

10. *The Charleston Daily News*, March 4, 1869; *New York Herald*, February 28, 1869. The hamlet of Camilla in southwest Georgia was the site of a weeklong killing spree in September 1868 that left more than a dozen Blacks dead and forty wounded. Democratic newspapers blamed armed Negroes while Republican newspapers correctly cited white vigilantes for having provoked the violence; see *The Daily Milwaukee News*, September 23, 1868; *New York Times*, September 23, 1868; Nicholas Johnson, *Negroes and the Gun: The Black Tradition of Arms* (Prometheus, 2014), 90–92.

11. *Racine County Argus* (Wisconsin), March 4, 1869.

12. Calhoun, *The Presidency of Ulysses S. Grant*, 66–68.

13. Mullett also designed the State, War, and Navy building next to the White House, known today as the Eisenhower Executive Office Building.

14. *The Brooklyn Daily Eagle*, March 6, 1869.

15. Scott, *Fortress of Finance*, 218–26.

16. Charles F. Adams Jr., "A Chapter of Erie," in Charles F. Adams Jr. and Henry Adams, *Chapters of Erie and Other Essays* (Henry Holt, 1886), 97. In 1905 when George Boutwell died, three hundred corporations controlled 40 percent of all manufacturing in America; Trachtenberg, *The Incorporation of America*, 4–7.

17. Samet, ed., *The Annotated Memoirs of Ulysses S. Grant*, lxix–lxxiii; Smith, *Grant*, 481.

18. According to Irwin Unger, "the problem of making almost half a billion dollars in greenbacks as good as gold was to become the largest single financial problem facing the United States after 1865"; Irwin Unger, *The Greenback Era: A Social and Political History of American Finance, 1865–1879* (Princeton University Press, 1964), 16.

19. William A. Richardson to William Robinson, April 13, 1869, *History for Sale*, www.historyforsale .com/william-a-richardson-autograph-letter-signed-04-13-1869/dc17333; Frank Warren Hackett, *A Sketch of the Life and Public Services of William Adams Richardson* (Washington, 1898), 62–72.

20. An observer at the time believed that "General Grant regarded the Secretaryship of the Treasury as the most important position in the Cabinet," even more so than that of secretary of state. "The Republic was at peace with other nations, and the military and naval forces, which had grown to such enormous proportions during the war, had been economically reduced, but the Treasury was an immense, overgrown organization, with its collections of customs and internal revenue duties, its issues of interest-bearing bonds and national bank-notes, the coinage of money, the revenue marine service, the coast survey, and the lifesaving stations, all of which had been expanded during the war until the clerks and employees were numbered by thousands." Treasury also had the second highest number of patronage positions, second only to those of the postmaster general. Poore, *Perley's Reminiscences*, 254–55.

21. *Report of the Secretary of the Treasury on the State of the Finances for the Year 1869* (US Government Printing Office, 1869) and *Register of Officers and Agents, Civil, Military, and Naval, in the Service of the United States, on the Thirtieth September 1869* (US Government Printing Office, 1869). There were hundreds of female clerks on the payroll, paid $900 a year compared to $1,200–$1,800 for their male counterparts. Likewise, a Black laborer in the Bureau of Statistics, Frances Lyles, was paid $360 per year while his white male counterpart, Charles C. Boyd, received $720. Boutwell's salary was $8,000 per year.

22. Boutwell, *Reminiscences*, 2:125. See also Stahr, *Salmon Chase*, and Susan Lee Guckenberg, *Hugh McCulloch: The Father of Modern Banking* (Allen County–Fort Wayne Historical Society, 2004).

23. Scaturro, *President Grant Reconsidered*, 18; Hugh McCulloch, *Men and Measures of Half a Century: Sketches and Comments* (C. Scribner's Sons, 1888), 349.

24. Adams admitted that his critique was "rather bitter, rather slashing, [and] very personal," in Henry Brooks Adams, "Civil-Service Reform," *North American Review* 109 (October 1869): 452–55. See also Brown, *The Last American Aristocrat* 109–11; Ari Arthur Hoogenboom, *Outlawing the Spoils: A History of the Civil Service Reform Movement, 1865–1883* (University of Illinois Press, 1968), 68–69.

25. Pulitzer singled out Boutwell as one of the "Republican executioners who swung the official ax." The *New York World* story was reprinted widely; see *Los Angeles Herald*, November 4, 1888.

26. Charles R. Douglass to George S. Boutwell, March 24, 1869, in *If I Survive: Frederick Douglass and Family in the Walter O. Evans Collection,* ed. Celeste-Marie Bernier and Andrew Taylor (Edinburgh University Press, 2018), 482. Charles Douglass would later have marital and debt problems, with creditors coming after his father; see Blight, *Frederick Douglass*, 571–72. Decades later, Charles Douglass would tell Black newspaper editor Thomas Fortune that Roscoe Conkling had insisted to Boutwell that he give Douglass a job, though Boutwell would not have needed any persuading; see *The New York Age*, March 22, 1917.

27. Quoted in Foner, *Reconstruction*, 507–8.

28. *Report of the Secretary of the Treasury 1869*, vii–viii, and Boutwell, *Reminiscences*, 2:126.

29. Boutwell's efforts paid off when Congress abolished moieties for Internal Revenue officers in 1872 and for customs officers in 1874; see *PUSG*, 20:24, and Nicholas R. Parrillo, *Against the Profit Motive: The Salary Revolution in American Government, 1780–1940* (Yale University Press, 2013), 221–24. Quote from *Report of the Secretary of the Treasury 1869*, xi.

30. Quoted in Guckenberg, *Hugh McCulloch*, 128; Unger, *The Greenback Era*, 44–45.

31. Noll, "Repudiation! The Crisis of the United States Civil War Debt, 1865–1870."

32. Allan Nevins spoke for Liberal Republicans when he wrote, "the unimaginative Boutwell had but a single passion. The one idea that flowered in his Sahara mind was the reduction of the national debt." See Nevins, *Hamilton Fish*, 288. See also White, *The Republic for Which It Stands*, 181–88.

33. Calhoun, *The Presidency of Ulysses S. Grant*, 114–16.

34. *New York Times*, August 21, 1876. Unger analyzes "hard" and "soft" money issues in *The Greenback Era*, ch. 2–4.

35. *New York Times*, May 10, 1869; "Mr. Boutwell as Secretary," *The Nation* 9 (July 1, 1869): 5–6.

36. Richard H. Timberlake, *Monetary Policy in the United States: An Intellectual and Institutional History* (University of Chicago Press, 1993), 194; Henry Adams, "The Session," *North American Review* 111 (July 1870): 36–37.

37. Elihu B. Washburne to Ulysses S. Grant, March 17, 1870, *PUSG*, 20:405; Unger, *The Greenback Era*, 192–93. Another modern favorable review of Boutwell's policy is James K. Kindahl, "Economic Factors in Specie Resumption: The United States, 1865–1879," *Journal of Political Economy* 69 (February 1961): 1.

38. Plagued by ill health and financial worries, Mullett committed suicide in October 1890, a few months after he and Boutwell had lost their case in the US Court of Claims. Mullett shot himself in an upstairs bedroom of his mansion on Pennsylvania Avenue within sight of what is today the Eisenhower Executive Office Building that he designed; see *The Evening Star* (Washington, DC), October 21, 1890. In preparing the Mullett case, Boutwell had written to Hamilton Fish, hoping but being disappointed in not finding written confirmation that Mullett had been promised extra compensation; see George S. Boutwell to Hamilton Fish, April 30, 1887, Hamilton Fish Papers, Correspondence, LC. For details on the case, see "Alfred B. Mullett," U.S. House of Representatives, Mis. Doc. 218, 51st Congress, 1st Session. After Mullet's death, his widow, Pacific Pearl Mullett, hired Boutwell to appeal to the US Supreme Court, which rejected their appeal in 1893; see *Mullett's Administratrix v. United States*, No. 121, US Supreme Court, October Term 1893, 566–72. Not one to give up, Pearl Mullett took her appeal to Congress many years later, but that was rejected as well; see *The Evening Star* (Washington, DC), March 9, 1908.

39. "An Act to Prevent the Extermination of Fur-Bearing Animals in Alaska," July 1, 1870, *CG*, 41/2, 5076 (July 1, 1870). Boutwell strengthened enforcement of the Act by stationing four Treasury agents on the remote and barren islands; see *New Orleans Republican*, June 8, 1872. See also Henry

W. Elliott, *The Seal-Islands of Alaska* (1881; Limestone Press, 1976). In 1888, Boutwell was mentioned by Ambrose Bierce in the latter's widely read newspaper column, "Prattle," in which Bierce castigated the current fur seal concession owners with clothing "their worthless entrails with fat belonging to the United States"; Ambrose Bierce, *The San Francisco Examiner*, January 29, 1888.

40. Dennis R. Means, "A Heavy Sea Running: The Formation of the U.S. Life-Saving Service, 1846–1878," *Prologue, Journal of the National Records and Archives Administration* 19 (Winter 1978): 4.

41. Whitley likely came to Boutwell's attention by having worked as an investigator for the impeachment effort against Andrew Johnson, looking into possible connections between the president and high-ranking Confederate officials; Charles Lane, *Freedom's Detective: The Secret Service, The Ku Klux Klan and the Man Who Masterminded America's First War On Terror* (Harlequin Books, 2019), 43–62. For Whitley's largely self-serving account, see Hiram C. Whitley, *In It* (Riverside Press, 1894), 83–91.

42. David R. Johnson, *Illegal Tender: Counterfeiting and the Secret Service in Nineteenth-Century America* (Smithsonian Institution Press, 1995), 69–77; Boutwell, *Reminiscences*, 2:129; "A Voodoo Doctor's Attempt to Fool Secretary Boutwell," Whitley, *In It*, 277–81.

43. *New York Times*, August 5, 1869. For more on the Miner case, see Lane, *Freedom's Detective*, 111–34. William Wood, the previous director fired by Boutwell, rejoiced in Whitley's legal difficulties; see "Letter of Wm. P. Wood, to the Hon. Geo. S. Boutwell, Secretary of the Treasury, Relating to One of His Favorite Officials, with Facts and Quotations for Reference and Study, New Year's Day, 1872," published as a broadside, *Printed Ephemera Collection*, portfolio 296, folder 23b, LC.

44. A. T. Akerman to Col. H. C. Whitley, August 18. 1871, *The Walt Whitman Archive*, nar. 02413; Johnson, *Illegal Tender*, 80–83. Whitley had successfully infiltrated the KKK in Georgia in 1868; see Lane, *Freedom's Detective*, 63–94.

45. *The Times-Picayune* (New Orleans), July 18, 1872. Boutwell refused to reveal the names of confidential informants, asserting that doing so would "diminish the power of the Government to discover and punish frauds." See George S. Boutwell to Hon. Schuyler Colfax, Vice President and President of the Senate, February 20, 1873, *USG Collection: Unpublished Correspondence*, S3.B12.-1.303, USGPL. See also *CG*, 42/3, 1636–37 (February 22, 1873).

46. Lane, *Freedom's Detective*, 224–47.

47. The most comprehensive account is Bordewich, *Klan War*.

48. Akerman, from Georgia, became attorney general when Grant asked Ebenezer Hoar to resign; Grant thus solved the problem of having two Massachusetts men in his cabinet while giving southern Republicans a cabinet position.

Chapter 12: The General and the Governor

1. James Russell Lowell, "The Vision of Sir Launfal," lines 33–34 (1848).

2. Local teenage Groton cornet player J. B. Raddin recalled decades later that band members "marched [Grant] up to Boutwell's house" but were then brusquely dismissed by Boutwell "to get them out of the way." It had been a long day and Grant admitted to being exhausted. "Recollection of J. B. Raddin, October 7, 1936," four-page typed memorandum, courtesy of family member Donald R. Black, Groton, Massachusetts.

3. Quoted in *Boston Daily Evening Transcript*, June 18, 1869. See also *Boston Post*, June 17, 1869; J. S. Gilmore, *History of the National Peace Jubilee and the Great Musical Festival in Boston, June 15–19, 1869* (Lee and Shepard, Boston, 1871), 307–8, 526–47; White, *American Ulysses*, 51.

4. *Fall River Daily Evening News*, June 18, 1869; Kara Fossey, Barbara Spiegelman, and Elizabeth Strachan, *Groton: Images of America* (Arcadia Publishing, 2009), 71.

5. See Greg Steinmetz, *American Rascal: How Jay Gould Built Wall Street's Biggest Fortune* (Simon & Schuster, 2022).

6. The best summary of the very convoluted Gold Ring affair is Calhoun, *The Presidency of Ulysses S. Grant*, 125–50, while the most entertaining, if flawed, account is Henry Adams, "The New York Gold Conspiracy," *Westminster Review* (American edition), October 1870. See also Kenneth Ackerman, *The Gold Ring: Jim Fisk, Jay Gould, and Black Friday, 1869* (Dodd, Mead, 1988); Steinmetz, *American Rascal*; Maury Klein, *The Life and Legend of Jay Gould* (Johns Hopkins University Press, 1986); and the scholarly analysis by Larry T. Wimmer, "The Gold Crisis of 1869: Stabilizing or Destabilizing Speculation Under Floating Exchange Rates?," *Explorations in Economic History* 12 (April 1975): 2.

7. Gould would buy gold on credit and loan it at lucrative rates to merchants and exporters who became ever more desperate for gold as the supply tightened. When the price then rose because of the gold shortage that Gould himself was engineering, he would sell for a handsome profit. Boutwell provides his own account of the affair, unfortunately in leaden prose; see *Reminiscences*, 2:164–82. See also James A. Garfield, *Investigation into the Causes of the Gold Panic*, House Report no. 31, 41st Congress, 2nd Session, 1870 (hereafter *Gold Panic*), and Brands, *The Man Who Saved the Union*, 437–46.

8. Calhoun, *The Presidency of Ulysses S. Grant*, 128–30.

9. Editor Caleb C. Norvell considered the story a self-serving press release and toned it down considerably; see *New York Times*, August 25, 1869. *Gold Panic*, 275–79; Boutwell, *Reminiscences*, 2:172–73. The letter "was a clever ploy to draw Boutwell out, but the secretary declined the bait with a noncommittal reply," Klein, *Jay Gould*, 104.

10. *Gold Panic*, 358–60. See Boutwell's testimony to the Garfield committee, 342–84. See also Boutwell, *Reminiscences*, 2:174, and Klein, *Jay Gould*, 105–8.

11. Quoted in Edmund Morris, *Edison* (Random House, 2019), 610.

12. *Gold Panic*, 15.

13. *Gold Panic*, 7–8.

14. Calhoun, *The Presidency of Ulysses S. Grant*, 145–50; *Gold Panic*, 19–20.

15. Boutwell, *Reminiscences*, 2:168 and 181.

16. Pleasonton schemed with the House Ways and Means Committee to seek a repeal of the income tax without consulting Boutwell, who was not only his boss but the man who introduced the tax in 1862; see Sidney Ratner, *American Taxation* (W. W. Norton, 1942), 130–33. Pleasonton sought in vain to keep his job, lining up support from congressmen, threatening a lawsuit, and pleading with Grant, but Boutwell prevailed. *PUSG*, 22:113–15; Boutwell, *Reminiscences*, 2:131–33; *New York Times*, August 9, 1871.

17. *New York Tribune*, July 15, 1869. Boutwell was able to convince the president that Dent was trying to win the Mississippi governorship with Democratic Party support; see William B. Hesseltine, *Ulysses S. Grant, Politician* (1935; Dodd, Mead, 1957), 184–85.

18. Richard White, *Railroaded: The Transcontinentals and the Making of Modern America* (W. W. Norton, 2011), 104. Bennett advised the president to "send Boutwell off to Germany or Spain . . . it is not wise or just for him [the president] to handicap himself and his party by carrying this inert, sluggish and narrow-minded Secretary," *New York Herald*, February 11, 1871; Ulysses S. Grant to Schuyler Colfax, December 16, 1870, *PUSG*, 21:94; Hesseltine, *Ulysses S. Grant*, 167.

19. The president "had long known and admired Mr. Boutwell, and when that gentleman became one of his Cabinet officers the strong friendship which had existed was more closely cemented," Grant interview in the *New York Times*, June 21, 1881. Georgianna A. Boutwell, "Washington," undated manuscript, Boutwell Collection, GHS, 2–4.

20. Orville Babcock to Mrs. G. S. Boutwell, January 17, 1871, asking Sarah and Georgie to assist the First Lady at a White House reception the following day; Boutwell Collection, GHS; Georgianna A. Boutwell, "Washington," 2–4.

21. Quoted in Ishbel Ross, *The General's Wife: The Life of Mrs. Ulysses S. Grant* (Dodd, Mead, 1959), 226. See also *Letters of Mrs. James G. Blaine*, ed. Harriet S. Blaine Beale (Duffield, 1908), 1:81.

22. George S. Boutwell, "The Late General Sherman," *Boston Sunday Globe*, March 1, 1891; Georgi-anna A. Boutwell, "Washington," 2.

23. Elihu B. Washburne to Ulysses S. Grant, December 8, 1869, *USGP*, 20:61; Hesseltine, *Ulysses S. Grant*, 167.

24. White, *Railroaded*, 1–38.

25. *The Sun* (New York), September 4, 1872. The paper's editor was Charles A. Dana, Boutwell's fellow commissioner adjudicating claims in the Western War Department in Cairo, Illinois in June 1862. Having been denied the lucrative position of collector of customs in New York, Dana became an ardent Grant foe. See also *New York World*, September 12 and 22, 1872.

26. *New York Tribune*, January 8, 1873. The congressional investigation concluded that Boutwell "never had any stock, or any dividend thereof; no money was paid by him for stock, or received by him for the same." See Jay Boyd Crawford, *The Crédit Mobilier of America: Its Origins and History, Its Work of Constructing the Union Pacific Railroad and the Relation of Members of Congress Therewith* (C. W. Calkins, 1880), 129–30.

27. Timothy Rives, "Grant, Babcock, and the Whiskey Ring," *Prologue: Quarterly of the National Archives and Records Administration* 32 (Fall 2000): 3.

28. Calhoun, *The Presidency of Ulysses S. Grant*, 494–501, 510–27, 539–44. See also the colorful if self-serving account of John McDonald, *Secrets of the Great Whiskey Ring and Eighteen Months in the Penitentiary* (St. Louis, 1880), 18–27, and Edward S. Cooper, *John McDonald and the Whiskey Ring: From Thug to Grant's Inner Circle* (Rowman and Littlefield, 2016). Illustrative of interlocking Gilded Age corruption, John McDonald had connections to Jay Gould, at one point asking Grant to support his claim against Gould's Erie Railway for losses suffered in a Pennsyl-vania train crash in July 1869, which the president rightly refused. See McDonald, *Secrets of the Whiskey Ring*, 18–19.

29. There is also no mention of the Whiskey Ring saga in the Thomas Brown biography, *George Sewall Boutwell*.

30. Motley did serve with distinction as US minister to the Austrian Empire during the Civil War, helping prevent European recognition of the Confederacy.

31. Boutwell told the oft-repeated story that Grant, when asked if he had ever heard Sumner con-verse, replied, "no, but I have heard him lecture," Boutwell, *Reminiscences*, 2:215.

32. Donald, *Charles Sumner*, 210; Boutwell, *Reminiscences*, 2:216.

33. See the Grant memorandum for acquiring Santo Domingo at *PUSG*, 20:74–76; Nevins, *Hamil-ton Fish*, 267–75; Ryan P. Semmes, "The United States on the World Stage: Foreign Policy During the Grant Administration," in *Grant at 200*, 137–38.

34. Memorandum of George S. Boutwell, November 12, 1877, *PUSG*, 28:308.

35. Calhoun, *The Presidency of Ulysses S. Grant*, 230–33; Chernow, *Grant*, 691–92.

36. Donald, *Charles Sumner*, 454.

37. Boutwell, *Reminiscences*, 2:217.

38. *PUSG*, 20:145; White, *American Ulysses*, 512–15.

39. In part to offset Sumner's influence in New England, Massachusetts senator Henry Wilson replaced Vice President Schuyler Colfax on the ticket with Grant, thus opening Wilson's Senate seat for Boutwell; see Donald, *Charles Sumner*, 551.

Chapter 13: A Most Trusted Cabinet Member

1. *New York Times*, March 24, 1871.

2. Orville E. Babcock to George S. Boutwell, March 23, 1871, Boutwell Collection, GHS.

3. *The Aberdeen Examiner* (Mississippi), March 15, 1871; *New York Tribune*, March 24, 1871.

4. Elaine Frantz Parsons, *Ku-Klux: The Birth of the Klan during Reconstruction* (University of North Carolina Press, 2016).

5. Bordewich, *Klan War*, 157, 184–85, 192–209.

6. Boutwell, *The Lawyer, the Statesman, and the Soldier,* 170–71. That same day, Democratic newspapers were gleefully reporting (erroneously) that Boutwell had lost Grant's confidence and would soon be resigning; *New York Daily Herald,* March 23, 1871.

7. Leonard, *Benjamin Franklin Butler,* 186–87. The president's message arrived on the Senate floor a little after 1 p.m. as Nettie Chase was saying her vows in St. John's Church; *CG,* 42/1, 235–41 (March 23, 1871).

8. Vernon Lane Wharton, *The Negro in Mississippi, 1865–1890* (Harper Torchbooks, 1947), 188–90; *Memphis Daily Appeal,* March 14, 1871.

9. Foner, *Reconstruction,* 454–59.

10. Lincoln had suspended the writ of habeas corpus during wartime, but it was ruled unconstitutional by Chief Justice Roger Taney in *Ex parte Merryman* on the grounds that only Congress, not the president, had such authority. President Grant *was* seeking congressional authority, but in *peacetime*; critics maintained that Klan violence did not constitute "Rebellion or Invasion" as prescribed by Article 1, Section 9 of the US Constitution. *The Cincinnati Enquirer,* April 27, 1871.

11. Frederick Douglass, *Life and Times of Frederick Douglass* (Citadel Press, 1983), 384.

12. An estimated 2,000 guests enjoyed the "lavish loveliness of the Sprague mansion." See *The Brooklyn Union,* March 25, 1871.

13. Quoted in "Hamilton Fish Diary, November 24, 1871." Earlier, the cabinet had been discussing the case of Absalom Markland, a Black postal official in Kentucky who was targeted by the KKK. The president had a special affinity for Markland, who during the war had served under Grant and was responsible for ensuring mail delivery to Union soldiers in the field as an important boost to morale; see "Hamilton Fish Diary, February 24 to March 24, 1871," Hamilton Fish Papers, Box 277, Reel 1, LC; and Candice Shy Hooper, *Delivered Under Fire: Absalom Markland and Freedom's Mail* (Potomac Books, 2023).

14. Lane, *Freedom's Detective,* 157–63; Allen W. Trelease, *White Terror: The Ku Klux Klan Conspiracy and Southern Reconstruction* (Harper and Row, 1971), 399–418.

15. *Report of the Joint Committee to Inquire into the Condition of Affairs in the Late Insurrectionary States,* 13 vols., House Reports, 42nd Congress, 2nd Session, no. 22.

16. Akerman was also undermined by his second-in-command, Solicitor General Benjamin Bristow, who was scheming to replace him; see Calhoun, *The Presidency of Ulysses S. Grant,* 322–27.

17. Charles Calhoun, *Conceiving a New Republic: The Republican Party and the Southern Question* (University Press of Kansas, 2006), 33–46.

18. Timberlake, *Monetary Policy in the United States,* 134, 249. A good joke at the time was that, "in spite of Boutwell, the currency isn't elastic. You can't stretch a \$5 to a \$10 bill, and if you try it you only demonstrate the legal tenderness of the paper." *Mower County Transcript* (Minnesota), May 15, 1873. See *Report of the Secretary of the Treasury for 1872* (US Government Printing Office, 1872), xx–xxi.

19. Unger, *The Greenback Era,* 16.

20. Stahr, *Salmon P. Chase,* 617–33.

21. Frederick J. Blue, *Salmon P. Chase: A Life in Politics* (The Kent State University Press, 1987), 304; *New York Tribune,* February 8, 1870. Boutwell wrote in his memoirs that Chase, fearing turmoil in the gold market, informed him of the *Hepburn* decision some two weeks before it became public, an action that could have led to Chase's impeachment. Boutwell disagreed with Chase's assessment and was correct; "the decision did not cause a ripple in the finances of the country." See Boutwell, *Reminiscences,* 2:208–10, and Jeffrey Boutwell, "When the Chief Justice Himself was the Supreme Court Leak," *The Baltimore Sun,* January 29, 2023.

22. Because these two new seats were already authorized, Grant did not engage in "court packing," despite criticisms from Henry Adams and others that the president was "destroying the independence of the Judiciary"; see Calhoun, *The Presidency of Ulysses S. Grant,* 119–23.

23. Boutwell, *Reminiscences,* 2:209–10; Stahr, *Salmon P. Chase,* 637–50. Boutwell was mentioned as a candidate to become chief justice when Salmon Chase died on May 7, 1873, but Grant picked

Ohio jurist Morrison Waite. In the *Slaughter-House Cases*, 83 U.S. 36 (1873), a case involving the rights of butchers in New Orleans to practice their trade, the court narrowly defined the Fourteenth Amendment as applying only to "privileges and immunities" protected by the federal government, thus giving state governments carte blanche to enact laws and regulations seriously undermining the safeguards of "equal protection" and "due process" for individuals.

24. Ratner, *American Taxation*, 132; Hamilton Fish to J. C. Hamilton, June 23 and October 1, 1870, Hamilton Fish Papers, Correspondence, LC.

25. Weisman, *The Great Tax Wars*, 99; Nevins, *Hamilton Fish*, 590.

26. Members of Congress were the worst offenders in demanding jobs for their constituents; it would take another decade for Congress to get serious about modernizing the civil service with the Pendleton Act of 1883 and the Civil Service Act of 1888.

27. Smith, *Grant*, 508; Donald, *Sumner*, 455–60. Boutwell had hoped that Britain's preoccupation with the Franco-Prussian War might induce her to shed her North American obligations; George S. Boutwell to Pres. Ulysses S. Grant, July 29, 1870, Boutwell Collection, GHS. Boutwell helped Grant during the negotiations by serving as an intermediary between the president and Charles Francis Adams (Sr.), the American member of the international arbitration panel who, as both an Adams and a prominent Liberal Republican, detested Grant; see Calhoun, *The Presidency of Ulysses S. Grant*, 355.

28. *The Times* (London), October 31, 1871.

29. *New York World*, August 19, 1872; *The Eaton Democrat* (Ohio), September 5, 1872.

30. Mark Wahlgren Summers, *The Ordeal of the Reunion: A New History of Reconstruction* (The University of North Carolina Press, 2014), 313.

31. Boutwell's speech in Greensboro received extensive coverage throughout the state, both pro, *The Carolina Era* (Raleigh), July 25, 1872, and con, *The Raleigh News*, July 23, 1872. Quote is from Calhoun, *The Presidency of Ulysses S. Grant*, 389. Boutwell was scheduled to appear at a major campaign rally in Richmond with Frederick Douglass and Henry Wilson on July 24, but had to return early to Washington; see *The Daily State Journal* (Richmond), July 20, 1872; *The Daily State Journal* (Alexandria), July 25, 1872.

32. Democratic newspapers hoped that "the taxpayers of the country" would relieve Boutwell of his duties as treasury secretary in the coming election; see *Buffalo Weekly Courier*, September 4, 1872; *New York Herald*, August 17, 1872; *New York Times*, October 27, 1872.

33. Douglass's support for Grant complicated his long friendship with Charles Sumner, who in July had called for Grant's impeachment; see "Letter to Washington's Colored Citizens, July 29, 1872," *The Works of Charles Sumner* (Lee and Shepard, 1883), 15:173–95. Douglass helped publish *Grant or Greeley—Which? Facts and Arguments for the Consideration of the Colored Citizens of the United States* (Washington, 1872), was an elector-at-large for New York state, and had the honor of delivering New York's thirty-five electoral votes to Grant when the final tally was made.

34. *New York Herald*, September 19, 1872.

35. White, *American Ulysses*, 528–37.

36. Brown, *George Sewall Boutwell*, 96–97. Rumor had it that Judge Richardson only wanted the title of secretary so he could resign after a few months and join the prestigious investment house of James Munroe & Co. in Paris so it could better compete with Jay Cooke & Co. in the selling of American bonds overseas. See *New York Times*, December 31, 1872; Henry Clews, *Twenty-Eight Years on Wall Street* (Irving Publishing, 1888), 692–98; Calhoun, *The Presidency of Ulysses S. Grant*, 415–16. Also see William A. Richardson to George S. Boutwell, May 13, 1873, Boutwell Collection, GHS.

37. *New York Tribune*, January 8, 1873. Boutwell tried to shut down double-dipping by the Union Pacific, which avoided paying interest on its government bonds while reaping handsome profits from carrying government troops, mail, and supplies. Union Pacific stocks and bonds fell by one-half and two-thirds on the news, but soon rebounded when Massachusetts congressman Henry Dawes championed an amendment allowing the railroad to forgo interest payments for thirty years. See White, *Railroaded*, 62–65.

38. *The Nation*, January 9, 1873.
39. Boutwell, *Reminiscences*, 2:223–24; Storey, *American Statesmen*, 423–24.
40. For Boutwell's defense of the gold standard, see his "The Mint Bill and the 'Crime of 1873,'" in *Reminiscences*, 2:150–63.
41. *Report of the Secretary of the Treasury*, December 2, 1872 (US Government Printing Office, 1872), xii.
42. *New York Daily Herald*, March 10, 1873.
43. Samuel DeCanio, *Democracy and the Origins of the American Regulatory State* (Yale University Press, 2015), 92–120.
44. DeCanio, *Democracy*, 100–105: White, *The Republic*, 264.
45. Walter T. K. Nugent, *Money and American Society* (Free Press, 1968), 160–65.
46. Boutwell, *Reminiscences*, 2:160.
47. James A. Garfield, "The Currency Conflict," *The Atlantic Monthly* 37 (February 1876): 235.
48. Milton Friedman and Anna J. Schwartz, *A Monetary History of the United States, 1867–1960* (Princeton University Press, 1963), 1172; Larry Margarsak, "Silver vs. Gold: William Steinway's Wedge Issue in the 1896 Election," *National Museum of American History*, October 29, 2014.
49. *New York Times*, January 25, 1873.
50. Michael Hiltzik, *Iron Empires: Robber Barons, Railroads, and the Making of Modern America* (Houghton Mifflin Harcourt, 2020), 80–84.

Chapter 14: Reconstruction Dying

1. Poore, *Perley's Reminiscences*, 287–88.
2. Chernow, *Grant*, 753–54.
3. Georgianna Boutwell, "Washington City Paper," 8–9.
4. Ulysses S. Grant, "Second Inaugural Address, 4 March 1873," LC.
5. Boutwell, *Reminiscences*, 2:236. In his final annual message to Congress in December 1876, Grant emphasized that the benefits of trade, a naval base, and hastening the demise of slavery in the Caribbean would have put the United States "in a more prosperous condition to-day, both politically and financially." Quoted in Calhoun, *The Presidency of Ulysses S. Grant*, 567.
6. *National Republican*, March 5, 1873; *New York Times*, March 5, 1873.
7. *New York Times*, March 18, 1873.
8. Donald, *Charles Sumner*, 563–71.
9. White, *American Ulysses*, 542; William A. Richardson to George S. Boutwell, May 13, 1873, Boutwell Collection, GHS; William A. Richardson to Ulysses S. Grant, August 28, 1873, *PUSG*, 24:214–15.
10. John M. Lubetkin, *Jay Cooke's Gamble: The Northern Pacific Railroad, the Sioux, and the Panic of 1873* (University of Oklahoma Press, 2014).
11. Grant was not staying at Cooke's mansion on the day of the collapse, despite accounts by Chernow, *Grant*, 776–77; White, *American Ulysses*, 541–42; and Smith, *Grant*, 575. The president had left Philadelphia on September 16 and was in Pittsburgh on September 17–18 for a reunion of the Army of the Cumberland; see *New York Times*, September 19, 1873; *The Brooklyn Union*, September 19, 1873; *The Philadelphia Inquirer*, September 17, 1873. Charles Calhoun points out this discrepancy in *The Presidency of Ulysses S. Grant*, 667n5.
12. White, *The Republic for Which It Stands*, 260–73.
13. Secretary Richardson to President Grant, September 19, 1873, *PUSG*, 24:214; White, *The Republic for Which It Stands*, 265.
14. White, *Railroaded*, 83.
15. George S. Boutwell to Ulysses S. Grant, October 2, 9, and 15, 1873, *PUSG*, 24:219–20.
16. George S. Boutwell, *The Currency-Specie Payments: Speech in the United States Senate, January 22, 1874* (US Government Printing Office, 1874), 4.
17. Calhoun, *The Presidency of Ulysses S. Grant*, 446–48.

18. William McFeely, in his biography of Frederick Douglass, wrote that Boutwell was the one person having the necessary expertise and commitment who might have saved the failing Bank by having it resume "the original policy of investing in safe government securities," but that devising such a plan "apparently did not occur to Boutwell, or to any other public figure." In truth, by the early 1870s, and especially after the Panic of 1873, there was no political will for rescuing the modest deposits of America's Black citizens. William S. McFeely, *Frederick Douglass* (W. W. Norton, 1991), 285.

19. Calhoun, *The Presidency of Ulysses S. Grant*, 482–85.

20. George S. Boutwell, "Silver as a Circulating Medium," *The Forum* 11 (March 1891).

21. Lemann, *Redemption: The Last Battle of the Civil War*, 4–29.

22. Leonard, *Benjamin Franklin Butler*, 201–3.

23. Rep. Alexander Stephens, *CR*, 43/1, 379 (January 5, 1874).

24. Rep. Robert Brown Elliott, *CR*, 43/1, 407–10 (January 6, 1874).

25. Frank J. Scaturro, *The Supreme Court's Retreat from Reconstruction: A Distortion of Constitutional Jurisprudence* (Greenwood Press, 2000), 178–88.

26. Sen. George S. Boutwell, *CR*, 43/1, 4115–16 (May 21, 1874).

27. Sen. George S. Boutwell, *CR*, 43/2, 1379 (February 17, 1875).

28. Sen. John W. Stevenson, *CR*, 43/2, 1380 (February 17, 1875); Alfred H. Kelley, "The Congressional Controversy over School Segregation, 1867–1875," *American Historical Review* 64 (April 1959): 553.

29. Douglass quote from *New National Era*, January 12, 1871, reproduced in Quarles, *Frederick Douglass*, 259; Foner, *Reconstruction*, 534; *The Civil Rights Cases*, 109 U.S. 3 (1883); Woodward, *The Strange Career*, 24–25; Luxenberg, *Separate*, 458–59, 477–87.

30. Lemann, *Redemption*, 84–91; White, *American Ulysses*, 550–51.

31. Calhoun, *The Presidency of Ulysses S. Grant*, 467–74.

32. *The New York Herald*, September 8, 1875, described armed whites arriving by train from Vicksburg prior to "slaughtering the negroes. All the colored men they could find were shot down. . . . It is estimated that fifty men were killed in this way in the county on Sunday." See also, Melissa Janczewski Jones, "The Clinton Riot of 1875: From Riot to Massacre," *Mississippi History Now* (September 2015).

33. Blanche Butler Ames, *Chronicles from the Nineteenth Century* (Colonial Press, 1957), 1:221, 283, 350.

34. Calhoun documents how Pierrepont actively undermined Grant's willingness to send federal troops; the attorney general and other party leaders feared that federal intervention in Mississippi would damage the party's prospects in the upcoming state elections in Ohio, which elected future president Rutherford B. Hayes as governor; see Calhoun, *The Presidency of Ulysses S. Grant*, 506–10; Chernow, *Grant*, 813–18.

35. Foner, *Reconstruction*, 559–63. C. Vann Woodward writes that Mississippi in 1954 took the lead in protecting southern segregation with a "third" Mississippi Plan to block implementation of the *Brown v. Board of Education* decision and "wage unremitting war in defense of segregation . . . just as she had in 1875 to overthrow Reconstruction and in 1890 to disenfranchise the Negro," *The Strange Career*, 152.

36. Blight, *Frederick Douglass*, 553.

37. Foner, *Reconstruction*, 554.

38. Coverage of the day's events in *National Republican*, April 15, 1876.

39. Harold Holzer, "Picturing Freedom: The Emancipation Proclamation in Art, Iconography, and Memory," in Holzer et al., *The Emancipation Proclamation: Three Views*, 130–36.

40. Frederick Douglass, *The Color Question: An Address Delivered in Washington, DC, July 5, 1875*, 4, LC; Ted Mann, "How a Lincoln-Douglass Debate Led to Historic Discovery," *Wall Street Journal*, July 4, 2020.

41. George S. Boutwell to Frederick Douglass, April 15, 1876, in *The Life and Writings of Frederick Douglass*, 4:98–99.

42. William Dudley Foulke, *Life of Oliver P. Morton, Including His Important Speeches* (The Bowen-Merrill, 1899), 365–76. Bayard had described Boutwell as a "bitter unreasoning fanatic" in a letter

to his father, James Bayard Jr., during the Johnson impeachment trial. The elder Bayard was a Delaware senator at the time who voted to acquit the president; his son succeeded him as senator in 1869, was a staunch opponent of Reconstruction in Congress until 1885, and then became secretary of state for President Grover Cleveland, whose election in 1884 as the first Democrat since before the Civil War further facilitated the triumph of white redemption in the South. See Thomas F. Bayard to James Bayard, April 28, 1868, Thomas Bayard Papers, vol. 14, LC.

43. *Mississippi in 1875: Report of the Select Committee to Inquire into the Mississippi Election of 1875*, United States Senate, vols. 1 and 2 (US Government Printing Office, 1876); Boutwell, *Reminiscences*, 2:279–80.

44. *New York Times*, May 2, 1876. Ames was interviewed by *Times* correspondent James Redpath, a Scots-born journalist who was doing double duty as the staff director for the Boutwell Senate Committee, prompting author Nicholas Lemann to observe that "occupational categories were not as strict then as now." Lemann, *Redemption*, 165. See also *New York Times*, May 2, 1876; "Extracts from Mississippi Democratic Journals," *Mississippi in 1875*, 2:161; *The Redpath Collection*, New York Public Library. Redpath lived an adventuresome life, having interviewed John Brown in Kansas in the 1850s and becoming the abolitionist's publicist; see Horwitz, *Midnight Rising*, 56–57; and John R. McGivigan, *Forgotten Firebrand: James Redpath and the Making of Nineteenth-Century America* (Cornell University Press, 2008).

45. Democrats Bayard and McDonald sought to suppress the telegrams, despite precedent that congressional committees had a right to see them; *Mississippi in 1875*, 1:380–420. The telegrams mentioned are found in *Mississippi in 1875*, 1:382, 393.

46. *Mississippi in 1875*, 1:403–6.

47. *CR*, 44/1. 5280 (August 8, 1876).

48. Allen J. Going, "Review, James B. Murphy, *L. Q. C. Lamar: Pragmatic Patriot* (Louisiana State University Press, 1973)," in *The Journal of Southern History* 39, no. 4 (November 1973): 602–4; Kennedy, *Profiles in Courage*.

49. *The People's Defense* (Jackson, Mississippi), June 24, 1876.

50. Anonymous letter to the Boutwell committee staff, June 18, 1876, *The Redpath Collection*, New York Public Library, quoted in Lemann, *Redemption*, 165.

51. *Mississippi in 1875*, 2:1031.

52. *Mississippi in 1875*, 1:420–21.

53. *Mississippi in 1875*, 1:306.

54. *The Clarion-Ledger* (Jackson, Mississippi), June 14, 1876. Refuting accusations that the Ames administration had squandered state revenues, Boutwell prepared detailed financial tables to demonstrate how Mississippi tax dollars for the first time ever were being used to fund public education, for both white and Black children. He also showed how white property owners sought to avoid paying taxes by assessing their property "far below its actual value." See "Boutwell Summary," *Mississippi in 1875*, 1:x–xi. See also William C. Harris, *The Day of the Carpetbagger: Republican Reconstruction in Mississippi* (Louisiana State University Press, 1979), 670–74.

55. "Boutwell Summary," *Mississippi in 1875*, 1:xiii; Johnson, *Negroes and the Gun*, 95–96.

56. "Boutwell Summary," *Mississippi in 1875*, 1:xiv.

57. *Mississippi in 1875*, 2:39.

58. "Boutwell Summary," *Mississippi in 1875*, 1:xiv. The 1884 election of Grover Cleveland as president helped cement the final victory of white Democratic control of Mississippi; *New York Times*, November 30, 1884.

59. *New York Times*, August 12, 1876; *New York Herald*, August 12, 1876. The Boutwell Committee majority and minority reports were presented on August 8, 1876; see *CR*, 44/1, 5274–98.

60. *Boston Daily Globe*, August 9, 1876; *Boston Post*, August 9 and 10, 1876.

61. *The Nation*, August 10, 1876. Godkin founded *The Nation* in 1865 and remained its sharp-tongued editor until 1899. Charles Dudley Warner of *Harper's Magazine* called it "weekly judgment day" when Godkin's editorials appeared each week.

62. White, *American Ulysses*, 576.

63. Chamberlain was an officer with the Black Massachusetts Fifth Cavalry Regiment in the Civil War and moved to South Carolina in 1866, becoming the Republican governor in 1874. Daniel Henry Chamberlain, "Reconstruction and the Negro," *North American Review* 128 (January 1879): 161, which issue also contained an article by Boutwell, "Substance and Shadow in Finance."

64. Calhoun, *Conceiving a New Republic*, 138.

65. George S. Boutwell to James Redpath, Esq., September 12, 1876, George S. Boutwell Collection, GA-73, RPHPL.

66. Richard E. Welch Jr., *George Frisbie Hoar and the Half-Breed Republicans* (Harvard University Press, 1971), 70–71.

Chapter 15: With Grant to the End

1. "Stephen M. Allen, Telegram to George S. Boutwell, January 19, 1877," Boutwell Collection, GHS, quoted in Welch, *George Frisbie Hoar*, 70n20. A good account of Boutwell's defeat is in Brown, *George Sewall* Boutwell, 100–102.

2. *Boston Globe*, January 20, 1877; George F. Hoar, *Autobiography of Seventy Years* (Charles Scribner's Sons, 1903), 2:1–4. Hoar served in the Senate until his death in 1904.

3. *New York Times*, January 24, 1877. William A. Simmons, described as "the most aggressive and ambitious as well as the most capable of Butler's henchmen," was nominated for the post in February 1874. See *New York Times*, February 17, 1874, and William D. Mallam, "Butlerism in Massachusetts," *New England Quarterly* 33 (June 1960): 192. Boutwell, *Reminiscences*, 2:283; Donald, *Charles Sumner*, 581–83. Ben Butler also blamed Boutwell for not fully supporting Butler's failed attempts at becoming governor of Massachusetts in the early 1870s; see Ames, *Chronicles from the Nineteenth Century*, 1:526, 556, 560.

4. Peter Pineo to George S. Boutwell, January 19, 1877, Boutwell Collection, GHS; Charles Eliot Norton to George Frisbie Hoar, February 14, 1877, *Hoar Papers*, MHS.

5. Hans L. Trefousse, *Rutherford B. Hayes* (Times Books, 2002), 78–83. Boutwell had preferred Hamilton Fish as the Republican nominee, as had Ulysses Grant, but Fish was not interested; George S. Boutwell to Richard H. Dana, June 19, 1876, Dana Family Papers, MHS.

6. Calhoun, *The Presidency of Ulysses S. Grant*, 552–64; Chernow, *Grant*, 843–50.

7. Ari Hoogenboom, *Rutherford B. Hayes: Warrior and President* (University Press of Kansas, 1995).

8. Georgianna Boutwell, "Washington City Paper," 9.

9. C. Vann Woodward, *Reunion and Reaction: The Compromise of 1877 and the End of Reconstruction* (Oxford University Press, 1951); Allan Peskin, "Was There a Compromise of 1877?," *The Journal of American History* 60 (1973): 1; Calhoun, *Conceiving a New Republic*, 105–36.

10. See "Miss Boutwell, 90, Dies in Groton," *Boston Globe*, September 22, 1933; *National Republican*, August 12, 1876, p. 4. In 1875 Georgie was elected to the Executive Board of the Miner School's parent organization, the Institution for the Education of Colored Youth, chartered by Congress in 1863; see George E. Baker, Secretary, to Georgianna Boutwell, January 30, 1875, Boutwell Collection, GHS.

11. *Second Edition, Revised Statutes of the United States* (US Government Printing Office, 1878); George S. Boutwell, *The Constitution of the United States at the End of the First Century* (D. C. Heath, 1895), described by the *Yale Law Journal* as a reference work that "cannot be surpassed and should be in the hands of every lawyer." See reviews in *Yale Law Journal* 5 (December 1895): 2; *Harvard Law Review* 9 (November 25, 1895): 4.

12. Georgianna A. Boutwell to George S. Boutwell, October 18, 1881, Boutwell Collection, GHS. See also Calhoun, *The Presidency of Ulysses S. Grant*, 369–70.

13. Though he never became a Justice, Boutwell did have a Supreme Court case bearing his name. In *United States v. Boutwell*, 84 U.S. 604 (1873), the court ruled that a suit brought against a government official (Boutwell as treasury secretary) may not be automatically carried over to his or her successor.

14. The day after Garfield was nominated, Grant thanked Boutwell while passing through Chicago on his way to attend a soldiers' reunion in Michigan, saying how he felt a "great responsibility removed from my shoulders" and that "I feel more indebted to my friends who gallantly stood by me than if they had succeeded in their endeavors." *New York Times*, July 2, 1880.

15. Boutwell, *Reminiscences*, 2:339. See David M. Jordan, *Roscoe Conkling of New York: Voice in the Senate* (Cornell University Press, 1971), 338–43; Kenneth D. Ackerman, *Dark Horse: The Surprise Election and Political Murder of President James A. Garfield* (Carroll & Graf Publishers, 2003), 124–31.

16. Boutwell was appointed by his old adversary from the Johnson impeachment trial, William Evarts, now secretary of state; see Boutwell, *Reminiscences*, 2:286–88. French and American Claims Commission, *The Final Report of the Agent and Counsel of the United States with Treaties and Schedules of Claims* (Gibson Brothers Printers, 1884), 119–23. For more on "Champagne Charlie," see Don and Petrie Kladstrup, *Champagne: How the World's Most Glamorous Wine Triumphed Over War and Hard Times* (HarperCollins, 2005).

17. Unidentified newspaper, June 29, 1880, Boutwell Collection, GHS; George S. Boutwell to Hamilton Fish, April 29, 1880, S3.B15-2.443, USGPL; J. R. Greene, *The Mass Central: Quabbin's Phantom Railroad* (Athol Press, 1996).

18. Chernow, *Grant*, 945–46. Frank, *The History of Lawrence Academy*, 151–54.

19. George S. Boutwell, "Last of the Ocean Slave Traders," *The New England Magazine* 23 (November 1900): 263–68; J. N. Leger, *Haiti: Her History and Her Detractors* (Negro University Press, 1970), 232–39.

20. Pelletier's death was reported in the *New York Daily Tribune*, June 22, 1885.

21. Foner, *The Second Founding*, 131–32.

22. The cottage was owned by a Grant family friend, the New York financier Joseph W. Drexel. For a moving account of Grant's final months, see Thomas M. Pitkin, *The Captain Departs: Ulysses S. Grant's Last Campaign* (Southern Illinois University Press, 1973).

23. The handwritten note is photocopied in Boutwell, *Reminiscences*, 2:253; it is also found in *PUSG*, 31:453. Georgie Boutwell wrote of Grant's response: "I had sent Mrs. Grant a New Year's card conveying pleasant wishes, but a mere trifle and not worth acknowledging." Georgianna A. Boutwell, "Washington," 5.

24. Grant enjoyed telling the story of riding from his army barracks outside St. Louis in 1844 to visit Julia at the Dent family residence prior to leaving for the Mexican War. Blocked by a rapidly flowing river, "I looked at it a moment to consider what to do. One of my superstitions had always been when I started to go anywhere, or to do anything, not to turn back, or stop until the thing intended was accomplished." Grant plunged his horse into the river. The two were almost swept away, but they ultimately made the far bank and the Dent house, where Grant "borrowed a dry suit from my—future—brother-in-law." *Ulysses S. Grant: Memoirs and Selected Letters* (Library of America, 1990), 38–39. Georgianna A. Boutwell, "Washington," 4-5.

25. *New York Times*, April 25, 1885; Georgianna A. Boutwell, "Washington," 6.

26. *New York Tribune*, August 9, 1885. For a moving account of Grant's funeral, see Waugh, *U.S. Grant*, 216–59.

27. *The National Republican*, August 9, 1885; Frank J. Scaturro, "The Odyssey of Grant's Tomb Through the Ages," in *Grant at 200*, 227–42.

28. Julia Dent Grant to Georgianna A. Boutwell, June 8, 1886, Boutwell Collection, GHS. In his novel, *The Gilded Age*, Mark Twain poked fun at Grant by having an elderly dowager look down her nose at the Jersey shore, sniffing that "only people of no position in society . . . and the President" would consider going to Long Branch rather than Newport (Rhode Island). Mark Twain and Charles Dudley Warner, *The Gilded Age: A Tale of Today* (American Publishing, 1874), 299. For example, Ida Honoré Grant to Georgianna Boutwell, March 25, 1889, thanking Georgie for her note congratulating Frederick Grant on his appointment as US Minister to Austria-Hungary, Boutwell Collection, GHS.

29. Ida Grant captured Georgie's spirit when she wrote, "I see you are the same thoughtful, devoted daughter upon whom your father and mother depend, absolutely doing good as you always did, thinking of others." Ida invited Georgie to come to New York to see "the wonderful tomb, built all voluntarily, for General Grant," which was dedicated on the seventy-fifth anniversary of Grant's birth in 1822. Ida Honoré Grant to Georgianna Boutwell, May 4, 1897, and the Grant Tomb invitation materials are in Boutwell Collection, GHS. For more on the mix-up with the invitation, see the *Boston Globe*, April 29, 1897.

30. *The National Tribune* (Washington, DC), April 26, 1888. One high profile Boutwell case was the court-martial of Maj. Garrett J. Lydecker of the US Army Corps of Engineers for mismanaging the building of the four-mile aqueduct from the Georgetown Reservoir to northeast Washington, DC. See *New York Times*, May 4, 1889.

31. *Utah Territorial Enquirer*, March 13, 1886. Boutwell's legal fee was reportedly handsome, given that the Mormons had "unlimited money . . . to conduct their fight." See *Brooklyn Daily Eagle*, June 7, 1886.

32. Hon. George S. Boutwell and others, *Arguments Against the New Edmunds Bill, Senate Bill No. 10, Before the Committee of the Judiciary of the U.S. House of Representatives, 49th Congress, 1st Session* (US Government Printing Office, 1886), 92–108. For one of the few times in his life, Boutwell was said to have been ill; his co-counsel read Boutwell's testimony for him. See *The Burlington Free Press* (Vermont), March 18, 1886.

33. William Lawrence, *Life of Amos A. Lawrence: With Extracts from His Diary and Correspondence* (Houghton, Mifflin, 1899), 270–71.

34. *Brooklyn Daily Eagle*, June 7, 1886; John Gary Maxwell, *Robert Newton Baskin and the Making of Modern Utah* (University of Oklahoma Press, 2013).

35. Visitors to the library will see a portrait of Boutwell inside the main entrance; other portraits of Boutwell hang in the US Treasury Building and the Massachusetts State House; see www.gpl.org. Virginia A. May, *Groton Houses* (Groton Historical Society, 1978), 97–100.

36. George S. Boutwell, "China and the Western Nations," *Boston Sunday Globe*, May 10, 1891.

37. George S. Boutwell, "Elections of the President and Vice-President," *Boston Sunday Globe*, July 3, 1892. Boutwell proposed a system used today in Nebraska and Maine, where electors are chosen by voters in congressional districts rather than statewide, thus eliminating the "winner take all" practice of each state giving all its electors to a candidate who might only win a bare majority of the votes.

38. George S. Boutwell, "Canada—Annexation," *Boston Sunday Globe*, January 16, 1890; "Parnellism and Crime," *Boston Sunday Globe*, July 7 and 14, 1889; "What the Communistic Idea Means," *Boston Sunday Globe*, July 1, 1890.

Chapter 16: Annexation of Hawaii and the Spanish-American War

1. Teddy Roosevelt idolized Ulysses Grant, ranking him with Washington and Lincoln as one of America's three great presidents; White, *American Ulysses*, 659.

2. *Pacific Commercial Advertiser*, March 8, 1886.

3. George S. Boutwell, *Annual Report of the Secretary of the Treasury on the State of the Finances for the Year 1872* (US Government Printing Office, 1872), ix–x.

4. *New York Times*, November 10, 1887.

5. Boutwell voiced his fears in a letter to the newly elected Massachusetts senator, Henry Cabot Lodge; see George S. Boutwell to Henry Cabot Lodge, December 20, 1895, Henry Cabot Lodge Papers, MHS.

6. "Coxey's Army Snowbound in a Grove," *New York Times*, April 11, 1894. Claims involving Wells Fargo and W. R. Grace adjudicated by the Chile Commission attested to America's growing corporate presence abroad. See Moore, ed., *International Arbitrations to Which the United States Has Been a Party*, 2:1469–84; George S. Boutwell to Georgianna A. Boutwell, April 24, 1894,

Boutwell Collection, GHS. Coxey's Army was likely spun as allegory by author L. Frank Baum in his *The Wonderful Wizard of Oz*. Dorothy was Coxey, accompanied by an American farmer (the Scarecrow), an industrial worker (the Tin Woodman), and populist leader William Jennings Bryan (the Cowardly Lion), all of whom are marching on Washington, DC (the Emerald City) to seek relief from the president (the Wizard). In Baum's original, Dorothy is wearing silver slippers, representing Bryan's advocacy of Free Silver instead of the gold standard, which is represented by the yellow brick road, which many blamed for causing the Panic of 1893. (In the movie version, of course, Dorothy is wearing ruby slippers, which were substituted for their cinematic effect in the early days of Technicolor.) See Henry M. Littlefield, "The Wizard of Oz: Parable on Populism," *American Quarterly* 16, no. 1 (1964), 47–58; Hugh Rockoff, "The 'Wizard of Oz' as a Monetary Allegory," *Journal of Political Economy* 98 (August 1990).

7. Hon. George S. Boutwell, "The Peril of the Treasury," *North American Review* 159 (October 1894): 419.

8. Michael Kazin, *A Godly Hero: The Life of William Jennings Bryan* (Anchor Books, 2007).

9. White, *The Republic for Which It Stands*, 841–49. To Lodge's credit, he was the sponsor of the Federal Elections Bill in 1891, the last best chance to protect Black voting rights until the civil rights era in the 1960s; the bill was defeated. Calhoun, *Conceiving a New Republic*, 235–59.

10. *Boston Daily Globe*, January 29, 1898; *Boston Post*, January 29, 1898. The *Post* story mistakenly had Boutwell going to his Boston office that day.

11. For more on the Lodge-Roosevelt friendship, see Lawrence Jurdem, *The Rough Rider and the Professor: Theodore Roosevelt, Henry Cabot Lodge, and the Friendship that Changed American History* (Pegasus Books, 2023); Karl Schriftgiesser, *The Gentleman from Massachusetts: Henry Cabot Lodge* (Little, Brown, 1944).

12. Quoted in Leon Wolff, *Little Brown Brother: How the United States Purchased and Pacified the Philippine Islands* (Doubleday, 1961), 14. Hearst is known for telling famed American artist Frederick Remington, who was in Cuba to illustrate the revolution but complained that not much was going on, "Please remain. You furnish the pictures and I'll furnish the war."

13. Kinzer, *The True Flag*, 32; *Boston Globe*, February 6, 1898; Edward Atkinson, "A Statesman of the Old School," *Boston Evening Transcript*, February 9, 1898.

14. Lodge was speaking metaphorically, one hopes, when he predicted to a friend, "There may be an explosion any day in Cuba which would settle a great many things," quoted in Wolff, *Little Brown Brother*, 38. Philip S. Foner, *The Spanish-Cuban-American War and the Birth of American Imperialism, 1895–1902*, 2 vols. (Monthly Review Press, 1972).

15. Navy secretary John D. Long, like Boutwell an ex-governor of Massachusetts, was famously absent from the office when Roosevelt unilaterally issued the order. Boutwell wrote to Long asking him to restrain the president from going to war; George S. Boutwell to John D. Long, March 29, 1898, John D. Long Papers, box 39, MHS.

16. George S. Boutwell to Justin S. Morrill, March 27, 1898, Justin S. Morrill Papers, Reel 27, LC.

17. George S. Boutwell, "War, and a Change of Our Public Policy," speech delivered at Kingston, Mass. on Memorial Day, May 30, 1898," reprinted in George S. Boutwell, *The Crisis of the Republic* (Dana Estes, 1900), 52, 57.

18. Lodge quoted in Ernest R. May, *Imperial Democracy: The Emergence of America as a Great Power* (Harcourt, Brace & World, 1961), 245; David Silbey, *A War of Frontier and Empire: The Philippine-American War, 1899–1902* (Hill and Wang, 2007), 54.

19. Kinzer, *The True Flag*, 49–67.

20. The anti-imperialist gathering drew little notice from the press, having to compete with news of the Senate voting on Hawaii annexation and the US Marines defeating the Spanish at Guantanamo in Cuba; see the *Boston Daily Globe*, June 16, 1898; *Boston Post*, June 16, 1898. George S. Boutwell to John D. Long, August 7, 1898, John D. Long Papers, Box 42, MHS.

21. Andrew Carnegie, "Distant Possessions—The Parting of the Ways," *North American Review* 167 (August 1898): 246.

22. George S. Boutwell, "Problems Raised by the War," speech to the Twentieth Century Club, Boston, October 8, 1898; quotes taken from reprinted version in Boutwell, *The Crisis of the Republic*, 65–85.

23. For more on the history of US-Cuban relations, and the Cuban independence struggle, see Ada Ferrer, *Cuba: An American History* (Scribner, 2021).

24. News of the meeting was overshadowed by Harvard defeating Yale 17–0 in football; Harvard grad, Teddy Roosevelt, was quoted as being "dee-lighted" with the result. See *Boston Sunday Post*, November 20, 1898; *Los Angeles Herald*, November 20, 1898.

25. Quoted in E. Berkeley Tompkins, *Anti-Imperialism in the United States: The Great Debate, 1890–1920* (University of Pennsylvania Press, 1970), 159; see also, Robert L. Beisner, *Twelve Against Empire: The Anti-Imperialists, 1898–1900* (McGraw-Hill, 1968). See George S. Boutwell, "Address to the Public," Anti-Imperialist League, *St. Louis Post-Dispatch*, May 7, 1899. Stephen Kinzer has written how "the simplicity of Boutwell's proposal, along with his many letters to civic and political leaders across the country, brought thousands of supporters to the anti-imperialist cause." Kinzer, *The True Flag*, 89.

26. W. E. B. Du Bois, "The Present Outlook for the Dark Races of Mankind," in Du Bois, *Writings by W. E. B. Du Bois*, 1:78; Quotes from Kinzer, *The True Flag*, 83–84 and 135–36.

27. *Speeches and Addresses of William McKinley from March 1, 1897 to May 30, 1900* (Doubleday & McClure, 1900), 166–72. See "Loyalty of the Southern People," *New York Times*, December 19, 1898; Ida B. Wells, *Southern Horrors: Lynch Law in All Its Phases* (The New York Age Print, 1892). From the 1870s through World War II, there were more than 4,400 lynchings of Black people nationwide. See *Lynching in America: Confronting the Legacy of Racial Terror* (Equal Justice Institute, 2017).

28. Boutwell, *Republic or Empire*, 19; George S. Boutwell, William Lloyd Garrison, and Thomas Wentworth Higginson, *How Should a Colored Man Vote in 1900* (Allied Trades Union Council, 1900), 1.

29. George S. Boutwell, "Imperialists or Republicans?" Address before the Essex Institute, Salem, Mass., January 9, 1899 (Anti-Imperialist League, 1899), 8.

30. Silbey, *A War of Frontier and Empire*, 197–201.

31. Kinzer, *The True Flag*, 137–42.

32. Christopher Benfey, *If: The Untold Story of Kipling's American Years* (Penguin Press, 2019).

33. Christopher McKnight Nichols, *Promise and Peril: America at the Dawn of a Global Age* (Harvard University Press, 2011), 96–97. Gompers quoted in *The Farmer and Mechanic* (Raleigh, NC), January 24, 1899. Woodward wrote that "As America shouldered the White Man's Burden, she took up at the same time many Southern attitudes on the subject of race," Woodward, *The Strange Career*, 72–74.

34. See *Letters of Henry Adams, 1892–1918*, ed. Worthington Chauncey Ford (Houghton Mifflin, 1938), 208.

35. Address by The Hon. George S. Boutwell, "Protest Against the Philippine Policy," Anti-Imperialist Meeting, Tremont Temple, April 4, 1899 (Anti-Imperialist League, 1899), 8–23.

36. Kinzer, *The True Flag*, 143–45.

37. *New York World*, July 15, 1899.

Chapter 17: Republic or Empire?

1. "Speech by George S. Boutwell, January 11, 1900," printed as *The President's Policy, War and Conquest Abroad, Degradation of Labor at Home* (American Anti-Imperialist League, 1900).

2. Kinzer, *The True Flag*, 162–65.

3. Tompkins, *Anti-Imperialism*, 214–15.

4. R. F. Pettigrew, *Imperial Washington: The Story of American Public Life from 1870 to 1920* (Charles H. Kerr, 1922), 324.

5. Boutwell, *Crisis of the Republic*, 211; William Bourke Cockran and George S. Boutwell, *In the Name of Liberty*, February 23, 1900" (New England Anti-Imperialist League, 1900), 11. Boutwell

agreed with his friend William Croffut that supporting McKinley now would be like "denouncing the crime and praising the criminal." William Croffut to George S. Boutwell, May 27, 1900, George S. Boutwell Papers, MHS.

6. *New York Times*, May 25, 1900. An adjacent story on the front page told of voters in Virginia approving a state convention "mainly for the purpose of disenfranchising the Negro voter." See also Boutwell, *Republic or Empire*, 21.

7. George S. Boutwell, *Bryan or Imperialism*, National Liberty Congress of Anti-Imperialists, Indianapolis, Ind., August 15–16, 1900 (New England Anti-Imperialist League, 1900).

8. *New York World*, October 6, 1900; *New York Herald*, October 15, 1900; *New York Tribune*, October 16, 1900; Philip McFarland, *Mark Twain and the Colonel: Samuel L. Clemens, Theodore Roosevelt, and the Arrival of a New Century* (Rowman & Littlefield, 2014), 62.

9. Mark Twain, "To the Person Sitting in Darkness," *North American Review* 172 (February 1901): 161–76.

10. *New York World*, July 20, 1900.

11. George S. Boutwell, *Free America, Free Cuba, Free Philippines*, Address to a meeting at Faneuil Hall, Boston, Massachusetts, March 30, 1901 (New England Anti-Imperialist League, 1901), 9–30 and 61–62.

12. Mark Twain, "A Defence of General Funston," *North American Review* 174 (May 1902): 613–24. In the same issue, Andrew Carnegie called upon President Roosevelt to be the "Man of Destiny" and pledge independence for the Philippines; see Andrew Carnegie, "The Opportunity of the United States," *North American Review* 174 (May 1902): 606–12. A local journalist in May 1900 reported seeing Governor Boutwell, always the farmer, "on the train Thursday morning. Suddenly he jumped up from his seat and went and sat down with another man. He asked him a question and what do you suppose it was? It wasn't about Aguinaldo, although its subject began with the letter 'A.' It was 'How's asparagus?' The distinguished president of the anti-imperialist league has a fine place up at Groton, and is quite a farmer." Asparagus was one of Boutwell's favorite crops. *Turner's Public Spirit* (Ayer, Massachusetts), May 26, 1900.

13. George S. Boutwell, "To the American People," American Anti-Imperialist League, July 4, 1901. In a case that involved import duties on sugar from Puerto Rico, the court decided that the "uniformity clause" of the Constitution did not apply if Congress had made a distinction between "incorporated" and "unincorporated" territories; this reasoning was applied as well to citizenship rights.

14. Hon. George S. Boutwell, "The Supreme Court and the Dependencies," *North American Review* 173 (August 1901): 154–60.

15. L. S. Rowe, "The Supreme Court and the Insular Cases," *Annals of the American Academy of Political and Social Science* 18 (September 1901): 55. *The Atlantic Monthly* captured the sentiment, noting that "if the stronger and cleverer race is free to impose its will upon 'new- caught, sullen peoples' on the other side of the globe, why not in South Carolina and Mississippi?"; quoted in Woodward, *The Strange Career*, 72.

16. "The Supremacy of the Constitution: Dissenting Opinion of Mr. Justice Harlan, In the Case of *Downes vs. Bidwell*, Before the Supreme Court of the United States, May 27, 1901," New England Anti-Imperialist League (Boston, 1901), 6. See also Canellos, *The Great Dissenter*. The issue is still with us today, given the unresolved citizenship status of the inhabitants of Puerto Rico and the Pacific islands. Despite the provision of the Fourteenth Amendment that "all persons born on U.S. territory and not subject to the jurisdiction of another state are native-born citizens," the three and a half million residents of these US territories continue to have only "statutory" citizenship granted by Congress and are denied the full protection of the US constitution, including voting rights and representation in Congress. See Lisa Maria Perez, "Citizenship Denied: The Insular Cases and the Fourteenth Amendment," *Virginia Law Review* 94 (June 2008): 4; Christina Duffy Burnett, "*Untied* States: American Expansion and Territorial De-annexation," *The University of Chicago Law Review* 72 (Summer 2005): 3.

17. David Starr Jordan, *The Heredity of Richard Roe: A Discussion of the Principles of Eugenics* (American Unitarian Association, 1911), 119.
18. Jordan later opposed US involvement in World War I on the same grounds, defining warfare as a "reversal of selection" by which "organisms best fitted to survive under normal conditions are destroyed, while inferior types are . . . left to reproduce the future." David Starr Jordan, *War and the Breed: The Relation of War to the Downfall of Nations* (Beacon Press, 1915), 10; Nichols, *Promise and Peril*, 79.
19. Quoted in Blight, *Race and Reunion*, 356.
20. *Boston Globe*, May 31, 1901; Greenidge, *The Grimkes*, 304.
21. In one incident, US troops killed as many as 1,000 Muslim Moros, including women and children, who refused to submit to American control in March 1906 at the site of the volcanic mountain of Bud Dajo; see Kim A. Wagner, *Massacre in the Clouds: An American Atrocity and the Erasure of History* (PublicAffairs, 2024); *New York Tribune*, July 5, 1901; *New York Times*, July 5, 1901.
22. Henry Cabot Lodge to William C. Endicott Jr., November 29, 1899, Henry Cabot Lodge Papers, letterbox no. 18, MHS.
23. See Beisner, *Twelve Against Empire*, 226–39.
24. Quoted in Kinzer, *The True Flag*, 210.
25. See Edmund Morris, *Theodore Rex* (Random House, 2001), 3–13; Schriftgiesser, *The Gentleman from Massachusetts*, 200.
26. *Affairs in the Philippine Islands, Hearings, Committee on the Philippines, January 31–June 28, 1902*, United States Senate (US Government Printing Office, 1902); *Proclamation 483, July 4, 1902: Granting Pardon and Amnesty to Participants in Insurrection in the Philippines*; *Washington Times*, July 5, 1902.
27. Quoted in Wolff, *Little Brown Brother*, 362–63; George S. Boutwell, "Address at the Twentieth Century Club," October 16, 1902, Boutwell Box, MHS; *Boston Globe*, October 24, 1902.
28. Georgianna A. Boutwell, "George Sewall Boutwell," Boutwell Collection, GHS, 14.
29. George S. Boutwell to Groton Tax Assessors, May 3, 1897, and documents relating to mining shares and the San Diego property, Boutwell Collection, GHS.
30. George S. Boutwell to Hon. George A. King, April 20, 1903, Boutwell Collection, GHS. King and Boutwell were law partners in the 1890s working on claims dating to the 1790s that were filed under the French Spoliation Act of 1885; see George A. King, "The French Spoliation Claims," *The American Journal of International Law* 6, no. 2 (April 1912). William F. Wharton to Rev. Endicott Peabody, January 20, 1905; R. Bayard Cutting to Rev. Endicott Peabody, January 11, 1905, Archive, Groton School. Cutting wrote how "very melancholy that such a man should feel a need of this kind." Wharton served as executor of the Boutwell estate on behalf of Georgie, while the King family later provided Georgie with an interest-free mortgage on the house. See *Probate of George S. Boutwell*, Schedule B, p. 2.

Chapter 18: A "New" Emancipation Proclamation

1. Warren, *New England Bound*, 58.
2. The Great Emancipation Meeting was extensively covered in the Boston press; among many accounts, see *Boston Evening Transcript*, January 1, 1903; *Boston Globe*, January 2, 1903.
3. Kerri K. Greenidge, *Black Radical: The Life and Times of William Monroe Trotter* (Liveright, 2020), 89–98.
4. "Rev. Joshua Young," in *The Purple and Gold*, Chi Psi Fraternity, June 1904, 21:283–85. Many in the audience were likely offended by Young's remark that, while he never regretted officiating at John Brown's funeral, he did suffer "an ostracism worse than that ever felt by a black man," in *Boston Globe*, January 1, 1903. In 1900, Boutwell and Georgie organized a twenty-fifth anniversary celebration of Young's tenure as pastor at the First Unitarian Church in Groton; see the *Boston Globe*, March 7, 1900.

5. *Boston Globe*, January 1, 1903.

6. *Boston Evening Transcript*, January 1, 1903; the full text of Boutwell's address is on p. 10.

7. Greenidge, *Black Radical*, 91–98; *Boston Globe*, January 1, 1903; *New England Farmer*, January 3, 1903; *Boston Evening Transcript*, January 1, 1903.

8. *Boston Evening Transcript*, January 1, 1903.

9. Greenidge, *Black Radical*, 95. Du Bois would make the same argument just prior to the 1920 national election in his famous article, "Republicans and the Black Voter." According to Du Bois biographer David Levering Lewis, the article "seems to have contained the first outlines of the balance-of-power concept that would become a staple of American Negro politics after World War II." To give them their due, Trotter and Boutwell were calling for it much earlier. David Levering Lewis, *W. E. B. Du Bois: The Fight for Equality and the American Century, 1919–1963* (Henry Holt, 2000), 27–28.

10. Quotes are in *New England Farmer*, January 3, 1903; *Boston Globe*, January 1, 1903; *Boston Evening Transcript*, January 3, 1903.

11. *Boston Globe*, January 2, 1903.

12. Morris, *Theodore Rex*, 52–58, 193–200. *Boston Evening Transcript*, January 12, 1903; *Fall River Globe*, January 14, 1903. On Lewis, see the *Boston Globe*, January 2, 1903.

13. Albert E. Pillsbury to George Sewall Boutwell, January 2, 1903, Boutwell Collection, MHS. Pillsbury later drafted the bylaws of the National Association for the Advancement of Colored People (NAACP), founded in 1909.

14. *The Sun* (New York), February 13, 1903.

15. *Boston Globe*, March 2, 1903; *Fitchburg Sentinel*, March 13, 1903.

16. *Boston Globe*, March 20, 1903.

17. *Boston Daily Globe*, May 25, 1904.

18. *Boston Post*, May 25, 1904.

19. Remarks by the Hon. A. A. Putnam, *Report of the Sixth Annual Meeting of the Anti-Imperialist League, November 26, 1904* (The Anti-Imperialist League, 1904), 28.

20. Remarks by the Reverend A. A. Berle, D.D., *Report of the Sixth Annual Meeting*, 23. William James, "Speech to the Graduate School at Harvard, January 9, 1902," in Ralph Barton Perry, *The Thought and Character of William James, As Revealed in Unpublished Correspondence and Notes, Together with His Published Writings* (Little, Brown, 1935), 2:298–99.

21. The quote is from *Henry IV*, 2:3, 11. Boutwell paid homage to Abraham Lincoln's well-known love of Shakespeare during the height of the so-called "authorship controversy," when Mark Twain, Henry James, and others were asserting that Shakespeare was not the real author of the plays and poems attributed to him, as these could only have been written by a university-educated gentleman. Boutwell compared Lincoln's and Shakespeare's upbringings and education, concluding that if "Shakespeare did not write *Hamlet*," perhaps "Lincoln did not compose the speech which he pronounced at Gettysburg." See Boutwell, *The Lawyer, The Statesman, and The Soldier*, 98; James Shapiro, *Contested Will: Who Wrote Shakespeare?* (Simon & Schuster, 2010); Michael Anderegg, *Lincoln and Shakespeare* (University Press of Kansas, 2015). Quotes from Boutwell, *Report of the Sixth Annual Meeting*, 3–9.

22. George S. Boutwell to Andrew Carnegie, December 20, 1904, Andrew Carnegie Papers, General Correspondence, Box 110, LC.

23. Georgianna A. Boutwell, "George Sewall Boutwell,", 14. "Last Will and Testament of George Sewall Boutwell, October 2, 1902." In an earlier will, Boutwell had put Georgie in charge of all his papers and manuscripts, along with $2,000, to manage their possible publication; "Last Will and Testament of George S. Boutwell, May 14, 1891." Both documents are at *Probate of George S. Boutwell, #67452*, Supreme Judicial Court Archives, Boston, Massachusetts.

24. "Ex-Governor Boutwell Died This Morning," *Boston Record*, February 27, 1905. *Last Will and Testament, Georgianna A. Boutwell, April 18, 1929*, Middlesex Probate and Family Court South, #196323, Woburn, MA; copy available at the Groton Historical Society, Groton, MA.

25. See *New York Times*, July 12, 1911, and *Award Pronounced by His Majesty King George V as "amiable compositeur" between the United States and the Republic of Chile in the Matter of the Alsop Claim, 5 July 1911* (US Department of State, 1911). The Alsop partners had originally lodged their claim against Bolivia, but the claim transferred to Chile following the conflict between the two countries in 1879 and Chile's seizure of the territory involved. *Distribution of Alsop Award by the Secretary of State* (US Government Printing Office, 1912). In September 1913, shortly after the Alsop award was transferred to Boutwell's estate, Georgie paid off, with interest waived, a $17,000 mortgage to Ellen King, whose husband George A. King had provided the gift of $3,000 to Boutwell in the final weeks of his life. See *Last Will and Testament, George S. Boutwell, October 2, 1902*, see *Probate of George S. Boutwell, #67452*, Supreme Judicial Court Archives, Boston, MA, copy available at the Groton Historical Society, Groton, MA.
26. *Boston Daily Globe*, March 3, 1905.
27. *Boston Daily Globe*, March 3, 1905. *The New York Age*, March 2, 1905; Thomas Fortune often published Boutwell's articles in the paper.
28. *Boston Post*, April 19, 1905; "George S. Boutwell," *The Nation* 80 (March 2, 1905): 169. E. L. Godkin, longtime editor and Boutwell bête noire, had died in 1902. The final quote is from a rather maudlin poem, "To an Old Heart in a New Cause: George S. Boutwell," written by author/historian William Roscoe Thayer, a classmate of Teddy Roosevelt's at Harvard in 1881.
29. Howe, *Portrait of an Independent*, 100.
30. David G. Haskins Jr., "Report of the Treasurer," and remarks by William Lloyd Garrison Jr., *Report of the Seventh Annual Meeting of the Anti-Imperialist League*, November 25–27, 1905 (The Anti-Imperialist League, 1905), 18, 20.
31. "The Report of the Secretary," Erving Winslow, *Report of the Seventh Annual Meeting*, 3–15.

Epilogue

1. George S. Boutwell, "Shade and Ornamental Trees in the Village of Groton," in Samuel Abbott Green, *Groton Historical Series*, vol. 4, no. 4, 297–301. Boutwell also led the effort in the 1840s and 1850s to plant elm and other beautiful shade trees along Main Street. See Joshua Vollmar, "Inspired by Mt. Auburn Cemetery: The Groton Cemetery at 175," *The Groton Herald*, December 23, 2022. *Boston Globe*, May 16, 1908.
2. "Address by Hon. Winslow Warren," *Commemorative Exercise: The Erection of a Memorial Tablet to George Sewall Boutwell, May 15, 1908*; Boutwell Collection, GHS.
3. George S. Boutwell Diary, Port Arthur, January 25, 1905, Boutwell Collection, GHS.
4. Blight, *Race and Reunion*, 7–12.
5. Scott Ellsworth, *The Ground Breaking: The Tulsa Race Massacre and an American City's Search for Justice* (Dutton, 2021).
6. The KKK march in Washington, DC on August 8, 1925, culminating at the foot of the Washington Monument, was one of many Klan gatherings around the country that spring and summer, some of which turned violent, including in the area surrounding Groton; see *The Sunday Evening Star* (Washington, DC), August 9, 1925; *The Fitchburg Sentinel* (MA), March 23, 1925; *The Berkshire Evening Eagle* (Pittsfield, MA), August 11, 1925. See also Linda Gordon, *The Second Coming of the KKK: The Ku Klux Klan of the 1920s and the American Political Tradition* (Liveright, 2018).
7. William Wolkovich-Valkavicius, "The Ku Klux Klan in the Nashoba Valley, 1840–1933," *Historical Journal of Massachusetts* 18, no. 1 (Winter 1990); Mark Paul Richard, *Not a Catholic Nation: The Ku Klux Klan Confronts New England in the 1920s* (University of Massachusetts Press, 2015).
8. Boutwell criticized Supreme Court decisions in the 1870s and 1880s for ruling that many individual rights and liberties remained "within the constitutional and legislative power of the states" and could not be protected by the federal government, a dilemma that continues today; *CR*, 43/2, 1379 (February 17, 1875).

Index